THE SOCIAL BASIS OF LAW

Second Edition

THE SOCIAL BASIS OF LAW

Critical Readings in the Sociology of Law
Second Edition

edited by
**Elizabeth Comack
and Stephen Brickey**

**Garamond Press
Halifax, Nova Scotia**

Garamond Press
Box 1298 North Stn.
Halifax, Nova Scotia
B3K 5H4

Cover illustration: Richard Slye
Cover design: Margie Bruun-Meyer
Design, typesetting and production: Beverley Rach
Printed and bound in Canada

Canadian Cataloguing in Publication Data

Main entry under title:

The Social basis of law: second edition

Bibliography: p.
ISBN 0 920059 95 3

1. Sociological jurisprudence - Addresses, essays, lectures. 2. Social legislation - Canada - Addresses, essays, lectures.
I. Comack, Elizabeth, 1952- II. Brickey, Stephen L., 1948-

KE3098.S63 1986 340'.115'0971 C86-093759-3

Contents

Acknowledgements

We are grateful to the following for permission to reproduce copyright material:

Butterworths & Co. (Canada) Ltd. for Reasons, Charles, Lois Ross and Craig Patterson. "Your Money or Your Life: Workers' health in Canada". In Reasons, Charles, Lois Ross and Craig Patterson *Assault on the Worker: Occupational Health and Safety in Canada* (Toronto: Butterworths, 1981).

Canadian Women's Studies for Turpel, Mary Ellen/Aki Kwe. "Aboriginal Peoples and the Canadian Charter of Rights and Freedoms: Contradictions and challenges" *Canadian Women's Studies* Vol. 10 nos. 2 and 3 (1989).

Journal of Human Justice for Sargent, Neil C. "Law, Ideology and Social Change: An analysis of the role of law in the construction of corporate crime" *Journal of Human Justice* Vol. 1 no. 2 (Spring, 1990).

Lester and Orpen Dennys for York, Geoffrey. "Defence of the North: The native economy land claims". In Geoffrey York *The Dispossessed: Life and Death in Native Canada* (Toronto: Lester and Orpen Dennys, 1989).

Queen's Quarterly for Boyd, Susan B. "Child Custody Law and the Invisibility of Women's Work" *Queen's Quarterly* Vol. 96 no. 4 (Winter, 1989).

Social Justice (formerly Crime and Social Justice) for Mandel, Michael. "Democracy, Class and Canadian Sentencing Law" *Crime and Social Justice: Issues in Criminology* Vols. 21-22, 1985.

Society for Socialist Studies for Calliste, Agnes. "Canada's Immigration Policy and Domestics from the Carribean: The second Domestic Scheme" In Jessie Vorst et al. (eds.) *Race, Class, Gender: Bonds and Barriers. Socialist Studies/Etudes Socialistes: A Canadian Annual* no. 5, 1990.

Studies in Law, Politics and Society for Snider, Laureen. "The Potential of the Criminal Justice System to Promote Feminist Concerns" *Studies in Law, Politics and Society* Vol. 10, 1990.

Contributors

Susan Boyd, Department of Law, Carleton University

Stephen Brickey, Department of Sociology, University of Manitoba

Agnes Calliste, Department of Sociology and Anthropology, St. Francis Xavier University

Elizabeth Comack, Department of Sociology, University of Manitoba

Michael Mandel, Osgoode Hall Law School, York University

Craig Patterson, Practising lawyer in Vancouver

Tannis Peikoff, Graduate student, Department of Sociology, University of Manitoba

Charles Reasons, Itinerant sociologist and law student in Vancouver

Lois Ross, Journalist in Gravelbourg, Saskatchewan

Neil Sargent, Department of Law, Carleton University

Russell Smandych, Department of Sociology, University of Manitoba

Laureen Snider, Department of Sociology, Queen's University

Mary Ellen Turpel, Faculty of Law, Dalhousie University

Jane Ursel, Department of Sociology, University of Manitoba

Geoffrey York, Parliamentary correspondent for the Globe and Mail

Preface

It has been five years since the publication of the first edition of *The Social Basis of Law*. During that time, theoretical and empirical work in the sociology of law has continued to develop. We hope that this second edition is in keeping with those developments. In this respect, there are a number of differences to be noted.

For one, the first edition contained works which we considered to be generic. The arguments put forward, while not specifically based on the Canadian experience, were considered to be applicable to the Canadian context. In contrast, all of the papers in this collection have a specific Canadian focus. Only four of the articles from the first edition have been retained, and eight new ones have been added. In selecting papers for inclusion, we were impressed by the variety and diversity of material that was available. Our choices of which articles to include were often difficult ones, but we are confident that the papers contained in this collection will provide students with a good sampling of some of the work currently being done in the sociology of law.

For another, readers will notice that the second edition is broader in its focus. While the first edition was more clearly centered around the issue of class interests and the law, the present collection is organized around the trilogy of class, race and gender inequalities as they pertain to an understanding of the law-society relationship. This is, in large part, a reflection of a shift in theoretical orientation which has occurred in the last decade.

Five years ago, our reading of the theoretical work in the sociology of law suggested that the structural Marxist approach was on the "cutting edge" of the sociological movement in law. Since that time, work within the Marxist approach has been refined and reformulated, mainly in response to the challenge of the feminist movement. For this reason, the present collection has been oriented around a socialist feminist framework. It is our belief that, of the variety of available frameworks, socialist feminism is the one which offers the greatest potential for theorizing the interconnection of class, gender and race.

In the Introduction, we provide an overview of the main theoretical approaches in the sociology of law — functionalism, liberal pluralism and Marxism — as well as the main feminist frameworks — the conservative approach, liberal feminism, radical feminism and socialist feminism. While it is ultimately up to the reader to decide which approach makes the most sense, we have not attempted to come across as presenting a "neutral" or "objective" presentation of these approaches. We question whether such a book would be possible. By historically situating the different theoretical approaches, and introducing some of the most current issues in the area, we believe that readers will be better challenged in coming to terms with the social basis of law. In the discussion sections, an attempt is made to provide a framework for that inquiry, and the Conclusion suggests further avenues that need to be pursued.

No book of this kind would be possible without the labour of many individuals. First and foremost, we would like to thank our contributors for allowing us to include their scholarship in the collection. Transforming the papers into manuscript form involved inumerable hours sitting in front of a computer. We would like to thank our friend Lana Maloney for taking on this arduous task, and for putting up with us in the process. We would also like to thank Errol Sharpe of Garamond Press, whose approach to this business of book publishing is always human and bears little relationship to the stereotype of "doing business." Finally, we would like to acknowledge the support of our families, and especially our partners, Wayne Antony and Janice Brickey. They perhaps had the most difficult job of having to live with us while the book was being created.

Introduction

Theoretical Approaches in the Sociology of Law

Introduction

Theoretical Approaches in the Sociology of Law

Law can be said to have a distinctly *social basis*; it both shapes — and is shaped by — the society in which it operates. It is this relationship between law and society which is the primary concern of sociologists of law. Indeed, the aim of this book is to generate an awareness of the theoretical and substantive issues pertinent to understanding the law-society relationship. In this regard, it is important to recognize that, just as there is not one but several competing theoretical approaches within sociology generally, so too are there different ways of making sense of the law-society relationship. Three approaches in particular have informed work in the area: functionalism, liberal pluralism and Marxism. Each approach is characterized by a set of assumptions about human nature — that is, each theory contains a particular conception of what we as human beings are like, about what is our innate or essential being. Each theory also includes, at a fairly abstract level, a particular image or conception of what society looks like; they each make sense of the form and organization of society in very different ways. These assumptions and images are significant in that they establish the criteria or point of view from which law is studied and theorized. It follows, therefore, that an important first step in the sociological study of law is an understanding of the three analytical frameworks.

It goes without saying that social theorists do not operate in a vacuum. They are very much influenced by the work of their predecessors and by events occurring in their society. With regard to the former, each of the theoretical approaches has its roots both in social and political philosophy and classical sociological thought. With regard to the latter, in different historical periods, certain theoretical approaches have received more attention than others by social analysts. Functionalism, which is an inherently conservative approach, predominated sociological thought in North America throughout the Cold War era of the 1950s. The popularity of the functionalist approach began to wane in the 1960s. Events such as the protests against the war in Vietnam, the Quiet Revolution in Quebec, and the increasing militancy of student and racial groups generated issues and questions which functionalism, because of its consensus-oriented assumptions about the nature of the social world, was unable to adequately address. Consequently, the liberal pluralist approach gained in prominence through the 1960s. Liberal pluralism, with its greater attention to power and conflict, opened the way for a more critical and radical approach to understanding the law-society relationship. However, by the 1970s, liberal pluralism increasingly came under scrutiny, and was found lacking. In response, attention shifted to a Marxist approach. Initially informed by an instrumental Marxism, and later a structuralist one, Marxist theorists raised questions about the class-based nature of law and legal order under capitalism.

Since the early 1980s, the Marxist study of law has been at the forefront of what Alan Hunt (1978) has termed the "sociological movement in law." As that movement has proceeded, however, so too has the theoretical understanding of the law-society relationship. New lines of inquiry have developed, each one stimulating further research and debate. In particular, one of the most significant challenges confronting the sociology of law in the last decade has been posed by the feminist movement. The significance of feminism lies in its endeavour to call attention to the extent to which gender inequality and women's subordination in society are reflected in and mediated by the law-society relationship. As a consequence, the fundamental problematic addressed in the Marxist study of law has undergone a considerable re-thinking and reformulation.

In order to gain a better understanding of the changes and developments which have characterized the sociology of law over the years, we need to investigate the specific elements of the three main theoretical approaches — functionalism, liberal pluralism and Marxism. In the remainder of the discussion, we will consider each of the approaches in turn, with a view to clarifying some of their key elements, and the kinds of issues, questions and debates that have informed the sociology of law.

Functionalism

Functionalism is rooted in the conservative tradition of social and political thought. For Thomas Hobbes, the 17th century social philosopher, humans were viewed as possessed of unlimited desires and appetites that need to somehow be controlled or brought into line. In short, we are "by nature" anti-social, self-interested and egotistical beings. It is only through our contact with society that we become "social beings." Through the socialization process, for example, we internalize or take as our own the norms and values of society. In this respect, *social control* — both internal (socialization) and external (police, prisons, etc.) — is necessary if society is to flourish.

Functionalists place heavy emphasis on order, stability and harmony in their theorizing. A basic assumption that informs their work is that there is a consensus or agreement in society on dominant norms and values. To use Emile Durkheim's term, there exists a "collective conscience" which consists of the "... totality of beliefs and sentiments common to the average citizens of the same society ..." (Durkheim, 1964:79). One implication to be derived from this approach is that *culture* is an important variable, especially in terms of producing social integration.

In their conception of what society looks like, functionalists adopt an *organic analogy*. In other words, society is considered to be very much like a living organism: it has evolved over time from simpler to more complex forms; it has a structure consisting of different parts; and each of the parts that make up the whole function interdependently with one another. For example, the different institutions within society — such as the economy, the family, religion, the state and the legal system — can be said to perform specific functions that contribute to the maintenance of the social whole, with each one functioning in harmony with the others. One implication of this conception is that, for analytical purposes, different institutions (like the legal system) can be separated out and studied independently in terms of their structures and functions (see: as an example, Friedman, 1977).

Because the focus in the functionalist view is so heavily centered on order and consensus in society, it is an approach which cannot handle an analysis of conflict very well. Conflict, when it is recognized, tends to be viewed as either pathological or temporary. For example, when social regulation does break down, and the controlling influence of society on the individual is no longer effective, individuals are considered to be in a state of "anomie" or a condition of relative normlessness. Such a condition, however, is not endemic to society, as the prevailing tendency is toward stability and equilibrium. Likewise, functionalists are not well prepared for an analysis of power. Domination, to the extent that it is incorporated into the analysis, is viewed in terms of "societal domination" or the power of society over the individual.

Since culture or the normative system of society is seen as a main source of social integration and cohesion, it follows that law is viewed as an important integrating mechanism. Law both represents and enforces the collective conscience of society. In applying the organic analogy, Durkheim suggested that law "plays a role in society analogous to that played by the nervous system in an organism. The latter has as its task, in effect, the regulation of the different functions of the body in such a way as to make them harmonize" (1964:128). In much the same way, Talcott Parsons, a modern functionalist, suggested that "the primary function of a legal system is integrative. It serves to mitigate potential elements of conflict and oil the machinery of social intercourse" (Parsons, 1980:61).

Durkheim's views on crime are also instructive. They not only provided the foundation for much of the later functionalist work in the area, but also give us some insight into the functionalist view of the modern state. Durkheim defined crime according to the sanctions imposed, that is, crime was an action which elicits punishment. The common characteristic of all crimes, regardless of the particular behaviours involved, was that they consist of "acts universally disapproved of by members of each society" (1964:73). Punishment against crime, according to Durkheim, takes the form of vengeance. Because crime shocks the collective sentiments of society's members, punishment provides a means of avenging the moral outrage which the criminal arouses. Crime, then, functions to maintain social solidarity. It is a means of defence for society and the collective conscience.

It is here where the role of the state comes to the fore. Because crimes are behaviours thought to be so serious that they threaten — not just the victim — but the entire society, it falls to the state, as representative of the members of society, to take action against the offender. In this respect, functionalism conceptualizes the state as a *neutral force* which operates on behalf of society as a whole. Its primary function is that of social control: ensuring individual conformity to the normative system.

Durkheim's views on crime are very much in keeping with the other aspects of the functionalist approach. For instance, the assumption of consensus on dominant norms and values in society is reflected in legal definitions of "what is criminal;" law is merely the institutional expression of the norms and values of the majority. Accordingly, within the functionalist framework, no attempt is made to question the political nature of crime: for example, whether, in fact, definitions of "what is criminal" provide a means by which one segment of the population controls another. Because of the assumption of consensus, there is no need to question the law *per se*, either in terms of its content or its origins. Instead, the focus moves to the *criminal offender* and the question of the causes of an individual's inability to conform to the norms and values which everyone else in society deems to be acceptable.

In their efforts to theorize the causes of crime, functionalists have generally framed their explanations in cultural terms. Crime is variously explained with reference to differing cultural beliefs (such as the existence of deviant subcultures), social disorganization, or inadequate opportunities for realizing cultural goals. Overriding these explanations is the assumption that crime is a *lower class phenomenon*. Since existing institutional arrangements in society are not questioned, problems such as crime come to be viewed as problems *of particular groups or individuals* who experience a lack of "fit" to the requirements of the social order. Solutions proposed, therefore, tend to revolve around policies of resocialization or rehabilitation, increased social control (for example, more police), and harsher penalties for wrongdoing (such as lengthier prison sentences and capital punishment).

Liberal Pluralism

Liberal pluralists derive their thinking about human nature from 18th century Enlightenment philosophers, like Jean Jacques Rousseau. In liberal thought, humans are viewed as naturally competitive and power-seeking beings; everyone wants the most out of life and aspires to "be number one." At the same time, however, individuals are possessed of certain innate human rights and freedoms that can only be realized through society. The task, therefore, is to ensure that the competition between individuals is "fair", and that society is organized in a way most amenable to realizing those rights and freedoms.

Liberal pluralists, in contrast to functionalists, do not make the assumption of consensus on dominant norms and values in society. Instead, society is viewed as consisting of a plurality of competing interest groups, each one intent on realizing their particular interests. In Max Weber's sociology, for example, this competition for power occurs within the stratification order of society. Weber conceptualized stratification along three different dimensions. In other words, power in society derives from three different sources, and the amount of power an individual possesses is related to his or her standing along each of the three dimensions: an *economic order* which features classes; a *social order* which features status groups; and a *political order* which features parties (Gerth and Mills, 1974). Since the sources of power are multidimensional, no one variable is seen as "determining." As such, liberal pluralism promotes a multicausal approach to understanding the sources of power differentials.

Liberal pluralism is better equipped than the functionalist approach to handle an analysis of conflict and power. However, conflict is viewed largely in *cultural* terms, as a conflict of interests between competing groups in society. Power, on the other hand, is viewed largely at the *interpersonal* level. For Weber, power was defined as the "probability that one actor within a social relationship will be in a position to carry out his (sic) own will despite resistance" (Weber, 1978:53). While conflict and power are seen as integral components in the liberal view of society, consensus is also prominent. Consensus is rooted in the idea that the system in which competition occurs is viewed as *legitimate.*

In this regard, liberal pluralists are inclined to view the state as an "umpire" whose job it is to channel and adjudicate social conflicts. Different groups and individuals will compete with one another to use the state to their advantage in the realization of their own interests. A primary role of the state, then, is to provide the rules of the game by which this competition is played out.

Liberal pluralists see law as an autonomous sphere in society. It can be influenced by economic factors, but will not necessarily be. Law can also influence economic activity. In Max Weber's sociology, for example, no one factor is singled out as *a priori*. The emergence of social structures such as capitalism, therefore, was to be understood, according to Weber (1958), in terms of an "elective affinity" between particular ideas and material interests.

Similar to their view of the state as an arena where political power is contested, liberals view the law as one other form or dimension of power.

According to Austin Turk, for example, law:

> ... is a set of resources for which people contend and with which they are better able to promote their own ideas and interests against others ... To say that people seek to gain and use resources to secure their own ideas and interests is, of course, to say that they seek to have and exercise *power* (Turk, 1980:108).

In contrast to the consensus-oriented view of the functionalists, then, liberal pluralism posits law as a reflection of power differentials in society. Accordingly, crime is not an inherent property of individuals, but is a *status* which is conferred on the individual by those who make and enforce rules. To cite Howard Becker: "Social groups create deviance by making rules whose infractions constitute deviance, and by applying those rules to particular people and labelling them as outsiders" (Becker, 1963:9). For the liberal pluralist, therefore, crime and deviance are *social creations*. As a result, the emphasis within liberal pluralism is shifted away from the etiology of criminal behaviour and toward the process by which particular acts come to be defined as criminal.

Becker, for example, went on in his work to argue that the process of creating deviance occurs much earlier than the application of labels to particular individuals. It is rooted in the inclinations of *moral entrepreneurs*, individuals in positions of power and privilege who take it upon themselves to arouse public concern and opinion around the need for new rules. In launching such moral crusades, moral entrepreneurs typically see their mission as a "holy" one, aimed at changing the behaviour of those less powerful in society. For liberal pluralists like Becker, then, "who gets defined as criminal" is ultimately a *political question*; it has to do with the nature of power relations in society.

By inserting the concepts of power and conflict into the analysis, liberal pluralism offers a number of advantages over the functionalist approach. For one, attention is directed toward the question of the origins of law. Becker (1963), for example, was led to an investigation of the factors surrounding the passage of the 1937 Marijuana Tax Act in the United States. Platt (1969) studied the origins of the juvenile court in Chicago. And Chambliss' work on the origins of the vagrancy laws "demonstrated the importance of vested interest groups in the emergence and/or alteration of laws" (Chambliss, 1964:77).

Another advantage of attending to the political nature of crime is that researchers have been led to investigations of the manner in which those who enforce and administer the law (police and judges) exercise their discretionary power. Researchers such as Piliavin and Briar (1964) and Cicourel (1968), for example, have documented the role of "extra-legal" factors like class, race, grooming, demeanour and perceptions of the "quality of parental control" in the imposition of delinquent labels.

Finally, by shifting the focus away from the criminal offender toward the question of the social creation of crime, liberal pluralism helps to mitigate the lower class bias found in traditional functionalist accounts.

Despite these advantages, however, the explanatory power of the liberal pluralist approach is limited, primarily because of the specific manner in which power and conflict are treated. First of all, there is a failure to adequately clarify the sources of power. In Turk's formulation, for example, society consists of authority (those in dominant social positions) and subject (those in relatively powerless social groups) relations. "How authorities become authorities" is deemed irrelevant. According to Turk, "(i)t is sufficient that a social structure built out of authority relations exists ..." (Turk, 1969:51). Moreover, the pluralistic view of society adds to the ambiguity of the approach. For theorists like Becker, it is enough to assert that the powerful enforce their rules on the less powerful: the old make rules for the young, men make rules for women, Anglo-Saxons make rules for racial minorities, and so on (Becker, 1963:17). The specific structure of inequality that exists in society is never fully examined.

While liberal pluralists have generated research on the operation of the criminal justice system (on the use of police discretion, sentencing practices and the like), the tendency to remain at the level of interpersonal relations has meant a failure to consider how the workings of the various social control agencies are influenced by the overall structure and operation of the state in modern societies. As well, without an explicit and well-developed understanding of the political process, liberal pluralists tend to simply identify agents of the state as politically powerful moral entrepreneurs. With respect to Becker's analysis of the Marijuana Tax Act, for example, Galliher and Walker ask:

> ... what are the consequences of blaming government officials for the passage of restrictive laws? The answer is that the American political process and economic structure remain unquestioned with the problem being isolated to a few bad people. In the tradition of liberal muckraking journalism, it is either Joe McCarthy, J. Edgar Hoover or Richard Nixon who is seen as the source of the problem, rather than the underlying political or economic system (Galliher and Walker, 1978:31).

In short, liberal pluralism fails to call into question the role of broader structural — social, political and economic — variables in the emergence of particular laws.

Finally, the reluctance of liberal pluralists to single out any one variable as "determining" or primary leads to an eclecticism when it comes to addressing questions about the relation between law and other structures in society (especially the economic sphere).

In response to the perceived shortcomings of the liberal pluralist approach, sociologists intent on studying the law-society relationship were increasingly drawn toward a Marxist analysis. Previous to the 1970s, much of the work on the law-society relationship had centered around the study of crime. The shift to a Marxist perspective, however, led to a very different orientation. Since Marxism is a theoretical approach which directs attention to the broader structural features of society, it became increasingly evident that to understand the phenomenon of crime required an investigation of the wider social, political and economic factors that impinge upon it. Consequently, the focus was no longer on understanding crime *per se*, but on situating law (both criminal and civil) within the broader structure of the state in capitalist society. In their examination of the law-society relationship, therefore, Marxists raised the issue of the class character of law in a capitalist society.

Marxism

Marxists view human beings as basically good. The problem is that they have created structures that limit the realization of their true potential, especially their creative capacity. Marx saw human beings as *homo faber*, or "man (sic) the creator." What distinguished humans from other animals, in other words, was *human labour power* — the intellect of people and their ability to create and transform their social world. For the Marxist thinker, human nature is not the source of the problem; it is the society and its structure which must be examined.

The Marxist approach starts out with the opposite assumption from the functionalist: instead of stability and consensus, society is characterized by conflict, antagonism and exploitation. Moreover, in contrast to liberal pluralism, conflict is rooted, not in cultural factors like "interests", but in the very structure of society. Key to the Marxist conception of society is the idea that the economic variable is the "determinant in the last instance." That is, in order to arrive at an adequate understanding of society, Marxists argue that the starting point must be an analysis of the nature of the economic system which prevails.

In the Marxist conception, society consists of an *economic base* or *infrastructure* out of which arises the *superstructure* or the other institutions and social processes in society (such as the legal, political, familial and religious spheres). The relation between the two is dialectical.

According to Marx, individuals begin to distinguish themselves from other animals as soon as they begin to interact with nature and produce their own means of subsistence. As this productive activity takes place, different *modes of production* will develop over time. The mode of production essentially refers to the way in which goods are produced and distributed in a society. This will depend upon the resources available in the environment and the level of skills and knowledge acquired. The mode of production will determine both the *means of production*, the tools and instruments used in productive activity, and the *social relations of production*, or how individuals relate to one another in the process of producing.

In class societies, two main groups can be distinguished: a dominant class, which owns and controls the material prerequisites for production, and a subordinate class which, given that it does not own and control the material prerequisites, can only gain access to them by means of the dominant class. Since the dominant class is in a position to appropriate the surplus products that are produced by the subordinate class, the relation between the two classes is one characterized by exploitation and conflict.

Historically, there have been a number of different modes of production. Under feudal societies, for example, production was organized around agriculture, with land, ploughs, livestock and the like comprising the means of production. The social relations of production under feudalism consisted of two main classes: the lords or nobility who owned the land and the serfs or peasants who were legally bonded to the lords. The exploitative nature of the relation between these two classes was revealed in the fact that, come harvest time, the serfs handed over the "tithe" or a proportion of the goods they produced.

Capitalist society is characterized by a different set of conditions and relations. Under capitalism, the mode of production is centered around the production and exchange of commodities. The means of production consist of the factories, capital and machines necessary to engage in productive activity. The capitalist class is that which owns and controls the businesses, factories, land and capital, while the working class must gain a livelihood by working for wages. The exploitative nature of the relationship is revealed in the fact that, while it is the labour of the workers which produces the products and, hence, the surplus or profits of the production process, the capitalist, because he possesses "rights of ownership," can appropriate the surplus value that is produced.

Given the position of dominance of one class over another in the economic sphere, the other spheres and processes in society will be organized to serve the interests of the dominant class. In other words, within the superstructure, the kind of legal system, the form of family, the nature of education and the like will operate in accordance with the interests of the dominant class. One implication of this approach is that, because the economic variable is viewed as primary, it is not possible for the purpose of analysis to study other segments of society, like law, in isolation from the economic. Rather, law must be understood *in relation to* the economic sphere.

Another implication is that, for the Marxist approach, conflict and power are viewed in structural terms, as *class conflict* and *class domination*. Accordingly, consensus is not a "natural" condition; it has to be continually manufactured.

With regard to the Marxist view of the state, Marxist thought has traditionally not concentrated on the formation of a coherent theory of the state. Marx himself never attempted a systematic study of the state, although he did consider it a subject worthy of study at a later date. His principal theoretical object was the capitalist mode of production. It has only been in relatively recent times that a coherent theory of the state has been defined as an explicit task by Marxist theorists. Generally speaking, theorists who have been working toward this end have all made the fundamental observation that the state in a capitalist society is one which broadly serves the interests of the capitalist class. This observation is usually placed in the context of Marx and Engel's passage in the *Communist Manifesto* that "the executive of the modern state is but a committee for managing the common affairs of the whole bourgeoisie" (Marx and Engels, 1975:82). From this similar starting point, two different theories of the state have been developed: the *instrumentalist* and the *structuralist*. Within the sociology of law, instrumentalism and structuralism were utilized to address the issue of the class character of law under capitalism. Chronologically, the instrumentalist approach was the first to gain prominence.

The instrumentalist position takes Marx and Engel's statement to mean that, apart from very exceptional circumstances, the state acts *at the behest* or command of the capitalist class. This interpretation is based on the idea that processes of the superstructure are determined by the economic base. As such, institutions within the state are tools that can be manipulated by the capitalist class as a whole. In essence, the instrumentalist position argued a direct correspondence between class power (ownership of the means of production) and state power. The principle support for this view consisted of inferring the power of the capitalist class from the class composition of personnel who hold key positions within the state (Miliband, 1969; Domhoff, 1970).

Within the sociology of law, the instrumentalist approach was used to argue that law itself was a weapon of class rule. The focus was on the coercive nature of law, whereby law and legal order were viewed as a direct expression of the economic interests of the ruling class — a means of protecting their property and consolidating their political power. Some writers even went so far as to claim that capitalist class members were immune from criminal sanction (Quinney, 1975; Chambliss, 1975b).

By directing attention to the linkages between class power and state power, instrumentalism called attention to the actions and behaviours of ruling class members. In particular, the legal definition of crime came under close scrutiny, especially in terms of the extent to which the criminal law excluded a range of behaviours which are harmful and threatening to members of the society. This led to an examination of "crimes of the powerful," including price-fixing, production of faulty consumer products, environmental pollution and government corruption (see: for example, Goff and Reasons, 1978; Snider, 1978; Pearce, 1978).

Instrumentalism, however, was not without its shortcomings. For one, viewing the state as an instrument or tool of the ruling class does not allow for any systematic analysis of how actions and strategies of various ruling class groups are limited by constraints inherent in the structure of society. For another, to say that law is a weapon of class rule implies, not only that the ruling class is a "united whole," but also that it is so powerful it will be able to ensure that the state will always legislate in its favour. While laws which ostensibly run counter to the interests of capital (in particular, anti-combines legislation) have been found to be weak in their wording and enforcement, instrumentalism cannot adequately account for a variety of other forms of legislation (such as employment standards, human rights legislation and workplace health and safety regulations) which seek to place limits on the capitalist class and hence are not in its immediate interests. Finally, instrumentalism displays an insensitivity to the conditions and processes whereby democratic capitalist societies are legitimated. Why is it, for instance, that a system which, according to the instrumentalist, is apparently so biased and coercive also appears to so many as "fair" and "just?" Is the belief in "equality of all before the law" false? Are legal rights "empty" or "illusory?" There is a need, in other words, to reconcile the assertion of the class-based nature of law with the existence of democratic ideals and principles which the legal order claims to uphold. Because instrumentalists portray legal enactments as unilateral declarations of a united ruling class, this seemingly paradoxical nature of law is never adequately addressed.

By the late 1970s, theorists were moving away from the conspiratorial formulation of the instrumentalist approach toward a more structuralist account of the role of the capitalist state. In rejecting the notion of the state as an "instrument" or "tool" of the ruling class, structuralists put forward the view that institutions within the state provide the means of reproducing class relations and class domination under capitalism. In this regard, Marx and Engel's formulation was interpreted to mean that, rather than acting at the behest of capital, the state acts *on behalf of* capital (Panitch, 1977:3-4). From this standpoint, the role of the state is one of "organizer;" it mediates between the two conflicting classes, capital and labour.

In carrying out its role as organizer and mediator, the state was seen to perform particular functions. These were broadly subsumed under the headings "accumulation" and "legitimation." Accumulation includes activities in which the state is involved, either actively or passively, in aiding the process of capital accumulation. In short, the state must try to create and maintain conditions under which profitable accumulation of capital is possible. Legitimation, on the other hand, refers to those activities of the state which are designed to create and maintain conditions of social harmony. That is, "(i)t must try to win the loyalty of economically and socially oppressed classes and strata of the population to its programs and policies, it must attempt to legitimate the social order" (O'Connor, 1973b:79). The relationship between accumulation and legitimation is dialectical: nearly every agency or institution within the state is (often simultaneously) involved in both activities.

In order for the state to carry out its role, it requires a certain degree of autonomy — not from the structural requirements of the economic sphere — but from direct manipulation of the state's activities by the dominant class (or fractions of it). In this way, the state is able to transcend the parochial interests of particular capitalist class members and thus ensure that the long term interests of capital are protected (Poulantzas, 1975). The relative autonomy of the state can therefore account for the presence of laws which favour workers (for example, legal limitations on the length of the working day and workplace health and safety legislation) and those laws ostensibly designed to control the actions of capitalists (such as anti-combines legislation).

Whereas instrumentalism concentrated on the coercive nature of law, structuralism extended the analysis to include an examination of the ideological nature of law and legal order. Law was a means of both coercive and ideological domination. It was part of the terrain on which hegemony is accomplished. "Hegemony" is a term used by Gramsci (1971) to refer to the "universalization of capitalist class interests" — the process by which the domination of the capitalist class is continually being reproduced. Gramsci noted that the exercise of hegemony depends, not solely on force, but on a combination of force *and* consent. In this sense, even law, as part of the coercive side of the state, must work through ideology.

As an ideological form, law acts as a legitimizer of capitalist social relations. One way in which this is accomplished, according to the structuralists, is in the *form* that law takes in a capitalist society, that is, the shape or structure of law under capitalism is one which provides the "appearance" of equality. This "appearance" of equality is achieved, in large part, through adherence to the "rule of law."

The "rule of law" is a doctrine which encompasses two broad claims. First, *everyone* is subject to the law, even the sovereign, since the law is presented as something separate and distinct from the interests of particular groups or classes. Second, the law treats everyone the *same* — as "legal equals." "Equality of all before the law" and "blind justice" are therefore the hallmarks of the "rule of law" (see: Hunt, 1976:178-187). The main effect of this particular legal form, then, is to provide a legal barrier against the arbitrary exercise of state power and a guarantee of the rights and liberties of individual citizens.

Nevertheless, structuralists are quick to point out that the rights and liberties embodied in the "rule of law" are *limited*. While the pivotal point in the "rule of law" is "equality of all before the law", the provision of formal equality in the legal sphere *does not extend* to the economic sphere. It is in this sense that only the "appearance" of equality is maintained, as the unequal and exploitative relation between capital and labour is never called into question. This peculiarity of the legal form is typically explained by invoking a quote by Anatole France:

> The law in all its majestic impartiality forbids both rich and poor alike to sleep under bridges, to beg in the streets and steal bread (France quoted in Hunt, 1976:184).

In essence, then, structuralists suggest that the law legitimizes the dominance of one class over another by appealing to the very democratic principles which are thought to guard against such a bias.

In many respects, the structuralist approach offered a more powerful analysis of the law-society relationship than instrumentalism. Instead of a monolithic ruling class, structuralism recognized the existence of "class fractions" within the dominant class. The state, as such, was not simply an instrument or tool, but an "organizer." Because consent was not an automatic condition, but had to be continually constructed, structuralists focused attention on the processes by which hegemony was realized. In this respect, the attention to the ideological role of law enabled the structuralists to better reconcile the assertion of the class-based nature of law with the existence of democratic ideals and principles (like "equality" and "justice") which the legal order claims to uphold.

Yet, structuralism also had its limitations. For one, while instrumentalism was criticized for its overemphasis on capitalist class input into and control over the state, it could be argued that the structuralist account went too far in the other direction: it is the constraints and limitations of the structure and not human agency which determine the direction of society. In a similar vein, the concept of "relative autonomy" has been viewed as problematic, in that the specific factors which determine the state's degree of autonomy from economic relations have not, at least to this point in time, been convincingly explained. How is it, for example, that the law, as a relatively autonomous entity, succeeds in continually reinforcing and maintaining the capital relation in a way that is functional for capital? As it stands, the focus on the accumulation and legitimation functions of the state leads to a kind of circular reasoning: any concessions made to workers are indicative of the legitimation function, while gains made by capital are attributed to the state's concern with maintaining capital accumulation.

During the 1980s, Marxist theorizing on law continued to be altered and reformulated. Debates around the relative autonomy of law, the need for theoretical and historical specificity, the ideological role of law and order issues in the manufacture of consent, and the potential of law as an agent for social transformation led to more sophisticated accounts of the class character of law and legal order (see, for example: Ratner and McMullan, 1987; Brickey and Comack, 1987; Snider, 1989a).

Yet, what was noteworthy about much of this work was that it framed the fundamental problematic in terms of *class relations*. By rooting inequality in the economic sphere, and defining power in terms of relations between dominant and subordinate classes, the Marxist formulation went beyond the functionalist and liberal pluralist accounts in clarifying the *systemic* nature of inequality and how it is reproduced at the superstructural level. In so doing, however, it effectively made *other* dimensions of inequality, specifically gender and race, into contingent variables. This feature was not lost on many of the Marxist analysts and, as the 1980s drew to a close, there was an increasing consensus among those working within this tradition that their fundamental problematic was in need of revision. The primary stimulus for the rethinking of the Marxist approach came from the challenge of the feminist movement.

The Feminist Challenge

While differing in their visions of what a society characterized by gender equality would look like, feminists all share a commitment to increasing women's autonomy. Starting from the premise that women's lives have value in and of themselves, feminists have explored the differing ways in which patriarchy, understood as a set of relations in which men are dominant, has restricted women. The result has been the formulation of a number of different feminist frameworks, each one endeavouring to provide "a comprehensive analysis of the nature and causes of women's oppression and a correlated set of proposals for ending it" (Jaggar and Rothenberg, 1984: xii).

Many of the frameworks that have been developed to explain women's subordination can be linked up with the various traditions of sociological thought. Conservatism, for example, is an approach which is compatible with functionalism. Its primary concern is, quite literally, with "conserving" traditional gender relations in society, that is, where men occupy the roles of breadwinner and key players in the public sphere and women are the homemakers and mothers in the private sphere. To this extent, conservatism does not offer a "feminist" analysis. Instead, women's subordination to men is both appropriate and biologically-based, and it is in society's interests to preserve this natural order by "keeping women in their place" (see: Dubinsky, 1987).

Liberal feminism, which is compatible with the liberal pluralist approach, is concerned with increasing women's power in society, especially in terms of their representation in the public sphere. Liberal feminists see the root of women's subordination, not in biology, but in their socialization into restrictive gender roles and the limited aspirations and opportunities for women. Women, therefore, should be "let in" to the corridors of public power and given their equal share of the pie. For liberal feminists, this entails changing gender roles and expectations and increasing women's access to facilities and opportunities that would allow them to better compete with men.

Liberal feminism, while perhaps the most publicized of the different frameworks, is not without its limitations. For one, it offers little in the way of an analysis of the structure of women's oppression in society. Gender inequality is viewed more or less as an historical accident that can be rectified by the implementation of appropriate policies and strategies. For another, in centering on the need to "let women in," liberal feminists tend to accept the rules of the game as they are presently constituted, that is, rules which are by and large male-defined and male-centered. To be successful in the present system, for example, means that women must be more competitive, more aggressive, more individualistic; in short, more "male." In effect, the aim is to give women a greater share of the pie, without calling the nature of the pie itself into question. Liberal feminism can also be criticized for its middle class bias. It amounts to a kind of "career feminism" which fails to adequately speak to and incorporate the experiences of working class women. For most of these women, aspiring to a career in law, medicine or politics is simply not a part of their lived reality. As well, by centering attention on women's access to the public sphere, there is a tendency to continue the practice of devaluing the work that women do in the home.

Radical feminism is an approach that does not readily connect with one of the traditional sociological approaches. It emerged largely as a critique of liberal feminism. For radical feminism, the main source of women's oppression is to be found in patriarchy; the fact that societies have historically been structured by men and for men. Radical feminists argue that patriarchy transcends specific economic systems. As such, they locate capitalism as but one manifestation of male dominance; its economic, social, religious and political institutions are cast as male-defined and male-centered. The only solution, therefore, is a "feminization" of society: the realization of a social order which is women-centered and focused on what are perceived to be women's inherent qualities. Such a society would therefore be a more nurturant, caring, cooperative and sharing one.

Radical feminism has the benefit of including within its scope an analysis of patriarchy. However, in giving priority to male power as a focus of both theoretical analysis and strategies for change, radical feminism encounters a number of difficulties. For one, there is a tendency to promote an "essentialist" view of the differences between men and women — that is, men and women are *by their very nature* different species. Such an assertion comes close to the "biology is destiny" claims of the conservative approach. For another, by giving priority to patriarchy as *the* source of inequality for women, radical feminism runs the risk of excluding working class women and women of colour from its purview. For these women, their ability to simply "opt out" of patriarchy (as writers like Sonia Johnson have advocated) are clearly limited. Moreover, such an assertion would imply that, in a women-centered world, inequalities of class and race would somehow disappear. Finally, since it is an approach which is so definitely women-centered, radical feminism effectively precludes men, especially the possibility of "feminist men."

Socialist feminism is a framework which has emerged in direct response to problems encountered within traditional Marxism. In particular, Marxism has come under heavy criticism for its "sex-blindness" (Hartman, 1981). By locating the key determinant of oppression within the productive sphere, Marxism subsumes reproduction and the family to production and the economy. In short, the oppression of women becomes merely a reflection of the apparently more important and fundamental class oppression. Socialist feminists have therefore engaged in the revision and reformulation of traditional Marxism in order to incorporate the *intercon-nection* between capitalism (class) and patriarchy (gender).

In traditional Marxist thought, the emphasis is on the sphere of produc-tion where the labour power of the worker is transformed to produce surplus value or profit for the capitalist. Socialist feminists, however, argue that an equally important labour process is that which takes place in the sphere of reproduction. This reproductive or domestic labour is seen as a *necessary complement* of the wage-labour/capital relation and involves four interrelated tasks: looking after adult members of the household (reproducing labour power on a daily basis); childbirth and childrearing; housework (cooking, cleaning and washing clothes); and the transforma-tion of wages into goods and services for household use ("making ends meet" by shopping, sewing clothes, growing and preserving food) (Luxton, 1980:18-19).

While reproductive labour is found in all societies, under capitalism the productive and reproductive spheres have been separated or divided into "public" and "private" realms. In the process, "house work" has become synonymous with "women's work." Moreover, while productive labour (working for wages) generally takes place outside of the home, reproduc-tive (or domestic) labour — previously integrated with the other labour of the household — has become "devalued." It is considered "unproductive" labour because it does not directly contribute to the surplus value or profit of capital.

By focusing on the interrelationship between the productive and repro-ductive spheres, socialist feminism is able to account for the specific nature of women's oppression in a patriarchal capitalist society. Attention to class leads to analyses of women's work in both the productive and reproduc-tive spheres. For example, although women have been entering the labour force in large numbers in recent decades, they have, by and large, been restricted to the lowest-paid, most monotonous and least-secure jobs (see, for example: Wilson, 1986). In addition, since domestic labour continues to be relegated to women, those who work for wages carry the burden of a double day's work.

Attention to gender leads to analyses of the particular ways in which men exercise their control over women and women's sexuality. This is done both overtly, through such means as the medicalization of childbirth, the objectification of women's bodies in pornography and violence against women in the form of rape and wife abuse, and covertly, in the form of a "monogamous heterosexuality" which historically has legitimated male control over children and property and legitimated the ideology that women are dependent on men for both their economic and sexual needs. Moreover, masculine dominance is maintained, not only by the family and economic system, but also by the state, media and religious and educa-tional systems. In other words, socialist feminists maintain that, like the class relations under capitalism, gender relations under patriarchy have both material and ideological dimensions.

By adopting a socialist feminist framework, we can begin to understand how women in patriarchal capitalist societies confront a "double oppression." Socialist feminism, therefore, has the potential of moving the analysis beyond a radical feminist framework. Upper class women and "career feminists," for example, may experience systemic discrimination because of their gender, but they are also privileged by their class position. In addition, while socialist feminists acknowledge the need for women to become "woman-identified" (much like Marx argued the need for the working class to become a "class-for-itself"), it does not preclude the possibility of working with men on a principled basis. Men-as-a-group also need to recognize that, while privileged by a patriarchal system, they too confront limitations. Conceptions of masculinity, for example, that subscribe to images of competition, aggression and "machismo" invariably distort men's true potential and their ability to communicate with each other, and with women.

In terms of its implications for the study of law, feminism has succeeded in broadening the scope of inquiry to include analyses of the complex ways in which the legal system operates to reinforce and reproduce the subordination of women (see: Sheehy and Boyd, 1989). Jane Ursel, for example, has suggested that, just as capitalism has proceeded through different stages of development, so too has patriarchy been altered and transformed over time. Ursel argues that, historically, there has been a shift from "familial" to "social" patriarchy, whereby the state itself has increasingly assumed a major role in maintaining reproductive relations. From this standpoint, it follows that, as social patriarchy develops, the law will become an increasingly important mechanism for the maintenance of patriarchal control. As such, developments in the areas of family law, labour legislation and even abortion legislation need to be situated in the context of the state's endeavour to manage reproduction.

Socialist feminism has highlighted the need to theorize the interconnection of class and gender in patriarchal capitalist societies. One other dimension that has been singled out for attention, however, is race. As some writers have demonstrated, racial oppression has historically worked to the benefit of capital. Split labour markets, for example, have proven to be effective barriers to the formation of working class consciousness (see: for example, Bonacich, 1980 and Li, 1979). And, as Thatcher (1986) has shown, "minority group disrepute" of Canadian native peoples has been highly effective in maintaining the capitalist enterprise. Moreover, as a cultural construction, the ideology of racism offers a most powerful weapon of oppression.

The inclusion of race into the analysis also raises important questions for feminists. For example, given the emphasis in much feminist work on the institution of the family as a main site for women's oppression in society, the addition of race into the equation raises the question of the extent to which the family has been uniformly oppressive for *all* women, or whether, for some women of colour, the family is more commonly experienced as a haven or shelter in a racist society (Sheehy and Boyd, 1989:3).

At the level of theory, the trilogy of class, gender and race has posed somewhat of a conundrum. While class and gender may be captured in a framework centering on the processes of production and reproduction, it remains unclear how race is to be situated theoretically. We would argue, for example, that it is not enough to simply suggest, as a liberal pluralist would, that class, race and gender are three important variables that may or may not become significant in any particular instance. Such a multi-causal (not to mention eclectic) approach does not take us very far in understanding the *systemic* nature of racism. While race has certainly not been ignored by Marxist and socialist feminist writers alike, there is clearly much more work to be done in the way of theoretically situating all three dimensions. As Mona Danner has recently noted:

> Patriarchy cannot be separated from capitalism, neither can racism, imperialism, or any other oppression based on "otherness." All are related dialectically. While we often separate them for analytical purposes, none can be separated in reality and it is increasingly questionable whether they should be separated in analysis (Danner, 1989:2).

The readings contained in this collection are representative of the kind of work now being conducted on the law-society relation. While significant divergences do exist, all of the papers share in common an attempt to examine some aspect of the class, race and gender trilogy. The readings have been organized around three central issues in the sociology of law. *Part One* focuses on the origins of law. The major question addressed is how to explain the emergence of specific pieces of legislation. Each of the papers in this section attempt to further our understanding of the social forces that were most influential in shaping the law. *Part Two* considers the operation of law. The readings in this section deal with the extent to which law reflects and reinforces inequalities of class, race and gender in society. *Part Three* examines the issue of change and reform through law. The theme of this section is the extent to which law can be an effective agent for bringing about substantive change in society.

Part One

The Origins of the Law

The Origins of Canadian Anti-Combines Legislation, 1890-1910

Russell Smandych

Within the last decade, Marxist accounts of law and crime have become the focus of critical debate in criminology. Basing their arguments on contentious theoretical assumptions, early proponents of the Marxist perspective in criminology argued that, in capitalist societies, the law was clearly designed to serve the interests of the capitalist ruling class (Chambliss, 1975a; Platt, 1974; Quinney, 1977; Taylor *et al.*, 1975). The advent of a "new" Marxist perspective on law creation in the 1970s met with a critical response from liberal criminologists who, pointing to the logical and empirical inadequacy of particular historical accounts (Hagan and Leon, 1977), predicted the rapid demise of Marxist criminology (Klockars, 1979).

The main thrust of the liberal critique of Marxist criminology in recent debates has been directed at exposing the "theoretical and empirical poverty" of Marxian-informed historical research (Klockars, 1979:479; Sparks, 1980). One of the major criticisms levelled at the Marxian approach to law creation is its inability to account *historically* for the enactment of social legislation that does not serve the immediate "objective interests" of the capitalist class (Bierne, 1979). Indeed, from the viewpoint of mainstream criminologists, the existence of various forms of social legislation — ranging from anti-combines legislation to product-safety laws — provides an apparent contradiction to the Marxist perspective's assumption that laws serve to promote the interests of capital.

Drawing on recent Marxist literature concerned with the capitalist state and the formation of state policies, this paper argues that the "objective interests" criticism of Marxian accounts of the creation of law is unsustainable because the specific criticism raised by liberal criminologists is based largely on an interpretation of instrumental Marxist theory, and fails to take account of recent developments in structural Marxism. In the attempt to shift the attention of academics to a more theoretically productive debate, I argue — through a critical examination of historical data — that the structural Marxist approach may fruitfully be employed to account for the existence of social legislation that does not serve the immediate interests of capital.

In support of this argument, the paper begins with a discussion of instrumental and structural Marxist theories of the capitalist state. This discussion is followed by an overview of foreign and Canadian literature in which the issue of class interests in the emergence of anti-combines legislation has been addressed. Subsequently, attention turns to a critical examination of historical data relating to the inception of early Canadian anti-combines legislation and the political and economic climate in which it emerged. On the basis of this examination an alternative interpretation is offered of the historical circumstances surrounding the emergence of anti-combines legislation in late 19th century Canada.

Instrumental Marxist Theory

Although there are differences in the specific propositions advanced by Marxists whose works are associated with the instrumental perspective (Gold et al., 1975), the basic features of instrumental Marxist theory are readily discernible. First, instrumental Marxist theory is predicated on the assumption that the state in capitalist societies is an instrument or a tool used by the ruling class to further its own interests. In instrumentalist terms, the ruling class or capitalist class is able to influence state policies by virtue of the "economic power conferred upon it" through its owner-ship and control of the means of production (Miliband, 1969:22). The economic power of the capitalist class is transformed into political influ-ence in the legislative process, according to instrumentalists, either "di-rectly through the manipulation of state policies or indirectly through the exercise of pressure on the state" (Gold, et al., 1975:34).

Informed by these theoretical insights, instrumentalist-based empirical research has focused on examining the mechanisms through which the unity of the capitalist class is maintained, and the specific manner in which it shapes state policy (Kerbo and Della Fave, 1979). In concrete terms, the ability of the capitalist class to affect state policies has been explained, at a personal level, by showing that its members actively participate in the policy formation process (Domhoff, 1970) and, at an ideological level, by demonstrating that the values and interests of the ruling class predomi-nate in shaping the "world view" of society at large (Miliband, 1969). Despite the difference in weight given to personal and ideological factors, instrumental Marxists nonetheless remain united in the view that the interests of the capitalist class are invariably reflected in the activity of the political apparatus of the state.

While recognized as having provided a noteworthy critique of pluralist conceptions of the state (Balbus, 1971; Stone, 1971), the writings of instrumental Marxists have also been subjected to pointed criticism. Notably, instrumentalist accounts have been criticized for creating a false image of ruling class unity (Greenberg, 1981), for failing to explain adequately the formation of state policy that is not in the "objective interests" of the capitalist class (Beirne, 1979), and for reproducing the liberal tendency to discuss politics in isolation from any consideration of the complex, structurally determined role of the state in capitalist society (Poulantzas, 1975). Significantly, therefore, the attack on instrumental Marxism is not solely the result of liberal dissatisfaction, but has also come from Marxists, who recognize that instrumentalists do not provide an analysis that succeeds "in establishing the real nature of the state in capitalist society and its inherent limitations as well as advantages for capital" (Jessop, 1977:357).

Structural Marxist Theory

In opposition to the instrumentalist view that the capitalist state is a pliant tool of the ruling class, structural Marxists contend that the state exercises "relative autonomy" in its relationship with the capitalist class members and their interests. Structuralists point out that the capitalist class—rather than being a cohesive entity — is a "highly fractionated class" with divergent political and economic interests (Gold *et al.*, 1975:37). While specific capitalists and members of class fractions may try to manipulate state policies, the success of such attempts is by no means guaranteed. Indeed, the state's ability to transcend the particular interests of individual capitalists, according to structural Marxists, is crucial in order for it to be able to protect "the long-run interests of the capitalist class as a whole" (Gold *et al.*, 1975:36).

Structuralist analysis begins with the observation that the class structure of capitalist society generates historically specific contradictions rooted in the capitalist economy. At the most general level, the capitalist economy is understood as the site of an "essential confrontation" between those who own and control the means of production (capital) and those who are forced to sell their labour power (labour) in order to survive (Wright, 1978:18). The continued existence of a system based on the creation of surplus value, structuralists argue, requires that the state function to reproduce existing social and economic relations (Wright, 1978) by attempting to "neutralize" or "displace" the contradictions inherent in capitalism (Gold *et al.*, 1975:36). The primary means by which the state attempts to resolve contradictions, and thereby reproduce the existing system, is through promoting capital accumulation and maintaining social harmony (O'Connor, 1973; Offe, 1975a; Poulantzas, 1975).

According to structural Marxists, the state has an "objective function" to perform in maintaining social harmony so that capital accumulation can proceed unhindered (Jessop, 1977:358). This somewhat contradictory role of the state precludes the pursuit of immediate interests of individual capitalists or class fractions. In a fundamental sense, therefore, the role of the state in capitalist society is seen to be broadly determined by the existing structure of society, the reproduction of which requires a continuous flow of capital accumulation (Offe, 1975a). Being a crucial component of the capitalist economic system, moreover, the process of capital accumulation is in itself subject to "impediments" or "constraints" that must be overcome in order for capitalist production to continue (Wright, 1978). The history of capitalist development, structuralists contend, is one of continuing attempts on the part of the state to find structural "solutions" to basic social inequalities that impede, or threaten to impede, profitable capital accumulation. The various "solutions" put forth by the state and reflected in state policies, however, rather than eliminating the problem altogether, merely help it to recede into the background. Thus, it is argued, the structural "solutions" proposed to overcome impediments to accumulation at a given stage in capitalist development will "generate new impediments which constrain the accumulation process" in the subsequent historical period (Wright, 1978: 112, 116).

With regard to methodology, Wright (1978: 10-13) has contended that the task of Marxist scholars is to develop empirical research agendas firmly rooted in the dialectical logic of structural Marxist theory. Empirical research must seek to establish a link between the "level of appearance," or observable social phenomena, and the "reality hidden behind those appearances," or the structural problems of capitalism. In a similar vein Panitch (1977a:8-9) has argued that Marxists can obviate the tendency toward "structuralist abstractionism" (cf. Poulantzas, 1975) by adopting a "concrete empirical and historical orientation" that directs attention to considering the "empirically given circumstances" in which the state functions to reproduce existing social and economic structures. According to Panitch (1977a:6): "Marxism may give us a method of analysis, but, as Marx himself pointed out ... this method has to be applied not as an overgeneralization but in a manner that will illuminate concrete empirical and historical circumstances."

Class Interests and the Creation of Law
From the viewpoint of liberal academics the enactment of legislation governing matters such as product safety, environmental protection, and corporate price-fixing represents an attempt on the part of the state to safeguard the interests of consumers, employees, and the general public. The frequent failure of such legislation *in fact* to protect the interests of society at large from the possibility of corporate misconduct is viewed by such academics as a consequence of inadequate legal controls — a situation that can be alleviated by the enactment of more effective regulatory and consumer law (Stone, 1977). This consensual view of the importance of class interests in the formation of social legislation, however, is not supported by recent historical research. The following overview of the contemporary foreign literature — concerned mainly with the issue of class interests in the emergence of anti-combines legislation — illustrates that, in recent years, various interpretations have been advanced to

account for the existence of social legislation that apparently does not serve the interests of the capitalist class.

In an examination of "the extent to which law is shaped by powerful economic interests," Hopkins (1979) presented data on a series of five anti-combines statutes enacted by Australian governments in the period from 1906 to 1977. While the earliest Australian anti-combines legislation passed in 1906 was unusual because it was aimed at protecting "indigenous" industries from the predatory behaviour of "foreign" monopolies (1979:70), subsequent legislation enacted in the 1960s and 1970s was directed specifically at eliminating the "anti-competitive practices engaged in by Australian businesses" (1979:72). In each of his five case studies, Hopkins revealed that organized business groups attempted vigorously to influence the content of anti-combines legislation. Significantly, however, the author found that business groups were not always successful in shaping the content of legislation because electoral pressures and counter-lobbying constrained governments from openly supporting the interests of capital. According to Hopkins' interpretation (1979:79-80), although Australian governments occasionally acted in ways "contrary to the immediate and perceived interests of powerful business groups," government members were well aware that intervention in the economy on behalf of consumer and small business groups would serve to legitimate the existing economic system, and thereby "safeguard the long term interests of capitalism."

In a similar study, McCormick (1979) examined the importance of "dominant class interests" in the emergence of American anti-combines legislation. Enacted in 1890, the Sherman Antitrust Act was justified in terms of the effect it would have on preventing "the economic system (of the United States) from coming under the powerful control of private interests" (1979:400). According to McCormick's research, however, the law's emergence and subsequent enforcement clearly served to "protect" rather than interfere with the interests of the American economic élite. Through examining the forces that motivated and shaped the legislation, McCormick found that the Sherman Antitrust Act originated in a political and economic milieu "in which the small independent entrepreneurship of the traditional middle class was in contradiction to the big business capitalist system of the rising corporate élite" (1979:413). In response to the demands of agrarian and small business groups that action be taken to deal with unfair corporate mergers and price-fixing, members of the United States Congress — many of whom "had strong ties with big business" — hastily drafted and enacted the Sherman legislation. Although ostensibly intended to place restraints upon the dominant economic élite, McCormick argued, the legislation "did little to restrain the continuing control of the élite over the political and economic sectors of society" (1979:413). Rather, as the legislators had actually intended, American anti-combines legislation served simply to "mollify and dispel mounting antibusiness sentiments" that threatened to interfere with the monopolistic activities of the rising capitalist class (1979:413).

Most recently, Barnet (1981) has produced a broadly based study concerned with accounting for why American corporations remain relatively immune from prosecution for violating regulatory laws that are supposedly intended to protect the interests of consumers, employees, and the general public. Barnett examined historical and statistical data on the enactment and enforcement of American product safety, environmental, anti-combines, and union labour laws. The relative weakness of these regulatory laws, according to Barnett (1981:4), could be understood in terms of "historical imbalance of power" — separating corporations and the victims of corporate wrongdoing — institutionalized in state-created "legal constraints." Historically in capitalist societies, Barnett argued, the state or government has functioned primarily to achieve two often contradictory goals: profitable capital accumulation and the maintenance of social harmony. Thus, he contended, the capitalist state is the site of a "dialectical process" in which those promoting public interests (that is, laws to control corporate wrongdoing) stand in contradiction to those promoting private interests (that is, increased corporate growth and stability).

Within the context of the United States, the imperative importance of maintaining the legitimacy of the state in the face of mounting public pressure to control corporate wrongdoing compelled the government to introduce legal constraints to regulate the corporate sector. However, Barnett (1981:7) contended that, in order for the government to continue to foster profitable capital accumulation, regulatory laws could not be made "so severe as to diminish substantially the contribution of large corporations to growth and employment." Thus, in Barnett's view, the capitalist state has little interest in creating laws that would effectively control corporate misconduct. Rather, according to his interpretation, corporate crime is reproduced on a continuing basis under conditions of corporate capitalism.

Prevailing Views on Canadian Anti-Combines Law

Whereas authors in other countries have moved noticeably towards developing structural Marxist explanations for the emergence of anti-combines legislation, relevant studies in Canada have tended towards adopting pluralist and instrumentalist interpretations (cf. Bliss, 1973; Goff and Reasons, 1978; Skeoch, 1966; Snider, 1979; Young, 1974). Despite the differences in interpretation, academics generally appear to agree on the immediate circumstances that surrounded the enactment of Canada's earliest anti-combines legislation in 1889. According to Skeoch, for instance:

> Canadian combines legislation had its origin in the report of the House of Commons appointed in 1888 to inquire into the existence of combinations and trusts in

Canada and their effect upon the Canadian economy. The Committee found that combinations inimical to the public interest existed in respect of a number of widely used commodities and services and recommended that legislative action be taken to curb such combinations. In 1889 an Act was passed, the parent of the present section 498 of the Criminal Code ... (Skeoch, 1966:6).

Moving from description to interpretation, more recent historians have pointed out that the manifestation of concern over the extent and effect of combinations in Canada was the direct result of lobbying activity on the part of small merchants, who felt "discriminated against by a grocer's combine" (Bliss, 1973:178). The concerns of these merchants, Bliss noted, were taken to Parliament by a single M.P., N. Clarke Wallace, who was subsequently appointed to head the Select Committee directed to investigate Canadian combines and trusts. After two months of hearings, Wallace, as chairperson of the Committee, introduced a bill in Parliament to deal with restrictive trade practices and price-fixing. According to the interpretation offered by Bliss, however:

> In truth the passing of the anti-combines act of 1889 was no more than a political sham, the central figure in which was Canada's self-proclaimed trust-buster, N. Clarke Wallace. He deliberately watered down his own bill until it was ineffectual. In April 1889 he withdrew the original bill, explaining that objections had been made to the possibility of a new offence being created, "and the judges might interpret the Bill more severely than was intended," and replaced it with a new bill ... which he explained was only intended to declare the English common law. He agreed that his bill would not prohibit cotton manufacturers from combining to limit production, and in later hearings he only singled out one particularly obnoxious salt combine, which his committee had not investigated, as an object of his legislation (Bliss, 1973:182).

Writing from an instrumentalist viewpoint, Young (1974:82) has attempted to document "the intimate relationship between the ruling class and the state" by examining the role of corporate interests and the state in shaping the Combines Investigation Act of 1910. Like Bliss (1973), Young (1974:71) argued that Canada's first anti-combines legislation, enacted in 1889, was the product of lobbying efforts by small businessmen concerned with protecting their firms from the combines. Despite the existence of this early *petit-bourgeois* inspired legislation, however, it was only after the movement towards corporate mergers reached a high point after 1909 that "the ruling class called upon the state to introduce legislation" to provide for the investigation of alleged combines (1974:73). The enactment of the Combines Investigation Act in 1910, along with subsequent amendments, Young (1974:73) argued, were prompted by the ruling class as a way of policing its own members during times when "the petit bourgeois felt squeezed out of the competition, or when working class discontent (such as that manifest in the Winnipeg General Strike of 1919 and during the economic depression of the 1930s) threatened severe disruption." That in practice the state worked directly to further the interests of the capitalist ruling class was, according to Young, evident in the continued growth of combines after 1910, the extent of price-fixing and supply control in heavy industries, and the active role played by the state in interfering with the administration of anti-combines legislation.

Goff and Reasons (1978) have also examined the circumstances surrounding the enactment of Canada's earliest anti-combines legislation. In line with the previous studies, Goff and Reasons (1978:35) argued that, although the 1889 legislation was introduced by the federal government for the express purpose of protecting "the public interest in economic competition," the legislation was largely a product of business interests and concerns. According to their analysis, the original demand for the legislation prohibiting the restraint of free trade "came not from the general populace but from small businessmen, who felt their firms were at the mercy of big business interests" (1978:42). As a consequence of the small-business lobby, and the political wisdom of the Macdonald-Conservative government — that giving support to anti-combines legislation would divert attention from its unpopular National Policy — anti-combines legislation was entered on the parliamentary agenda. Evidently, however, the authors found that the specific content of the 1889 legislation was determined largely by representatives of the Canadian banking and financial establishment, who played an active role in the debates preceding enactment (1978:44). The result, according to Goff and Reasons (1978:xiii), was that Canada's first anti-combines statute became an unenforceable and "expressive law" that served merely to convince "certain segments of the public that something was being done" about protecting economic competition.

Focusing more on subsequent revisions to the original 1889 Act, Snider (1979) examined the numerous attempts that have been made to strengthen the enforcement provisions of the legislation. Although, as Snider (112) reported, strict "proconsumer and procompetition" amendments to Canadian anti-combines legislation have been proposed over the years, at each stage proposals "were weakened or eliminated in the face of business opposition" (110). The inability of small entrepreneurs and consumer groups to effect significant legislative reforms, Snider (118) argued, was largely the result of the corporate sector's direct "control over the life chances of most Canadians through [its] dominance over the health of the economic system." Recognizing the important role played by the dominant economic élite, the state, according to Snider, exists "ultimately to defend and further the interests of the ruling class"(106).

The thrust of Canadian research, as we have seen, has been directed at documenting the immediate circumstances surrounding the enactment of Canada's earliest anti-combines statutes, and the enforcement and effect of the legislation. In general, authors supporting both pluralist and instrumentalist interpretations appear to agree that the anti-combines legislation was the product of intra-capitalist conflict, manifested in the struggle between small business interests and growing corporate concerns. Also, there seems to be a general consensus that the advent of anti-combines legislation had negligible impact on the activities of major firms that were known to be involved in merger and price-fixing agreements. Given the documentary evidence forwarded by various authors, the conclusion that early Canadian anti-combines legislation was ineffectual and seldom enforced is difficult to dispute.

Re-Examining the "Origins" of Anti-Combines Legislation

While the historical "facts" presented by previous writers can hardly be disputed, there is considerable evidence to suggest that their substantive interpretations are remarkably incomplete. Without exception, historical accounts of the "origins" of Canadian anti-combines law have focused largely on examining the immediate political events surrounding the enactment of early legislation. Remarkably, not even the most critical authors have moved beyond the level of immediate events and circumstances to examine the broader political and economic context within which Canada's first anti-combines statute emerged. Such an examination, as we shall soon observe, leads to a strikingly different interpretation of the social and historical forces that influenced the character of anti-combines legislation in late 19th century Canada.

It is a significant, although almost totally neglected, fact that the emergence of anti-combines legislation in Canada coincided with the rise of industrial growth in the latter part of the 19th century. Centred mainly in Ontario, industrial growth in the latter part of the 19th century led to a dramatic increase in the number of large-scale urban factories, and a concomitant breakdown in the traditional agrarian social and economic structure of society. Palmer, in describing the manner in which "industrial capitalism sank deep roots in Canadian soil," has noted that:

> The hallmarks of capitalist production, large factories employing workers by the hundreds, dotted the landscape of many early industrial cities. With time the process accelerated. Between 1870 and 1890 establishments capitalized at $50,000 and over increased by about 50 percent, and machines became increasingly common. By the 1880s a period of concentration had begun, marking the demise of the manufactory and the rise of the

corporate concern, centralized, bureaucratized, and
linked to its suppliers and distributors through a network of horizontal and vertical integration (Palmer,
1979:5).

The demise of the small manufacturing establishment at the hands of
growing corporate concerns resulted in a vast increase in both the size of
Canada's urban working class and the number of workers who were
forced to sell their labour to large corporations. For instance, Kealey
(1980:307), in his study of the response of Toronto workers to the rise of
industrial capitalism, reported that in the period from 1871 to 1891 the
number of workers employed in major Toronto industries increased from
9,400 to over 24,000. Of the more than 24,000 workers employed in 1891,
Kealey further noted, over 14,000 were working in the city's ten major
industries. Toronto's industrial development closely paralleled that of
other Ontario cities such as Hamilton where, in the period from 1871 to
1891, capital investment in industry grew from about $1,500,000 to over
$8,000,000. During the same period, the number of "hands employed" in
Hamilton's machine factories rose from around 4,500 to 9,500 (Palmer,
1979:17). For the province of Ontario as a whole, aggregate data compiled
more recently by Kealey and Palmer (1981:376) indicate that, in each
decade between 1870 and 1890, capital investment in Ontario more than
doubled, while "the number of hands employed increased 90 per cent over
the twenty year period."

As the centre of industrial capitalist development in Canada, Toronto
and other Ontario industrial cities also became the centre of Canadian
labour organization and militancy in the late 19th century. Although craft
unions were an undeniable feature of Canada's early industrial heritage,
union organization in the 1870s and 1880s began to reflect a heightening
class consciousness and a growing class antagonism between capitalists,
who owned and controlled the means of production, and workers, who
were subjected to capitalist control (Palmer, 1979). In the 1880s, the
growing confrontation between labour and capital was concretely displayed in the emergence of vocal trade unions — such as the Knights of
Labor — that appealed to the working masses. Regarding the growing
prominence of the Knights of Labor in Toronto, Kealey noted:

In four short years the order organized approximately 53
locals and, at its peak strength in 1886, it represented
almost 5,000 workers. The order led the city's most
dramatic strike in spring 1886, and then initiated the
massive independent labour campaigns of 1886-87. For a
brief moment, the Toronto working class stood together
united, with the Knights providing both the ideological
and organizational vehicles for this new unity (Kealey,
1980:176).

Although the immense gains obtained by the Knights of Labor in Toronto in the mid-1880s stemmed from their commitment to organize "all workers" regardless of craft, ethnicity, sex, and skill (Kealey, 1980:181), the growing prominence of the order in Canada was not directly related to this effort. Rather, according to Kealey:

> The order came to Canada on the telegraph lines... It was the international telegrapher's strike of 1883 that brought the order to prominence in Canada. The strike against the monopolistic telegraph companies, symbol for much that was despised in the new industrial capitalist society, received much support from the general public and the resurgent trade-union movement (Kealey, 1980:177).

It is of crucial significance that the rise of the militant trade unions in Canada owed as much to labour's hatred of monopolistic companies as it did to labour's desire to improve working conditions. Hand in hand, during the 1880s, trade unions pressed for better factory legislation, reduced work hours, child-labour laws, and the elimination of industrial capitalist combines. Indeed, contemporary documents are replete with demands by workers that steps be taken to protect the working class from the ravages of industrial capitalism (Cross, 1974; Kealey, 1973). As the following evidence suggests, the possibility that worker demands for the elimination of combines went unnoticed by the government of the day is extremely doubtful.

The most telling evidence that the Macdonald-Conservative government was acutely aware of the threatening confrontation between labour and capital is contained in the *Reports of the Royal Commission on the Relations of Labor and Capital,* issued in 1889. Created for the purpose of investigating industrial conditions in Canada, the Commission interviewed and recorded the testimony of numerous trade-union representatives and workers. Most notably, one Toronto trade-union advocate, when asked by the Commission if there was "any means by which the Legislature should interfere in the distribution of wealth for the benefit of the masses of the people?" responded:

> Only by ways I have spoken of — by doing away with those systems of monopoly — I do not mean any ordinary systems of work, because monopoly has controlled practically the circulation of the country, and the railways have controlled the distribution of the products, and then our land system is a first tax on every man's labor (cited in Kealey, 1973:68).

In an equally forthright manner, a leading figure in Hamilton's Knights of Labor movement reported to the Commission that his organization was guided by the following principle:

> The alarming development and aggressiveness of great capitalists and corporations, unless checked, will inevitably lead to the pauperization and hopeless degradation of the toiling masses. It is imperative, if we desire to enjoy the full blessings of life, that a check be placed upon the unjust accumulation and the power of evil of aggregated wealth (cited in Kealey, 1973:162-63).

It is no mere coincidence that the Royal Commission on Labor and Capital issued its report in the same year that Canada's first anti-combines statute was enacted. Indeed, under the surface appearance of separate concerns, both may be interpreted as pragmatic attempts on the part of the government of the day to find "solutions" to constraints that threatened to hinder the profitable accumulation of capital. The mounting protest by labour against "the evil of aggregated wealth," and the government's response in the form of anti-combines legislation, was but one manifestation of the basic structural contradiction of capitalism — namely, the confrontation between labour and capital. That, indeed, the Macdonald-Conservative government viewed anti-combines legislation as a necessary step in promoting social harmony (or placating the working class) is eminently possible, given the political influence wielded by prominent trade unions, and especially by the Knights of Labor.

In their recent research on the Knights of Labor in Ontario, Kealey and Palmer (1981) reveal that during the 1880s the Order was directly involved in politics at all levels of government. Furthermore, the authors contend that the Knights of Labor was seen to pose a direct threat to the hegemony of the federal Tory party. According to Kealey and Palmer:

> Macdonald in assessing the political climate in the summer of 1886 worried that the Conservative party was "not in a flourishing state." The "rock heads" which threatened the Tory "ship" were "Riel, Home Rule, the Knights of Labor and the Scott Act." The Knights thus specifically merited "the old chieftain's" close attention and two of the three other threatening reefs were movements intimately tied to the Order and its ideals ... (Kealey and Palmer, 1981:397).

Throughout the 1880s, the Knights of Labor and other trade unions controlled and directed a significant percentage of the working man's vote (Kealey, 1973, 1980; Kealey and Palmer, 1981). In order for the Macdonald-Conservative government to maintain its image as "the people's party," to foster social harmony, and to promote profitable capital accumulation, it had no choice but to take action — at least symbolically — in support of labour's demands and against offensive monopolistic companies. It is, therefore, not unreasonable to claim that the first flourishing of Canadian anti-combines legislation was the product of an "essential confrontation" between labour and capital, and of the state's effort to find an acceptable "solution."

Conclusion

The interpretation of anti-combines legislation offered in this paper differs substantially from those advanced by both liberal pluralists and instrumental Marxists. The historical evidence presented here provides considerable support for the structural Marxist premise that the state functions to reproduce existing social and economic relations by attempting to "neutralize" or "displace" the contradictions inherent in capitalism. As the evidence indicates, the ordinary worker in late 19th century Canada (the victim of industrial capitalism) assertively endeavoured to influence the enactment of effective anti-combines legislation. However, as we have seen, monopolistic companies of the period — by virtue of their crucial importance in capital accumulation — wielded immense economic and political power. The ultimate consequence of this situation was the state's enactment of a symbolic but ineffectual law that served only to foster the reproduction of combines activity in the late 19th century.

This paper offers a more broadly-based interpretation of the origins and impact of early Canadian anti-combines legislation than those offered by contending liberal pluralist and instrumental Marxist writers. In addition, it illustrates the added theoretical and historical insights to be gained from adopting a structural Marxist approach in examining the creation of various forms of social legislation. While both liberal pluralists and instrumental Marxists have effectively pointed out that the emergence of Canada's first anti-combines statute was *in part* the result of a noticeable conflict between *petit bourgeois* and monopoly capitalists, the structural Marxist approach points to additional evidence that the creation of anti-combines legislation in Canada was influenced by a threatening confrontation between labour and capital. To date, no single theoretical orientation, with the exception of that advanced by structural Marxists, draws us towards examining the broader political and economic context within which various forms of social legislation have emerged. In directing attention to previously unexamined evidence, the structural Marxist approach brings into view valuable information concerning the historical circumstances underlying the formation of legislation that does not serve the immediate interests of capital.

"We will get some good out of this riot yet:" The Canadian State, Drug Legislation and Class Conflict

Elizabeth Comack

Prior to 1908 in Canada, there were no legal restrictions imposed on either the sale or consumption of opiates, whether for medicinal or pleasurable purposes. The importation of opium was subject to a standard duty for drugs, and manufacturers had to pay a licensing fee. A variety of opium-based tonics, elixirs and cough syrups were freely prescribed by doctors and dispensed by druggists across the country. In addition, prepared smoking-opium was manufactured and sold by Chinese opium merchants on the west coast (see Solomon and Madison, 1976-77). Beginning in 1908, however, this state of affairs was altered quite drastically, when the Canadian Parliament began passing legislation to criminalize the use of opiates. The standard or accepted description of the events immediately leading up to the passage of the legislation runs as follows:

In September of 1907, an anti-Asiatic riot took place in Vancouver, British Columbia. In response, the government sent William Lyon Mackenzie King, who was at that time Deputy Minister of Labour, to investigate the incident and provide reparation to Asiatics who had suffered losses. In the course of his investigation, King was "somewhat surprised" to receive claims of $600 each from two Chinese opium merchants for six days loss of business as a result of the rioting. Upon further investigation, King discovered that prepared smoking-opium was being manufactured in Victoria and New Westminster as well as Vancouver. In his report of the losses sustained by the Chinese, King concluded that there was a need to prohibit the importation of crude opium and its manufacture in Canada "save in so far as may be necessary for medicinal purposes."[1] Further to this, King submitted a report to the government in July of 1908 entitled *The Need for the Suppression of the Opium Traffic in Canada*.[2] Less than three weeks later, Canada's first criminal prohibition of a drug was put into effect.[3]

The origins of Canadian drug legislation is a subject which has received a considerable amount of attention within the literature.[4] To date, the analyses offered to explain the decision to criminalize opiate use have typically taken their lead from labelling theory and/or some version of the pluralistic-conflict approach. Accordingly, certain key explanatory variables have been singled out: the racial conflict which existed between the "British type" in the population and the Chinese; the enterprising efforts of individuals like Mackenzie King to generate particular "definitions of the situation"; and, more generally, the attempts of high status, powerful groups to control the behaviour of low status — in this case the opium-smoking habit of the Chinese — powerless groups.[5]

These explanations reveal that the issue of opium use in Canada was intricately connected with the "Chinese question."[6] For although a large number of Caucasians were dependent on opium-based products that were being manufactured by Caucasian-owned pharmaceutical companies, it was the Chinese opium-smoker and the Chinese opium factories that were singled out for criminal sanction.[7] Nevertheless, explanations couched in labelling and pluralistic-conflict terms fail to consider the connection between the drug laws and the "Chinese question" in any detail.

In contrast, a Marxist approach would offer a very different kind of analysis than what is presently available. The Marxist perspective is one which directs the researcher's attention to the nature of class relations in a particular historical period and the significant and variable role of the state in mediating those relations. As such, a Marxist analysis would call into question a number of factors as they pertain to the drug laws. One such factor is the class position of the Chinese: how did the Chinese figure with the labour market and economic developments of the late 19th and early 20th centuries in Canada? Another is the role which the Canadian state played in bringing about the legislation. A third factor is the correspondence between the drug legislation and the political and economic developments occurring in Canada at the same time. In short, a Marxist approach would endeavour to situate both the drug laws and the Chinese question in their *historical context*.

The purpose of this paper, therefore, is to present a Marxist analysis of the factors and conditions which led to the decision to criminalize opiate use in Canada. Accordingly, the discussion will be organized into two parts. The *first* will locate the "Chinese question" within the economic, political and ideological dynamics of the rise and consolidation of industrial capitalism in Canada. The *second* will situate the drug legislation within the larger issue of the "Chinese question."

The "Chinese Question" and the Rise of Industrial Capitalism in Canada

The basis for the emergence of industrial capitalism in Canada was laid in the mid 19th century. Much of the impetus for this development came from the construction of transportation facilities — railways and canals — which stimulated the growth of cities, the formation of a socialized labour force and the development of a domestic market, thus welding the country into an economic unit. By the 1870s the process was well underway:

> Purely extractive industry was overlaid with a secondary development involving an elaborate transportation system, a capitalistic agriculture, an extensive list of manufacturers that appear to have been efficient in their day, and a creditable finance structure (Pentland, 1950:457).

It was in the 1870s that large scale production began to take root in Canada. Between 1870 and 1890, investment in machines increased and more and larger factories emerged. In 1879, for example, there were approximately 38,000 manufacturing units in Canada. By 1890, their numbers had increased to 70,000. During the same period, the number of firms with a capital of $50,000 or more nearly doubled, thus increasing manufacturing output (Rinehart, 1975:31). By the 1920s, the giant corporation had replaced the small scale enterprise as the central feature in the Canadian economy. Employment conditions had become increasingly bureaucratized. Manufacturing units, which had numbered 70,000 in 1890, were reduced to 20,000 in 1920, and manufacturing investment reached a peak in 1929 which would not be surpassed until the 1950s (Lowe, 1979:22). In short, industrial capitalism had arrived. Evidently then, the late 1800s and early 1900s was a crucial period for the rise and consolidation of industrial capitalism in Canada.

Capitalist Ascendancy and Workers' Control

Central to the rise of capitalism as a dominant mode of production is a series of struggles over control of the production process. The supremacy of the capitalist class requires, for example, not only the ability to set wages but, more importantly, the "flexibility" to organize and reorganize the work process in its own interests. Such organization and reorganization entail the regulation of the pace of work, its scheduling and assignment, the supply of new workers, and the introduction of innovations into the work process (mechanical or otherwise) (Kealey, 1976; Marglin, 1974).

During the initial phases of capitalist development in Canada, control over the production process by capitalists was by no means assured or complete. Despite the existence of privately-owned corporate firms, workers in many industries still maintained considerable domination over production, thus acting as barriers to expanded profit-making and capital accumulation. Capitalist ascendancy, therefore, necessitated breaking the last vestiges of workers' control.

In this respect, one of the major developments characterizing the period of capitalist ascension in Canada was increased rationalization of the production process through mechanization and application of scientific management techniques (Heron and Palmer, 1980). This development had a number of consequences for workers' control, the most important being the general "deskilling" of the labour force that accompanied it. By substituting machine power for human labour, and by reducing the production process to its constituent parts, capitalists were continually able to employ more and more "bucks" or "greenhands" (Kealey, 1976).

The use of unskilled labour can not only reduce the wage bill and workers' control (through diminishing the dependence of production on the skills and knowledge of the workers), it can also create important divisions within the working class. In essence, a "split labour market" may develop in which unskilled, cheaper labour is used to create new industry (having substantially lower costs than the rest of the labour market); to act as strikebreakers or replacements to undercut organized, skilled labour; or generally to create a reserve labour pool (Bonacich, 1976). The introduction of cheaper labour into the labour market can be perceived as threatening to higher paid, skilled labour, who fear that their jobs and wages are being undermined. In the case of Canada, where the supply of "greenhands" was very often made up of recent immigrants, the labour force was also split along ethnic or racial lines (Heron and Palmer, 1980).

In the context of the pattern described above, the "Chinese question" in British Columbia becomes explicable.

The Role of Chinese Labour

The immigration of Chinese people to Canada began around 1858 with the discovery of gold on the Fraser River. Initially, like other miners, they moved up the west coast from California; but within a few years of their first appearance in British Columbia, the Chinese were emigrating directly from China (Woodsworth, 1971).

As the gold rush subsided, many Chinese began serving the settler class (working as farm labourers, domestics, and the like) or laboured on public works. With the discovery of coal at Cumberland, B.C. in 1864, the Chinese went to work in the mines, and with the rapid development of the fishing industry after 1878 many took up positions in the salmon canneries. By the end of the 1870s the Chinese were shouldering much of the unskilled work in the province. When the construction of the Canadian Pacific Railway (CPR) began in 1881, Chinese labourers were recruited in large numbers.[8] As Li (1980) has noted, Chinese immigration, like other international migrations, was tied to poor economic opportunities in the home country and a labour demand in the receiving country. The vast majority of Chinese coming to Canada originated from the province of Kwangtung in south eastern China, an area which had suffered the repercussions of decades of foreign intrusion, economic hardship and political unrest. Most of the immigrants were male "sojourners" who, like many of the central European immigrants who came to Canada (Avery, 1975), were attracted by the potential opportunities for making enough money to improve their economic situation once they returned home.

On the other side of the coin, the initial development of the resource industries — mining, timber and fishing — in British Columbia and the infrastructure necessary to sustain it (especially the railroad) were all labour intensive endeavours which required the presence of an industrial army. In addition, an adequate — or at least potential — supply of labour was needed to induce capital investment to the west coast. It was not simply labour, however, but *cheap* labour that was required. This was particularly true in resource production where labour cost was the primary factor in determining the viability of a given industry because resource commodities carried a large export component and had to remain competitive with world prices. Chinese labour clearly fit the bill, since the Chinese would work for low wages and China seemed to offer an endless supply of potential recruits. The presence of Chinese labour, however, was both a "blessing" and a "threat," depending upon one's position in the production process.

From the capitalist's point of view, the Chinese were indeed a blessing. The major industries in British Columbia all profited directly from Chinese labour. In mining, for example, Robert Dunsmuir, owner of the Wellington Mines, testified before a Royal Commission in 1885 that "... if it were not for the Chinese labour, the business I am engaged in specially, coalmining, would be seriously retarded and curtailed."[9] Moreover, Andrew Onderdonk, Chief Contractor for the Canadian Pacific Railway, argued that without the Chinese, the construction of the railway would be delayed "twelve years longer than necessary."[10]

While British Columbia capitalists and backers of the CPR viewed the Chinese as a cheap and reliable labour source, Canadian workers saw them as a serious threat. This threat, however, was both real and imaginary. On the one hand, there is no doubt that the Chinese worked for lower wages.[11] In addition, immigrant Chinese were one group — although not the only one — who were used as strikebreakers, often on threat of deportation (Phillips, 1967). On the other hand, it could be argued that the threat posed by the Chinese was really "imaginary" since, by and large, the Chinese were actually segregated from other workers by industry and occupation.[12] Much of the impetus for the fears of Caucasian workers actually came from the capitalists. Onderdonk, for instance, argued that:

> ... if Chinese labour was prohibited, white men instead of finding work at high wages, would find very little work to do at all, because the theory of high wages for all precludes the possibility of high wages for any.[13]

Nevertheless, the "threat" posed by the Chinese, whether real or imaginary, did promote racial antagonism within the British Columbia working class, because the "definition of the situation" promulgated by employers was that the presence of cheap Chinese labour — not the capitalist quest for profit and control over production — produced wage differentials and conflicts within the work place.

Consequently, Chinese labour played an integral role in the general assault on workers' control which was at the heart of the rise of industrial capitalism in Canada. Owing to a combination of factors, the immigrant Chinese proved to be an easily exploitable group in the hands of the British Columbia capitalists, who used them in a variety of ways to undermine the position of skilled labour. The tendency for unskilled labour to be drawn from particular racial and ethnic groups and the resulting hostility from Caucasian workers placed the Chinese in an especially precarious position within the British Columbia society.

Needless to say, Canada's and British Columbia's working classes did not passively accept the changes in, and direction and consequences of, industrial development. The strategies employed and the intensity of working class response were varied and complex — but respond they did.

Response of the Working Class

Generally speaking, most Canadian workers came to accept the increasing use of mechanization as an inevitable addition to the workplace. They did, however, attempt to control its ill-effects through a variety of means: "staunch enforcement of union rules, the introduction of training programmes, petitions for the establishment of training schools and, *above all else*, ... the organization of their craft" (Heron and Palmer, 1980: 53, emphasis added). A major offensive and defensive thrust of workers' conflict with capital was work stoppages of various sorts. Both organized and "wildcat" strikes provided a potentially effective vehicle for backing workers' demands. Union recognition was one major source of work stoppage. The increasing use of greenhands, typically supplied through immigration, also gave rise to a good deal of working class discontent. For skilled labour, greenhands and immigration undermined the very foundation of their control since "the strength of craft bodies ... traditionally resided in their ability to limit labour's availability" (Heron and Palmer, 1980:63).

Until the 1980s, union membership in British Columbia was relatively low, and strikes tended to be few and local. General unions (such as the Knights of Labor) were evident, but the prevailing trend was towards the formation of separate craft bodies that were loosely coordinated by congresses and city councils.[14] In addition, labour organizations at this time were essentially conservative in nature and hesitant to engage in more direct forms of political action. When a political ideology did surface, it tended to centre around the immigration policies and practices of the period.

While labour groups across the country vehemently opposed the increasing immigration of unskilled labour (Watt, 1959; Ostry, 1960; Craven and Traves, 1979; Kealey, 1980), in British Columbia the opposition to immigration meant an *anti-Asiatic* and *Oriental exclusion* stance. Indeed, the issue of Chinese immigration was one of labour's main cohesive bonds during this early period (Saywell, 1951) because it provided fuel for labour's defence against the erosion of their control over the production process. The anti-Chinese posturing of organized labour in British Columbia was, therefore, not a purely racist reflex but part of a general strategy to oppose the immigration of the unskilled.

Beginning in the 1890s, there is evidence of a marked change in both the form and intensity of the working class response. An increasing number of workers were becoming unionized; in addition to the traditional craft bodies, industrial unions were forming.[15] Perhaps most notable, however, was the increasing *militancy* and *radicalism* on the part of organized labour.

By the turn of the century, relations between management and labour were reaching a crisis situation (Saywell, 1951). Indeed, the first two decades of the 20th century can be characterized as a period of intense and violent labour unrest. Of fourteen large and intense strikes in Canada between 1901 and 1913, six occurred in British Columbia (Jamieson, 1968:67). The situation in B.C. had become so severe that "Ralph Smith, Laurier's labour lieutenant, described British Columbia society as "being divided into two armed camps" just as Marx had predicted" (Robin, 1972: 76). Increased militancy was accompanied by the appearance of socialism in the province. While the late 19th and early 20th centuries saw the growth of socialism across the country, it appears that "Canadian socialism came of age in British Columbia ... fledgling socialist organizations emerged across the country, but British Columbia became the dynamic centre of the movement" (McCormack, 1977:18).

The reasons behind these developments are many. The cyclical and seasonal fluctuations of British Columbia industry, depending as it did on the world market, meant high job insecurity for workers. Workers south of the border were experiencing more benefits and higher wages, and government giveaways to industry, especially in the form of land grants, were not being well received by labour. Also important was the predominance of isolated, single industry communities. In the mining camps, for instance, the division between mine managers and workers was most stark. When the miners (who were subjected to unhealthy working conditions, a preponderance of accidents and deaths, and unenforced safety regulations) attempted to establish unions, they were met with strong resistance from management. The mine operators perceived unions as illegitimate, as placing restrictions on their freedoms, and used a variety of means — including blacklists, spies and militia — to undermine worker's attempts to organize (McCormack, 1977; Phillips, 1967).

The more radical, industrial unions accounted for a large proportion of the labour unrest. Their influence was especially evident in the mining industry. In 1901, The Western Federation of Miners (an industrial union based on a militant socialist philosophy) struck at Rossland, B.C. The WFM was involved in a series of strikes in the Vancouver Island Collieries in 1903 and also struck in sympathy with the United Brotherhood of Railway Employees that same year (Jamieson, 1973; Phillips, 1967).

The socialist influence also prompted a more direct political involvement on the part of labour. In general, labour's political agenda included such issues as the single tax and public ownership, but the socialist agenda was most distinct. The 1903 platform of the Socialist Party, for example, included the transformation of all capitalist property into the "collective property of the working man (sic);" the management of industry by workers; the gradual establishment of production for use and not for profit; and the conduct of public affairs in such a manner as to promote the interests of the working class alone (Saywell, 1951:148). Moreover, while the moderates within the labour movement could not be characterized as "cooperative" with management (as the struggle for control over production indicates), they were certainly not advocating the overthrow of capitalism as were the socialist unions and parties. The manifesto of the Socialist Party, for example, read:

> Labour produces all wealth and to labour it should justly belong ... in order to free the working man from his slavery to the Capitalist the wage system must be abolished and to this and other ends labour must take the reigns of government away from capital (cited in Saywell, 1951:148).

The socialists could also be distinguished from the more conservative labour element by their *lack of support for the popular anti-Oriental stance*. In the provincial election of 1900, for example, labour candidates generally stood on a platform that had become a traditional labour program — including the eight hour day, safety legislation and anti-Orientalism — but as Phillips (1967:31) notes: "(T)he socialists differed mainly over the issue of Oriental exclusion, which they did not basically support." As well, the Industrial Workers of the World, whose organizing drives were directed towards the unskilled, itinerant, immigrant workers, "even advocated the organization of Asiatics in British Columbia ... [reflecting] the Wobblies' [the I.W.W.'s] commitment to the proletarian solidarity of the working class" (McCormack, 1977: 101-2). For the socialists, in other words, the "enemy" was the capitalist class and its state — not cheap Oriental labour.

By the first decade of the 20th century, then, the political-economic situation in British Columbia had changed markedly: the working class was better organized, and the increasing militancy and radicalism of the labour movement had altered the nature of class relations in the province. The presence of a socialist element within the working class posed a serious threat to the economic and political stability of British Columbia society, since the socialist unions and political parties, unlike the more conservative craft bodies, were intent on defining labour issues in class, rather than ethnic or racial, terms.

The Canadian state occupied a very central, although precarious, position in the conflict between capital and labour. Its policies and practices aided capital accumulation and, hence, the ascendancy of the capitalist class. In addition, it was primarily to the state which fell the task of meeting organized labour's challenge to capitalist hegemony, a task exacerbated by the fact that the state itself was often responsible for precipitating and/or intensifying working class discontent. The following section examines the role of the state in more detail.

The Role of the Canadian State

It is clear that the activities of the Canadian state — at all levels — assisted the rise of industrial capitalism in Canada. John A. Macdonald's National Policy of 1870, for example, which guided state activity for many years, was essentially aimed at fostering and enhancing economic growth along a capitalist path. Government grants in the form of cash, land and resources notably speeded up the process of monopolization in Canadian industry (Robin, 1972; Myers 1975), and the tariff provided protection for Canadian industry against foreign competitors (Craven and Traves, 1979). An even more critical component of the National Policy, however, was its stand on immigration.

The success of the great projects of industrialization depended upon a steady supply of cheap unskilled labour. Consequently, the federal government actively encouraged immigration (through government agencies and advertising abroad and through government-sanctioned, private labour-contract firms) and, when forced to, summarily disallowed any attempts by provincial legislatures to restrict immigration. This was especially the case in British Columbia, where attempts by the provincial government to restrict Chinese immigration and employment throughout the late 1800s came into direct conflict with the intent of the National Policy.[16] Chinese labour was seen as indispensable, among other things, to the completion of the railroad. Indeed, Macdonald himself argued in 1883 that "it will be all very well to exclude Chinese labour, when we can replace it with white labour, but until that is done, it is better to have Chinese labour than no labour at all."[17] That the state played a significant role in aiding capital accumulation and hence the ascendancy of the capitalist class is evidenced by a number of state policies and practices during the initial phase of capitalist development. But the state could adhere to the interests of capital to the neglect of labour only at the risk of generating or exacerbating working class discontent. In short, the Canadian state had the task of not only aiding or enhancing capital accumulation but *legitimating* it as well. In essence, the state was involved, simultaneously, on two fronts: aiding the ascendancy of the capitalist class and meeting the challenge of the working class response. As mediator of class conflict, the state had to contend with the increasing organization and unrest on the part of labour. That such a task was carried out and the manner in which it was executed can be gleaned by an examination of the nature and degree of state intervention into capital-labour relations.

While the history of state involvement with the "labour problem" antedates the turn of the century in Canada, the first decade of the 20th century provides an appropriate focal point for an examination of state intervention into capital-labour relations. This is so for a number of reasons, not the least of which was the increasing militancy and radicalism of the working class during this period. In addition, the year 1900 brought with it the passage of the Conciliation Act. The Conciliation Act established the Federal Department of Labour and, at the same time, "marked the entry of the Federal Parliament into the field of legislation for the conciliation of industrial disputes" (Lorentson and Woolner, 1950:147). The remainder of this section, therefore, will centre on the role which the state played — via the Department of Labour — in the conflict between capital and labour during the first decade of the 20th century.

The development of the Department of Labour and state activity as a whole with regard to industrial relations during this period cannot be approached without discussing William Lyon Mackenzie King. Indeed, as Craven suggests:

> To write about the development of Canadian labour policy without discussing William Lyon Mackenzie King would be like mounting a production of *Hamlet* without the prince (Craven, 1980:11).

King was the Deputy Minister of Labour and Editor of the *Labour Gazette* from the time of the department's inception in 1900 until 1908, and then Minister of Labour from 1909 until the defeat of the Laurier government in 1911. As Ferns and Ostry (1955:51) note: "He was from the first the star of the show, and the impression was created that he was the author of all thought and action relating to labour." Indeed, King can be considered as the embodiment of the strategic position the state occupied in the conflict between capital and labour during this period. He devised a whole new theory of the role of the state in industrial relations and put that theory into practice on a number of different occasions. It becomes important, therefore, to devote some attention to King's perceptions of the capital-labour conflict and the role which he saw for the state within that conflict.

Above all else, Mackenzie King saw himself as a conciliator (Fern and Ostry, 1976) whose duty it was to "mediate between the two conflicting classes to restore the natural equilibrium in the political economy" (Whitaker, 1977:152). In other words, while aware of class conflicts, King held to a liberal vision of a fundamental harmony between capital and labour in which both were viewed as legitimate parties in the productive process, with their respective returns regulated by the market. From this view it followed that since there was no fundamental conflict between capital and labour, disputes arose from a lack of communication between the parties involved (Whitaker, 1977) and any problems that did arise could be resolved through ideological or normative measures.

Not surprisingly, such an outlook gave rise to another significant premise in King's conception of labour relations and the state's role in them. King believed that unions had a place in labour relations—but only those unions that were willing to cooperate with capital. All others were perceived as illegitimate — "to be fought with every weapon at the concerted disposal of capital and the state" (Whitaker, 1977:153-4). For King, this meant an explicitly *anti-Socialist* stance. At one point in his diary, for example, King wrote: "... while my love is mostly for the working classes ... I am on the whole opposed to 'Socialistic Schemes'."[18] In short, while King expressed some sympathy with labour, his views ultimately rested with the long-term interests of capital. And a working class — or sections of it — which challenged the very basis of his vision of a liberal society could simply not be tolerated. As Rudin (1972:44) has observed: "The whole problem, as King perceived it, is fitting the worker to the requirements of the capitalist system."

That King adhered to this particular world view is evidenced by his actions and reflections during his tenure with the Department of Labour, especially in terms of his involvement with conflicts in British Columbia. Indeed, King's exposure to the situation in British Columbia came very early in his career. As Ferns and Ostry (1955:56) state: "Almost from the first moment of his entry into the new Department of Labour, Mackenzie King found the problem of British Columbia at his doorstep."

In 1901, for example, King was sent to British Columbia to investigate and report on the industrial unrest centred at Rossland, where the Western Federation of Miners (WFM) was on strike. Rossland was King's first encounter with a socialist union, and the experience left him uneasy. King felt that the WFM was a "gang of alien radicals" who had to be beaten back at all costs to protect the mining interests of the province (McCormack, 1977:40). As he wrote in his diary: "All of Canada can learn from British Columbia, the province speaks a note of warning in strongest terms against the dangers of labour democracy."[19] King's first impression of the WFM was to be a long-lasting one, and was significant in shaping the state's response to militant industrial unions in 1903.

As the magnitude and intensity of industrial conflict in British Columbia increased, so did the demand from business groups in the province for some sort of action on the part of the state to resolve it. The government responded by appointing a Royal Commission on Industrial Disputes in the Province of British Columbia in April of 1903. Mackenzie King was appointed as secretary of the Commission.

Despite the broad title of the Commission, most of the evidence collected and the findings and recommendations reported concerned the strikes by the Western Federation of Miners and the United Brotherhood of Railway

Employees. The manner in which the investigation was carried out led one prominent socialist to comment that it "was not an investigation but that the WFM and kindred international organizations were on trial" (cited in Saywell, 1951:140). Indeed, the numerous grievances expressed by the workers were either ignored or dismissed as misleading or irrelevant. Instead, the Commission concluded that the unrest was the work of a conspiracy among the affiliates of the American Labour Union to disrupt British Columbia industry. The miners had been "tricked" or "intimidated" into joining the WFM and had not joined or gone on strike because of legitimate grievances. Moreover, the WFM and UBRE were roundly denounced as not being legitimate trade unions at all, but "conspiracies against society" and "secret political organizations" which distributed "incendiary and scurrilous literature" and in whose ranks were "socialistic agitators of the most bigoted and ignorant type." In fact, one of the most significant outcomes of the Commission was the distinction it endeavoured to make between "good" and "bad" unions.

> And here ... lies the essential difference between the legitimate trade unionist and the revolutionary socialist: the former realizes that he has a common interest with the employer in the successful conduct of the business; the latter postulates an irreconcilable hostility and is ever compassing the embarrassment or ruin of the employer, all the while ignoring the fact that capital and labour are the two blades of the shears which, to work well, must be joined together by the bolt of mutual confidence, but if wrenched apart, are both helpless and useless.[20]

Nevertheless, the Report of the Royal Commission did not — as it was intended to do — retard the growth of the militant industrial unions. If anything, it produced the opposite effect in that the overwhelming reaction by labour was one of indignation and an increased hostility toward, and suspicion of, the federal government (Jamieson, 1968; McCormack, 1977).

As evidenced by the preceding discussion, Mackenzie King was very much the personification of the strategic position which the state occupied in the conflict between capital and labour during the first decade of the 20th century. His perception of the "labour problem" and his involvement in industrial disputes during this period provide ample documentation of the Canadian state's concern with the long-term interests of capital and the need to not only aid in capital accumulation, but meet the challenge which organized labour posed to capitalist hegemony as well.

The Drug Legislation and the Chinese Question
As noted previously, concern over Chinese immigration, particularly from the ranks of organized craft workers, antedated the turn of the

century. One of the moves taken by the federal government to appease those calling for Oriental exclusion was the passage of a Restriction Act in 1885 which imposed a $50 head tax on Chinese immigrants (Munroe, 1971). Despite the head tax, the number of Chinese entering Canada began to increase at the turn of the century.[21] In addition to the increase in Chinese immigration, there were a large number of Japanese and East Indian immigrants.[22]

With the increase in Asiatic immigration, anti-Asiatic sentiments in British Columbia mounted. Calls for the restriction of Asians intensified during the summer of 1907. In July, for example, the Victoria Trades and Labor Council appealed to Prime Minister Laurier to bring a halt to Japanese immigration.[23] As well, MacPherson, the Liberal MP for Vancouver, wrote to Laurier to express his concern over the number of Japanese labourers arriving in Vancouver and the strong sentiments of organized labour against them. Laurier, however, was not to be moved. In his reply to MacPherson he stated:

> The question is simply this: you have a scarcity of labour
> in British Columbia and there are parties in the Province
> with the tacit approbation of a large section of the Popu-
> lation, who are making constant efforts to bring in Asi-
> atics to work your lumber mills, your fisheries and your
> mines, and also as domestic servants ... I sympathize
> deeply with you in the delicate position in which you are
> and you may be sure that as far as it is possible for me to
> do I will not complicate matters.[24]

The B.C. legislature made an effort to stop the influx of Japanese immigrants by passing a restriction act, but James Dunsmuir, the Lieutenant Governor, would not give assent to the act. The Wellington Collieries, owned by Dunsmuir, had recently entered into a contract with the Canadian Nippon Supply Company of Vancouver to procure 500 Japanese labourers under contract.[25] It was charged that Dunsmuir's business interests were overshadowing his role as lieutenant governor. Calls were made in the legislature for his removal, but were ruled out of order. The same restriction act was subsequently passed, and this time assent was given. But it was promptly disallowed by the federal government.

Such recalcitrance on the part of the federal government and the apparent impotence of the provincial legislature in taking action led many Caucasian workers to conclude that there was no political agency that would effectively respond to the perceived threat posed by Asiatic labour. As such, in August, the Vancouver Trades and Labor Council formed an Asiatic Exclusion League (AEL) to further their cause (Ward, 1978).

It was alleged that several hundred Japanese would be arriving by steamer on September 8th. To demonstrate their protest, the AEL organized a parade on the evening of September 7th. Between eight and nine thousand people paraded to the city hall, where an effigy of Lieutenant Governor Dunsmuir was burned. A meeting presided over by Von Rhein of the TLC then heard speeches and passed a number of resolutions, including one condemning Dunsmuir for refusing his assent, another requesting the resignation of Premier MacBride, and several others demanding an immediate end to all immigration from Asia. The crowd then moved on to the Chinese and Japanese quarters nearby and within minutes a riot was in progress — precipitated by a rock thrown through the window of a Chinese store. A few persons were hurt and substantial property damage was incurred by Chinese and Japanese businesses. In all, it took the police four hours to restore order. Although a crowd gathered again the next day, police had blocked entrance to the area. As well, Japanese and Chinese residents had armed themselves in preparation for another onslaught; but the trouble was effectively ended.

The federal government responded to the riot in a number of ways. For one, an Order in Council was passed appointing Rudolphe Lemieux, the Minister of Labour, as a special envoy to Japan to meet with the authorities there on the subject of Japanese immigration to Canada.[26] For another, Mackenzie King was appointed Commissioner to investigate the losses sustained by the Chinese and Japanese as a result of the riot.[27] King heard Japanese claims for two weeks beginning late in October. While he was still in Vancouver, Parliament passed an Order in Council naming King as Commissioner to investigate the methods by which Oriental labourers had been induced to come to Canada.[28] In March of 1908, King was sent to England to confer with the British authorities on the subject of immigration from India.[29] The investigation of losses suffered by the Chinese as a result of the riot did not take place until May of 1908. It was during the course of the Commission's hearings that King heard testimony from two opium manufacturers. In the conclusion to his report on the losses sustained by the Chinese, King made mention of the need to prohibit the importation and manufacture of opium in Canada for other than medicinal purposes. He then followed up this suggestion with a report on the opium traffic in Canada which was submitted on July 1, 1908. On the strength of King's report, Lemieux introduced Bill 205 in the House of Commons, "An Act to Prohibit the Transportation and Sale of Opium for other than Medicinal Purposes." With only one minor amendment, the Opium Act was passed on July 20, 1908.

At first glance, one could interpret the situation in British Columbia in the early 1900s as primarily a "race problem." The apparent growth in magnitude of the "Oriental question" had reached a point where some form of action became necessary. From this perspective, the Canadian state responded to the riot — and the intensity of the unrest which it symbolized — by a variety of measures designed to restrict the Asian population in British Columbia.

However, interpreting the situation as strictly a "race problem" overlooks several factors. One of these is that concern over Asian immigrants was not aimed at restricting *all* Asians but only one *class* of Asians: labourers. This is evident in the list of Chinese who were exempt from paying the head tax — which includes officials, merchants, tourists, men of science and students, but not labourers.[30] Indeed, during King's mission to the Orient in 1908-1909, he conferred — in an effort to determine the attitude of the Chinese authorities on the matter of regulating immigration to Canada — with a member of the British delegation who led King to believe that, "He did not think the Government [of China] cared a whit about the coolie classes, or how they were treated, but were very sensitive in regard to their gentry."[31]

Another factor is that while the number of Asians entering British Columbia had increased during the first decade of the 20th century, that increase had not kept pace with the number of Caucasians entering the province. From 1891 to 1901 the percentage of Asians to the total population in British Columbia rose from 9.1 to 11, but had decreased to 7.8 by 1911. More significant, however, is that during this same period the percentage of Asians to the white population in B.C. *declined* from 16.5 in 1891 to 14.6 in 1901 and 8.9 in 1911.[32] Consequently, the exact magnitude of the "race problem" falls into doubt and one could argue that the Asian "threat" was more imaginary than real. It will be argued that to comprehend fully the nature of the "Chinese question" and the decision in the early 1900s to criminalize opium use, one must consider a key variable: the change in form and intensity of the British Columbia trade union movement which had dramatically altered the nature of class relations in that province.

To elaborate, rather than a "race problem," the situation in British Columbia in this period can be considered a "labour problem." As noted earlier, a serious political crisis of legitimacy dawned in the early 20th century British Columbia as the socialist movement grew in strength. The re-establishment of working class consent, which was imperative if capitalist industrialization was to proceed, depended greatly on the repression and discrediting of the socialist movement.

Thus, from 1900 onward, not only an economic — but an ideological — conflict intensified. The main battlelines in this ideological struggle to define the situation were drawn between the socialist unions and political parties on the one side and the capitalist class and its state on the other. In essence, what ensued was a class-based battle to define the "relevant properties" of the social environment. The socialists were intent on furthering a definition of the situation along class lines. "Problems," as such, were rooted in the exploitative nature of the capitalist relations of production. The state, on the other hand, in meeting the challenge which organized labour posed to capitalist hegemony, endeavoured to further a "moral" and "racial" perspective regarding the source of economic and social problems. That is, the unrest and discontent of the era were due to the "moral laxity" of various groups — particularly "foreigners" or "aliens" — in the country. From this perspective, solutions to the country's ills lay not in a fundamental realignment of the material basis of Canadian society, but in the manipulation of consciousness. And it is here where the Oriental question and the drug legislation must be located: as part and parcel of an ideology founded on "racism," "aliens" and "immorality" utilized in the manufacture of consent to resolve a legitimation crisis in the early 1900s.

There is little doubt that racism was employed in a politically opportunistic manner. Incidents of racial hostility in British Columbia appear to have figured prominently when economic conditions deteriorated and competition for jobs increased. Just as important, public campaigns endorsing anti-Asiatic prejudice were often associated with elections. Even the notorious James Dunsmuir, for example, when running for office in the 1900 provincial election, pledged to replace all of his Chinese workers with Caucasians if elected (Ward, 1978). In most cases, anti-Chinese organizations were short-lived, and in one instance the organization died immediately after its instigator was elected to office (Robin, 1972).

The press also played a significant part in promoting an ideology of racism in British Columbia. Newspapers often carried inflammatory stories and editorials warning of the "Yellow invasion" and the havoc it would wreak on B.C. society. During the months preceding the Vancouver riot, for instance, the urban press in the province "featured daily comment on the 'invasion' reports which grew more sensational with every passing week" (Ward, 1978:30). Many of the leading newspapers in British Columbia had direct political party links[33] and, needless to say, the press was not above promoting racism to further political ends.[34]

In these ways, the Chinese (and all Asians) were consistently and continually portrayed by politicians and the press as an "alien group" who were undermining the prosperity which British Columbia had to offer its Caucasian citizens. This definition of the situation was in direct contrast to the view of the socialist movement, which identified the capitalist class and its state as the culprits behind the unrealized expectations of the working class in B.C. But while anti-Asiatic sentiments did not hold sway with the socialists, racist appeals did find support among the more conservative craft unions, especially given their explicit and implicit anti-immigration connotations. In this respect, promoting a definition of the situation couched in racial terms helped to maintain a distance between the so-called "legitimate" and "illegitimate" unions in their perception of the economic situation — but it did little to quell the unrest. If anything, anti-Asiatic sentiments became a source of unity for the conservative unions in British Columbia.

The 1907 riot signified the intensity of the labour situation in B.C. That the riot was an incident of "labour unrest" was noted by the British Ambassador, Claude MacDonald, in correspondence with Governor General Grey:

> There can be, I think, no doubt that the whole difficulty

> on the American Continent is purely a labour difficulty;
> all the sensational newspaper articles against immoral-
> ity, unsanitary habits, etc. appear to be written with the
> object of obscuring the real issue and are, in any case,
> entirely beside the mark and for the most part quite
> untrue; the plain fact is that those in possession of the
> labour market object to the competition of men who are
> willing to do the same work as themselves for a lower
> wage or to do more work for the same wage. This
> objection is somewhat natural and the incident now
> reported shows that it is held quite strongly ...[35]

Moreover, that Mackenzie King played such a significant role in the events following the riot was not surprising. It was only logical for the federal government to send its Deputy Minister of Labour to investigate what had been defined as a "labour unrest," especially since King had been a central figure in the state's ideological offensive against the socialist movement, and had been actively involved in mediating capital-labour conflict generally. King's views on the labour question, particularly his distinction between "good" and "bad" unions, have already been discussed in some detail. The views which King held on the Chinese question are also significant.

During his trip to B.C. in 1901 to investigate the WFM strike at Rossland, King remarked in his diary on the "suitability" of Chinese labour:

> Everywhere in the houses in Rossland, one sees the
> Chinese servants and what I have seen of them makes me
> feel they are suited perfectly for this work. White labour
> should go into industries and trades and leave the lower
> grades of work to these people who enjoy it and do it
> well.[36]

Nevertheless, although realizing the advantages that had been gained from the presence of Chinese labour in British Columbia, King was also keenly aware of the prevailing opposition to the Chinese. In 1901 he wrote:

> The Oriental labour question is the big one for British
> Columbia and our West, whether it can be made as good
> a thing as slavery seems doubtful, because it wear (sic)
> the semblance of free contract. I think this country is well
> rid of the Mongolian classes, but it looks as if they were
> destined to become our slaves. It is a serious problem for
> the West.[37]

But King — ever the conciliator — was likewise intent on striking a balance between the demand for Chinese labour and the opposition which its presence generated. For example, in a letter to a Mrs. Fitzgibbon, whom King had met when in B.C. in 1907, he continued a discussion they had on the Chinese question. King was of the opinion that the head tax should remain in force, but that a law be enacted

> which would restrict the occupations into which Chinese coming to Canada would be permitted to enter, beginning possibly with the two occupations of agriculture and domestic service and advocating that the Chinese entering Canada to engage in these occupations might take out a license which would entitle them to exemptions from the poll tax ... By keeping the law regarding the Chinese upon the statute books you would not encounter the same opposition of those who are interested in excluding Chinese labour and by advocating exemption in the case of agricultural and domestic service only the proposal would receive a pretty general support.[38]

King's views on the Oriental question, when added to his position on the "labour problem," give us some insight as to the kind of philosophical and experiential baggage which he brought with him to Vancouver in 1908 when he investigated Chinese claims.

Upon concluding his examination of one of the opium manufacturers who, King said, had given "interesting and valuable evidence," he added: "We will get some good out of this riot yet."[39] While the intention here is not to impute conspiratorial motives on King's part (although, given his political cunning, he should not be underestimated), what is being suggested is that the subsequent decision to criminalize opium use must be seen in terms of the *historical process* in which the drug laws emerged. The Canadian state was confronted by a crisis of legitimacy — a threat to the system that had to be responded to in some fashion. The increasing intensity of the labour unrest in British Columbia was emanating from two fronts: the socialists, who were intent on defining labour issues along class lines, and the more conservative craft unions, as represented by the TLC. Although the socialists did not adhere to an anti-Asiatic stand, the Asiatic Exclusion League had been formed in the summer of 1907 by members of the Vancouver TLC and the AEL was seen as responsible for the riots that followed shortly afterward.

Following the theoretical reasoning of the Marxist approach, for the state to mediate class conflict successfully, such threats must be dealt with in *other* than class terms. In the case of the 1907 riot, and the intensity of the unrest that it symbolized, the conflict was managed in a number of ways.

For one, an effort was made to pin the responsibility for the riot on "foreign agitators." Shortly after the riot occurred, Governor General Grey wrote to Laurier: "I hope the result of the investigation by the Govt. into the causes of this abominable outbreak may be to show that it was not spontaneous but the work of Seattle, and other American organizations."[40] In an effort to further such a definition of the situation and gain evidence to that effect, the government hired T.R.E. McInnes as an "agent provocateur" to report on the activities of the AEL.[41] For another, the conflict was interpreted as a "race problem" stemming from the influx of Asiatics into the province. Accordingly, Rudolphe Lemieux was sent to Japan to negotiate an agreement that would regulate the flow of Japanese labourers to Canada, and King was sent to Britain to confer with the British authorities on Indian immigration. In addition, the establishment of the Royal Commission on the methods by which Oriental labourers had been induced to come to Canada further reinforced the "race problem" interpretation and gave the appearance that the government was taking action to resolve the growing opposition to Oriental immigration.

Finally, as a result of King's investigation, the situation in British Columbia was defined as a "moral" or "normative" problem because of the opium trade carried on by the Chinese and all of the "immoral" connotations associated with it.

In short, the definition of the situation generated by the state was that an "alien element" was responsible for the deteriorating situation in British Columbia. It was not, in other words, the fundamental material conflict between capital and labour that gave rise to problems and tensions within the system but the invasion of "foreign agitators," "immoral outsiders" and the like.

The Opium Act further reinforced this definition of the situation. In essence, the criminalization of opiate use amounted to the creation of a social problem by the state. Before the 1908 Act, opium use was not generally defined in the public mind as a social problem (Solomon and Madison, 1976-7; Green, 1979). The state was aware of opium use as early as the 1880s (Munro, 1971) and both the federal and provincial governments collected considerable revenue from opium imports, indicating an awareness and implied condonement of the practice. Moreover, one could argue that prohibiting the importation and manufacture of opium for non-medicinal purposes in 1908 was, in some ways, akin to beating the proverbial dead horse. By 1907, the tonnage of crude opium imports was at a level almost equivalent to that of 1884, whereas in the decade 1885 to 1895 import levels had been almost twice as high (Solomon and Madison, 1976-7:243). Furthermore, a relatively insignificant amount of imported opium was prepared for smoking in comparison with that used by Caucasian-owned pharmaceutical companies.

The result of criminalizing opiate use was that the drug trade was driven underground and prices skyrocketed, creating a profitable market for smugglers (Chan, 1983:77). It would seem, therefore, that official prohibition simply increased the gravity and changed the nature of the problem of drug use, rather than correcting or controlling it. Singling out opium use among the Chinese also served the purpose of providing an avenue for bringing about the restriction of Chinese immigration. On the subject of regulating Chinese immigration to Canada, King noted that "visiting China to attend the Opium Commission [in 1909] afforded an opportunity to quietly discuss the situation with the Chinese authorities and find out their feelings on the matter."[42]

There appears to be a clear and inescapable connection between legislation aimed at the "immoral" habit practised by the Chinese and the ideology that an "alien element" was responsible for the deteriorating situation in British Columbia. Opium-smoking became an easy symbol for the dangers and evils embodied in the fantasy of the "Yellow Peril," and the opium legislation helped to affirm Oriental immigrants as a major cause of social problems. Consequently, one could argue that the drug legislation was not so much directed at the Chinese but rather helped to identify them as a major source of the problems confronting B.C. society. In doing this, the law de-legitimized further the competing view of the socialist movement, which insisted on defining labour issues in *class*, not racial terms. Moreover, the continuing identification of unrest with aliens was more-or-less a symbolic concession to the "legitimate" conservative unions, which were willing to cooperate with capital (as contrasted with the so-called "illegitimate" socialist unions that were more hostile to capital). In this fashion, the drug legislation drove another wedge, however small, into working class unity.

Canada's first drug law emerged in the midst of growing class conflict in which the Canadian state was clearly involved. As that conflict intensified, so did the need for the state to respond to it; not simply by force, but by ideological and normative means as well. The drug legislation can be seen as part of a much wider effort by the state to respond to a legitimation crisis in order to maintain and reproduce the social relations of capitalism in the early 1900s.

It has been argued that a full understanding of the circumstances surrounding the emergence of Canada's first drug law cannot be reached without situating the drug legislation and the "Chinese question" in their historical context. As the foregoing discussion has demonstrated, a Marxist approach is capable of offering such an analysis and, consequently, can provide a more powerful explanatory scheme than those presently available.

Notes

1. Canada, *Sessional papers* (1907-8), No.74f, "Report on W.L.M. King on losses sustained by the Chinese Population of Vancouver, B.C." pages 15-16.
2. Canada, *Sessional Papers* (1908), No.36b.
3. The Opium Act (1908, 7-8 Edw VII c 50) prohibited "the importation, manufacture and sale of opium for other than medicinal purposes" and made it an indictable offence to import, manufacture, sell, offer for sale, or have in possession for sale, opium.
4. See, for example, Solomon and Madison (1976-77); Green (1979); Trasov

(1962); and Chapman (1979).

5. See, especially Small (1978).

6. The "Chinese question" is a term which was prominent around the turn of the century and used to refer to the perceived problems generated by the presence of Chinese immigrants in Canada (See, for example: Woodsworth, 1972:Chapter 15).

7. Parliament did pass the Patent and Proprietary Medicines Act in 1908 to deal with the indiscriminate use of medicines, but the penalties were not severe and any medicine that had the formula on the label of the bottle was exempt from the act (see Small, 1978).

8. Between 1881 and 1885 over 15,000 Chinese were brought to Canada under labour contracts. More than half arrived during 1882-83 when the demand for labour was at its height (Cheng, 1931).

9. Canada Sessional Papers (1885), No. 54A, "Report on the Royal Commission on Chinese Immigration," page 129.

10. Public Archives of Canada (PAC), J.A. Macdonald Papers, vol. 321, page 144776, Onderdonk to Macdonald, 14 June 1882.

11. For example, the average wage for Chinese in the collieries was $1.25 per day for 8 hours underground and $1.50 per day for 10 hours on the surface. The average earnings of Caucasian workers was $4.00 per day (Carrothers, 1928:223-4).

12. The Chinese were predominantly employed in industries requiring lesser skills (the domestic/service industry, for example) or in the lowest-level occupations in the major industries (as miners' helpers and general labourers in mining, for example).

13. PAC, J.A. Macdonald Papers, vol. 321, page 144780, Onderdonk to Macdonald, 14 June 1882.

14. For example, the Canadian Trades and Labor Council (formed in 1886) and its American counterpart, the American Federation of Labor. In 1889 the Vancouver Trades and Labor Council affiliated with the CTLC (see Saywell, 1951).

15. For example, The Western Federation of Miners, the United Brotherhood of Railway Employees, the Industrial Workers of the World and the United Mine Workers of America all had an increasing influence in British Columbia (see Phillips, 1967). The United Mine Workers of America, which by 1903 had taken over jurisdiction in the coal industry, grew from a membership of 10,000 in 1897 to 400,000 in 1913 (Avery, 1979:56).

16. For a discussion of such attempts see: Cheng (1931); Robin (1972); Munro (1971); Ward (1978).

17. Canada House of Commons Debates, 1883, page 905.

18. PAC, WLM King Diaries, page 1342, 23 January 1900.

19. Ibid., page 1688, 19 November 1901.

20. Canada, Sessional Papers (1903) No.36A2 "Report of the Royal Commission on Industrial Disputes in the Province of British Columbia," pages 65-66.

21. The number of Chinese in British Columbia steadily increased from

4,483 in 1880 to 8,910 in 1891 and approximately 16,000 in 1901 (Canada, *Sessional Papers* (1902) No.54, "Report of the Royal Commission of Japanese and Chinese Immigration") An increase in the head tax to $500 in 1903 reduced Chinese immigration for a time, but between July 1907 and June 1908 their numbers increased again as 1,482 Chinese paid the head tax (PAC, *WLM King Papers*, vol. 80, page C61347).

22. While only 354 Japanese entered Canada in 1905, this figure rose to 1,922 in 1906 and to 10,358 between July 1906 and October 1907 (PAC, *Governors General Numbered File*, file 332, volume 200, "Report by Hon. R. Lemieux, Minister of Labour, on the subject of the Influx of Oriental Labourers into the Province of British Columbia" (hereafter cited as the Lemieux Report), page 11. While East Indian Immigrants had begun to arrive in Canada in very small numbers at the turn of the century, a sudden surge in their immigration brought 4,747 to British Columbia between July 1906 and March 1908 (Cheng, 1931:138-9).

23. PAC *Laurier Papers*, vol. 479, pages 127065-7, Swertz, Secretary of the VTLC to Laurier, 29 July 1907.

24. *Ibid* vol. 479, pages 127063-4, Laurier to MacPherson, 8 August 1907.

25. See: PAC *Governors General Numbered File*, file 332, vol. 199, McInnes to Oliver, 2 October 1907.

26. See: The Lemieux Report *op.cit.*

27. Initially only Japanese claims were to be considered, as the federal government was concerned with its diplomatic relations with Japan. However, the Chinese were eventually included in the investigation due, in part, to Imperial considerations: the British government feared it would hamper similar efforts to obtain compensation for British subjects in China.

28. See: Canada, *Report of WLM King, Commissioner to Enquire into the Methods by which Oriental Labourers have been Induced to come to Canada.* Ottawa: King's Printer, 1908.

29. See: Canada, *Sessional Papers*, No. 36A, "Report of WLM King on his Mission to England to Confer with British Authorities on the Subject of Immigration to Canada from the Orient and Immigration from India in Particular."

30. See: Canada, *Statutes* 48-49 Vict., c.71.

31. PAC, *WLM King Diaries*, "Mission To The Orient," page c-2215473.

32. These figures are adapted from Ward, 1978:169.

33. The *Trail Herald*, the *Victoria Colonist*, the *Vancouver News Advertiser* and the *New Westminister Columbian*, to name a few, were owned and operated by the Conservative Party or its members (see Robin, 1972).

34. One clear example of this was an episode which occurred during the provincial election campaign of 1907. A few days before the election, the *Vancouver Daily Province* ran a front page banner article claiming the Grand Trunk Pacific and the federal government had plotted to unload 50,000 Japanese in the province as labourers on the railway line. The editor thanked W.J. Bowser who was Premier MacBride's prospective Attorney

General and boss of the city's Tory machine for exposing the plot. In truth, however, Bowser himself was actively aiding the importation of Oriental Labour, as he acted as a solicitor for a Japanese labour contractor who was bringing in railway workers in contravention of the Alien Labour Act (Robin, 1972:101).

35. PAC *Governors General Numbered File,* file 332, vol. 199, Claude MacDonald to Sir Edward Grey, 1 October 1907.

36. PAC, *WLM King Diaries,* page 1687, 19 November 1901.

37. *Ibid.* page 1665, 30 September 1901.

38. PAC, *WLM King Papers,* vol. 6 page 5985, King to Mrs. Fitzgibbon, 25 November 1907.

39. Cited in the *Vancouver Province* 3 June 1908.

40. PAC *Grey of Howick Papers,* 501-2 Grey to Laurier, 13 September, 1907.

41. See for example, PAC *Governors General Numbered File,* file 332, vol. 199, McInnes to Oliver, 7 October, 1907. Numerous telegrams and letters between McInnes and Laurier, Gov. Gen. Grey and several other members of the federal government can be found in the Public Archives all dealing with the subject of the Oriental question.

42. PAC, *WLM King Papers* (1908-1909), "Mission to the Orient," page G2215.

Creating Precious Children and Glorified Mothers: A Theoretical Assessment of the Transformation of Childhood

Tannis Peikoff and Stephen Brickey

Take care of the children ... and the nation will take care
of itself (Reverend J. Edward Starr, 1895).

A transformation in the day-to-day lives of children and in the concept of childhood took place in Canada in the period extending from the mid-19th century to the 20th century. This change is evident not only in the increase in rhetoric concerning children but also in the number of legislative reforms in areas such as education, child labour practices, the treatment of dependent children, and adoption. During this time, social reformers devoted more energy to children than in any other period in history. Within a few decades, children had become the symbol of a growing spirit of reform in Canada.

Prior to the 19th century, the concept of childhood as a distinct stage in the life cycle did not exist. Parents did not invest emotionally in their offspring, and children were not considered to be especially vulnerable or in need of special attention (De Mause, 1974). By the end of the 19th century, however, children came to be seen in a different light. Not only was childhood "discovered," but it was widely believed that the future of Canadian society was linked to the welfare of children. As a result, comprehensive measures for the welfare of children were backed by legislative action.

Although theoretical accounts have been offered to explain the emergence of the changes in the treatment of children, there is a tendency in the literature to examine these changes in isolation from one another (Minge-

Kalman, 1978; Hurl, 1985) or to attribute their cause to the most visible source calling for change: the various social reform movements that were in existence during the latter half of the 19th century (Morrison, 1976; Sutherland, 1976; Kealey, 1979; Zelizer, 1985). What is needed is a theoretical approach that is capable of uncovering the commonalities that are at the root of these changes and revealing the structural factors that were responsible for bringing about a transformation in all of the major dimensions of children's lives. In the following discussion, it will be argued that a socialist feminist framework provides such an approach.

The paper is divided into two sections. In the *first* section, an historical description is given of three aspects of children's lives that underwent significant change: the participation of children in the labour force, the treatment of dependent children, and the introduction of compulsory education. Particular attention is given to the role of the state in enacting legislation that produced and legitimated these changes. Although these areas do not encompass all of the changes in childhood that took place during this period, they have been selected to illustrate the fundamental and pervasive nature of the transformation that was occurring. The *second* section of the paper presents a brief discussion of socialist feminism and demonstrates how the historical changes described in the first section can be best understood by attending to the conceptual linkages made explicit in this theoretical approach.

The Transformation of Childhood
i. Changes in the family and the nature of work
In the early 19th century, Canada was a rural society, composed primarily of lower class agrarian families. By the time of Confederation, eighty-five percent of Canada's population still lived on farms or in small communities (Connelly, 1977). Commodity production, other than agriculture, consisted of small workshops operated by skilled artisans and craftsmen (Olsen, 1984:27). In the areas of farming and small scale commodity production, the household was the basic unit of economic production. The family income was based on the assumption that children would contribute their labour from the earliest possibility. Women and children, while not considered equal to the male head of the family, played economically essential roles. Not only were women responsible for the care of children, but they also worked as a production unit with their children, engaging in essential tasks such as caring for the livestock, producing clothing, tending gardens and preparing food for the family (Johnson, 1974). In this form of economic organization, the patriarch of the family derived economic benefits from a large family. Children were an asset in that they assisted in production and there was a close link between the number of children in a family and the relative ability of the patriarch to manage a family-based economic enterprise.

With the advent of industrial capitalism in the latter half of the 19th century, the nature of production and work changed. Complex skills were broken down into simple repetitive tasks and muscle power was replaced by machine power. The type of skilled labour previously performed by craftworkers was gradually replaced by low-paid unskilled labour resulting in the increasing separation of skilled workers from the control of their labour process. With fewer craftsmen self-employed, the apprentice system gradually broke down and children no longer had the benefit of the vocational training that they had previously received from parents or in apprenticeships (Bradbury, 1982; Palmer, 1983; Hurl, 1988). There was little advantage to training children in a trade as they now operated machinery which required little skill, or worked at tasks such as stoking fires or fetching materials to assist adults. As Bradbury notes:

> The reorganization of work coincident with factory production was rendering old skills obsolete ... Apprentices no longer learned how to make a commodity from beginning to end. They had become cheap sources of labour for employers interested only in maximum, rapid production. Women and children as well as men were drawn into the new and usually tedious kinds of jobs created by the mechanization of old processes. Skilled workers faced competition from unskilled workers and from women and children in jobs that might retain their old names but were fundamentally altered in their content (Bradbury, 1982:111).

Families became increasingly dependent upon an uncertain and seasonal labour market and in most working-class households additional wage earners were a necessity. Typically, however, it was the children who were relied upon for extra income as married women were required for their labour in the home (Bradbury, 1982). Although the majority of child labourers who were employed in factories came from the early adolescent age group, smaller children were employed in tasks which required small hands or statures (Hurl, 1988:90). In some cases, children worked in sweat shops[1] under contract for large retail and wholesale outlets (Bullen, 1986).

By 1871, children under 16 represented 8.1 percent of the total workforce in all Ontario industrial establishments (Census of Canada, 1871, Vol.3, cited in Hurl, 1988:99). Together with women, they formed 34.2 percent of the labour force in Toronto (Kealey, 1980). One in three workers in Ontario's three leading boot and shoe production centres in 1871 was a woman; one in seven was under 16 years of age. Women and children made up 42 percent of the industrial workforce in Montreal in 1871 where approximately one in every four boys aged 11 to 15 was employed in wage labour. In Montreal, the proportion of women and children in the shoe-making and clothing industries increased 50 and 80 percent respectively between 1861 and 1871. Across the country, more women and children than men worked in tobacco manufactories in 1881 (Palmer, 1982).

The conflict over the implementation of legislation to restrict women and children from the labour force entailed a struggle involving business, labour unions and reformers. Because women and children formed a cheap labour pool, business, for the most part, supported policies which permitted their labour. From the mid-19th century on, however, the state was faced with increasing pressure from both labour unions and social reformers to impose restrictions on both women and children in the labour market.

As the wages of women and children were less than men's, male workers became concerned about the loss of their own jobs and/or reductions in pay. The first opposition to the employment of children came from skilled workmen as early as the 1830s when the introduction of machine technology resulted in a decreasing need for skilled craft workers (Hurl, 1988). As a result of a reduction in the need for skilled labour and the ensuing decline in apprenticeships, children who had formerly worked as apprentices to craftsmen now competed with them for work in factories. Confronted with this problem, as well as other insecurities that arose as capitalists imposed new conditions of work and payment, skilled workers began to formally organize. In 1881, the first Canadian local of the Knights of Labor, which was a general craft union representing unskilled as well as skilled workers, was founded. Both the Knights of Labor and the Trades and Labor Congress (formed in 1883) called for the abolition of child labour under 14 years of age in factories (Hurl, 1988).

Although trade unions openly and persistently advocated the abolition of child labour, they were torn between three different positions concerning women. As workers, male unionists saw women as dangerous competitors. Thus, some unions openly advocated women's exclusion from the labour market. On the other hand, as trade unionists, men were committed to the protection of all workers, including women, and some opted for working class solidarity (Connely, 1977:230). As men, however, most union members also accepted the traditional moralistic definition of a woman's place as being in the home, as it ensured male privilege and familial order (Johnson, 1974).

Social reformers, most of whom came from middle class backgrounds, were not intent on undermining the structure of the new economic order itself. Rather, they concentrated their efforts on the disorganization of the family that was caused by wage labour, and on perceived disruptions in the maternal functions of women, reflecting their commitment to the moral standards of their class. While the stance taken by reformers resembled that of the trade unionists, their underlying motives were somewhat different. For example, as work was consistent with the strong Protestant orientation of most reformers, they were more concerned with the conditions of child labour than with the concept of labour itself. In fact, for reformers, the employment of children in factories was preferable to their idleness or appearance as "street children." Thus, while reformers condemned the conditions under which children worked, they did not reject the concept of child labour (Hurl, 1988:108). In the case of women, reformers were concerned with the apparent transformation in the lives of working class women who worked outside the home in physically danger-ous and potentially morally corrupting conditions. Therefore, several middle class reform groups, such as the National Council of Women and the Women's Christian Temperance Union, vigorously promoted protec-tive legislation for women and children in the factories. As Klein and Roberts note:

> The major focus of their concern was the woman as a future mother — the sacrifice of whose health would degrade the community — not as a worker. Their obses-sion with separate lavatories, considered one of the key goals of factory inspection, demonstrates their focus on issues pertaining to the maintenance of purity, modesty and other necessary qualities of wifely and motherly virtues. Another key issue, seats for shopgirls, brings this concern into sharp relief; seats were deemed important because extended periods of standing up were thought to be harmful to the reproductive organs (Klein and Roberts, 1974:225).

Although reformers had a number of concerns that applied to women, none of them addressed the discrepancy in women's wages. Rather, they focused on issues of women's morality, reproductive capacity and moth-erhood. The purpose of restrictive legislation, as they saw it, was to change the immoral environment confronting working women, to alleviate dan-gers to reproduction, and to bring an end to the inadequate provision of a home environment that was thought to be typical of working women. Factory work was seen by middle class reformers as making women unfit for their more important role of motherhood. This notion was reinforced by the medical journals of the Victorian era, which maintained that women should not work because they "need to conserve their energies for the vital tasks of reproduction" (Kealey, 1974, cited in Olsen, 1984:51). Goldwin Smith, a prominent social commentator of the period, expressed this concern in the following way: "They want, some of them say, to live their own lives ... as though the life of a woman could be perfect without domestic affection" (*Weekly Sun*, Dec.6, 1903, in Klein & Roberts, 1974:218).

Prior to the passage of the Factory Acts, state intervention in the labour force took the form of acts to repress and to police labour in the interests of employers (Ursel, 1986:202). However, in response to the demands of the trade unions and reform groups, a commission was appointed "to enquire into the working of mills and factories of the Dominion, and the labor employed therein" (Canada, *Sessional Papers*, 1882, no.42, cited in Splane, 1965:225). The 1882 *Report of the Royal Commission on Mills and Factories* suggested that the hours and nature of work constituted "too heavy a strain on children of tender years." Poor ventilation, overcrowd-ing, dampness, bad sanitary provisions, and accident hazards were re-ported by the Commissioners to be common in a large number of the factories they visited. The Commissioners also voiced special concern for women's vulnerability in the areas of health and reproduction and recom-mended a work environment that would take this into consideration. In 1884, following the presentation and withdrawal of a number of bills proposing the regulation of women and child workers, the first Canadian Factory Act was passed in Ontario. The Act prohibited the employment of boys under twelve and girls under fourteen years of age. Boys between twelve and fourteen and girls between fourteen and eighteen, as well as women, were not to be employed for more than ten hours a day or more than sixty hours a week. In 1888, the Shops Act was passed which limited the number of hours that children could work in wholesale and retail establishments (Splane, 1965:257). However, while both the Ontario Fac-tories Act of 1884 and the Shops Act of 1888 restricted the work hours of children in industrial and commercial establishments, both pieces of legislation specifically exempted work in the home (such as paid domestic labour or piece work) from any type of regulation (Bullen, 1986:173).

Much of the content of the first and subsequent Factory Acts was aimed specifically at women. The legislation required that special consideration be made for women in the areas of sanitation and comfort so that the conditions of their labour would not have an adverse effect on their morality or their ability to bear and nurture children. Under the Shops Act of 1888, for instance, the owner of any shop employing females was required to provide a suitable chair for women. As Ursel (1986) notes, the architects of this legislation clearly had a one-dimensional definition of womanhood: women as mothers. The special considerations that were made for women had the effect of discouraging employers from employ-ing women in non-traditional roles, thus reducing competition with male workers.

However, the Factory Acts and the Shops Act contained a number of loopholes and were not adequately enforced. Data show that while in 1881 children represented 7.6 of the labour force in Ontario, they still repre-sented 6.2 percent of the workforce in 1891. It was not until around the turn of the century that a marked decrease in child labour occurred. By 1901, a census report showed that only 3.6 percent of the workforce was com-posed of children (Census of Canada, 1891 Vol 3, cited in Hurl, 1988:116).

ii. Changes in the treatment of dependent children

At the beginning of the 19th century, the only means by which the state assumed responsibility for dependent children[2] was by providing for their apprenticeship or by placing them in institutions. The first legislation that was passed for the protection of children in Upper Canada was the Orphans Act of 1799, which was intended to provide for the education and support of orphans or children deserted by their parents. The means provided by the Act for the attainment of this objective was that of binding children out as apprentices[3] by town wardens or by mothers whose husbands had abandoned them. Although the Act was intended to provide for the care of children, it was deficient in that it failed to include adequate safeguards against their exploitation or abuse (Splane, 1965:215).

The state in early 19th century Canada provided for those dependent, neglected, and delinquent children who were not apprenticed by the same means as it provided for marginalized adult populations. Children were placed alongside adults in almshouses, poorhouses, houses of industry, penitentiaries and asylums. Whenever possible, the children were auctioned off or apprenticed to craftsmen and farmers (Aiton, 1961; Splane, 1965).

The harsh conditions of dependent children did not evoke much comment until the mid-19th century, when, for the first time, children were separated from adult paupers and placed in separate facilities such as orphanages. This movement to separate relief for children was due mainly to the efforts of women from influential families and coincided with the growth of philanthropic organizations such as the Ladies Aid Societies and the Women's Christian Temperance Union (Splane, 1965:223; Rooke and Schnell, 1982). While many of the children's institutions received grants from the provincial government, there was no guarantee of provincial aid and a number of institutions were sponsored by charitable funds. Although the acts incorporating the first children's institutions did not mention the placement of children as apprentices, provision was made for their apprenticeship shortly thereafter and subsequent children's institutions followed suit. It was not uncommon for children's services to be advertised on the doors of the institutions or in the local press. Commissioners, who had the right to reclaim the children if certain conditions (such as board and some education) were not met, rarely did so. Even in orphanages, conditions were such that children were:

> ... moved about all day like pieces of machinery and their education consisted chiefly of scolding, fault finding ... No real attempt was made to find homes for the children until they reached the age of twelve when they were apprenticed out as servants (Kelso Papers, MG 30, Vol 8, in Rooke and Schnell, 1982:93).

By the second half of the century, the undependable nature of wage labour led to the increase in a class of urban poor. Some families that could not cope abandoned their children. Increasing numbers of children were left to their own resources and came to be labelled "street arabs" or "street urchins" (Bradbury, 1982).

Towards the end of the 19th century, a "child-saving" movement arose which focused on the assumed detrimental effects of urban life on lower class children.[4] Reformers argued that most criminal offenders came from urban areas, were poor, and were reared in "neglectful" families, and the city came to be depicted as a "breeding ground for criminals." The urban poor were identified as crime-prone, and in an attempt to return to traditional stability, rural family life and agricultural labour came to be associated with morality (Platt, 1969; West, 1984:30). The growing belief in the influence of environment in controlling crime led reformers to the assumption that crime could be prevented by removing neglected and dependent children from their supposedly detrimental environments. Not only "street arabs," but also dependent and delinquent children[5] were lumped together under the category of "pre-delinquent" and placed in industrial schools or in rural families as labourers (Parr, 1980; Platt, 1969; West, 1984). Although reformers preferred to place children in the countryside, a small percentage were placed in middle class homes. Despite efforts to ensure adequate affection and education for the children, it was the child's ability to work that was often the decisive factor in placement (Bullen, 1986:80).

By the end of the 19th century, child saving strategies had changed radically. Where reformers in the 1850s believed in institutionalization as the best means for caring for dependent and delinquent children, by the latter part of the 1880s, reformers questioned the advantages of institutional care and looked to a "wholesome family environment" or suitable foster home and attention was turned to the possibility of developing other arrangements to give children the opportunity of growing up in a family setting (Sutherland, 1976; Bullen, 1986).

Although steps had been taken on behalf of children in the middle and later decades of the 19th century, it was not until the end of the 1880s that comprehensive measures for the welfare of children were backed by legislative action. As the belief in the "moral" family environment gained momentum, the state gradually increased its intervention into the functioning of the family. By so doing, the relations between families and the state were re-ordered.

Prior to 1874, Manitoba and Ontario welfare law consisted of only two statutes: the Apprentices and Minors Act of 1851, which amended the Orphan's Act in an attempt to provide adequate safeguards for the indenture of children who were orphaned or abandoned, and the Charity Aid Act of 1851, which made provision for provincial support for institutions (Ursel, 1986; Splane, 1965). The end of the 19th century, however, marked an increase in legislative activity in the areas of family law in Ontario and Manitoba. In 1874, the Ontario legislature passed the Industrial Schools Act, which established schools to lodge and to provide industrial training for neglected and truant children under the age of 14 committed to the school by police magistrates. In addition, in 1891, the Children's Aid Society of Toronto was founded in response to the perceived necessity for a type of child welfare agency that had adequate authority to take action for the protection of children. In 1893, the Children's Protection Act empowered the Children's Aid Society to act as a regulatory agency to inspect homes, apprehend children and place them in foster homes. In an 1884 amendment to the Industrial Schools Act, philanthropic societies were permitted to take the initiative in the establishment of industrial schools and added "delinquent" children, or children who, in the opinion of the magistrate, should be sent to an industrial school instead of to a reformatory. Both the Child Protection Act and the Industrial Schools Act contained clauses permitting the state to sue the parent for support of the children while in government institutions.

Over the next two decades, the state considerably increased the conditions under which it could assume wardship, the number of institutions and programs available for children, and the regulatory agents for supervising both public and private institutions of child care (Ursel, 1986). During this period, the state also extended its authority over the care of children in other areas. Whereas, in the past, the only indicators of the state's concern for the child's best interests were laws prohibiting infanticide or severe physical abuse, the state now became involved in the welfare of children in areas such as health care and education. Following the establishment of the Humane Society in 1891, extra provisions, such as a Children's Fresh Air Fund which provided outings for poor children and the Santa Claus Fund which provided parties for them at Christmas, were established by the reformer J. J. Kelso (Splane, 1965). In 1909, a Special Committee on Infant Mortality and a Royal Commission on Milk called for greater government initiative in ensuring the welfare of children (Splane, 1965; Ursel, 1986).

iii. Changes in the practice of adoption

As we have shown, provision for dependent children at the beginning of the 19th century showed only minimal concern for their welfare and it appeared as though their intrinsic value was solely dependent upon their economic value. By the end of the century, however, concern for the welfare and adequate socialization of children had escalated considerably. The changes that took place in the practice and philosophy of adoption illustrate the change in the perceived value of dependent children.

Although legalized adoption has been practised since the beginning of recorded history as a means of continuing a family line, there was no legal provision for its practice in English Common Law due to the importance of blood lines to inheritance. *De facto* adoption, however, was widely practised among the lower classes throughout Europe, as there was considerable reliance on extended family and neighbours in times of crisis. This was an informal arrangement without legal sanction (Middleton, 1971:237).

The use of the term "adoption" in 19th century Canada was somewhat ambiguous in that the distinction between adopting a child and taking the child under contract for labour as an apprentice was not clear. However, it appears as though "adoption" broadly referred to placement schemes for homeless children (Parr, 1980; Sutherland, 1976; Rooke and Schnell,

1982). Andrew Doyle, sent by the British government in 1874 to investigate the situation of British emigrant children placed in Canadian homes, quoted one child as having said, "Doption, sir, is when folks gets a girl to work without wages" (British Parliamentary Papers 1875, LX111, p.12).

Although adoption was mentioned as an alternative to apprenticeship in two of the statutes incorporating institutions in the 1860s, no separate legislation was passed governing adoption or indicating the responsibilities it entailed. Any legal problems that may have been encountered were left to the common law for resolution (Splane, 1965:225).

As stated earlier, due to the efforts of child-savers in the latter half of the century, "waifs," "street arabs" and "delinquent" children were lumped together with orphans and illegitimate children, removed from their urban environments, and placed in rural family homes. This scheme was also adopted by British philanthropists, and between 1868 and 1925, 80,000 homeless and neglected children were sent to Canada for "adoption" by rural families. Usually the families of children aged 3 to 8 were paid by the agency[6] for the board of the child. Between the ages of 8 and 14, as children were just strong enough to earn their keep, the family was not reimbursed. From age 14 on, children were considered to be capable of adult labour and were therefore given a wage by the family. In most cases, children were not considered to be members of the family, which is evidenced by the fact that children were often exchanged depending on the economic situation and/ or needs of the family in which they lived. For instance, it was common for struggling families in marginal farm districts to exchange children when they got older if they could not afford to pay the wages required for an older child's labour (Parr, 1980).

Although ostensibly brought in on humanitarian grounds, the reason for the ready acceptance of the British children into Canada was almost entirely in answer to a desperate need for agricultural labourers and domestic servants. Indeed, correspondence and newspaper advertisements emphasized a child's ability to perform specific domestic tasks (Bullen, 1986:181). No legal regulations were in place to control the distribution of children to uninvestigated homes where they were used as cheap labour. Descriptions of a number of adoptive situations attest to drudgery, inadequate clothing, exploitation, and lack of concern for the emotional effect of displacement on the children (Rooke & Schnell, 1982; Hurl, 1981; Parr, 1980). In 1874, Andrew Doyle reported an intolerable incidence of ill-treatment, overwork and physical abuse (Doyle Report of 1875, cited in Parr, 1980). In the words of one witness, the goal of the foster parent appears to have been to take the children and "drill them into usefulness" (Sutherland, 1976:9). While some homes took children aged 3 to 8 for "trial adoption," which more closely resembled adoption as we know it today, in many cases the families could not accept the children as their own and so they were returned (Parr, 1980).

As infants were rarely taken in for "adoption," mothers of unwanted children often placed their babies in poorhouses or orphanages. The mothers of children born out of wedlock, however, had fewer options. The stigmatization of illegitimacy was such that even these institutions were known to refuse unwed mothers and their "bastard" children (Rooke and Schnell, 1982:87). In such instances, mothers had the choice of either abandoning their children in public places and foundling asylums, or placing them in baby farms, which were profitable enterprises run by middle-aged women who charged a fee to take in mostly illegitimate babies. Those mothers who could afford the entrance fee required by baby farms were assured of a good home for their infants. However, the promised prospect of adoption for the infant was seldom fulfilled. Various investigations revealed "a disgraceful system of dealing with illegitimate children" (Ontario Sessional Papers no.29, 1895). Only a small minority of the children that were taken in by baby farms, poorhouses, or foundling asylums survived the first few weeks. For instance, of the more than 600 abandoned in 1863 in a foundling home in Montreal, records show that only 10 per cent survived (Bradbury, 1982:114). In 1883, the Bethlehem Home for the Friendless in Ottawa recorded 199 deaths in a year where there had been 224 admissions (Splane, 1965:242).

No action was taken to remedy the conditions of infant boarding houses until 1887, when the Ontario legislature passed an act calling for the licensing and supervision of all homes in which children under the age of one year were boarded (Splane, 1965). Throughout most of the 19th century, unwanted babies were more likely to die than be adopted. In effect, these infants were a worthless commodity, given their stigmatization as "bastards" and the fact that they were too young to work. The desire for a useful child put a premium on strong older children.

The structural changes that took place in adoption were marked by increasing state intervention into the adoptive process. In 1887, an Act for the Protection of Infant Children was introduced. The 1897 amendment to this Act required that the Children's Aid Society supervise the adoption of children under one year of age from these homes. A 1912 amendment gave the Children's Aid Society authority over adoption of all children under three born in these homes. With the passing of the first Adoption Acts in British Columbia and Ontario, and subsequently throughout most of Canada,[7] the state expanded its authority from the supervision of adoption cases which fell under the authority of the Children's Aid Society to the assumption of complete authority in all adoption cases (Ursel, 1986). Prior to these statutes, the state's authority over adoption was limited to cases under the supervision of the Children's Aid Society, which typically involved only unwed mothers.

The increase in state intervention into adoption was accompanied by a specific push by reformers to change its ideological basis. Child welfare workers now sought to establish a new sentimental approach to adoption. By the end of the 19th century they had begun their campaign against the established instrumental approach to child care and stressed the "Christian" motive in child care and the value of a "genuine" home where a child would be taken in for love rather than for his/her instrumental value (Zelizer, 1985:176-7).

By the time the majority of the provincial statues legalizing adoption were instituted, the ideology as well as the practice of adoption itself had changed radically. Structurally, it had changed from a form of indenture to an institution that made children full members of the adopting family. Ideologically, it changed from taking a child for his/her instrumental value to raising a child for the joy and satisfaction that children were purported to bring. As a result, the need for children as domestic labourers came to be an illegitimate motive for adoption.

In the early decades of the 20th century, adoption gradually gained in popularity. In fact, by the third decade of the 20th century, the demand for children had undergone a complete reversal. Infants were now in the greatest demand and, deprived of their former economic value, adolescents were difficult to place.

iv. Changes in education

In the primarily agrarian society of 19th century Canada, lower class children were taught necessary skills by their families or masters through actual labour. In contrast, the aristocracy provided its children with a classical education (Johnson, 1974:21). Female members of the aristocracy were taught by tutors and governesses while male children were taught in private schools or in government financed grammar schools. The small number of grammar schools which existed at the beginning of the 19th century were attended primarily by upper class children (West, 1984:27).

The Common School Act of 1816 was significant in that it marked the first assumption of responsibility by the state for the education of the lower classes. The Act provided for funds to help pay the salary of a teacher for the residents of any town who could collect twenty students. Most parents, however, could not afford to pay the fees required to supplement the legislative grant, and the school remained largely out of the reach of the poor (Wilson, 1978:24; West, 1984:27). Although in 1817, there was a debate in Nova Scotia concerning the provision of education for the lower classes, the proposal met with considerable opposition on the grounds that education was unsuited to the type of manual labour the lower class workers performed (Pentland, 1981:135).

The push for mass education was initiated in the 1830s by Egerton Ryerson, who was later to become the first superintendent of education for Upper Canada. Ryerson justified public education as a means of instilling social control among the Irish Catholic immigrants, whose poverty and alleged immorality were seen as potentially dangerous to the social order (Schecter, 1977:373).

In the years between 1836 and 1850, several attempts at school reform were made, but they were blocked by both Tory and Reform administrations (Houston, 1975:33-48). By the mid-19th century, however, the effects of the shift in the Canadian economy from an agrarian based society to one of industrial capitalism resulted in increased concern for the maintenance of the social order. The appearance of "street children" and a heavy influx of famine Irish in 1847 raised further concern about the development of a restless and potentially dangerous class.

Ryerson and other reformers stressed this concern as the main rationale, particulary to the propertied classes, for promoting mass education. In 1847, Ryerson lobbied for the introduction of a compulsory assessment on all property to finance a system of public education. In order to convince the bourgeoisie that investment in educational reform was beneficial, the social control function of the school was stressed. Mass education was promoted as a panacea on the grounds that criminality was directly connected to ignorance, illiteracy, and "an influx of criminal elements from outside the country, and particularly from Ireland" (Graff, 1978:189). Since "immorality" rather than the social structure was defined as the problem, reformers promoted an expanded school system that would teach all children a common moral code.

Ryerson used an additional rationale when addressing the *petite bourgeoisie*, who were composed of propertied, skilled artisans and merchants. To this class, educational reform was promoted mainly as a means to enhance opportunities for upward social mobility. As many had suffered reversals with the advent of industrial capitalism, Ryerson played upon their uncertainty as to their future social status (Schecter, 1977).

In 1850, the efforts of the educational reformers were rewarded with the passing of The Common School Act of Ontario which inaugurated a centralized provincial school system and provided free common schools for the masses. The purpose of central authority was to "Canadianize" all elements of society through central control of the curriculum in the form of authorized textbooks, common programs of studies and external examinations (Child, 1978:285). The curriculum, which included instruction in morality, was designed for a society in which individuals were trained to know their proper "place" and to recognize and accept what is "right" and "good" (MacDonald, 1978:104). However, as G.A. Barber, the Toronto superintendent of schools, made clear in his report of 1857, the implementation of free education did not solve the problem of the children of the lowest classes for whom it was intended. Rather, the schools were attended mostly by the children of industrial mechanics and tradesmen, and not by the children of the poor. Upper class children continued to rely on private tutors or to attend grammar schools (Schecter, 1978; Houston, 1978; Davey, 1975).

The absence of urban poor from the schools did not, however, appear quite so dangerous to the upper classes as the persistence of "street children." Consequently, as Houston (1978) notes, despite the fact that the numbers of children attending schools increased slightly, school promoters paid a heavy price for promoting mass education as a mechanism for social control. Pressure to justify the public's investment in free schooling increased as complaints mounted against the persistence of "street arabs," and the credibility of the system was called into question (Houston, 1978).

It appears as though reformers had miscalculated the success of free schooling in several ways. One problem was that there was little in the common school system to attract the children who had been labelled "street arabs," particularly since the schools emphasized the virtues of cleanliness, discipline, and punctuality. To complicate the issue further, it was generally believed by the 1860s that "street urchins" had no place in the city schools and that forcing these children to attend public schools might result in the objection and flight of the "respectable" working classes (Houston, 1978). In 1865, Justice Haggarty stated to the Grand Jury: "Those who know the poor can testify how they too shrink in their filth and tattered clothing from Church and School" (cited in Houston, 1978:266). In 1867, it was suggested that "the only way ... is by asking for the enactment of some law which shall deal with their ignorant and disordered condition as itself a species of crime, less indeed their own than that of their parents and guardians." (The Journal of Education, no. 10, 1867, cited in Houston, 1978). Another problem for reformers was that they did not allow for the fact that children's earnings were fundamental to the working class family economy (Bradbury, 1982; Bullen, 1986). Therefore, even those children who did attend school did so on an irregular basis (Davey, 1975; Houston, 1978). A school census taken in 1863 showed that while attendance had reached an all-time high, fewer than half of the children of school age who were registered for a six month period were on the registers of the common school at any one time (Houston, 1978).

As the socializing potential of the common school was one of the main premises of mass education, reformers attempted to justify compulsory taxation by concentrating their efforts on adequately socializing the children of the respectable working classes. To this end, compulsory education was instituted in Ontario in 1871. It provided free, universal, Protestant education that was controlled mainly by a central authority. It required that each municipality provide free common schools which children between the ages of seven and twelve years of age were required to attend four months a year. For working class children, it was intended to allow for employment rather than to replace it (Prentice, 1975). The purpose of the short term was to accommodate children's participation in the labour force or in domestic labour. The rationale behind the introduction of compulsory education, therefore, was no longer that of urban reform; rather its stated objective was to reduce lateness and absenteeism among pupils already enroled.

Working class response to the introduction of mass education appears to have been mixed. Some sectors of the working class (particularly skilled craftsmen) saw education as a vehicle to upward social mobility, but with the worsening of their economic position, could only send their children on a part-time basis (Davey, 1975). Other members of the working class were largely ambivalent. The fact that the school curriculum clearly favoured bourgeois interests made the school seem irrelevant and unnecessary to making a living performing unskilled labour (Davey, 1978; West, 1984). Although records show no defiance to compulsory education on the part of parents (Annual Report of the Local Superintendent for 1872, cited in Hurl, 1988:118), the reality of working class existence and the possibility and/or the relative importance of classical grammar school education was such that the provision of compulsory education was not immediately effective in getting children to attend. As Davey (1975) notes, this was exacerbated by the emergence of mechanized factory production in the 1860s which increased economic insecurity and at the same time devalued the importance of education by creating opportunities for unskilled employment for both children and adults. Child and adolescent labour, both in the sweatshop and on the farm, was often a necessary factor in the family's struggle to survive.

As capitalism progressed, and the demand for skilled labour increased, the long-term benefits of education in terms of both the children's and family's interests resulted in longer and more regular attendance by working class children. However, full-time attendance was a luxury that the majority of families could not yet afford (Houston, 1978; Hurl, 1988), so the implementation of compulsory education was not immediately effective in getting children to attend. Data show that the average daily attendance between 1866 and 1880 only increased from 42.9 percent to 43.5 percent (Historical Statistics of Canada, cited in Hurl, 1988:92, 99). It was not until the last decade of the 19th century that the numbers of children attending schools and the average daily attendance began to increase significantly. By 1895, the average daily attendance had increased to 52.5 percent (Hurl, 1988).

Although compulsory education provided a vehicle for reformers to force children of the working class to attend schools, it did not immediately solve the problem of destitute and vagrant children. Following considerable debate on the delegation of responsibility for lower class children, an Industrial Schools Act was passed in 1874 which created an institution to fill the void between the public school and the reformatory (Splane, 1965). By housing the children in rural cottages with a matron and a guard that were to act as "mother" and "father," industrial schools were intended to be analogous to middle class Protestant homes. Admission to an industrial school was limited to children under the age of fourteen committed to the school by police magistrates, who were authorized to commit any children found begging, wandering the streets, destitute, orphaned, or without adequate parental control (Splane, 1965:249-250). The right to establish such schools was conferred on the boards of public or separate school trustees.

As there was no assurance of provincial financial support, however, school trustees were unwilling to assume new financial burdens and the Act remained ineffective until its amendment in 1884. The amendment provided for annual grants and empowered school trustees to delegate "powers, rights and privileges" to any incorporated philanthropic society

(Splane, 1965:254). It also provided for the inclusion of delinquent children in the industrial schools. The main purpose of the Act was to train neglected and destitute children into usefulness and to teach them the values of discipline and middle-class morality.

A Socialist Feminist Analysis

Before providing an explanation of the significant shifts that took place in the lives of children in the latter half of the 19th century, it is first necessary to couch this explanation in a theoretical context that is sensitive to economic changes that were occurring during this period, as well as to the relationship between these economic changes and the transformation of relationships within families, specifically working class families. It will be argued that, by focusing on the changing mode of production and the concomitant changes in the family during this period, a clearer understanding can be gained of the scope and the timing of the wide range of legislative and policy changes that were to affect children. The approach we are proposing as the most appropriate for accomplishing the above tasks is a socialist feminist analysis of the transformation of childhood.

Although there are a variety of specific theoretical approaches that fall under the category of socialist feminism (Eisenstein, 1979; Ursel, 1984; Burstyn, 1985), the common thread uniting these writings is the assumption that an adequate explanation of society requires a reworking of the Marxist perspective which allows for the problematic of organizing reproduction. For Marx, the fundamental fact in social life was human labour, and the structure of social relations within society was understood as derived from the way that labour was organized and controlled. By giving conceptual primacy to economic relations, all other elements of social life, such as the subordination of women to men, were seen as being the result, directly or indirectly, of the mode of production that was prevalent within a particular society. In the language of the metaphor used to convey this primacy, the mode of production is the base or infrastructure and all other social relations are in the superstructure. Thus, patriarchy, or the hierarchical sexual division of men and women in society, was a form of inequality that would disappear with a change in the mode of production.

For socialist feminists, the flaw in Marx's analysis is the failure to recognize that reproduction is equally necessary to production if societies are to exist. Not only must individuals labour to produce clothing, shelter, food, etc., but they must also procreate and care for future human beings to replace the existing population. The reconceptualization of Marxism which places reproduction at a level equal in importance to that of production is referred to as the dual systems theory (Eisenstein, 1979). Instead of starting from the premise that the mode of production has priority over the organization of reproduction, socialist feminists begin from the assumption that there is a dynamic interplay between the two which is characterized by a relationship of codetermination, or what Eisenstein calls "mutual dependence" (1979:22). Any significant change in production or reproduction within a society will invariably affect the other. As Ursel states: "Any given economy or productive capacity ... is itself determined by the existing demographic composition (labour supply) of the community, which in turn is a product of prior interactions between the productive and reproductive modes" (1986:153). Thus, just as it would be absurd for Marxists to explain the subordination of classes without reference to the mode and relations of production in a society, it would be equally absurd, socialist feminists argue, to explain the subordination of women without reference to the mode and relations of reproduction in that same society. More importantly, these theorists argue that to focus only on capitalism or patriarchy is to ignore the fundamental interdependence of production and reproduction within any social system.

It is this idea that there is a mutual dependence or codetermination between production and reproduction that is crucial to understanding the transformation of childhood in the historical period under study. In the remainder of the paper, the argument will be made that the transformation of the Canadian economy to industrial capitalism not only created profound changes in production, but also created a crisis in the organization of reproduction that required, among other things, unprecedented state intervention in the areas of child labour, education and the treatment of dependent children. The changes in both the material condition of children and their ideological portrayal were the result of this intervention. As we will show, these policies were initially directed at the socialization and nurturing aspect of reproduction and were later expanded to encompass policies that were designed to have an impact on procreation.

i. The Onset of Capitalism

By the 1850s, the nascent development of an industrial capitalism was evident in Canada. Although agriculture continued to be a predominant component of the economy, the shift to an urbanized, industrialized society was starting to take form. From 1852 to 1861, the number of people engaged in industrial production was facilitated by a growing urban population that had started in the first part of the century. For example, Pentland (1981:135) notes that Kingston tripled in population between 1829 to 1851; Hamilton grew by nine times between 1835 and 1853, and Toronto increased four and a half times between 1830 and 1851. Montreal started to experience rapid growth somewhat later, almost doubling its population between 1851 and 1871. The rapid increase in urbanization stemmed more from immigration than a movement from rural areas, with the greatest proportion of the immigrants being the famine Irish.

The consequence of this economic shift was that more families, particularly in the urban centres, were becoming dependent on wages for their subsistence. For these families, the household was no longer an autonomous economic unit. Rather, the ability to sell one's labour power for wages was increasingly becoming the means for a family to survive. With the advent of a wage-labour system, the economic viability of the roles of women and children underwent a marked change. There was a variety of responses to this disruption. One response was for women and children to enter the labour market and to earn wages that would contribute to the family's economic survival. Since the predominant gender ideology was that of familial patriarchy, where the woman's proper place was in the home engaging in domestic labour and caring for children, most women factory workers were single. Married women who needed to supplement their husband's wage engaged in home-centred industries and sweat shops, where women and children worked under contract to produce clothing and other goods for large retail outlets (Bullen, 1986). Working class children would also contribute to the family's income by working at a number of street trades, such as selling fruit, polishing shoes and selling newspapers (Bullen, 1986). The necessity of working class children working outside of the home meant that the nurturing role played by the family for these children was being diminished. Children could now be seen operating independently on the streets without parental supervision and control.

It was during this initial transition period of the 1840s and 1850s that we find pleadings from Ryerson and other reformers to encourage the children of the working class to attend school. In addition, reformers were arguing that the state should provide the costs of these educational institutions (Gidney, 1975). As noted earlier, a number of reasons were given by reformers to support their push for public education. Behind these claims, however, seemed to be a pervasive concern that public institutions were required to appropriately provide social control and instill proper values in children in a new economic order where family socialization was no longer sufficient. The public school was intended to be more than simply an institution that taught literacy: it was to be a moral agency that would provide an environment conducive to the proper (in middle class terms) upbringing of the poor. As Houston notes: "Ryerson promoted public education to accomplish the tasks for which the social conservative would instinctively use it: to prevent pauperism, crime, vice, ignorance and contribute to the increased productivity of the labour force" (1975:45).

This emerging trend to involve the state and the use of public monies in the care of children was necessitated by the transition to industrial capitalism. In an economic system where the household was the primary economic unit, socialization of children to the roles they were to perform could best be taught by the parents. However, in a society where an increasing amount of labour took place in settings outside the home, there were concerns that the young were not being instilled with the work habits and values that were necessary for these new roles. In addition, the large number of Irish immigrants arriving in the cities sparked fears that, without proper training, the children of these new immigrants would not readily fit in to the new industrial regimen. According to Ryerson, immigrants were "as notoriously destitute of intelligence and industry as they are of means of subsistence" (Graff, 1978:188).

The policy initiatives directed toward child labour, the treatment of dependent children and compulsory education occurred later in the 19th century and were brought about by a further impact of industrial capitalism on the reproductive sphere. This impact was the lowering birth rate in the country.

ii. A Crisis in Reproduction

Although industrial capitalism began to develop in the mid-19th century, it was not until the 1880s that an "industrial revolution" took place, "almost overnight" (Johnson, 1974). Between 1881 and 1891, the number of industrial firms in Toronto more than tripled, the number of workers doubled, and the amount of capital invested increased two and a half times (Palmer, 1983:97). Since industrial production was concentrated in the cities, the proportion of the population that lived in urban areas continued to increase. For example, Toronto grew from 56,000 in 1871 to over 144,000 in 1891 (Kealey, 1980:99). The textile industry experienced a "minor industrial boom," which created factory employment for women (Cross and Kealey, 1982; Olsen, 1984). Employment for women was also provided by the expanding boot and shoe industry, as well as the tobacco industry (Olsen, 1984).

With the growth of the wage-labour system, the economic viability of the roles of women and children in the home continued to deteriorate. The response to this in the latter half of the 19th century was for women and children to enter the industrial labour market and earn wages that would contribute to the family's economic position. This transition, however, did not result in the familial patriarch continuing to receive economic benefits in proportion to the size of his family. Because women and children had historically been subordinated to adult males under a system of patriarchy, it was considered natural that factories would provide them with a lower wage, even though the work might be identical to that performed by men. Thus, the wages that women and children received were often insufficient to offset the costs of food, clothing and shelter that they required (Ursel, 1984). Although their incomes certainly helped to offset the costs of their maintenance, it soon became apparent that children in working class families were no longer an economic asset; they were now economic liabilities.

Another difficulty that emerged with the influx of women and children into the labour force was that now they were in direct competition with the patriarch for wages and jobs. Male-dominated labour unions in the late 19th and early 20th centuries repeatedly expressed concerns over the problem of competition with women and children. Although there were some who called for higher wages for women, the predominant strategy was for unions to adopt a gendered ideology to argue that women and children should be taken out of the work force and that men should receive a "family wage" to enable them to support their wives and children.

In the latter decades of the 19th century, there were growing signs that industrialization was producing major consequences in the area of reproduction. Since the individual patriarch was no longer benefitting from large families, these consequences were consistent with the realigning of the patriarch's new economic self-interest. One of these consequences was a trend, starting in the 1870s, of declining birth rates.

The initial impact of industrial capitalism on family size appears to be that of increasing the birth rate among working class families. Thus, in the 1850s and 1860s, while the bourgeois and *petty bourgeois* classes began to limit the number of children they had, the birth rate among the families of skilled workers and labourers significantly increased. Palmer has argued that this increase in fertility rate was the result of working class families' attempting to increase their economic chances by expanding the number of workers they could put into the wage-labour pool (Palmer, 1983:82). This is a plausible argument, given both the marginal economic position of working class families at this time, and the logic that had been established prior to industrialization in which families could count on improving their economic lot by having a large number of children to assist in the family-based production unit.

By the 1870s, however, the evidence suggests that the impact of the new economic mode of production was to reduce the birth rate throughout the country in all social classes. Between 1871 and 1901, the fertility rate in Canada declined by 24 percent (McLaren and McLaren, 1986). The rate of change was greatest in Ontario, where the fertility rate dropped by approximately 44 percent during the same time period. It became increasingly evident that there was little, if any, advantage for a family to produce a large number of children.

Despite the steady decline in the fertility rate, the population continued to grow at a significant rate during this period. Between 1881 and 1920, the population in Canada increased from 4.3 million to 8.5 million (McLaren and McLaren, 1986:16). Given the decreasing birthrate, it is apparent that immigrants comprised the bulk of this increase. For example, between 1900 and 1914, 2.9 million immigrants were admitted into the country (Connelly, 1977:229). To accommodate the needs of employers for an expanded labour pool, the Canadian government developed an immigration policy that opened the doors to Europeans and Asians on an unprecedented scale. The massive scale of this immigration, and the fact that most of the immigrants came from ethnic and cultural backgrounds quite distinct from the ruling Anglo-Saxon population, created concerns that the new "foreign" element would seriously undermine the Canadian way of life. Consequently, the fear was expressed by middle class reformers and echoed in newspapers of the day that Canadians were engaging in "race suicide" (McLaren and McLaren, 1986), and nothing less than the future of the country was at stake.

Demographic changes taking place in the last decades of the 19th century are the key to understanding the structural and ideological transformation of childhood that occurred during this period. One of the major consequences of the growth of the capitalist economic system was the over-exploitation of labour to meet the voracious appetite of emerging industries. Working class women and children, unable to continue their contribution to family production within the home, and forced to find ways to supplement the low wages of the husband, looked for work within the new factory system. Because of the deskilling of labour that accompanied industrial production, women and children were welcomed by employers who were in need of cheap labour. Dickinson (1986) has argued that this over-exploitation of labour, or the consumption of labour at the point of production at a faster rate than it can be reproduced domestically, is a common feature of industrial capitalism in its early stages.

One way for the state to mitigate the dilemma of increasing labour demands and decreasing fertility, was to initiate an immigration policy that facilitated a large influx of workers. The more long term solution was the intervention of the state in restricting the labour of women and children in production and the support of an ideological shift that defined children as precious creatures of intrinsic value and women as inherently suited to the role of nurturing these precious creatures. The eventual exclusion of children from the factories and the setting of restrictions on the maximum hours of work and conditions of the work site for women served to ensure the industrial workplace as a male domain.

Although they had somewhat different objectives, the unions' struggle for a family wage and the elimination of the competition of women and children from work supported the state's actions. As early as the 1870s, labour newspapers sent a clear message to women by providing advice on raising children and increasing domestic happiness (Hurl, 1988). An article in the *Toronto Labour Day Souvenir Book* for 1907 entitled "The Influence of Women in the Labour Movement" dealt exclusively with the role that women as consumers, wives and mothers could play in the union movement by supporting the union label (Klein and Roberts, 1974:220). Similarly, an article in the *Labor Gazette* reported that:

> Towards the end of his address the lecturer spoke of the great aim of labor legislation being the establishment of the home on a solid basis. Every effort must be made to keep the mother in the home, she being the natural and primary factor in education and in the development of good citizenship (1914:1158).

The other state policy which reduced the availability of children for work was the enactment of compulsory education. Instituted to accomplish a number of objectives, one consequence of compulsory education was to limit the time when children could work. Employers were initially discouraged and later legally prohibited from permitting children to work during school hours (Seccombe, 1986). In addition to delimiting children's time, compulsory education was an important ideological tool. Not only was the school valuable in inculcating the large number of immigrant and working class children with a middle class Protestant morality that would be compatible to the demands of a working life within an industrial economy, it was also seen as a powerful ideological force for instilling familial values for future generations: "If Canadians were to improve social conditions," explained Mrs. Hoodless, they had to "go to the root" which was the "HOME." "The school," she continued, "must become the agent that shaped the homes of the next generation" (Hoodless Papers, 1902, in Sutherland, 1976:173).

The other area of legislative initiative described earlier, the treatment of dependent children, is also consistent with the argument that the state was placing the issue of reproduction as a priority in the late 19th and early 20th centuries. Given the lowering birth rate of Canadians, the plight of unwanted and orphaned native-born children could no longer be ignored. The same middle class that was raising fears about "race suicide" was also successfully advocating new policies that would redefine children as objects of precious value that must be protected. Clearly, the high mortality rates that were commonplace in baby farms and orphanages were no longer tolerable.

The state's recognition of the Children's Aid Society as its agent in 1893 signalled a growing interest in the welfare of unwanted and poor children. In addition, greater scope was now given in defining those children in need of protection. Ursel (1986) notes that, from the beginning, the majority of state wards were not orphans or abandoned children, but were children apprehended by the Children's Aid Society from "undesirable" homes. Moreover, providing basic food and shelter for a child was no longer sufficient in the state's new conception of adequate care. The fact that some working class parents resisted this intrusion of the state is indicated by an amendment of the Child Protection Act in 1895 which made it a criminal offense for a parent to encourage a child to leave an institution or home to which the child had been committed (Ursel, 1986:201).

Conclusion

The changes that occurred in the lives of Canadian children from 1850 to 1920 were dramatic. The restrictions on child labour, the move toward compulsory education, and the increased surveillance of and state sanctioned guidelines for the treatment of dependent children are indicative of the transformation that occurred during this period. We have attempted to demonstrate that this change was not simply a reflection of the emergence of "enlightened attitudes" toward children; nor can it be understood by an exclusive focus on the economic changes that were occurring at this time. Rather, it is only by examining both the changes in the workplace and the changes in the home that we can develop an adequate understanding of the material and ideological shift in society's approach to children. Put simply, the onset of industrial capitalism in the latter half of the 19th century produced a crisis in reproduction. Indications of this crisis were a declining birth rate and the increasing reliance on immigration to meet capital's labour needs, and the conflicting demands on women to be industrial workers and domestic labourers.

The response of the state to this crisis of reproduction was to enact legislation and implement social policies that would have the effect of making the state itself an active participant in the care of children and the structuring of the home. Ursel (1986) refers to this process as the movement from familial patriarchy to social patriarchy. The direction of state intervention was twofold: to reinforce the ideology of patriarchy by restricting women's participation in the workforce and by lending tacit support to defining women's proper place as being in the home, and to alter patriarchy itself by transferring some control of women and children from the individual patriarch to the state. The state was now seen as having a legitimate interest in what had previously been the exclusive domain of the individual patriarch: a child's involvement in labour, the extent of a child's formal education and the standards of minimal care for children. The consequences of these structural and ideological changes were to transform children into precious creatures in need of special care and to transform motherhood into a sacred position best qualified to providing much of the special care required by these new precious creatures.

Notes
This article is a revision of a paper presented at the Multidisciplinary Workshop on Historical Research Concerning Children and Youth, University of Manitoba, February, 1990. The writers would like to thank Gregg Olsen, Elizabeth Comack and Rick Linden for their helpful comments.

1. The term sweat shop refers to a small workplace, occasionally attached to the home, where women and children worked under contract or subcontract for retail and wholesale outlets of the clothing industry (Bullen, 1986:170).
2. As used in this paper, "dependent children" will refer to any children who were orphaned or abandoned by their parents.
3. Apprenticeship was widely practised in England since the middle ages as a means for middle and lower class children to learn a trade. This practice was carried over into America where children typically left home between the ages of 7 and 14 to work in richer homes as domestic servants, labourers or apprentices (Minge-Kalman, 1978).
4. This concept was originated by Sir Charles Loring Brace in New York in 1853. Canadian child savers emulated this scheme in the latter part of the century.
5. "Dependent" children consisted of illegitimate children in foundling homes, orphans, and children of the poor that were bound out into orphanages or houses of industry. "Street arabs" and "waifs" were chil-

dren who were "neglected" by their parents and survived by selling newspapers, pilfering, or begging. "Delinquent" children were children between the ages of 7-14 found guilty of breaking a municipal, provincial, or federal statute (Sutherland, 1976).

6. "Agency" refers to the philanthropic agencies maintained by the child-savers.

7. Although the first Canadian adoption statute was passed by the province of New Brunswick in 1873, its focus was mainly on inheritance disputes. It was followed in 1896 by a more elaborate adoption statute in Nova Scotia. A period of nearly a quarter-century then elapsed before adoption legislation was passed in B.C. in 1920, Ontario in 1921, Manitoba and Saskatchewan in 1922, Quebec in 1924, Alberta in 1927, and Prince Edward Island in 1930.

Canada's Immigration Policy and Domestics from the Caribbean: The Second Domestic Scheme

Agnes Calliste

Employment in domestic service was one of the few ways by which black women from the Caribbean could immigrate to Canada before 1962. The role of domestic service in the immigration of Caribbean blacks has been historically significant. In the period 1922 to 1931, 74 percent of the 768 Caribbean blacks who immigrated to Canada came as domestics. Between 1955 and 1961, domestics comprised 44 percent of the 4,219 independent Caribbean immigrants; many of these immigrants also sponsored the entry of their family members to Canada.[1] The proportion of Caribbean domestics is even higher than these statistics indicate, since many of the sponsored wives of immigrants who are listed as "dependents" entered the labour market; they had to work because of economic necessity given their husbands' low wages (Arnopoulous, 1979; Leah, 1980; Confidential interviews, May–August, 1982: July 12, 1988). Despite the significance of domestic service for the immigration of Caribbean blacks, little has been written on Caribbean domestics in Canada.[2]

This study examines the Caribbean Domestic Scheme in Canada from 1955 to 1967 and argues that the growing demand for cheap domestic labour in Canada was the crucial stimulus for the Scheme. At the same time, other economic and political factors played a role in the initiation and continuation of this immigration scheme. Caribbean people, both in Canada and in the Caribbean, had pressured the Canadian Government to liberalize its discriminatory immigration policy and regulations against people from the area. The Department of Immigration agreed to the Domestic Scheme in order to maintain Canada's preferential trade and investment in the British Caribbean; this agreement also reflected imperial ties between Canada and the Caribbean.[3]

The Domestic Scheme did not indicate liberalization of Canada's immigration policy. On the contrary, it indicated the racial, patriarchal and class biases underlying Canadian policy. Prior to 1962, the entry of black immigrants had been severely restricted except when they were needed as a cheap pool of labour. They provided a reserve army of labour for predominantly unskilled work which white workers were not willing to do (these jobs included working in the coke ovens in the Sydney steel plant and working as domestics).[4] As the Superintendent of Immigration, W.D. Scott, stated to the Minister of Immigration: "Coloured labour is not generally speaking in demand in Canada and it is not only regarded as the lowest grade, but it is the last to be taken on and the first to be discharged in most enterprises."[5] Scott's description of the 1918 situation was still relevant in 1955. Despite the critical shortage of labour during the post-war industrial boom (Green, 1976), Canada turned to the Carribean as a source of cheap domestics only when it became evident that Europe could not satisfy the urgent demand for domestics. Adding to the problem, many Europeans who emigrated as domestics left domestic work soon after their arrival in Canada. Utilization of the Domestic Scheme reflected some of the strategies adopted by Caribbean women (as well as other immigrant women) to enter Canada in order to improve their economic and social position.[7] These developments also provide some insights into race, class and gender relations in Canada. We will begin by outlining the conceptual framework for this study of the Domestic Scheme. Next we will discuss Canada's immigration regulations and policy in relation to Caribbean blacks, focusing on those factors which influenced the Domestic Scheme. Finally, we will examine the operation of the Scheme and look at its impact on the lives of Caribbean women.

Conceptual Framework

Canada's immigration policies have been shaped by the demand for cheap labour, as well as racial, ethnic, gender and class biases which have discriminated against women of colour, particularly black Caribbean women. Recent studies (Burawoy, 1976; Castells, 1975; Miles, 1982; Portes, 1978) suggest that international labour immigration is a result of uneven capitalist development: massive accumulation of capital and concentration of productive resources in some countries and underdevelopment and dependence on those countries by others (i.e., the "centre-periphery" relationship). This dependence is partly the product of direct exploitation by the centre of the periphery's resources through colonialism and imperialism. Sixteenth century European settlers in the Caribbean first tried to enslave indigenous people to cultivate tobacco. When this population proved unsuited, the settlers brought over indentured workers from Europe. With the change of the primary crop from tobacco to sugar cane in the mid-17th century, settlers began to import African slaves as a cheap, abundant and easily controllable labour force to work on the sugar plantations. After emancipation, indentured workers were imported predominantly from China and India (Augier, et al., 1960; Williams, 1966). Colonialism and slavery moulded plantation societies in the Caribbean in the interest of the metropolitan countries. Their economic legacy in the Caribbean has been underdevelopment, with high levels of unemployment (over 25 percent in some countries),[8] limited opportunities, low wage levels, and poverty for the majority of the population (Beckford, 1972). Governments in the Caribbean encouraged emigration as a means of reducing overpopulation and unemployment, as well as improving the economic conditions of emigrants and their families.[9] Thus, Caribbean people have had a migratory tradition since the time of emancipation, as they responded to employment opportunities within the Caribbean (for example, migration from the smaller Windward and Leeward islands to Trinidad, Guyana and Panama) and opportunities abroad to support themselves and their families (Beckford, 1968).

The legacy of slavery produced a low status for blacks. While Africans were enslaved for economic reasons (Williams, 1968) the ideology of racism (that blacks were inferior) was used to justify slavery. Colour was also used as an effective means of social control (Beckford, 1968); the colour stratification in the Caribbean, which associated blackness with class disprivilege and powerlessness, was maintained after emancipation. In the Caribbean, as well as in Canada, blacks remain one of the most disadvantaged groups due to institutional racism and systemic discrimination. Colonialism and slavery have affected labour migration, race relations and gender relations. People from colonial and less developed societies, particularly blacks, were more vulnerable to exploitation; they were more likely to retain their subordinate position in the country of immigration and to be subjected to economic, political and social control. Working class women of colour from colonial societies were the most vulnerable.

Despite Canada's demand for cheap labour, its immigration policies were selective in terms of race, ethnicity and gender in accordance with the needs of the labour market. Race and gender ideologies were used to justify the domination, exclusion and restriction of blacks and other people of colour, particularly women. For example, prior to 1955, stereotypes about black women being promiscuous and single parents were used to restrict the immigration of Caribbean domestics.[10] Moreover, the ideology of racism was not only constructed to justify slavery, colonialism and imperialism, as this ideology was reproduced it perpetuated the belief that different racial and ethnic groups had inherent attributes which suited them to particular jobs. In this way, racism interacted with sexism and class exploitation in the labour market.

Prior to the mid-1950s in Canada, black men were pictured mainly as porters and black women as domestics. The latter reflected the stereotype of the "black mammy" or the traditional Aunt Jemima.[11] In 1911, for example, some employers in Québec recommended the immigration of domestics from Guadeloupe, not only because they were cheap, but also because they were "fond of children" and "knew their place."[12] The Québec mistresses' evaluation of their domestics also reflected class relations and the fragmentation of gender along class lines.

The ideologies of racism and sexism were so pervasive that even some British Caribbean people seemed to have shared the stereotypical conceptions about black women. For example, a Caribbean trade official in Canada criticized Canada's discriminatory immigration policy against British Caribbean people because of its refusal to admit domestics into a "field of employment" he believed to be "admirably suited to the West Indians" (Bodsworth, 1955:127). Similarly, another Caribbean minister made a proposal to the Department of Immigration to recruit Caribbean women as "children's nurses" because they were "temperamentally well suited" for these positions.[13]

In advanced capitalist and patriarchal societies, racism and sexism are used to maximize profits in several ways: through segregated labour markets in which racial minorities and women (particularly women of colour and immigrant women) are concentrated in low status and lowpaying jobs; and through the split labour market where women of colour are paid less than white workers and men for doing the same work (Bonacich, 1972, 1975 and 1976; Phizacklea, 1983). Specifically, Caribbean domestics have been paid less than their Canadian and European counterparts. In 1910-11, for example, Caribbean domestics received a monthly wage of $5.00 compared to $12.00-$15.00 paid to other domestics. Even when we add the $80.00 cost of transportation from Guadeloupe to Québec, Caribbean domestics were still cheaper to hire since they had two-year contracts.[14]

The classic cycle of structural discrimination reproduces itself. Discrimination in employment affects the wider society; discrimination in the areas of education, housing and immigration serves to perpetuate inequality. Blacks were stigmatized as inassimilable and undesirable for permanent settling because of racist ideology. The Department of Immigration used the depressed conditions of blacks in Canada, particularly in Halifax, to justify its restrictive immigration policy against Caribbean people.[15] In reality, the low socio-economic position of blacks in Nova Scotia and in Canada generally reflects a history of oppression: slavery, discrimination in employment and housing, and segregated schools. Black poverty, a result of structural conditions, was attributed by many whites to cultural and personal characteristics, such as laziness and an inability of blacks to maintain themselves (The Black Worker, March 1952; Clairmont and Magill, 1970; Corbett, 1957; Tulloch, 1975; Winks, 1971).

Organized labour — feeling threatened by a cheap pool of non-union-ized workers that might depress wages and partly because of racism[16]— has historically discriminated against blacks (including those from the Caribbean) and other people of colour by formally excluding them from unions or by relegating them to auxiliary and segregated locals (Calliste, 1987 and 1988; Marshall, 1965; Northrup, 1944). Labour opposed liberal immigration policies. Thus, the working class was fragmented along racial lines.

Working-class immigrant women of colour face a four-fold oppression. Their immigrant status interacts with race, class and gender. Many immigrant women have been relegated to the worst jobs, such as domestic service (Leah, 1980; Phizacklea, 1983; Rothenberg, 1988). With its low wages, social isolation and undesirable working conditions (Arnopoulos, 1979; Leslie, 1974) domestic service is increasingly being performed by women from the Third World (particularly the Phillipines and the Caribbean) on work permits. Live-in domestics are super-exploited. As Arnopoulos points out (1974:23), "[they] usually earn less than half the minimum wage, work long hours with little time off, and are clearly the most disadvantaged group among immigrant women in the Canadian labour market."

As in other aspects of the gender division of labour, the racial and class position and the immigrant status of women affect their reproductive role. The stereotype about working class Caribbean women as single parents has been used to justify the restriction and exclusion — even deportation — of Caribbean domestics since 1911. In that year, for example, seven domestics from Guadeloupe were barred from entry because they were single parents. The immigration officer surmised that they were likely to become pregnant again and would probably become a public burden.[17] The stipulation that Caribbean domestics who came on the Scheme were to be young (ages 21 to 35), single and without children[18] had economic advantages for both employers and the state. The women were likely to be strong and healthy. Without their families in Canada, they would be more dependent on employers. This also represented a substantial saving in social capital such as housing, schools, hospitals, transportation and other infrastructural facilities (Burowoy, 1976; Miles, 1982). Such restrictions reflected the double standard in society, as well as an ethnocentric and patriarchal bias in immigration policy. As Leah and Morgan (1979) point out, male immigrants and migrants were not required to be single and without children. Immigration regulations and policy which prohibited the entry of Chinese women (except for the wives of those classes of Chinese that were exempt from the Act, that is, members of the diplomatic corps, merchants and students)[19] and of American, black, migrant porters' wives and families prior to 1943 (Calliste, 1987), suggest racial, class and patriarchal biases in immigration policy which have inhibited the reunification of families of people of colour. These biases in Canadian immigration policy have also shaped the migration of black women from the Caribbean as domestics.

Canadian Immigration Policy and the Domestic Scheme

Caribbean blacks began migrating to Canada in very small numbers at the turn of the century. In Nova Scotia, they came to work predominantly in the Cape Breton steel mills and in the coal mines. The Caribbean women

were in great demand as domestics: with industrialization and urbanization, Canadian women were leaving domestic service to work in the
emerging manufacturing and service sectors (for example, in factories and
shops) which provided higher status and greater freedom because their
work time was clearly established.[20]The first Caribbean Domestic Scheme
consisted of the recruitment of approximately 100 women from Guadeloupe in 1910-11 to help fill the demand for cheap labour in Québec.[21]
Despite favourable reports from employers, who recommended that the
Scheme be continued as a solution to the chronic shortage of domestics, it
was stopped ostensibly because of rumours that some women were single
parents.[22] Another reason for discontinuing the Scheme was the view that
domestic service was not vital to the economy.

In his recommendation to the Minister that the Scheme be discontinued,
W.D. Scott, Superintendent of Immigration, also emphasized the need for
the exclusion of black immigrants, especially from among the Americans
who were going to Saskatchewan and Alberta as homesteaders.[23] An
Order-in-Council (P.C. 1324 of 1911) was passed to prohibit black immigration for one year. However, the order was cancelled because "it was
inadvertently passed in the absence of the Minister."[24] Such an order
would have raised undesirable diplomatic problems with both the United
States and the Caribbean. It would also have antagonized black voters in
Ontario and Nova Scotia who had traditionally supported Liberal candidates. Moreover, the informal restrictions instituted by the Department
were probably considered sufficient to exclude blacks.[25]

Some of the domestics from Guadeloupe and the British Caribbean were
subsequently deported when it seemed likely they would become public
charges. This occurred particularly during the recession in 1913-15, when
it was reported that there were scores of unemployed Canadian women in
the cities and towns who were willing to do the domestic work. Moreover,
immigration officers were instructed to exclude all Caribbean blacks (on
the grounds that they were likely to become public charges) even though
they complied with the Immigration Act.[26]The deportation of domestics,
particularly from Guadeloupe, was used for decades to justify the restricted entry of Caribbean women.[27]

Even when there was a demand for Caribbean domestics (for example,
during the wars), their immigration was strongly discouraged because
they were not regarded as a "permanent asset."[28]Blacks were stereotyped
as lazy, backward, more criminally inclined and less productive than
whites (Winks, 1971:292-8). During the economic slack, they were likely to
be fired to make room for unemployed whites. As Scott argued during
World War I, when there were many requests to nominate Caribbean
domestics:

> It seems to me that Canada would be adopting a very
> short-sighted policy to encourage the immigration of
> coloured people of any class or occupation. At its best it

would only be a policy of expediency and it is altogether unnecessary, in view of the present upheaval in Europe, which will unfortunately throw upon the labour market a large number of women of a most desirable class, who can be utilized for the permanent advantage of Canada ... there is no use booking these coloured domestics because they are bound to meet with difficulties.[29]

One of the most effective regulations used to restrict the immigration of Caribbean blacks was Order-in-Council P.C. 1922-717, which prohibited the landing of immigrants except farmers, farm labourers and domestics, the wife and minor children of residents in Canada, and British subjects from white English-speaking countries (Britain, Newfoundland, New Zealand, Australia and South Africa) and American citizens.[30] This regulation practically excluded all Caribbean blacks except dependents and domestics going to assured employment.[31] Thus, in the period before World War II, the entry of Caribbean blacks was small and sporadic. Altogether, between 1904 and 1931 only 2,363 were admitted — largely as labourers and domestics.[32] Immigration almost ceased during the depression.

In the immediate post-war period, the immigration of Caribbean blacks was restricted to sponsorship by close relatives.[33] Section 61 of the 1952 Immigration Act gave the Governor-General-in-Council authority to exclude people on the basis of nationality, citizenship, ethnic origin, occupation, geographical area of origin and probable inability to become readily assimilated.[34] This section of the act was rigidly applied to restrict black immigration. For example, Order-in-Council P.C. 1950-2856 defined British subjects eligible for admission as those born or naturalized in Britain, Australia, New Zealand and South Africa. British subjects from the Caribbean and other non-white countries could enter only under special arrangement or quota, or if they satisfied the Minister that they were suitable immigrants (for example, that they could be integrated into the Canadian community within a reasonable time after their entry).[35] The Order reduced immigration of Caribbean blacks from 105 in the fiscal year 1949-50 to 69 in 1950-51, although the number of applications had doubled. Ethnic origin, not geographical area, mattered. Whites from the Caribbean were admitted. In 1951-52, 414 whites compared to only 65 Blacks entered Canada.[36] Since miscegenation (racially mixed marriage) was unacceptable in Canada, immigration policy required married white applicants to supply family photographs in order to avoid non-white wives and children coming through chain migration.[37]

Pressures for Increasing Immigration from the Caribbean

The restriction of blacks and other people of colour from the British Caribbean antagonized Caribbean people, particularly after World War II. They put pressure on the Canadian trade commissioners in Jamaica and

Trinidad to liberalize Canadian immigration regulations and policy. This intensified pressure resulted from the movement toward self-govern- ment, an increasing level of education, and high unemployment[38] (espe- cially after the McCarran Walter Act of 1952 further restricted Caribbean immigration to the United States). The trade commissioners recommended to the Department of Immigration that it should develop a tolerant immigration policy which would permit the entry of a restricted number of people from the British Caribbean, irrespective of their ethnic origins. The commissioners also called for greater diplomacy in responding to applicants, particularly the influential professional and business people, in order to develop closer commercial relations. As the Canadian Trade Commissioner in Trinidad, T.G. Major, stated to the Acting Director of Immigration in 1950:

> We must be very careful not to offend local susceptibili- ties ... It must always be kept in mind that the peoples of the British Caribbean when not hampered by exchange difficulties buy up to $40 per head per annum of Cana- dian goods, even now the figure is close to $25 per capita or about $43 million per annum. As the colonies are moving steadily in the direction of self government and federation Canadian public relations must be handled with care ... There have been occasions when I have not been too happy about the phraseology used in "refusal" letters sent directly from Ottawa and have had to sooth ruffled feelings ... Canada is looked upon as the "big brother" of the British Colonies in these parts ... the accumulated good will is such a valuable asset to Canada that it must be carefully tended. Sooner or later immigra- tion from the British Caribbean will have to be dealt with in accordance with a yet to be determined policy rather than on an ad hoc basis.[39]

In the period following World War II, Canada had, indeed, more trading and investment interests in the Caribbean than in any other Third World country. Over 1,500 Canadian firms and companies had commercial connections in the Caribbean with a volume of exports which, despite exchange difficulties during the war and immediate post-war period, ranged between $30 and $80 million dollars.[40] Canada-Caribbean trade was especially significant to the Atlantic provinces. The Caribbean was the most important market for salt fish; Nova Scotia's exports in 1963 to the English-speaking Caribbean were valued at over $14 million or 10.8 percent of the province's total exports for that year. Moreover, Canada imported raw materials (for example, petroleum, bauxite and sugar) from the Caribbean. But more important to the Canadian economy was Cana- dian investment, particularly in the field of banking and insurance. Canadian banks began to move into the British Caribbean in 1889 to serve the bilateral trade and quickly spread throughout the area. For many years, three Canadian banks (Royal Bank, Bank of Nova Scotia and Canadian Imperial Bank of Commerce), together with the Barclays Bank of England, had a monopoly of the banking business of the Caribbean. While intended to serve the interests of Canadian traders, these Canadian Banks soon became an indispensable internal banking system for the Caribbean—but only on the deposit side, since loans were generally restricted to traders (Fergusson, 1966:32; Nash, 1960). Consequently, "the West Indies suffered a net drain in funds that helped [to] perpetuate their underdevelopment" (Naylor cited in R. Chodos, 1977:110) at the same time that the Canadian economy was being developed. Moreover, the banks' entry into consumer loans in the 1950s and 1960s reinforced the region's heavy dependence on imports.

Canadian insurance companies began to move into the Caribbean in 1880, and controlled approximately 70 percent of the insurance business in the region by the 1950s. Since 1955, Canadian investment has also played an important role in mining and manufacturing, particularly the Aluminum Company of Canada (ALCAN). In its Jamaican operations alone, ALCAN has invested more than $130 million (Callender, 1965; Chodos, 1977; Fraser, 1966).

Given Canada's economic interests in the Caribbean, it was important to appease Caribbean people, whether in the Caribbean or in Canada (such as the Negro Citizenship Association in Toronto), who were very critical of Ottawa's discriminatory immigration policy. Thus, in 1951 the Departmental Advisory Committee on Immigration recommended to the Minister that Canada establish an annual quota of 150 Caribbean blacks who were professionals, skilled workers, or close relatives sponsored by residents and who would contribute to the economic and cultural development of this country. The committee expected such immigrants to become exceptional citizens and help in making blacks more acceptable in Canada.[41] Although the cabinet did not agree to a formal quota, it decided to admit a small number of immigrants from the Caribbean "of exceptional merit" (that is, professional and skilled immigrants) on humanitarian grounds and by executive direction.[42] Out of 122 applicants from the Caribbean admitted in 1952-53, for example, 56 were skilled and professional immigrants.[43] This class bias in immigration policy was designed to serve the needs of the Canadian economy.

Canada's refusal to agree to a Caribbean quota (similar to those for India, Pakistan and Ceylon)[44] reflected racism against blacks. It probably also reflected the Caribbean's colonial status, which increased the likelihood that Caribbean people would be perceived as inferior (that is, that they could not govern themselves). Moreover, as colonies, they did not have representatives at the United Nations who could help to put international pressure on Canada. Besides admitting immigrants of "exceptional merit," the Department of Immigration decided to be more diplomatic and, if possible, more specific when explaining the rejection of Caribbean applicants on occupational grounds (that is, where it appeared that applicants had either no employment offer nor a skill which would make them readily employable in Canada).[45]

Given the insatiable demand for domestics, it became increasingly difficult to reject Caribbean domestics on occupational grounds. As labour force opportunities grew for women — with the shift from primary to secondary industries — women tended to leave domestic work because of undesirable working conditions, low wages and the low value placed upon domestic work (Arnopoulos, 1976; Connelly, 1976). The increased participation of women in the paid labour force (Connelly, 1976), the affluence which accompanied the post-war industrial boom, and the baby boom also strengthened the demand for domestics. Canadians, particularly those who had visited the Caribbean, put pressure on the federal government for the admission of Caribbean domestics as a cheap and reliable labour supply.[46] The publicity given to the exclusion of Caribbean domestics[47] probably also served to pressure the Canadian government to modify its immigration policy with respect to Caribbean domestics.

The pressure to change immigration regulations and policy came increasingly from within the Canadian black community. In the immediate post-war period, this group had assisted Caribbean immigrants in trouble, particularly those threatened with deportation, and facilitated the immigration of relatives of residents in Canada. By 1954, the community had developed a program to challenge immigration policy. The Negro Citizenship Association co-ordinated the efforts of existing black organizations with the support of mainstream organizations, such as church groups and the Ontario Labour Committee for Human Rights.[48] The association focused attention on immigration policy, arguing that it demonstrated second-class status and was a structural barrier to integration. The black community held public meetings and invited Caribbean politicians visiting Canada to give public lectures. They also demonstrated and sent petitions to Ottawa. A delegation presented a brief to Prime Minister Louis St. Laurent in 1954 with explicit proposals for policy reform: equal treatment of applicants from the British Caribbean with other British subjects, definition of "exceptional merit," and the need for an immigration office in the Caribbean.[49]

Racial provisions in the immigration regulations were challenged before the Supreme Court of Canada in 1955 when Narine-Singh's family was ordered deported to Trinidad because Caribbean people of South Asian origin could not be admitted to Canada unless they were sponsored by close relatives.[50] Although the appeal was dismissed with costs on the basis that the immigration regulations which permitted exclusion or restricted entry because of ethnicity were legal, "the regulations were amended and 'Asian' was deleted." Thus, women of South-Asian origin were eligible to apply to Canada on the Domestic Scheme. As the Director of Immigration informed the Labour Commission in Guyana, "there would be no objection to including a few" of them in the Domestic Scheme.[51] The discriminatory immigration policy against British Caribbean people was also periodically attacked by the official opposition.[52]

However, the Immigration Department did not liberalize the regulations and policy. It simply sought "to eliminate certain irritants."[53] Thus, the Domestic Scheme was designed and shaped by both economic and political interests. In addition to serving the needs of the Canadian labour market, the scheme was intended to further Canada's economic interests through trade and investments in the British Caribbean. It was also influenced by local and international politics, and by the need to appease the official opposition and people from the British Caribbean, both in Canada and in the Caribbean.

The Second Caribbean Domestic Scheme

The second Caribbean Domestic Scheme was based on the Canadian government's racist and sexist assumptions about black Caribbean women. Given that black women were perceived as promiscuous or as single parents likely to become a public burden, the Domestic Scheme began as an experiment with black immigration acceptable only under certain conditions: a limited number of migrant workers would be allowed as a short-term solution to the chronic shortage of domestics. The Department of Immigration's original intent was to admit Caribbean domestics as migrant workers for one year, with a possible one year extension on the understanding that they would remain in domestic service. The ministers of Trade and Industry of Jamaica and Barbados, who negotiated the Domestic Scheme with the Department of Immigration through the Colonial Office, had guaranteed the return of the domestics at the end of their contract.[54] Such a migrant system was economically advantageous to employers and the state in that it gave them the greatest possible degree of control over labour power: it could be utilized only for domestic service and for no longer than justified by economic demand. The use of migrant domestics would thus ensure that Canada did not have to meet the cost of their original production (nurturing and educating them), nor the expense of maintaining them in times of recession (Burawoy, 1976; Miles, 1982). Furthermore, the Department of Immigration did not want the Domestic Scheme to open the door to Caribbean immigration. As late as January 1955, the Director of Immigration blatantly argued against an immigration agreement with the British Caribbean. In his words:

> It is from experience, generally speaking, that coloured people in the present state of the white man's thinking are not a tangible asset, and as a result are more or less ostracized. They do not assimilate readily and pretty much vegetate to a low standard of living ... many cannot adapt themselves to our climatic conditions. To enter into an agreement which would have the effect of in-

creasing coloured immigration to this country would be
an act of misguided generosity since it would not have
the effect of bringing about a worthwhile solution to the
problem of coloured people and would be quite likely to
intensify our own social and economic problems.[55]

However, the Immigration Department decided to admit Caribbean
domestics as landed immigrants. This change was made for two reasons:
first, in response to criticisms that admitting domestics as migrant labour
was a discriminatory policy similar to indentured labour; and second,
because officials thought that, unlike Europeans, Caribbean domestics
were not likely to leave domestic service at the end of their one-year
contract. Moreover, the Department felt that administrative controls would
provide sufficient sanctions to prevent abuse of the Scheme. For example,
any domestic found "undesirable" (for instance, who might become
pregnant during her first year) or who broke her contract was to be
deported at the expense of the Caribbean government.[56]

The perception of Caribbean women as career domestics was based on
discrimination in the labour market and the stereotypical perception of
black women. In 1963, for example, when the Ministry of Development,
Trade, Industry and Labour in Barbados offered to recruit 300 nurses to
supply the growing demand in Toronto, the Central District Superintendent assumed that Barbados could not afford to send so many trained
nurses. Based on a racist stereotype, the superintendent suspected that
these women were either domestics or at best nurses' aides.[57]

The emigration of skilled labour actually indicated the limited job
opportunities available in Barbados; such emigration caused a brain drain
from Barbados to Canada — an economic loss incurred by Barbados from
educating and training professional and skilled people who subsequently
migrated without contributing directly to the country's economic activity.
Canada, on the other hand, economized on the reproduction of high-cost
labour by importing ready-made workers, since it was cheaper and
quicker to import foreign nurses than to produce them domestically.

Caribbean governments facilitated the brain drain. They instituted a
rigorous selection process to ensure that candidates for the Domestic
Scheme would establish a good name for Caribbean people in Canada. In
this way, the Domestic Scheme would continue. It was also felt that the
selection process would reduce or eliminate the probability of Caribbean
governments having to pay the return fare of any domestic who might be
deported during the first year after her arrival in Canada.[58] Unlike preferred immigrants from northern and western Europe, Caribbean domestics were not eligible to apply for interest-free travel loans from the
Canadian government under the Assisted Passage Loan Scheme of 1950.[59]
Since the Domestic Scheme provided almost the only opportunity for
many black women from the Caribbean to enter Canada, and given the
lack of educational and employment opportunities in the Caribbean, some

skilled and semi-skilled workers (for example, civil servants, nurses and teachers) used the Scheme to immigrate to Canada in order to further their education and to seek other fields of employment.[60] Henry (1968) found in her study of 61 domestics in Montréal who came on the Scheme that only 12 percent of those previously employed had worked as domestics. According to *The Trinidad Chronicle,* the selection process placed greater emphasis on the women's educational background and ambition than on their domestic skills.[61] This policy of brain drain from the periphery to the centre to do unskilled work was depicted in a cartoon about Caribbean girls' aspirations: "I'll be a Civil Servant when I grow up and get a chance to go to Canada as a Domestic Servant!"[62]

In 1956, the Department of Labour described the Scheme as an excellent experiment that had provided the best group of domestics to enter Canada from any country since World War II. According to the government, all of the 100 women were still in domestic service and 84 percent were still in their first job approximately nine months after their arrival. Those who had transferred did so for higher wages and better working conditions or to be located closer to friends. Employers were enthusiastic about the Scheme. They found their employees to be more educated, "fond of children," obliging and less demanding than other domestics.[63] Thus, the scheme was extended from 100 in 1955 to 200 in 1956 and to 280 by 1959 to include Guyana and the islands of the Caribbean Federation. Between 1955 and 1966, 2,940 domestics came to Canada on the Scheme.[64]

Unlike their employers, many Caribbean domestics were very disappointed. They found the work harder, the working hours longer, and the pay much less than they had expected. They were surprised that Canadians hired only one domestic — a general domestic — instead of several who would share the work load and perform specialized duties. The first group found it more difficult than subsequent groups to leave domestic work at the end of their contract. This might be attributed to several factors, including: greater inequality in employment; the lack of recognition of education, skills and work experience from non-European countries; the stigma attached to people engaged in domestic work; and the lack of networks among Caribbean women. Thus, three years after their arrival, many of the women were still working as domestics: they were trapped in dead-end jobs.[65]

However, by the late 1950s, different areas of employment were becoming accessible to blacks, due in part to post-war social changes and legislation. As a result, some blacks were able to leave domestic service.[66] Caribbean domestics developed their own networks in order to be supportive of one another and to prepare new arrivals for work in Canada. They met these women at the airport or train station, quickly exchanged addresses and telephone numbers, and tutored them on working conditions and wages in order to put them on their guard. One domestic told a new arrival:

> If you don't like your bosses, you are allowed to switch
> right away ... Thursday is the regular day off; they will try
> to change it when it's convenient for them, don't let them
> do it. For big jobs such as washing windows, walls and
> scrubbing floors, let them bring in a char.[67]

Members of succeeding groups were more likely to assert their rights, to ask for higher wages, to transfer from one domestic job to another (because of unsatisfactory working conditions or isolation in the suburbs or because it was too far to travel to night classes), and to leave their position at the end of their contract.[68]

Those who were skilled or semi-skilled in other occupations (approximately 25 percent) tended to leave domestic service at the end of one year; others did so at a lower rate — as they upgraded their education through night classes or correspondence courses or tried to save their money to sponsor some members of their family. Sixty percent of the 1958 group, for example, left domestic service in less than two years. Less than 25 percent of each group remained in domestic service after three years.[69] Caribbean women found employment in the following areas: the service sector; secretarial services; the textile industry; laundry; hairdressing and restaurants; as nurses and nurses aides in hospitals; and, to a lesser extent, in sales, accounting and teaching. In some cases, the new job was more physically exhausting and the net pay was lower than in domestic service, but the women's work time was clearly established and they had greater freedom.[70]

The educational qualifications required of Caribbean domestics were changed from Grade 8 to some high school in 1961 to prevent the immigration of low-skilled people from the Caribbean through sponsorship and to facilitate the retraining of domestics, if necessary.[71] This change reflected the general educational upgrading of the labour force; it also recognized the likelihood that Caribbean women might leave domestic work.

Although Caribbean women remained in domestic service longer than Europeans who came on similar schemes, some officials of the Departments of Immigration and Labour were disappointed by the former group's high mobility rate out of domestic service, particularly during the downturn in the economy and the high unemployment rates in semi-skilled and unskilled jobs in 1958-59. Even more disturbing to the officials was the sponsoring by some women of their family members.[72] Although the number of Caribbean applications was negligible compared to the influx of unskilled immigrants from Southern Europe (Levitt and McIntyre, 1967), immigration officials complained that Caribbean immigrants were swelling the semi-skilled and unskilled labour force through chained migration. In 1961, there were 107 applications from the 1959 and 1960 groups of Caribbean domestics to sponsor their fiances and close relatives, including five "illegitimate" and three "legitimate" children.[73] Since only single women without children were allowed on the Scheme, mothers with children, who had failed to list their children on their application forms, needed legal counsel if they wanted to sponsor them.[74] The eventual case of the "Seven Jamaican Women" (who were ordered deported in 1977 when they applied to sponsor their children) occurred during a period of economic decline and after the establishment of a new policy of recruiting domestics on work permits. At this time, Caribbean women were considered to be expendable (Leah, 1980).

Immigration officials' negative attitudes toward Caribbean women's sponsorship of their families reflected race, class and gender biases: the nuclear, patriarchal family was regarded as the norm in Canada and men were expected to be the main wage-earners. Order-in-Council, P.C. 1950-2856 provided for a resident to sponsor the entry of his fiancee "provided the prospective husband is able to support his intended wife."[75] This assumed that immigrant women were likely to be dependent. However, the evidence suggests that because of immigration policy regarding Caribbean blacks, namely, a predominance of single women as domestics (and nurses), women were more likely to sponsor their prospective spouses and other relatives.[76] Some of the Caribbean men who came to Canada, sponsored by women already immigrated on the Domestic Scheme, had difficulty finding work (Clarke, 1967; Bled, 1965). In these cases, the women were the main wage-earners. Black women have always worked (for wages) proportionately more than white women. Similarly, black women have had responsibility for financially supporting their children and grandchildren more often than have their white counterparts (Brand, 1984; Davis, 1983).

The need for professional and skilled immigrants, as well as ethnic selectivity in immigration policy, militated against the immigration of low-skilled Caribbean men. The Negro Citizenship Association made representations to the Department of Immigration to admit a comparable number of Caribbean males to balance the sexes. The Department responded that it would prefer to admit professional and skilled Caribbean men to better meet the needs of the labour market. Given the class differences between the sexes, such immigration would not satisfy the women's needs for companionship and marriage.[77]

The loneliness and isolation of Caribbean domestics were partially counteracted by community and women's organizations, and by the women's own initiative. Some domestics in Toronto, Montréal and Ottawa organized their own clubs, which met at the Young Women's Christian Association (YWCA). Some domestics in Montréal started two netball teams. Another group, the Pioneer Club, met at the Negro Community Centre (NCC) where community workers organized activities such as sewing and craft classes, and arranged for visiting speakers. The Pioneer women organized some social functions at the NCC such as talent shows. The group which met at the YMCA in Ottawa occasionally attended the Pioneer Club's functions, thus widening the network.[78] The initial contact between the Centre and domestics was made by some employers in

Québec living outside of Montréal (e.g., in Chateauguay) who were concerned about their employees' loneliness on Thursday afternoons. The Department of Labour's evaluation of the Domestic Scheme in 1956 indicates that some employers had expressed concern about the limited social contacts that domestics had outside of employment.[79]

Caribbean domestics traditionally preferred to work in Montréal and Toronto. These cities had higher wages, a greater demand for domestics, and better educational and employment opportunities; the women were also more likely to have friends and/or relatives in these cities. Between 1955 and 1961, 580 out of the 1600 women chose Montréal (Bled, 1965). After 1958, deliberate efforts were made to place domestics across the country, albeit in small numbers. Based on a racist supposition, this was done to prevent racial concentration: domestics tended to band together. Immigration officers sometimes spirited women away from their friends (meeting them at the airport in Montréal) who might have influenced them to remain in the city.[80] This manipulation of Caribbean domestics was probably intended to make them more controllable; it also served to fill requests for domestics in small towns in Western Canada.[81] Despite the wider placement, some domestics migrated to Montréal and Toronto. In the 1959 group, for example, 34 moved to Toronto during their first year.[82]

Criticisms of the Domestic Scheme

By 1961, the Department of Immigration was becoming ambivalent about the benefits of continuing the Domestic Scheme. Some officials suggested that the Scheme should be discontinued because the "rapid movement" out of domestic service did not serve the long-term economic need for domestics. Moreover, the Scheme, like other special group programs, was perceived to have become unnecessary because of the proposed changes to immigration regulations in 1962 which emphasized education, skills, the ability of immigrants to establish themselves successfully in Canada (for example, with pre-arranged employment), and the elimination of explicit racial qualifications for admission.[83] This view was also supported by the Caribbean Association in Ottawa, which argued that "to enter into a formal agreement with a government of a predominantly white country in which non-whites enter this country in a socially inferior role" encourages racism. The Association suggested that since there was no apparent need for the continuation of the Domestic Scheme, which labelled and condemned Caribbean women to second-class status in Canada, Caribbean governments should cancel it and domestics should be treated as a skilled group under Canada's preferred immigration policy.[84] In the Caribbean government's assessment, though, eliminating or reducing the quota of Caribbean domestics would likely cause greater tension in Canada-Caribbean relations, since the new regulation had not led to a substantial increase in Caribbean immigration to Canada.[85] This was due partly to the administration of the regulations, as the evidence suggests that, apart from the Domestic Scheme, Canada did not actively recruit or officially encourage immigrants from the Caribbean until 1967, when immigration offices were open in Jamaica and Trinidad.[86]

The Scheme had other political benefits for Caribbean government officials who did the initial selection of domestics.[87] Although the Department of Labour wanted the Scheme to continue because of the need for domestics, some immigration officials thought that professionals and skilled immigrants would be more beneficial to the Canadian economy.[88] The Canadian government's dilemma was well expressed by G. F. Davidson, Deputy Minister of Immigration:

> Our chief dilemma seems to be that we are ambivalent as to what it is we are trying to do. Are we trying to pick domestics whose attitude to household service is good and who will continue to be content to remain in household service and be good domestics on a career basis? Or are we using the domestic movement as a means of selecting a higher class of girl (sic) who will not stay in domestic service any longer than necessary but will move out after a year into the occupation for which she is best suited, and be in the long run a greater credit to herself, her race, and to Canada?[89]

Support for the continuation of the Domestic Scheme as a means of maintaining Canada-Caribbean relations also came from Canadian government representatives in the Caribbean. For example, the assistant Under-Secretary of State for External Affairs in British Guyana, Arnold Smith, was very patronizing in his support for the Scheme. In his words:

> ... nothing that Canada has ever done for B.G. is so well and favourably known, or has given Canada as much kudos as this Domestic Workers Plan, which has had the very modest achievement of sending for the past 10 years a total of 30 B.G. (per year) girls (sic) to work in Canadian homes as servants. I have noted Department of Immigration rumblings somewhere to the effect that they are considering discontinuing the plan. Notation is made here that if this becomes a real intention it must be combatted in the strongest possible fashion. Why should such a mild scheme - which is working in doing something towards filling a labour shortage in Canadian homes, is doing much to prove no discrimination because of colour, and which is pleasing to the B.G. people - be eliminated?[90]

Smith did not recognize the race, class and gender biases of the Domestic Scheme. However, these were clear to blacks, particularly during the Civil

Rights Movement and the movement for political independence in the Caribbean.

The immigration issue was a constant source of embarrassment and friction in Canada-Caribbean relations, particularly on the politically independent islands. Eric Williams, Prime Minister of Trinidad and Tobago, criticized Canada and other predominantly white Commonwealth countries for discriminating against people of colour as if they were "poison or disease:"

> Today the world has worked out the curious hybrid of
> juridical equality of states and racial inequality of people
> ... Canada eases its conscience by accepting a handful of
> domestic servants; in Britain the contemporary slogan is
> "keep Britain white," the very Britain which was built up
> by African and Asian labour in Africa, Asia and the West
> Indies. Whatever the Commonwealth may be in theory,
> it is in practice being increasingly tainted with a racial
> limitation.[91]

Williams' criticisms prompted a Canadian Member of Parliament, David Orlikow, to propose the issuing of a White Paper to amend the Immigration Act and regulations, eliminating racial discrimination and convincing people of colour that the Canadian government believed in racial equality.[92]

Some blacks criticized the Scheme as a form of indentured labour in which Caribbean domestics were expected to work harder at much less pay than their Canadian and European counterparts. One critic estimated the wage difference at $150 per month.[93] Blacks argued that the benefits of the Scheme were questionable for several reasons. First, the small number of women who emigrated under the scheme could not significantly reduce unemployment and population pressure in the Caribbean. Second, the Scheme did not provide great opportunities for black women, since they did not have time to upgrade their education. The evidence suggests that after the initial surprise at domestics' attending night classes, many employers agreed to give their employees time off for this purpose, even though they thought that the women's educational and occupational expectations were too high. Some employers, though, refused to do so; in a few cases the relationship became very strained once employers had found out that domestics were attending classes. Obviously, some employers held very negative stereotypes about Caribbean women which influenced their perceptions about what jobs were appropriate for them.[94] These negative stereotypes and employers' attempts to limit their employees' educational and occupational expectations reflected race, gender and class biases, as well as the desire for cheap and controllable labour. A third criticism of the Scheme was that Caribbean domestics were being treated as third-rate citizens in Canada who were not allowed to integrate.

Caribbean governments were criticized for their sexism and for supporting the centre-periphery relationship by sending young women—including skilled and semi-skilled workers—to Canada as domestics. The editor
of *The Barbados Advocate*, for example, argued that pay inequity in the
Caribbean was pushing skilled and semi-skilled women to emigrate on the
Domestic Scheme. He called for pay equity for women and an end to the
brain drain.[95] Thus, both Canadian and Caribbean governments were
being asked to re-examine the effects of the Domestic Scheme.

Despite these criticisms, the Domestic Scheme seemed to be popular in
the Caribbean.[96] It gave some women the chance to emigrate to a legendary
land of opportunity, and it enabled them to send much needed remittances
home.[97] Emigration was also perceived as a relief from unemployment and
overpopulation.

In a remarkable development, Guyana relinquished its annual quota of
30 domestics in 1965 as part of its repatriation program. The Guyanese
government asked Ottawa to implement a program which would educate
Guyanese women and men, and which would be mutually beneficial to the
Canadian and Guyanese people (for example, by training 25 women as
stenographers and 25 men as agriculturalists to help meet the country's
development needs).[98] This request reflected a policy shift in Canadian-
Caribbean relations — from trade preference to an aid program.[99]

The Caribbean Domestic Scheme was approved annually by Order-in-
Council until 1967. In that year, it was announced that the Scheme would
be discontinued effective January, 1968. Domestics would continue to
enter under the points system.[100] Since 1973, the Canadian Employment
and Immigration Commission (CEIC) has been admitting domestics (and
seasonal agricultural workers) predominantly on temporary work permits. This policy shift reflects two factors: the number of women leaving
domestic work at the end of their contracts and the lack of industrial
expansion. The goals of the new system are two-fold. First, it ensures that
the women's labour power is utilized only for domestic work. Second,
because domestics from the Third World are regarded as expendable, they
can be sent back to their home countries when the demand for domestics
falls. Thus, women on permits are even more marginalized than those
women who came on the Scheme.

Caribbean women seem to be even more vulnerable than some Third
World women. Recruitment of domestics from the Phillipines has increased significantly in recent years, while there has been a decrease from
the Caribbean. For example, 30 percent of the 5,021 new entrants in 1985
were from the Phillipines compared to 13 percent from Jamaica and
Guyana, the two Caribbean countries included in the ten leading source
countries. Filipinos comprised 42 percent of the 8,175 new entrants in 1987,
with Jamaicans comprising only 2 percent. In 1986 and 1987, Jamaica was
the only Caribbean territory in the ten principal countries of origin for
domestics.[101] Plausible explanations for the employers' preference for
Filipinos compared to Caribbean domestics are: the former tend to be

younger, they are probably cheaper, and they are more likely to show, if not to feel, deference to their employers.[102]

Under the 1981 regulations, live-in domestics who have been here for two years and who have achieved a potential for self-sufficiency are allowed to apply for landed immigrant status. However, older Caribbean women with children are less likely than others to be granted immigrant status.[103] These disadvantages experienced by Caribbean women have several causes. Racism may be a factor, given that blacks are lower on the stratification ladder and have more negative stereotypes (for example, they are likely to be single parents) than Asians. Moreover, CEIC officials may evaluate older Caribbean women with dependent children as less likely to become self-sufficient. Further research is needed on the current immigration policy, its implementation, employers' preference for domestics and the question of whether types of domestic service vary by ethnicity.

Conclusions and Evaluation

Although the Domestic Scheme provided opportunities for some Caribbean women and their families to emigrate to Canada, it reinforced the racial, class and gender stereotypes about black women being inherently suited to domestic work. This did not stop Caribbean women in their struggle for upward mobility. They upgraded their education and moved into jobs with higher status and pay. Currently, some of the women are in nursing, teaching, accounting, small businesses and secretarial services. At least one studied medicine after teaching for a number of years and two are educational administrators. Some of the women migrated to the United States.

On the whole, though, the Domestic Scheme reinforced the oppression of black working-class women. It also contributed to the Caribbean's dependency on Canada. While some Caribbean governments recognized that the Scheme was demeaning to black women, they regarded it as a partial solution to such domestic problems as unemployment and over-population. Despite some advantages of emigration, it could not significantly reduce unemployment or provide a solution to the Caribbean's under-development. Indeed, by sending some skilled and semi-skilled women on the Scheme, Caribbean governments were perpetuating their under-development and dependency through the brain drain. Caribbean women were thus being oppressed by colonialism and neo-colonialism in the Caribbean, and by racism, sexism and class bias in Canada.

Although we do not know the long-term psychological effects of the Domestic Scheme on the women and their families, there is a suggestion that some domestics — particularly those from a higher social class background in the Caribbean and those whose families had employed domestics themselves — found such work very demeaning. Some Caribbean domestics described their jobs as being in prison - they felt as if they were trapped. Moreover, the stigma attached to doing domestic work, and the racism, sexism and class bias that the women had to endure, may well have contributed to psychological problems. Some women who have achieved upward mobility will not admit that they came on the Scheme; they would prefer to forget about it.[104]

Keith Henry's study of black politics in Toronto indicated that the overwhelming majority of females — particularly domestics — were politically disadvantaged because of racism and sexism; women's participation occurred predominantly in the church and social clubs (Henry, 1981:35). While this may have been the case in the 1950s and early 1960s, since the late 1960s —with the increased influx of people from the Caribbean to Canada and policies promoting multiculturalism — some Caribbean domestics, whether current or former, have been very active on the boards and executives of community and women's organizations. A few former domestics have even been elected national presidents of organizations, and some have served on provincial and federal advisory councils.

This paper on Canada's immigration policy and the second Caribbean Domestic Scheme provides some of the historical background for understanding the experiences of some black Caribbean women in Canada. There is a need, however, for further research on the social consequences of the Domestic Scheme for Caribbean women and their families, the effects of immigration policy on ethnic stratification, and the policy implications for the aging of Caribbean women. Given that domestic service was the job open to many black women before the late 1950s, it would be interesting and useful to conduct a comparative analysis of Caribbean domestics and indigenous black Canadian domestics. Such a study might focus on the experiences of black Nova Scotians who work in white communities adjacent to their black communities. Special attention should then be directed to the implications of domestic service for the family and the community.

Notes

1. Canada, Department of Immigration and Colonization, *Annual Report*, 1922-1931; Canada, Department of Citizenship and Immigration, *Annual Report*, 1955-1961; Public Archives of Canada (Hereafter PAC), Immigration Branch Records, RG 76, Vol. 475, File 731832; Vols., 566-67, File 810666; Vol. 830, File 552-1-644: Vol. 838, File 553-36-563.

2. For preliminary work on the case studies on Caribbean domestics, see Bled (1965); Henry (1968); Silvera (1983); Turritin (1976).

3. PAC, RG 76, Vol. 830, File 552-1-644; Vol. 838, File 553-36-556; File 553-36-644..

4. Canada, Department of the Interior, *Annual Report*, 1906-1917; Department of Immigration and Colonization, *Annual Report*, 1918-1931; Department of Citizenship and Immigration, *Annual Report*, 1955-1961; PAC, RG 76, Vol. 566, File 810666, W.D. Scott to L.M. Fortier, August 10, 1916; Vol. 830, File 552-1-644; Vol. 838, File 553-36-556; File 553-36-644; RG 76, Acc. 83-84/349, Box 107, File 5750-5, Part 1, the Director of Immigration to Crerar,

Minister of Immigration, Apr. 17, 1942.

5. PAC, RG 76, Vol. 566, File 810666, W.D. Scott to W.W. Cory, Apr. 25, 1918.

6. PAC, RG 76, Vol. 838, File 553-36-644; Iacovetta (1986).

7. Canada, House of Commons, *Debates*, 1948, Vol. 6, pp. 5811-12; PAC, RG 76, Vol. 838, File 553-36-644; Iacovetta (1986).

8. The official unemployment rate of 25 percent disguises seasonal patterns and underemployment.

9. PAC, RG 76, Vols. 566-67, File 81066; Bodsworth (1955).

10. PAC, RG 76 Vol. 475, File 731832; Vol. 566-67, File 810666; RG 76 Acc. 83-84/349, Box 107, File 5750-5, Pt. 1, the Director of Immigration to Crerar, April 17, 1942.

11. Davis, (1983); Hooks, (1981); *The Winnipeg Tribune*, August 4, 1904; August 20, 1905; January 30, 1906.

12. PAC, RG 76, Vol. 475, File 731832, G.A. Marsolais to W.D. Scott, May 20, 1911; E. Dufrersne to W. D. Scott, May 20, 1911; F.X. Dupuis to W.D. Scott, May 22, 1911; R. Morin to W.D. Scott, May 22, 1911; A Rivet to W.D. Scott, May 22, 1911; C. Laurendeau to W.D. Scott , May 23, 1911; G. Boudrias to W.D. Scott , May 23, 1911.

13. PAC, RG 76, Vol. 847, File 553-110, the Office of the Commissioner for Canada to the Under-Secretary of State for External Affairs, December 29, 1961.

14. *The Montreal Herald*, April 8, 1911. See also PAC, RG 76, Vol. 475, File 731832; Vol. 566, File 810666; Clarke (1967); *The New Nation*, May 31, 1964.

15. PAC, RG 76, Vol. 830, File 552-1-644, the Director of Immigration to the Minister, September 12, 1951.

16. PAC, RG 76, Vol. 830, File 552-1-644, the Director of Immigration to the Minister, September 12, 1951.

17. PAC, RG 76, Vol. 475, File 731832, W. Klein to W.D. Scott, July 21, 1911.

18. PAC RG. 76, Vol. 838, File 553-36-644, L. Fortier to the Permanent Secretary, Minister of Labour, Jamaica, August 1955; C. Smith to R. Mapp, Minister of Trade, Industry and Labour, Barbados, July 25, 1956.

19. "An Act respecting Chinese Immigration," *Statutes of Canada* (Ottawa, 1923), Chapter 38, pp. 3-4.

20. PAC, RG 76, Vol. 475, File 731832, M.D. to L.M. Fortier, c. May 22, 1911; Vol. 566, File 810666 F.B. Williams to W.D. Scott, June 29, 1909; J. Gilchrist to W.D. Scott, April 1, 1915; Barber (1980); Leslie (1974).

21. PAC, RG 76, Vol. 475, File 731832, E.B. Robertson to G.W. Elliot, August 5, 1910; G.W. Elliot to W.D. Scott, September 10, 1910; Regimbal to W.D. Scott, April 10, 1911; R. Morin to W.D. Scott, May 22, 1911; *La Patrie* [Montréal], April, 1911; *The Montreal Herald*, April 7, 1911.

22. PAC, RG 76, Vol. 475, File 731832, W.D. Scott to F. Oliver, June 2, 1911.

23. Ibid.

24. PAC, RG 2/1, Vol. 769, P.C. 1324, "Prohibiting Negro Immigrants from landing in Canada," August 12, 1911; Vol. 772, P.C. 2378, October 5, 1911.

25. Canada, House of Commons, *Debates*, 1911, Vol. 1, col. 608; Brown and Cook, (1974:62).

26. West Indians had the highest deportation rate, particularly in 1913-15 when 91 were deported. Between 1909 and 1916, one in every 30 West Indians was deported. PAC, RG 76, Vol. 556, File 810666, L. Fortier to W.D. Scott, June 30, July 27, 1914; W. Egan to J. Cormack, April 24, 1925; *The Canada Year Book 1915* (Ottawa, 1916), p. 114.

27. PAC, RG 76, Vol. 556, File 810666, W.D. Scott to E. Mousir, secretary, the Canadian-West Indian League, September 8, 1914; Scott to W. Givens, November 11, 1914; Scott to Melville-Davis Steamship and Touring Company, September 24, 1915; Scott to Knight, April 25, 1916; RG 76, Acc. 83-84/349, Box 107, File 5750-5, Pt. 1, the Director of Immigration to Crerar, April 17, 1942.

28. PAC, RG 76, Vol. 556, File 810666, W.D. Scott to Pickford and Black, June 17, 1915.

29. PAC, RG 76, Vol. 475, File 731832, W.D. Scott to Hone and Rivet, May 11, 1915.

30. P.C. 1922-717 was amended several times, e.g., P.C. 1923-183, P.C. 1931-695, P.C. 1950-2856. PAC, RG 76, Acc. 83-84/349, Box 107, File 5750-5, Pt. 1, April 17, 1942; Cameron, (1943); Canada, House of Commons, *Debates*, 1922, Vol. 3 pp. 2514-17; cited in *Debates*, 1931, Vol. 4, pp. 3124-25.

31. Canada, Department of Immigration and Colonization, *Annual Report, 1922-31*; PAC, RG 76, Vol. 556, File 810666, F.C. Blair to the Royal Mail Steam Packet Company., September 20, 1922.

32. Canada, Department of Citizenship and Immigration, *Annual Report, 1954*. Department of the Interior, *Annual Report, 1906-17*. Department of Immigration and Colonization, *Annual Report, 1918-31*.

33. An average of 82 West Indian Blacks were allowed annually in the fiscal years 1945-52. Canada, Department of Mines and Resources, *Annual Report, 1945-49*; Department of Citizenship and Immigration, *Annual Report, 1950-52*; PAC, RG 76, Vol. 830, File 552-1-644.

34. "An Act Respecting Immigration," *Prefix to Statutes, 1952*, (Ottawa: Queen's Printer), p. 262.

35. Canada, House of Commons, *Debates*, 1950, Vol. IV, pp. 4449-50; *Debates*, 1922, Vol. 3, pp. 2514-7; *Debates*, 1931, Vol. 4, pp. 3124-5; Cameron (1943); Moore (1985); PAC, RG 76, Acc. 83-84/349, Box 107, File 5750-5, the Director of Immigration to Crerar, April 17, 1942.

36. PAC RG 76, Vol. 830, File 552-1-644, "Immigration from the British West Indies since World War II showing partial breakdown of ethnic origin," January 1, 1958.

37. PAC, RG 76, Vol. 567, File 810666, C. Smith to A. Joliffe, May 28, 1948.

38. PAC, RG 76, Vol. 567, File 810666, T. Major to H. Choney, January 26, 1948.

39. PAC, RG 76, Vol. 830, File 552-1-644, T.G. Major to the Acting Director of Immigration, May 17, 1950. See also, T.G. Major, "Immigration from the British Caribbean," August 31, 1951; E.M. Gosse to the Director of Immigration, October 9, 1951.

40. PAC, RG 76, Vol. 830, File 552-1-644, T.G. Major, "Immigration form the

British Caribbean," August 31, 1951; E.M. Gosse to the Director of Immigration, October 9, 1951.

41. PAC, RG 76, Vol. 123, File 3-33-21, L. Fortier to Cabinet, October 13, 1951.

42. PAC, RG 26, Vol. 123, File 3-33-21, P. Baldwin to the Deputy Minister, December 22, 1951; C. Smith to the Deputy Minister, March 28, 1952; W. Harris, Memorandum to Cabinet, June 10, C. Smith to the Deputy Minister, May 26, 1954; 1952; D. Moore , *Don Moore.*

43. Canada, Department of Citizenship and Immigration, *Annual Report, 1953*, pp. 34-35.

44. After India, Pakistan and Ceylon became independent, Canada agreed to accept 150, 100 and 50 immigrants from these countries, respectively. This decision was a result of international pressure. PAC, RG 26, Vol. 123, File 3-33-21, L. Fortier to Cabinet, October 13, 1951.

45. PAC, RG 76, Vol. 830, File 552-1-644, the Director of Immigration to the Minister, September 12, 1951.

46. PAC, RG 76, Vol. 567, File 810666; Vol. 838, File 553-36-644.

47. Bodsworth (1955); "Here's Ottawa's Side of the Negro Ban Story" *The Financial Post.* July 12, 1952, p. 12.

48. For information on the Ontario Labour Committee on Human Rights, see Bruner (1979) and Calliste (1987).

49. PAC, RG 26, Vol. 123, File 3-33-21, the Director of Immigration to the Deputy Minister, May 26, 1954; Vol. 830, File 552-1-644 Brief presented to the Prime Minister by the Negro Citizenship Association, April 27, 1954; *The Worker* (March 1952); Moore, (1985:87-120).

50. Harry Narine-Singh was a draughtsman who applied for landed immigrant status when he was on a visit to Canada. "Immigration and 'Race'," *Canadian Labour Reports* July–August 1955), p. 4.

51. PAC, RG 76, Vol. 830, File 552-1-644, the Director of Immigration to the Deputy Minister, September 12, 1958.

52. Canada, House of Commons, *Debates*, 1952, Vol. 3, pp. 2803-4; *Debates*, 1952-53, Vol. 4, pp. 4348-53; *Debates*, 1957-58, Vol. 4, pp. 3382, 3670-71; Hawkins (1972).

53. PAC, RG 76, Vol. 830, File 552-1-644, the Director of Immigration to the Deputy Minister, September 12, 1958.

54. PAC, RG 76, Vol. 830, File 552-1-644, W. Dawson to A. Brown, May 10, 1955.

55. PAC, RG 76, Vol. 830, File 552-1-644, the Director of Immigration to the Minister of Labour, January 14, 1955.

56. PAC, RG 76, Vol. 838, File 553-36-644, Department of Citizenship and Immigration to Cabinet May 1955; interview, January 26, 1989.

57. PAC, RG 76, Vol. 847, File 553-110, Pt. 2, Central District Superintendent to the Acting Chief, Settlement Division, April 3, 1963; Note, April 17, 1963.

58. PAC, RG 76, Vol. 838, File 552-1-644, The Department of Citizenship and Immigration to Cabinet, May 1955.

59. The Assisted Passage Loan Scheme provided interest-free loans —

initially to single workers and heads of families migrating from Europe, and since 1955 also to their wives and dependent children — to cover the cost of passage to their Canadian destination of those immigrants who qualified because they were in occupations which were considered to be in short supply in Canada.

60. PAC, RG 76, Vol. 838, File 553-36-644, Pt. 2, G. Haythorne to L. Fortier, Mar. 13, 1956.

61. *The Trinidad Chronicle,* October 28 and November 2, 1956.

62. *The Evening News,* May 30, 1960.

63. One woman who had changed jobs three times was making the highest salary in the group: $125.00 per month compared to the average wage of $75.00. PAC, RG 76, Vol. 838, File 553-36-644, G. Haythorne to L. Fortier, Mar. 13, 1956.

64. Computed from PAC, RG 76, Vol. 838, File 553-36-563.

65. Confidential interviews, July 9-16, 1988.

66. Canada, *Prefix to Statutes, 1952-53* (Ottawa: Queen's Printer, 1953), pp. 27-29; Potter (1949); confidential interviews, May – August, 1982, 1983; July 15, 1988.

67. Confidential interview, July 13, 1988.

68. PAC, RG 76, Vol. 838, File 553-36-563, The West Indian Domestic Scheme, November 20, 1963; interviews, July 9-17; King (1958:173-183); Bled (1965).

69. PAC, RG 76, Vol. 838, File 553-36-556, W. Baskerville to R. Smith, January 15, 1960; File 553-36-560, C. Isbister to the Minister of Immigration, November 20, 1963; File 553-36-563, A. Ewen, "Household Service Workers from the West Indies and British Guiana," October 6, 1961.

70. Confidential interviews, July 9-17, 1988.

71. PAC, RG 76, Vol. 838, File 553-36-560, W. Baskerville to R. Smith, December 12, 1961.

72. PAC, RG 76, Vol. 838, File 553-36-563, A. Ewen, "Household Service Workers from the West Indies and British Guiana," October 6, 1961.

73. PAC, RG 76, Vol. 838, File 553-36-563, A. Ewen, "Household Service Workers from the West Indies and British Guiana," October 6, 1961.

74. Confidential interviews, July 16, 1988.

75. Canada, House of Commons, *Debates,* 1950, Vol. 4, p. 4450.

76. Interviews, July 12-16, 1988.

77. PAC, RG 76, Vol. 838, File 553-36- 563, The West Indian Domestic Scheme, November, 20, 1963.

78. PAC, RG 76, Vol. 838, File 553-36-644, Pt. 2, G. Haythorne to L. Fortier, March 13, 1956; Bled (1965); Das Gupta (1986:57); King (1958); interviews, July 9-17, 1988.

79. (Interviews, December 1988). The immigration policy of recruiting single women, causing the black community to experience and imbalanced sex ratio in certain age categories, has implications for aging: in the next decade some of the women who came on the Domestic Scheme will have become Senior Citizens - without having any immediate family in

Canada. There is need for further research in this area.

80. PAC, RG 76, Vol. 838, File 553-36-563, Location of West Indian Domestics, 1961; interviews, July 24, 1983; July 16, 1988.

81. Historically, it was difficult to get domestics to work in small towns and rural areas (PAC, RG 76, Vol. 566, File 810666, J. Gilchrist to W.D. Scott, April 1, 1915; Barber, 1980).

82. PAC, RG 76, Vol. 838, File 553-36-563, Location of West Indian Domestics, 1961; interviews, July 28, 1983; July 16, 1988.

83. Order-in-Council, P.C. 1962-86. Canada, House of Commons, *Debates,* 1962, Vol. 1, pp. 9-12.

84. PAC, RG 76, Vol. 839, File 553-36-644, B. Myers to the Chief Minister, St. Lucia, December 2, 1964.

85. PAC, RG 76, Vol. 838, File 553-36-560, C. Isbister to the Minister of Immigration, November 20, 1963.

86. In 1961, 1,126 West Indians were admitted; in 1962, the number increased to only 1,480 and in 1963 to 2,227. In 1964, Canada permitted 112,606 immigrants to come to Canada. Of these only 1,493 were from the Caribbean. Canada, House of Commons, *Debates,* 1966, Vol. 6, p. 5963; *The Globe and Mail,* November 5, 1963; Hawkins (1972); Levitt and McIntyre (1967:93).

87. PAC, RG 76, Vol. 838, File 553-36-560, C. Isbister to the Minister of Immigration, November 20, 1963; File 553-36-563, the Deputy Minsiter of Immigration to W.R. Baskerville, June 16, 1961; W. Baskerville to the Deputy Minister, June 27, 1961; September 26, 1961.

88. PAC, RG 76, Vol. 838, File 553-36-563, W. Baskerville to the Deputy Minister, June 27, 1961; September 26, 1961.

89. PAC, RG 76, Vol. 838, File 553-36-563, G. F. Davidson to the Acting Director of Immigration, August 29, 1961.

90. PAC, RG 76, Vol. 838, File 553-36-560, A. Smith to C. Isbister, July 3, 1964.

91. Canada, House of Commons, *Debates,* 1966, Vol. 3, p. 2319; Vol. 6, p. 5963; *The Globe and Mail,* May 21, 1965.

92. Canada, House of Commons, *Debates,* 1966, Vol. 3, p. 2319.

93. *The New Nation,* May 31, 1964.

94. Bled (1965); interviews, July 24, 1983; July 12-16, 1988.

95. *The Barbados Advocate,* April 1964; *The New Nation,* May 31, 1964.

96. PAC, RG 76, Vol. 838, File 553-36-560, S. Hubble to the Under-Secretary of State for External Affairs, May 7, 1965.

97. For a discussion of the importances of remittances to the Gross Domestic Product in the Caribbean, See: Lewis (1968).

98. PAC, RG 76, Vol. 838, File 553-36-560, C. Merriman to M. Gregg, May 3, 1965; R. Curry to H. Moran, July 13, 1965; Note for file, July 13, 1965.

99. Canada's aid program in the British Caribbean began in 1958 with the West Indian Federation (See: Chodos, 1977; Fraser, 1966).

100. PAC, RG 76, Acc. 83-84/349, Box 135, File 5850-3-533, R.N. Adams to D. Henderson, April 5, 1972.

101. Canada, Employment and Immigration, "Foreign Domestic Movement: 1985 Highlights"; "Foreign Domestic Movement Statistical Review, 1986" (July 1987); "Foreign Domestic Movement Statistical Highlight Report, 1987 (December 1988); Interview, June 26, 1989. In both years England and Germany ranked second and third respectively of the top leading source countries. In 1987 seven European countries and Australia accounted for 32 percent of the new immigrants.

102. Research has shown that employers expect submissiveness from domestic workers (Martin and Segrave, 1985; Rollins, 1985).

103. Ramirez (1983) Silvera (1983:29); *Winnipeg Free Press*, November 25, 1983; interview, June 26, 1989.

104. PAC, RG 76, Vol. 839, File 553-36-644, L. Fortier to A. Brown, June 8, 1960; Bled (1965), interviews, July 12-16, 1988.

Discussion

The four papers in this section share in common a concern with situating law within its broader historical context. In the following discussion, we will attempt to integrate these different analyses into a wider framework for understanding the historical conditions pertinent to law creation in Canada.

One of the main premises of the Marxist approach is that capitalism is a system founded on a basic contradiction which is rooted in the exploitative relationship between the two major classes: capital and labour. This contradiction makes for an inherently unstable system, as it creates conflicts and crises of varying forms and levels of intensity. As the capitalist project unfolds, for example, subordinated and disposessed classes and groups will be intent on resisting the changes that occur. We can expect to find, therefore, that different historical periods will be characterized by their own persistent conflicts, crises and dilemmas.

The inherently unstable nature of the system and the tendency for conflicts and dilemmas to occur points to the role of the state under capitalism. In structural Marxist terms, the capitalist state has as its main purpose the maintenance and reproduction of the capitalist system. It acts as an organizer to ensure that capital accumulation runs smoothly and as a mediator between the conflicting groups and classes to produce social harmony. The capitalist state, as an organizer, will therefore have as its main goal the maintenance of the capitalist path of development. As a mediator, it will also be the responsibility of the state to contain the unrest and dissent that is generated. One of the mechanisms available to the state in carrying out this role will be law creation.

In his analysis of the process by which the state engages in law creation, William Chambliss (1986) makes the point that the state will act to resolve, not the basic contradictions of the system, but the conflicts, dilemmas and crises which those contradictions create. In this respect, law making can be viewed as a "symptom-solving mechanism," with law creation itself contingent upon a host of historically specific factors. Chambliss' work takes its lead from the traditional Marxist formulation, which gives priority to the sphere of production in the determination of the organization of society. However, if we adopt a socialist feminist framework, which directs attention to the spheres of production *and* reproduction, then we need to expand our analysis to include a consideration of the ways in which the interrelationship between productive and reproductive spheres operates to create certain conflicts, dilemmas and crises for the state. In particular, we will need to be sensitive to the historically specific ways in which class, gender and race interconnect with one another.

Prior to 1850, Canadian society was essentially a "pre-capitalist" social formation. Production was centered around farming and small-scale commodity production, and the family was the major unit of productive activity. The period from 1850 to 1890 can be described as Canada's "Age of Industry" (Cross and Kealey, 1982). With the emergence of industrial capitalist production after 1850, more and more people were entering the labour force to work for wages, bringing about the creation of an industrial working class. During this time, the number of large scale urban factories increased dramatically, and competition between the many small firms intensified. The period after 1890 was one of the rise and consolidation of monopoly capitalism in Canada. Capital became more concentrated (as individual capitalists expanded the amount of capital under their control) and centralized (as existing capitals were merged together).

What is most remarkable about this development is how, within a relatively short period of time, Canadian society underwent such a dramatic transformation. Not only was the very nature of the labour process being altered (for example, by mechanization and the use of scientific management techniques), the sexual division of labour and the respective roles of men, women and children both within the home and at work were reconstructed. Even as these changes were unfolding, however, the capitalist path of development was by no means assured. Workers, for example, organized to resist the changes that occurred as capital asserted its control over the workplace. The monopolization of Canadian industry drew complaints from not only small business, but labour as well. And the perceived threat of women, children and immigrants to the jobs of white males led to calls for restrictions on immigration and demands for a family wage system. As the transformation occurred, therefore, the state was increasingly drawn in as a key player to respond to the conflicts, dilemmas and crises that were generated by capitalist development.

Russell Smandych's analysis points to the role of the state in responding to a particular set of conflicts and dilemmas that were rooted in the changing class dynamics that accompanied capitalist development. By the 1880s, the process of monopolization of Canadian industry was underway. This created *intra*-capitalist class conflict as small business, feeling the effects of this trend, lobbied for relief from the restrictive trade and price-fixing practices of the larger corporations. At the same time, industrialization had contributed to a vast increase in the size of Canada's working class. As the class consciousness of workers rose, *inter*-class conflicts intensified. As Smandych notes, the militancy of the early labour organizations stemmed not simply from their desire to improve working conditions, but from labour's hatred of monopolistic companies. Consequently, organizations like the Knights of Labor used their increased political strength to put pressure on the state to eliminate industrial capitalist combines.

The conflicts generated by the monopolization of Canadian industry posed a real dilemma for the Canadian state in the late 1800s. In its role as organizer, Macdonald's government was hesitant to interfere with the capitalist project, especially since monopolistic companies wielded immense economic and political power. As a mediator, however, the government had to somehow contend with the mounting protest, particularly from the ranks of labour. In the end, the solution chosen was the creation of a symbolic law which gave the appearance of doing something to protect economic competition yet, in actuality, only fostered combines activity.

Situating Canada's first drug law in its historical context requires recourse to a different configuration of factors. The early 1900s was a period of consolidation and entrenchment of the capitalist class. The erosion of workers' control over production which capitalist dominance signified intensified class conflicts. This was especially the case in British Columbia, where the labour movement had grown in strength. As Elizabeth Comack's analysis indicates, however, the conflicts which occurred had a basis not only in *class*, but in *race* as well. Assisted by the immigration policies and practices of the state, the Chinese were brought to Canada in order to meet capital's demand for an abundant supply of cheap labour. The perceived threat of Chinese labour generated working class dissent. However, while the more conservative craft unions perceived their main threat to be the "Oriental Menace," the socialist unions and political parties were more intent on defining issues in class rather than racial terms. In combination, these conflicts amounted to a "legitimation crisis" for the state.

If capital accumulation was to proceed, the re-establishment of working class consent was imperative. In resolving this dilemma, Comack argues that the state endeavoured to further a "moral" or "racial" perspective regarding the source of economic and social problems. With Mackenzie King's "discovery" of opium use among the Chinese population in British Columbia, the Opium Act became part of a more general effort by the state to promote this particular definition of the situation. To the extent that the drug law helped to identify the Chinese as a major source of the problems confronting British Columbia society, it de-legitimized further the competing view of the socialists while offering a symbolic concession to the more conservative unions.

In focusing on the transformation of childhood, Tannis Peikoff and Stephen Brickey draw attention to the changes in the reproductive sphere that accompanied the emergence and development of capitalism. In the pre-capitalist period, the home was the major unit of productive activity. As Peikoff and Brickey indicate, while women and children were not considered equals to the male head of the family, they did play economically useful roles. The emergence of capitalism brought about a dramatic separation of home and work which created new roles for women and children. Initially welcomed as a source of cheap labour for the emergent factory system, women and children increasingly came to be seen as a threat to male workers, who argued for a "family wage" to support their dependents. As industrialization proceeded, children were no longer seen as an economic asset, but an economic liability for the familial patriarch. By the 1870s, therefore, a "crisis of reproduction" was brewing, reflected in large part by the declining birth rate.

The state's response to this crisis of reproduction was complex and varied. In the short term, the population decrease — with its corresponding threat to the labour supply — could be supplemented through immigration. In the long term, however, the response consisted of a material and ideological shift that dramatically affected the lives of women and children. Materially, the implementation of labour laws and compulsory mass education restricted the availability of women and children as workers. Ideologically, the concern over the family resulted in the promotion of an image of children as "special creatures" whose value was primarily sentimental, not economic, and of women as "nurturers" whose proper place was in the home.

As Peikoff and Brickey note, the response of the state to this crisis of reproduction had the effect of making the state *itself* an active participant in the care of children and the structuring of the home. In the process, patriarchy was also transformed, as some of the control over women and children was transferred from the individual patriarch to the state. In this respect, the manner in which the state chose to deal with the crisis ensured that patriarchy, albeit in a new guise, remained the dominant form of gender relations.

The paper by Agnes Calliste brings our understanding of historical development further into the 20th century by analysing the ways in which the Canadian state has endeavoured to respond to labour market demands. As Calliste informs us, international labour migration has been the result of uneven capitalist development, whereby the more "developed" countries exploit the resources (including labour power) of the "underdeveloped" countries through colonialism and imperialism. For the underdeveloped countries, emigration is often viewed as one way to reduce unemployment and overpopulation. For the emigrants, it is perceived as a means of improving their life chances. It is in this context that Calliste locates the history of one aspect of Canadian immigration policy: the Carribean Domestic Scheme. In particular, she documents how the Canadian state's immigration policies have been shaped by racial, class and gender biases.

The first Domestic Scheme, which brought 100 women from Guadeloupe in 1910-11, was designed to fill the shortage of domestic workers in Québec. These women were seen as aptly suited for the job: not only were they cheap, but they were "fond of children" and "knew their place." Calliste notes, however, that when economic conditions deteriorated and demand for labour decreased, immigrant workers were often fired to make room for whites and deported for fear that they would become public charges. Following World War II, as Canada's trade and investment in the Carribean increased, the need to appease the demands for a more "liberal" immigration policy became more accute. In addition, the increasing participation of women in the labour force and the post war baby boom resulted in a greater demand for domestic labourers. As a result, the second Domestic Scheme was implemented in 1955. Because of the assumption that black women were promiscuous or single parents likely to become public charges, Carribean women were admitted on the condition that any domestic found "undesirable" was to be deported at the expense of the Carribean government.

For Carribean women, the Scheme offered virtually the only opportunity to enter Canada. Given the lack of educational and employment opportunities in their home country, many used the Scheme to improve their situation. As single women were the preferred immigrant, many had to leave their own children behind. Most faced long hours of work, poor pay, and extreme loneliness and isolation. Many sought to improve their situation by upgrading their education and finding other employment. Since the Canadian state had expected Carribean women to be "career domestics," the long term benefits of the Scheme for Canada were questioned. By 1973, domestics were being admitted under temporary work permits. This meant that they could be deported when demand for domestic labour fell and ensured that those who immigrated would remain in domestic work. Under 1981 regulations, domestics who have been in Canada for two years and have achieved a potential for self sufficiency are allowed to apply for landed immigrant status.

As Calliste demonstrates, Canadian immigration policies have historically been fueled by both racist and sexist ideologies. Blacks in general were depicted as lazy, more criminally inclined, backward, unassimilable, and possessed of inherent attributes that "suited" them to particular jobs. Black women in particular were stereotyped as "temperamentally well suited" for domestic work. In combination, such ideologies provided the rationalization for segregated and split labour markets in which racial minorities and women were concentrated in low paying and low status jobs. In these ways, racism and sexism has proven profitable for the capitalist enterprise. Moreover, systemic discrimination based on race and gender has meant that immigrant women of colour remain as one of the most socially disadvantaged groups in Canadian society: they confront a fourfold oppression in which their immigrant status interacts with race, class and gender.

The four papers in this section have sensitized us to the different ways in which the law historically has operated to reproduce inequalities of class, race and gender. In the next section, we will explore these issues further by investigating the operation of law in its contemporary Canadian context.

Part Two

The Operation of Law

Your Money and Your Life: Workers' Health in Canada

Charles E. Reasons, Lois Ross
and Craig Patterson

I'm only a broken down mucker
My life in the mines I have spent
I've been fooled and played for a sucker
My back's all broken and bent

But I realize now that I'm older
I used my back where he used his brains
The drifting machine done for my hearing,
The mine glasses dimmed my sight.
I know my last days are nearing
But I'll rally for one last fight (Thomas, 1979).

"Industry Kills." "Job Accidents Nearing a Crisis." "Serious Ailments Found in Workers." "Occupational Health Official Warns of Reproductive Injuries." "Crushed Miners Had Little Warning." "Asbestos Cases Showing Up." "Government May Be Failing To Keep Cancer Out of Work Place." "On Job Death Rate Has Labor Upset." The titles of these newspaper articles suggest that working may be dangerous to our health. We are just beginning to realize that our job brings us not only a periodic paycheque, but often death, injury and disability due to disease or accident. Between 1978 and 1987 one work disabling injury (involving lost time) occurred, on average, every 15.1 seconds and a non-disabling injury occurred more frequently, every 12.9 seconds. One out of every ten workers in Canada will be hurt on the job each year and one in every 16 workers will spend at least one shift away from work because of an occupational accident. In 1987, about six times as much time was lost from work because of occupational injuries and illnesses as was lost from work because of strikes and lockouts, and yet media attention is focused on the latter. Canada lost about 25 million person-days due to work injuries and illnesses in 1987 as compared with about 4 million due to work stoppages. For the period 1985 through 1987, occupational fatalities have averaged approximately 907 per year in Canada.[1] What this means is that, as Canadian workers, we are much more likely to meet violence through injury or illness in the workplace than in our streets.

On the Nature of Violence In Canada

Most people think of violence as something bad and illegal which is perpetrated by a person or persons against another person or persons. Therefore, when someone sprays mace in our face it is violence, while when one is forced to inhale asbestos dust at work it is uncomfortable, but not violent. According to the *Concise Oxford Dictionary* violence is the "unlawful exercise of force." To "violate" is to disregard, fail to comply with, act against the dictates or requirements of such things as an oath, treaty, law, terms, or conscience. While the inhalation of asbestos dust may not be unlawful, it *violates* the health of the worker. Mary Beyer has pointed out the difficulty of defining violence:

> The problem has perhaps been that while violence is a word we hear every day, it is rarely clearly defined, and the listener quickly learns to associate the word violence with the word bad. While cultural and socioeconomic class differences tell us something about the nature of crime, what is perceived as violence is frequently a matter of interpretation. From this perspective violence is in the eye of the beholder (Beyer, 1978:1).

Many more Canadians die yearly from violent deaths due to cancer, automobile accidents, heart disease, suicide, and occupational injuries than from murder and manslaughter, but we tend to focus upon the latter categories. Of course, homicide has a readily identifiable victim and offender and is included under the Criminal Code. We also have criminal statutes concerning automobile accidents and suicide, but not concerning occupational death. Nonetheless, the yearly toll in lives for occupational carnage is much higher than that for murder. If we look (in Figure 1) at how Canadians die, we find that Canadians are three times as likely to die from occupational hazards as from murder. It must be emphasized that this is a very conservative estimate of occupational death, since it only includes deaths from industrial accidents and excludes deaths from other industrial diseases, such as lead poisoning, heart disease due to work-related stress and lung disease such as asbestosis or mesothelioma. These diseases have a long latency period and are often not diagnosed as work-related diseases.

While Canadians often pride themselves on the fact that they are less violent and more civilized than people in the United States, statistics suggest otherwise. According to the 1988 *Year Book of Labour Statistics,* Canada has a relatively higher industrial fatality rate than does the United States.[2] It would appear that it is safer to work in the United States than in Canada in many industries, especially in mining where there were 900 fatalities in Canada in 1985 compared to 500 in the United States in 1986.[3] Nearly twice as many Canadian miners died in mining accidents as did their American counterparts. While Americans are much more likely to be victims of murder outside the workplace, death from the job is more common in Canada. It may be that, as Canadian historian Kenneth McNaught explains, "Canada has a history of violence enacted through legitimate institutions, in contrast to a pattern of individual and group violence in the United States" (Beyer, 1978: 1). Much of the violence we experience in Canada may be through legitimate institutions such as work.

It's a Crime
Dr. Samuel Epstein describes his book entitled *The Politics of Cancer* in the following terms: "I view it as a book on white-collar crime on the one hand and also on the failed democracy ..."[4] Henri Lorraine, past president of the Canadian Paperworker's Union says employers have killed workers by refusing to invest profits to improve working conditions.[5] Why do these men call it white-collar crime and not killing or assault when workers die or are injured and disabled from work? We have been taught to think of crime as involving an easily identifiable victim and offender. For example, if our spouse poisons us and we subsequently die then we have been murdered by our spouse, who is liable to prosecution for murder. However, if our company causes us to be exposed to toxic substances and we subsequently die from this exposure, the company is not criminally liable for our deaths and will at most be cited for violations of health and safety regulations. For example, it has been revealed that asbestos companies continued to expose workers to that substance in spite of the fact that they had had evidence concerning its fatal effects for some thirty years. Such conscious, premeditated, and rational behaviour undoubtedly led to thousands of deaths and disabilities. Nonetheless, asbestos companies are only liable to civil lawsuits.[6]

Another example is Quasar Petroleum Ltd. of Calgary, which was found guilty of violating job site safety regulations, resulting in the death of three men. The law provided for a maximum of $5,000 fine and/or imprisonment of up to six months. Quasar was fined $5,000 for killing the three men, who were single and in their early twenties. How did Quasar kill the young men? The company did not provide respiratory protective equipment and an external gauge on an enclosed tank; thus, the men had to go inside the tank without protective equipment and subsequently were overcome with toxic fumes. Furthermore, the company had not trained the workers concerning the hazards of the job and the need for such equipment.[7]

Table I
Industrial Deaths Compared to Homicides
Canada, 1982 and 1985

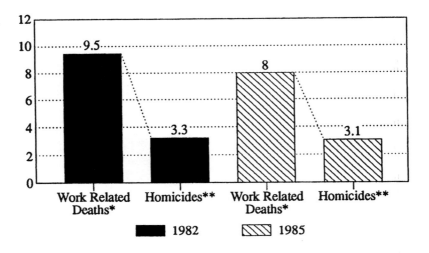

* rate per 100,000 workers. It should be noted that this is a conservative estimate.
The figures exclude workers not covered by compensation (likely 25%) and the
estimated 20% of cancer deaths which are occupationally related.
** rate per 100,000 adult population

Source: *Year Book of Labour Statistics* 48th Edition, International Labour Office,
Geneva, 1988.

Isn't this just an unfortunate "accident"? No, the deaths of these three
young men could have been avoided if the proper training and equipment had been provided. While the company undoubtedly did not
mean to kill these specific three men, it established the conditions for
their death by violating the law. By analogy, we could view murder
during an armed robbery as an accident. Most armed robbers do not
intend to kill the robbery victim but merely want to make some money.
However, their act of robbery with a dangerous weapon sets the
conditions for such violence. Likewise, a company saving money by not
purchasing safety equipment may be merely pursuing profit, but its
action establishes the conditions for an "accident" or "disaster."

> The private corporation (and many crown corporations)
> exists first and foremost to earn a reasonable profit and
> return on investment for their shareholders. Occupa-
> tional health, and other costs, unless they can be passed
> on to the consumers, are ultimately an expense which
> reduces profit, at least in the short run (Doern, 1977: 18).

Should the company which threatens the workers' safety and health for profit be any less culpable when death occurs than the armed robber who also threatens violence for economic profits? We think not!

The violation of safety and health standards and/or the failure to establish adequate standards is usually a rational, premeditated, conscious choice concerning capital expenses and business profits. In the public sector, it is usually a political decision to streamline a budget. In both the private and public sectors, the consequences are the same. While deaths and job injuries on the worksite are usually thought of as accidents caused by worker carelessness, research suggests otherwise. It has been estimated that approximately 39 percent of job injuries in the United States are due to illegal working conditions while another 24 percent are due to legal but unsafe conditions. At the most, a third of accidents are due to unsafe acts (Ashford, 1976: 107-15). However, the maintenance of unsafe conditions is rational since the likelihood of detection is low and penalties are relatively small. The attitudes among many safety and health personnel reflect a lenient approach toward such law violaters. One provincial head of inspection states that:

> We are not dealing with criminals when we take people
> to court. A guy who breaks into your house knows what
> he is doing and knows the consequences and probably
> has been through the process before. To be dragged
> before a judge and be sentenced to twelve months in jail
> is not pleasant to him, but it is not unexpected, and it isn't
> demeaning to him; he will stand there with a smile on his
> face and be defiant. When we are talking about individu-
> als or entities being prosecuted for infractions of Occupa-
> tional Health and Safety legislation, we are talking about
> an entirely different animal. We are talking about a
> person who basically is honest and an upright citizen.
> We are talking basically of a person who finds this
> process of being prosecuted and having that process
> publicized extremely distasteful (Reschenthaler, 1979:
> 82-83).

In this manner, the government enforcer of safety and health laws rationalizes why heavy fines or even imprisonment are not as important as the stigma of the court process. However, this same official goes on to say that violaters are prosecuted only after serious and/or repeated violations.

> People who go to court have refused to apply regula-
> tions they know exist and have in the past been or-
> dered to and instructed — advised — to put those
> things into effect and they have decided they are not
> going to. So they are not strangers to the law (Reschen-
> thaler, 1979: 82-83).

Using the above logic, since a murderer is a solid citizen 99.9 percent of the time and only murders 0.1 percent of the time, we should not view him or her as a criminal! We must look at the consequences of one's actions or inactions. If violating safety and health laws does not cause a death then the penalty should be less than if it does take a life, just as the penalty for armed robbery is less than that for murder. Unfortunately, current penalties for health and safety violations do not adequately consider this distinction between the law violation and subsequent violence and death. This may be due, in part, to the above image of the white-collar criminal who is not considered a criminal.

The Canadian public has tended to view corporate crime as economically harmful but not physically dangerous. The image of the corporate criminal is that of the business person who commits fraud, income tax evasion, bribery, embezzlement, price fixing or some other crime for personal economic gain. This approach fails to consider that organizations are legal entities which may commit crimes against us. For example, if a construction company speeds up work and fails to observe proper safety and health rules, it may kill or seriously injure workers.[8] Two criminologists have defined organizational crime in the following manner:

> Organizational crimes are illegal acts of omission or
> commission of an individual or a group of individuals in
> a legitimate formal organization in accordance with the
> operative goals of the organization, which have serious
> physical or economic impact on employees, consumers
> or the general public (Schrager and Short, 1978: 411-12)

By making the distinction between corporate and organizational crimes we are recognizing the daily impact private and public organizations have upon our lives as workers, consumers and members of the general public. Therefore, the behaviour of individuals is placed within the context of the organization. For example, while an employee who embezzles from the employer is guilty of a corporate offence, the same employee may be involved in safety and health violations as part of the policies, practices and/or procedures of the organization. In the latter offences, the corporate offender is carrying out organizational goals. This distinction forces us to look at organizational changes and control as a means of addressing workplace violence rather than solely individual sanction. For example, punishing a worker for not wearing safety equipment or failing to follow health and safety procedures may not deter the behaviour if the organizational goals and practices of the company and management reinforce such behaviour.

Attention to organizational crime has largely been upon violations of competition legislation which, although having criminal penalties, are not generally viewed as criminal (Goff and Reasons, 1978; Snider, 1982). This is largely due to the fact that only economic harm occurs. However, does the public view violence from organizational law violation in the same way? No, according to an analysis of public survey data by two criminologists. They found that the public ranks organizational crimes having physical impact much higher in seriousness than those with merely an economic impact. Therefore, "causing the death of an employee by neglecting to repair machinery" is as serious as impulsive homicide or arson which kills someone (Schrager and Short, 1980). Thus, the belief that the public does not view organizational crimes as crimes is wrong, particularly when they entail violence and death.

We should criminalize many of these organizational acts which involve "victims without crimes." Two Canadian lawyers have made a case for applying the Criminal Code to violations of health and safety laws. They assert that criminal negligence, duties of master to servant, assault, criminal breach of contract, traps likely to cause bodily harm, causing mischief, common nuisance, conspiracy, and murder all may be used for prosecuting violations (Glasbeek and Rowland, 1979). For example, an assault is committed when a person either applies force intentionally to another person or, by an act or a gesture, causes another person to have reasonable grounds to believe that there will be an interference with his or her physical integrity. The daily interference with the physical integrity of workers evidenced in injury and disease statistics amounts to a massive assault on the Canadian workforce. However, one may argue that the victims of workplace hazards really do not see themselves as victims of an assault or other type of crime since they may contribute to their own injuries. In discussing occupational deaths Jeffrey Reiman states:

> To say some of these workers died from accidents due to their own carelessness is about as helpful as saying that some of those who died at the hands of murderers asked for it. It overlooks the fact that where workers are careless, it is not because they love to live dangerously. They have production quotas to meet, quotas that they themselves do not set (Reiman, 1984: 56).

Do injured workers view themselves as victims of crime? The following case study tells the story of one worker who was injured in the high-risk construction industry.

Profile: Stolen Health

Throughout the 1970s Alberta was seen as the land of prosperity, where employment was plentiful, money abundant, and life euphoric. In quest of black gold, corporations needed the support of thousands of employees. Oil companies fuelled the growth of other, indirectly related corporations. Petroleum created the boom economy. But most employees failed to recognize a grim principle behind economic booms. Just as a company can provide a worker with a sizable paycheque, it can also create, in the name of production (that is, profits), an unsafe workplace.

Alberta's growing need for homes and office space prompted developers to promote highrise construction. In 1979, Alberta's construction workers suffered through a record-breaking 17 percent increase in injuries, making construction one of the most accident-prone industries in the province. Those who gravitate to construction work are, by and large, young, strong, and unhampered by mortgages or family responsibilities. Such was the situation of eighteen-year-old Hubert Maisonneuve. When he arrived in Calgary in the fall of 1978, he planned to work for a year or so, then return to his native French community in Ontario where, hefty bankroll in hand, he would start up a bakery, a trade he had learned from his father.

After two months of unemployment, Hubert was hired by a small construction firm and put to work "flying the forms" on a highrise building, though he was non-unionized and inexperienced in highrise construction. One month later Hubert lay in a coma in a southwest Calgary hospital.

On a chilly December day, Hubert was working on the forms for the highest level of the escalating highrise. As he reached over to grab a cable — an innocuous movement at ground level — he slipped, flew over the edge, and fell nine floors — a full 120 feet — onto a pile of steel below.

Whisked to the hospital and life-support systems, he lay in a coma for sixteen days. His sturdy muscles had turned into molten rubber from the impact. One of his lungs had collapsed and a tracheotomy was performed. Two months after his fall, no doubt to the surprise of onlooking doctors, Hubert was beginning to test his strength in the halls of the hospital. He had aged visibly. His weight had dropped from 150 pounds to less than 110. Tasks that had once been automatic had to be relearned. Walking or the use of any muscle now required concentration, but his concentration had also been severely weakened by the shock. Six months after his fall, having undergone hours of therapy, Hubert considered it an achievement to be able to withstand the physical onslaught of a ten-minute walk in the fresh air.

Most of the day I slept. I slept for 20 hours sometimes. Then I started to go outside, sometimes for five minutes, then for ten minutes, and one day I went out for a whole half-hour. That was really something. I just had to get out.

More than two years after the accident, Hubert was still coaxing his body to perform, and trying to regain the stamina and capability he had prior to his fall. While the visible physical signs of his accident had disappeared, his thought processes, along with his gait, had slowed and his speech was cautious.

Obviously, Hubert's fall would not have occurred had he not accepted the job. But his money was running out and, despite his lack of experience, the foreman offered to hire him. Hubert fell, but he believes it could have happened to another worker just as easily. There is no hesitation as he points to the company for failing to provide equipment and to educate workers to protect themselves. Also at fault was the government for failing to enforce standards on the job site.

Hubert was not wearing a mandatory safety belt when he slipped. According to him, workers on the site were not briefed on what kind of gear was necessary and most of the crucial safety equipment was lacking. "The company had three safety belts for thirty workers," he explains. Besides preventive measures, Hubert wonders about sanctioning practices. No charges were ever laid against the company for failing to comply with safety regulations by providing adequate equipment, nor was an inquiry into the "accident" ordered by the Workers' Compensation Board (WCB). Since then, the company has gone bankrupt. What's the sense of having safety standards if a company is allowed to violate them with impunity?

Hubert equates the WCB with a cheap insurance scheme for companies, recognizing one major difference — once a company is covered by the WCB, its employees relinquish their rights through the courts, for either prosecution or compensation. The Board is the only authority allowed to handle such details.

Since the accident, Hubert has been receiving 75 percent of his wage — $850 a month. He has undergone assessments to see whether he is fit to return to work. So far he has not been, but Hubert doesn't know when the board may conclude he is fit to take on "light duties." At that point a decision will be made as to whether he is permanently or only temporarily disabled. Once a worker's condition "plateaus" (stabilizes), the WCB decides whether an accident has permanently or only temporarily disabled the worker. If harm is considered permanent, meaning if it will hinder a worker's future earning power, a pension is granted. The pension is based on a percentage of the disability, but no one is quite sure of the board's criteria in arriving at that figure.

Whether Hubert will be covered for future problems stemming from the accident is hard to determine. Muscle damage may lead to premature arthritis ... but how does one prove the disease had its roots in an accident? Doctors advise that serious head injuries often lead to epilepsy ... but how does one show unequivocally the cause?

Hubert looks on, well aware of having been robbed of his health, and warns other workers to refuse dangerous tasks and to demand necessary safety equipment. Hubert considers mandatory safety committees who would check worksites daily as priority instruments of safety control.

But one pain will linger — the first-hand knowledge that the government does not enforce safety standards by fining those companies which break the law. Hubert would like to force the issue, but that would mean proving the government's laxity in his case. "But I can't sue the government. You just can't go after the government."

For Hubert, the message from his experience is clear: "Government compensation isn't acting for human rights."

Whose Risk? Who Pays?

The question in occupational health and safety is not necessarily whether a risk will be taken or not, but rather who decides to take what type of risk which endangers whom and for what purposes. There are three sides involved in every hazardous condition or situation: those who create it, those who experience it, and those who regulate it (Ravetz, 1977: 598). In the past, workers have, knowingly and unknowingly, experienced innumerable risks which they did not create and had no control over. Management created the risks, workers assumed them, and subsequently health and safety officials have attempted to regulate them.

As Dr. Ravetz notes, "a hazardous environment (at work or at home) is part of social powerlessness." The traditional view of management and government was that the worker voluntarily assumed the risks of a job by accepting it. This ignorance of economic reality is no longer accepted and workers are increasingly demanding safer and healthier workplaces. Those workers most subject to physical abuse, including death, have been largely powerless to do anything about it. Canadian journalist Lloyd Tataryn concludes that:

> The principal victims of unsafe environments created by industries generally come from the ranks of the working-class and the poorest segments of society. Consequently the victims do not have the resources to mount the concerted scientific and political campaigns necessary to alter their environmental circumstances (Tataryn, 1979: 156).

Notes

This is a revised version of Chapter One of *Assault on the Worker: Occupational Health and Safety in Canada*. Toronto: Butterworths, 1981. We would like to acknowledge the work of Lana Maloney in updating some of the data found here.

1. Cited in *Labour News: Employment Injuries and Occupational Illnesses*, May 25, 1990.
2. Cited in *Year Book of Labour Statistics* 48th Edition, International Labour Office, Geneva. 1988. Chart 4.2.
3. In the reporting of international labour statistics, different years are cited for occupational fatalities in the *Yearbook of Labour Statistics*, 1988
4. Quoted in *Canadian Health and Safety News*, June 11, 1979, p.3.
5. "Industry Kills — Union Head", *Calgary Herald*, November 13, 1979.
6. "The Asbestos Industry on Trial". *The New Yorker*, June 10, 1985; Tataryn (1979); U.S. House of Representatives (1980).
7. *Canadian Occupational Health and Safety News*, July 23, 1979, p.3.
8. "Workers Walk Off Job After Steel Jack Falls," *The Calgary Herald*, July 24, 1980.

Democracy, Class and Canadian Sentencing Law
Michael Mandel

The central thesis of the Marxist theory of state and law is that there is an organic connection between state and legal institutions on the one hand and the structure of the social relations of production (e.g., the relation of capitalist and worker) on the other. This is the case no matter how much it may be concealed by such ideological distinctions as that between "public" and "private" spheres (Wood, 1981). According to Marx, "legal relations as well as forms of the state are to be grasped neither from themselves nor from the so-called general development of the human mind, but rather have their roots in the material conditions of life." The "real foundation" of society is [t]he sum total of [its] relations of production ... on which rises a legal and political superstructure" (Marx, 1977: 389). The connection between "base" and "superstructure" has been described by G. A. Cohen (1978) in "functional" terms, namely that it is the function of the state and law to maintain the structure of productive relations by providing norms and institutions which allow those relations to flourish. This is subtly, though importantly, different from merely saying that the state and legal institutions exist to protect the "status quo," because it specifies the aspect of the status quo protected, not the legal or democratic status quo of equal citizens but the productive relations status quo of massive inequality, dominance, and subordination.

It is sometimes argued that one of the main ways in which the law is superstructural (that is, supports the social relations of production) is, paradoxically, via the very notion of "equality before the law" in both its material and ideological effects (Balbus, 1977). From this point of view, the virtually exclusive and greatly disproportionate use of prisons and other intrusive forms of punishment for social groups subordinated in production relations is due to the application of an equal law to persons in unequal circumstances, with the usual invocation of Anatole France's line about the law in "its majestic equality" forbidding both the rich and poor from sleeping under bridges (Balbus, 1977: 577). Ideologically, this is said to also promote a false unity which suppresses the real inequality of social relations.

The problem with this line of reasoning is that it runs contrary to the general results of research into the actual bases for the invocation of criminal sanctions, which is quite overwhelming in the conclusion that the criminal law is applied in anything but an equal manner and that it is this that accounts for the severe social skew in prison. This phenomenon occurs at all levels of the system including the judicial sentencing stage (Hogarth, 1971; Jankovic, 1978; Kruttschnitt, 1981; Warner and Renner, 1981). While there is a tendency among researchers to apply the Anatole France line of reasoning by attributing the phenomenon to or characterizing it as taking into account "extra-legal" factors (Hagan, 1974; Warner and Renner, 1981), it is quite clear that this lets the law off too lightly, at least if Canadian sentencing law is representative.

Though no reference is made in Canada to class factors in the statutes defining offences, these merely open the door in virtually all cases to a wide range of sentences in the "discretion" of the court (*Criminal Code of Canada*, S.645). These sentences, in turn, have been subject for most of the century to a system of appeals against sentence on the basis of their "fitness" (S.614). In the reasons for judgement on sentencing appeals, we find a more or less complete common law of sentencing articulated by the senior levels of the judiciary. These reasons serve the dual function of instructing sentencing courts on how to structure their practice and of legitimating that practice. As courts are obviously the central legitimators of modern criminal law systems, it is worth paying some attention to what they have to say in this context.

In the reasoning of the courts of appeal, we find a clear recognition of the legitimacy of varying punishment not only according to the *offence*, but also according to the *offender*. In addition to the "gravity" of the offence (which includes quantitative matters such as the amount of property, drugs, etc., the severity of violence, the degree of *mens rea* and premeditation, as well as qualitative matters such as the victim-offender relationship), great importance is attached to the offender's "character." A crucial feature of this is the presence, extent, and nature of the offender's criminal record. However, the criminal record is only one feature of what courts deem worthy of note. Reasons for sentence and, indeed, the pre-sentence reports written by probation officers often cited in these reasons generally contain a complete rundown of the offender's social history. Essential to this is the offender's relation to the productive apparatus, that is, his or her employment status, employment history and occupation. Examples from various courts over charges ranging from theft, robbery, conspiracy to fraud, rape, attempted murder to criminal negligence causing death evince a consistent interest in all aspects of the offender's socioeconomic status.[1] Courts are interested in the degree of occupational success attained, but also in the responsibility and reliability of the offender as a worker (often relying in this respect on representations from employers), and even in the sheer quantity of employment (at least at the lower levels). However, failure as a worker itself need not count against the offender to the extent that it is not his or her "fault" (*Pruner*, 1979; *Stein*, 1974). Even in the decision as to the period of ineligibility for parole beyond the minimum ten years in second degree murder, an offender's "good employment record" will count in his or her favour (*Rouse* and *McInroy*, 1981).

So it is clear that the courts recognize it as a legitimate part of the sentencing function to determine the severity of the sentence on the basis not only of the nature of the offence, but also of the nature of the offender, not as offender but as *social being*. Part of this has to do with the criminal record but a good part of it has as well to do with the extent to which the offender fulfils his or her role in the productive apparatus. Whether this *accounts* for or merely *reflects* the observed class bias in sentencing, it would be rather strange if the law did not take some official notice of it. But, naturally, the law does not merely take notice of it, it also *defends* it. In the following pages, I wish to investigate this defence, because in my opinion it is a good way to understand the superstructural nature of criminal law.

The general legitimation framework set up by the courts of appeal concerning the execution of the sentencing function is fairly easy to state. There is a set of prescribed *purposes* which sentencers are to seek to fulfill. These purposes determine whether a given circumstance or factor is relevant to sentencing, and include social factors either explicitly or implicitly. Under various names the prescribed purposes fall into three main categories: (1) denunciation; (2) reform (or rehabilitation), individual (or "special") deterrence and incapacitation; and (3) general deterrence.

Denunciation

Denunciation is the modern successor to retribution as the principal aim and justification of punishment. Retribution's principle of just deserts is modified in denunciation by giving it (theoretically) a *social* origin and function. In the words of one court, "the sentence imposed must be one which expresses the *public* abhorrence for such conduct and a refusal to countenance it" (*Ingram and Grimsdale*, 1977, Ontario Court of Appeal, emphasis added). It is society's justice, not abstract justice, that is enforced. But the social origin of denunciatory justice, as with the abstract (or divine) origin of retributive justice, turns out to be largely theoretical:

> Society, through the courts, must show its abhorrence of
> particular types of crime, and the only way in which the
> courts can show this is by the sentences they pass. The
> courts do not have to reflect public opinion. On the other
> hand, courts must not disregard it. Perhaps the main
> duty of the court is to lead public opinion (*Sergeant* (1974)
> U.K., quoted in *Atkinson, Ing and Roberts*).[2]

This statement also gives us a glimpse of the judiciary's idea of the social *function* of denunciation, which another court has put as follows:

> The denunciatory sentence plays an important part in maintaining the righteousness of social values. The community demands that certain conduct be heavily punished and when the Courts fail to satisfy this demand to support core values, the public, in my view, can justifiably complain that the Courts have failed in their duty. (*Wood* (1975), Alberta Court of Appeal).

The Law Reform Commission of Canada, which has made denunciation the cornerstone of its approach to criminal law, has provided a vivid articulation of the notion in *Our Criminal Law* (1976):

> Criminal law, then, primarily has to do with values. As such — as wrongful acts — they demand response ... To be fully human and to hold certain values means responding when they are violated. Such violation requires public condemnation, and this is preeminently the job of criminal law.

> This job — condemning crime — is not an end in itself. It is part of the larger aim of producing a society fit to live in. Such a society is less one where people are too frightened to commit crimes than one where people have too much respect for one another to commit them. Fostering this kind of personal respect is a major aim of parents, teachers, churches, and all the other socializing agents. One such agent, though far less important than the others, is the criminal law. In its own way the criminal law reinforces lessons about our social values, instills respect for them, and expresses disapproval for their violation. This — what some call "general deterrence" — is the moral, educative role of criminal law.

So denunciation has to do with vindicating the social values challenged by the crime. It would seem for this reason that the point of reference for punishment would be the offence. However, that would be to take denunciation at face value (!). Remember that denunciation vindicates social values by *punishing the offender* and thus the central value being vindicated is really that of individual responsibility for crime. This is the logical result of treating crime as a clash of *values* instead of *interests* in the first place. To use the punishment of the transgressor against a value as the method by which value is to be taught is at the same time to provide an explanation of crime in the irreducible failure of some malefactors to accept these values. The main message remains that of Stephen (a favourite of the report's authors): "The criminal law thus proceeds upon the principle that it is morally right to hate criminals, and it confirms and justifies that sentiment by inflicting upon criminals punishments which express it" (Stephen, 1883:81).

If it is true that at the heart of denunciation is an assessment of the degree to which the offender deserves condemnation for a transgression of social values, this would naturally entail an assessment of the degree to which he or she deserves praise for adherence to (other) social values. If the point of denunciation is to assess an individual's worth, and not in any simple or direct way to prevent crime, *everything*, not only the crime committed, must be considered. Has he or she been generally law-abiding? Has he or she been a good worker? And so on. This seems to be the best way of reading those otherwise non-specific statements which advance as mitigating or aggravating factors the offender's praiseworthy or discreditable social history. For example, in *McNamara*, the offender's "contributions to the community" were "placed on the credit side of the ledger in considering what penalty ought to be imposed for the injury done to society by the offences." In *Stein* (1974), the offender's upgrading of her education in order to obtain some post-conviction employment and to make some partial restitution mitigated the sentence because it "displayed an exemplary sense of responsibility." And in *Shanower* (1972, Ontario Court of Appeal, rape), the offender's character ("a good father, a good husband and a good citizen in his community"), it was said, "stands him in good stead on an occasion such as this."

For relatively high status offenders, reference is liable to be made to the loss of status presumed to flow from the opprobrium of the conviction. This apparently mitigates the sentence by lessening the need for additional suffering through additional penalties in order to achieve a just proportion between offence and penalty. In *Hinch and Salanski* (1968, British Columbia Court of Appeal, conspiracy to obtain by false pretences), it was said in mitigation of sentence:

> These respondents had been persons of substance and position in the community in which they live and work. They were family men and prior to their connection with Mead they had been active and blameless citizens in their community. Any conviction and sentence of imprisonment, apart from the fines imposed, would be almost totally destructive of these respondents in the small community. It is likely that the learned Magistrate had under consideration what might be called the side effects of conviction and sentence such as the restrictions on travel and emigration to another country and the limitation of future employment.

In dissent, this argument was countered as it frequently and sometimes successfully is (*Johnston and Tremayne*, 1970; *Gingera*, 1966) by the argument that they "should have known and in fact did know better." However, even the dissenting judge in *Hinch and Salanska* felt that "men whose environments have been such as those of the respondents will probably find it harder to bear any given term of imprisonment." The same sentiment was expressed in *Legare*. We have a right to be skeptical about this notion of "They've already suffered enough" for reasons I will outline shortly. But that apart, one cannot help remarking how the courts in these cases treat elevated socioeconomic status and the comforts thereof as matters of property and not as continuing commensurate rewards for continuing contributions. In other words, the courts never point out "on the other hand" that the offender will no longer have his or her "onerous" responsibilities to carry out, even though these are the usual (if only partial) justifications even under capitalism for continued high levels of income.

In some situations, the relevance of class to denunciation will be via an *explanation* of the offence. The dissonance between explaining crime as caused by a rejection of social values and being confronted with an offender who otherwise adheres to those values is resolved by emphasizing an explanation which mitigates the offence by reducing the level of culpability. Alcohol often plays this role. For example, in *Morrissette* (1970, Saskatchewan Court of Appeal, rape), we read the following:

> It is difficult to understand how a young man with no previous record of wrong doing, with a good work record and a responsible family history, such as James Morrissette had, would become involved in such an offence. There is no doubt but that on the night in question liquor had been consumed by those at the party. There is no suggestion that they were intoxicated, but it may be that the alcohol consumed by James Morrissette aroused his passion and clouded his judgement. This, of course, would be no justification for his actions, but may be an explanation.

One court has gone so far as to say that consideration of alcohol or drugs as mitigating factors "is normally confined to cases where the actions of a person are completely out of character" (*Breen*, 1982, robbery). *Sawchyn* (1978) and *MacArthur* (1978) invoke similar notions. In the latter case, the P.E.I. Court of Appeal felt that a "domestic" shooting was mitigated by the fact that the offender was a "progressive businessman [sic] in the community with no criminal record, who was under some considerable personal strain, having earlier in the evening been informed that he and his companies were close to bankruptcy."

Reform

The second group of justifying aims, namely, reform of the offender, is much more obviously connected with the social characteristics of the person before the court, and it is on this basis that the relevance of class factors is usually justified. On the other hand, as more than one court has pointed out (see, for example, the cases of *Warner*, 1946 and *Ko*, 1979), the circumstances of the offence also shed light on the character of the offender.

The unifying feature of this group of aims is their reference to the future behaviour of the very offender before the court. The sentence is to be determined on the basis of what he or she is likely to do if one or another measure is used. The main concern of courts here is clearly with *criminal* behaviour. And reasons for sentence indicate that past behaviour is considered to be the best guide in this respect. In the classic formulation of *Warner, Urquhart, Martin, and Mullen* (1946, Ontario Court of Appeal, manslaughter):

> Wilful persistence in the deliberately acquired habit of crime marks the offender as an enemy of society in proportion to the extent of such persistence. An individual's actions may indicate his permanent tendencies, or, on the other hand, they may merely be the result of transient moods or momentary impulses. Where we find an individual, over a period of time, pursuing a course of conduct, it is thereby possible reasonably to determine his or her character or mental attitude. That is why Judges consider the previous record of a delinquent in determining the penalty to be imposed upon him.

But courts also consider the offender's *social* history as independently important in predicting his or her criminal future. In *Demeter and Whitmore*, the social histories of the offenders showed the offence to be "completely out of character." There was "no reason to believe that these two youths had set upon a course of criminal activity as a pattern for their future. Indeed, the contrary appears clear." The same was true of *Shanower*: "this was an isolated incident in his life, not likely to be repeated." In *Cedras*, the court seems to have felt that the offender's character made it "unlikely that [he] would commit such a crime again." And in *Hardy* the character information was a prelude to the following statements:

> Sergeant Detective David does not think the accused is dangerous and would have him as a friend ... The accused does not represent in any way, a threat to society and ... there would be no substantial likelihood of Mr. Hardy committing any further criminal offence.

Sometimes, however, courts express an at least partial concern for the offender's social (productive) future as well. In *Morrissette*, the reference to social history and the alcohol explanation quoted above were followed by:

> On the other hand there is every reason to believe that he will not repeat such an offence and upon release will again become a *useful* and law-biding citizen. A sentence should therefore not be imposed that may destroy both his hopes and plans for the future (emphasis added).

This question of disruption or destruction of the offender's successful integration into the productive apparatus is the usual basis for a reference to the social future of the offender. It is meant to mitigate a punishment that would otherwise be warranted (for denunciatory or deterrent purposes) on the ground of this disruption. The notion of rehabilitation in sentencing seems, in fact, to be most often used in this negative sense. An extreme example perhaps, is *A.* (1974, Ontario High Court). The offender, unnamed in the report of the case (apparently to protect his business), was convicted of indecently assaulting an employee. He was sentenced to pay the victim $1,000 and put on probation. The court reasoned as follows:

> Imprisonment would be of no assistance to the accused. It is likely it would ruin his one-man business. To him the conviction itself forms a substantial portion of the punishment ... While the solution I propose to follow here cannot be adopted in all cases, because the offender is usually without funds, here the offender is a man of modest means ... I propose to make compensation of the victim part of the process of rehabilitation. After all it has long been recognized that restitution for wrong done is rehabilitation.

Here it will be noted that class operates in two ways. First, naturally, there is the question of funds to buy oneself out of trouble. The fine option prison sentence when combined with the bizarre notion that fines cannot be increased on the basis of wealth[3] operates in much the same way. Second, and more important for our purposes, is the role in production played by the *petit bourgeois* in a capitalist economy (indispensable) compared to that of the worker in a situation of structured unemployment (dispensable).

Another example is the "intermittent" sentence (*Criminal Code*, s. 663[1][c]), a much milder form of imprisonment with a 90-day maximum invented precisely for working offenders (see Canadian Committee on Corrections, 1969: 203, *Wortzman*, 1979; *Kischel*, 1979). Of course, it may be argued that the intermittent sentence has resulted in more working offenders going to jail than would otherwise have gone. Nevertheless, the invention of this sentence proves the reluctance of the courts to use imprisonment against the employed.

Finally, there are some cases in which rehabilitation is used positively against the unemployed, though it is rare to see such sentiments expressed. In *Maclean* (1978, Ontario Court of Appeal), a case of breaking and entering and theft in which a sentence of nine months imprisonment was reduced to one of four months, we read: "He is seventeen years of age. His work record has been sporadic and the trial judge felt that he needed to be in a structured situation."

A very important aspect of the relevance of good character to sentencing is as a guarantee against future criminality. In this way, good character is held by sentencing courts to lessen the need for official penalties meant to protect the public by incapacitating the dangerous offender (see Hardy, for example) or, in less extreme cases, to deter future criminality. In *Ruddock* (1978, Nova Scotia Court of Appeal, bribery), we read:

> By his conviction the appellant has lost his employment with the Government which he had since February 1, 1968. He doubtless has suffered great humiliation and embarrassment. The pre-sentence report indicates that he has suffered great emotional strain as a result of this matter. He is a man of 46 years of age, married with two grown sons and has no previous criminal record. His conviction for this offence with all the attendant ramifications thereof, some of which I have referred to, has, no doubt, graphically brought home to him the gravity of the matter.

In *Legare* (1978, Que. C.A., theft):

> What appellant has already suffered is in all probability sufficient to deter him from committing any such crime again. Rehabilitation is hardly a factor in this case ... [He] had no prior criminal record, has a family of three children and was highly considered by his fellow citizens: the fact of being found guilty and of being sentenced to 30 days' imprisonment in these circumstances constitutes a severe penalty and I do not think that society would profit by completely destroying the appellant by a sentence of imprisonment which was too long, which would make any rehabilitation very difficult.

Thus good character — which means, as we have seen, properly fulfilling a valued role in the productive apparatus and also something not to be interfered with in itself — is a guarantee against future criminality since it dispenses with the need for more severe guarantees. In this way, reform operates in a similar manner to denunciation. Those who exhibit a proper integration into the productive apparatus *deserve* some "credit" for their adherence to *social* values and they also *require* less punishment to ensure their continued adherence to legal values. This is partly because their "character" continues to be a guarantee against future criminality, but it is also because of these extra, non-official punishments which accompany the conviction of persons of their status.

For reasons which will become obvious a little later on, the question of whether these non-official penalties actually do enhance individual deterrence is a very important one. It should be noted that it is different from the question of the relationship between class and recidivism. There is ample evidence of a relationship between recidivism and class and also between recidivism and other demographic variables including criminal record (Gendreau et al., 1979; Cockerill, 1981; van der Werff, 1981), and all are in the direction we would expect from judicial practice. But these relationships seem to be quite independent of the sentence. That is, while a judge can *predict* recidivism from these variables, his or her choice of sentence has little if any *effect* on recidivism. And where it does, the effect is precisely the opposite of what one would expect from judicial practice. That is, other things equal, recidivism is *enhanced*, not reduced, by custodial sentences: longer sentences enhance it more effectively than shorter ones (Hood and Sparks, 1970, Chapter 6; Walker, 1972, Chapter 6; Brody, 1976; van der Werff, 1981).

Thus, the available empirical evidence provides little support for the individualization of sentences in the interests of preventing recidivism, and what support it does provide suggests a strategy of leniency to those *most likely* on the basis of demographic variables (including class) to be reconvicted, the exact opposite of the actual current approach. But, of course, the established relationships are between *official* recidivism and class, which naturally begs the question of how the police go about determining who to arrest and charge. We know very well that both class and record play an important role in these choices, as well (Ericson, 1982, Chapter 6; Hagan, 1978).

So the question remains at least partly theoretical and it is this: what is our guarantee that Ruddock and Legare will not commit the same or similar offences again? The courts argue that the unofficial penalties are an important reason. They have lost their jobs and their social reputations. But isn't it obvious that if this were true the exact opposite would occur? That is, if they really had so much less to lose now than they had before the conviction, wouldn't it be *more* likely that they would repeat their offences in the future? There seems, in fact, to be a hidden assumption in all this that bears a closer resemblance to reality: they probably have not lost that much at all, at least economically and socially speaking, and it is their *continued* high status that provides the court with its guarantee. Those qualities that made Ruddock a desirable high status employee before will continue. And the same will probably hold for Legare despite his financial setback.

There are indeed some famous cases were leniency was justified on the basis that the offender had already "suffered enough" which demonstrate this point quite dramatically. A particularly striking example is the former Solicitor General of Canada, Francis Fox, who was not prosecuted for forgery partly on the grounds that he had suffered enough.[4] In fact, it was not long before he was overwhelmingly re-elected and once again a Cabinet Minister with a Cabinet Minister's salary. Another recent example is the case of a rich Toronto sports entrepreneur, Harold Ballard. His conviction for theft and a three-year penitentiary sentence in 1972 (*Globe and Mail*, October 21, 1972) neither interfered with his class position nor his social standing, unless one can be said to suffer "opprobrium" when the Mayor celebrates your birthday at City Hall and the Prime Minister sends you presents (*Toronto Star*, July 29, 1983).

Even in those cases where there might be some loss suffered by virtue of the conviction itself, why should it be assumed that it increases with class status? What evidence there is indicates that, on the contrary, the loss is inversely related to status (Schwartz and Skolnick, 1962). It seems that people on the economic margins of society are more likely to suffer from the stigma of conviction in their employment prospects than those at the economic centre. As for "humiliation," the degradation which accompanies subjection to the naked power of the police and the deferential attitude required by courts also seems to vary *inversely* with class, and there is no reason to suppose that it is any less irksome than the public humiliation of the prominent. So the tender attitude displayed to high status offenders by sentencing judges seems merely to betray their sympathy for the problems associated with their own class and their insensitivity to those of the working and marginal classes.

General Deterrence

The third category of official purposes to be fulfilled by sentencers in exercising their discretion is general deterrence. The basic idea is fairly straightforward:

> The governing principle of deterrence is, within reason and common sense, that the emotion of fear should be brought into play so that the offender may be made afraid to offend again *and also so that others who may have contemplated offending will be restrained by the same controlling emotion.* Society must be reasonably assured that the punishment meted out to one will not actually encourage others (*Willaert*, 1959, Ontario Court of Appeal, emphasis added).

In Holmes' classic description: "The law threatens certain pains if you do certain things, intending thereby to give you a new motive for not doing them. If you persist in doing them, it has to inflict the pains in order that its threats may continue to be believed" (Holmes, 1881).

General deterrence figured in Bentham's utilitarian theory of punishment as the "chief end of punishment, as it is its real justification" (Bentham, 1775:396). This may surprise some because Bentham is best known in modern criminology for his Panopticon invention, a device which, as Foucault has pointed out, epitomizes the "disciplinary" (reformative, individualizing, etc.) orientation of modern penal systems. Nevertheless, Bentham was quite firm and consistent in his preference for general over individual prevention. When they conflicted, individual effects had to give way to general effects.[5] The reason for this was that, according to Bentham, punishment was an *evil* because it inflicted suffering on the offender who was also "a member of the community ... His welfare is proportionately the welfare of the community — his suffering the suffering of the community" (398). Consequently, it could only be endorsed if the suffering it prevented outweighed that which it inflicted so that the result was an increase in the net balance of "happiness." The "inconsiderable benefit which might result in the way of disablement or reformation" (399) would rarely outweigh the suffering imposed on the offender or be of any counterweight to what the deterrence of potential offenders could achieve. Punishment for Bentham, using the imagery of the English *petit bourgeois*, was an "expense" which had to be outweighed by the "profit" accruing from it. Furthermore, "frugality" was of the essence, no more should be expended than was absolutely necessary (398).

One of the most striking things about general deterrence as it figures in the legal rationale of sentencing discretion in Canada is that it is almost completely detached from any utilitarian context of expense, profit, and frugality. Cases where an attempt is made to verify the general deterrent effect of a given sentence are almost nonexistent (one pathetic example is *Paterson*, 1963, British Columbia Court of Appeal, a classic case of *post hoc ergo propter hoc* reasoning). For the most part, courts blithely accept, albeit implicitly, the assumption that increased severity of sentence enhances the general deterrent effect in reducing crime (for example, *McNamara, Campbell*, 1981; *McEachern, Wickham*, 1978; *Johnson and Tremayne*). On the other hand, it seems that when a court is bent on a lower-than-usual sentence for other reasons, it can safely assume that this will not diminish the deterrent effect. For example, in *Doughty* (1978, Prince Edward Island Court of Appeal), MacDonald, J., wrote:

> On the facts of this case, I cannot say that it warrants a sentence greater than three years. There would appear to be an excellent chance for the rehabilitation of the offender and I do not believe that incarceration for one or two years more would have any greater effect as a deterrent on other prospective offenders. (See also *Atkinson, Ing and Roberts*.)

There seems also to be some confusion as to whether factors relative to the offender as well as to the offence are relevant to the general deterrence question. In *Morrissette,* it was said that "objective" factors were relevant to general deterrence and "individual" factors were relevant to specific deterrence of the offender. On the other hand, some courts have considered it proper to take into account individual factors in connection with general *and* specific deterrence (for example, *Demeter and Whitmore,* age; *Ruddock,* class). This has been done on the assumption that factors such as youth and class status, which are thought to reduce the need for punishment in order to prevent repetition by the offender, likewise reduce the need for the threat of punishment as a deterrent to offenders sharing the same characteristics.

Among these contradictions, general deterrence has had a rather precarious existence as an official purpose in sentencing. The British Columbia Court of Appeal rejected it in *Harrison and Garrison* (1978) only to bring it back in *Campbell* (1981). Even in the latter case, one member of the five member Court felt that deterrence often meant denunciation and two others seemed to think that both aims could be fulfilled by the same sentence.

The reason for the confusion seems to me to be that in the current Canadian sentencing system, general deterrence can only be a *pseudo-purpose.* That is, while it can be a justification or defence of *any* sentence, it cannot function as a *guide* to a judge in deciding *which* sentence and cannot, therefore, justify distinctions *between* sentences. This is not because the so-called "severity hypothesis" is absolutely invalid. In fact, there are good grounds for supposing that in certain circumstances and within limits, increased severity of punishment does enhance the deterrent effect (Fattah, 1976) — though these limits are probably greatly exceeded by the savage prison sentences meted out in Canada (American Friends Service Committee, 1971: Chapter 4). It is rather because of the *design* of the sentencing system. In order for variations in penal severity to affect crime — that is, for one penalty to be a more effective deterrent than another — that penalty, the variation, or whatever must be *known* by potential offenders. But in the Canadian system, with its enormous discretion (even leaving parole apart), penalties are virtually unpredictable. Certainly they cannot be gleaned from the statutes, except for the one mandatory penalty and the few mandatory minimum penalties. So uninterested is the system in making even the range of penalties known that sentencing statistics have not been published for ten years!

But knowing the range of penalties wouldn't do any good anyway, because the penalties vary enormously from judge to judge. For example, Hogarth found that one could predict the length of a prison sentence five times more accurately by knowing a few things about the judge and nothing about the case, than by knowing everything about the case and nothing about the judge (Hogarth, 1971:351). Furthermore, there are a whole set of factors besides the offence which affect the sentence in quantitatively unpredictable ways, including post-arrest behaviour and the personal characteristics of the offender. And since the sentences vary unsystematically on these bases, it is impossible ever to determine (by observing any variation in the incidence of crime) whether more punishment is being inflicted than is necessary to prevent what crime can be prevented through the threat of punishment. Though it bears repetition, what we know suggests Canadian sentences are far more severe than necessary to achieve what can be achieved by way of general deterrence.

Thus, the design of the Canadian system necessitates its evident lack of concern with general deterrence except as it may incidentally follow from its denunciatory and reformative, incapacitive, etc. purposes. In my opinion, this is a point of enormous significance because it is precisely in those respects in which it departs from general deterrent principles that the Canadian system departs from democratic principles, even in the limited bourgeois (or "liberal" or "political") sense of democracy.

Utilitarian general deterrence presupposes a *two-step* procedure. First, one must determine what penalty is *warranted* for a given crime. This involves an evaluation of the amount of harm which the crime does to its victims.[6] No more than this can be imposed on the offender, or the evil inflicted by the punishment will outweigh that sought to be prevented by it. But not every *warranted* penalty is *necessary*. Whatever can be accomplished in the way of crime prevention through deterrence by a warranted penalty might also be achieved by a lesser one. The capital punishment debate is instructive in this regard. Those who opposed capital punishment on the basis that it failed to deter assumed that if it saved more lives than it cost, it would be *warranted*. However, they thought that because life imprisonment could achieve whatever prevention of murder capital punishment could achieve, the lesser penalty was required. There is an empirical question embedded in the general deterrence program or, as Zimring and Hawkins have put it, there is a "moral duty to do research" (Zimring and Hawkins, 1973:43).

Now, in order to determine what penalty is not only warranted but also necessary, it seems that the warranted penalty would have to be varied downward systematically so that its effect, if any, on the incidence of crime could be observed. But systematic variation of penalty cannot occur where there is individual judicial discretion. For any variation in penalty to have an effect, as we have already pointed out, the penalties must be knowable in advance and flow automatically from conviction. Penalties must therefore be fixed by legislation or regulation and not vary from court to court. But once penalties become legislative, they become more within popular control. And when judges are bound by rules, their personal power over offenders is thereby considerably diminished, making the criminal law consistent with the maxim of a government of laws and not of "men."

It should not be surprising that Bentham was also opposed to judicial discretion in sentencing and for the same basic reasons (Bentham, 1775:516):

> The legislator ought, as much as possible, to determine
> everything relating to punishments, for two reasons: that
> they may be *certain*, and *impartial*. 1. The more com-
> pletely the scale of punishments is rendered certain, the
> more completely all the members of the community are
> enabled to know what to expect. It is the fear of punish-
> ment, in so far as it is known, which prevents the commis-
> sion of crime. An uncertain punishment will therefore be
> uncertain in its effects, since, where there is a possibility
> to escape, escape will be hoped for.
> 2. The legislator is necessarily unacquainted with the
> individuals who will undergo the punishment he ap-
> points; he cannot, therefore, be governed by feelings of
> personal antipathy or regard. He is impartial, or, at least,
> appears to be so. A judge, on the contrary, only pro-
> nouncing upon a particular case, is exposed to favour-
> able or unfavourable prejudices, at least to the suspicion
> of such, which almost equally shakes the public confi-
> dence.

However, Bentham equivocated on this issue. In almost the same breath he observed:

> There may, however, often arise, either with regard to the
> offences themselves, or the person of the delinquent,
> unforeseen and particular circumstances, which would
> be productive of great inconveniences, if the law were
> altogether inflexible. It is therefore proper to allow a
> certain latitude to the judge, not of increasing, but of
> diminishing a punishment, in those cases in which it may
> be fairly presumed that one individual is less dangerous,
> or more responsible than another; since, as has been
> before observed, the same nominal punishment is not
> always the same real punishment — some individuals,
> by reason of their education, family connections, and
> condition in the world, presenting if we may so speak, a
> greater surface for punishment to act upon.

So Bentham thought that class was (slightly) relevant to general deterrence and thereby permitted some (slight) mitigation in penalty, thus
opening the door to discretion (if only slightly). We have seen that some
Canadian courts have agreed with this. A good example is *Ruddock*,
discussed earlier under the issue of individual deterrence and class. The
court reasoned as follows on the "general, or third party deterrence" issue:

> In the present case the main consideration is to impress

upon Government officials and employees (and indeed
those who have dealings with the Government) that if
they accept anything (without the written consent of
their department head) from the people doing business
with the Government, they have breached the criminal
law. As a result of accepting money from Mr. Boudreau,
without the required consent, the respondent has lost his
employment with the Government, a fact apparently not
definite when he was sentenced by Judge O'Hearn, and
has acquired a criminal record which may adversely
affect his ability to acquire new employment. Certainly I
think it fair to assume that he will not again be employed
by any Government. All these circumstances no doubt
are now well known to other civil servants. If such do not
act as a deterrent to others in the Government service
then I frankly doubt whether the addition of a term of
imprisonment will do so. This, to me, is the crux of the
matter.

In my opinion, Bentham and the Court in *Ruddock* were both wrong in
thinking that high status offenders should be treated any differently in the
interests of general deterrence. The issue does not seem to differ analyti-
cally from the issue with respect to individual deterrence which was
discussed earlier. There is no plausible argument that unofficial penalties[7]
which flow from conviction increase, at least relatively speaking, with
class. While it is true that the likelihood of conviction varies inversely with
class (Bell-Robertson and Boydell, 1972: Tables 17 and 18), it could hardly
be argued that it is unofficial penalties which account for this. A much
more likely explanation is a selection process on the part of police and
prosecutorial authorities which operates on a similar basis to the sentencing system, thereby tending to protect relatively high status offenders
from prosecution for the sort of crime with which police usually deal
(Hagan, 1978; Ericson, 1982). This also happens to be the sort of crime
which workers and poor people tend to commit because of their material
circumstances and opportunities (these are what the Law Reform Commission of Canada calls "true-crimes"). Naturally, the same selection
system also tends to deal non-punitively with the sort of crime that the
bourgeoisie and the rich tend to commit ("regulatory offences") (Braithwaite, 1979, Chapter 10; Snider, 1978).

Hence, there is no reason why general deterrence need take class into
account and no need for a special judicial discretion on this ground.
Bentham seems to have been betraying his own "feelings of [class] antipa-
thy or regard" here. Indeed, as Marx pointed out, Bentham's major fault
was to assume "with the dryest naivete ... that the modern petty bourgeois,
especially the English petty bourgeois, is the normal man" (Marx, 1976:
759n). In any event, a system based on utilitarian general deterrence, that

is, the prevention through general deterrence of the harm caused by crime, insofar as possible and at the least social cost, would need to eliminate discretion and base punishment entirely on the conduct sought to be prevented, not on the "character" (class) of the offender. It would thus fulfill as closely as class society permits the democratic ideals of equality before the law and the separation of the public and private spheres.

Finally, a punishment system which was utilitarian in the sense that its goal was the prevention of "harm to others" as opposed to the assessment of offenders' adherence to social values would be, it seems to me, more egalitarian in its treatment of *victims*. The relative social (that is *judicial*) characterizations of, for example, robbers (*Nichol*) and drug traffickers (*Zizzo, Vetrovec, Maruska*) on the one hand, and wife killers (*Hardy, Mac-Arthur*, 1978) and motor manslaughterers (*Cedras*) on the other, lead to sentences of stunning severity for the former and stunning leniency for the latter when denunciation and rehabilitation are the goals. When the relative dangers of the two types of activity to potential victims are assessed, however, the relative warranted punishment or, in Bentham's words, "the expense which it may be worthwhile to be at, in the way of punishment" (1780: 88) is completely reversed.

The same reasoning applies to police crimes, especially of the massive political sort practised under the leadership of the RCMP, which not only had real victims but also stabbed deeply at the democratic process in Canada. In the only case yet to reach a disposition in this affair,[8] the accused pleaded guilty to a carefully concocted charge under S. 115 of the *Criminal Code*, which substantially diminished the normal penalties for breaking, entering, and theft. They were given absolute discharges because, in the words of the judge, they "acted in good faith and for a noble cause, the security of the state and the protection of the public" (*Coutellier, Cobb and Cormier*, 1977). This case should be contrasted with *Parrot* (1979), where the union leader's "honest belief in the righteousness of [his] cause" got him a sentence of three months in jail under the same provision of the *Code* for an offence usually punished *less* severely and one which was far less harmful in its consequences than those committed by the RCMP. Nor did the difference between the two cases lie in the sincerity of the motives, or in the "premeditation," or in the "lack of remorse" (though these last two matters were naturally mentioned only in Parrot's case). The difference was only in the consistency of the motives with the extant relations of production and their political superstructure: Parrot was acting on behalf of workers (actually, refusing to act against them) and the RCMP was acting against the Québec independence movement and other working class interests advocated by l'Agence de presse libre du Québec and the Mouvement pour la défence des prisonniers politiques québecois.[9]

So when compared with a system based on utilitarian general deterrence, the current Canadian system appears very undemocratic indeed, and this is precisely because it concerns itself with the preservation of the social status quo of class relations and not the protection of individuals from the harmful effects of crime at the least social cost. This means that the class features of Canadian sentencing practice and law cannot be success-fully legitimated by reference to such democratic objects. It also explains the weak commitment to them by reformers and by the judiciary.

I should emphasize that it is not my argument that it is simply a mistake in penal philosophy which has brought us to this position. My point is rather that the class function of the sentencing system — a mechanism partly responsible (along with an ensemble of mechanisms having the same function) for the class nature of Canadian punitive practices — is best revealed by comparing it to a system organized for the technical function of prevention of crime at the least social cost, which is what one would expect of the neutral state that Marxism claims to be a myth. If it were possible, a neutral state in a class society might indeed vary its repression according to class, but only in as much as *crime* varied according to class (á la Anatole France). In the Canadian system, it is *punishment* which varies according to class. The Canadian system is therefore "superstructural" in the sense that it is concerned with the strengthening of class relations and of the *social* status quo as distinct from the defence of the *legal* status quo.

Notes

1. See, e.g. *Legare* (1978, theft); *McNamara et al.* (1981, conspiracy to defraud); *Sawchyn* (1981, rape); *Hardy* (1976, manslaughter); *McEachern* (1978, theft); *Blake* (1978, perjury); *Cedras*; (1981, criminal negligence causing death); *Demeter* and *Whitmore*; (1976, robbery); *Paradis* (1976, attempted murder).
2. See also *Gamester* (1978), where the Prince Edward Island Court of Appeal prohibited a judge from inviting the public to appear before him and make known their opinions about the sentence he should impose on a fatal drunk driving case.
3. The prevailing view seems to be that poverty is a mitigating factor but wealth is not an aggravating factor in assessing the amount of a fine (*Wells*, 1977). Nor can a jail sentence be substituted for a fine where the guilty person is so rich that a fine would be meaningless: "If the Court can discriminate according to class in imposing sentence, then there is nothing to prevent it from imposing punishment based on race, creed, color or society status of the accused" (*Johnson*, 1971). On the other hand, the mere fact that the fine option for this reason inevitably results in poor people going to jail for offences for which the affluent pay fines, even when they get the same sentence, does not violate the principle of (equality before the law): "In being subject to imprisonment in default of the payment of the fine imposed, the appellant has not been treated differently to others. A poor man who is fined inevitably suffers more than a rich man ... In my opinion, "equality before the law" has no relation to such matters and things as these" (*Natrall*, 1972).
4. In explaining his decision not to prosecute, the Attorney General of Ontario said:

> To launch a prosecution in this case would be to bring disproportionately harsh consequences to a person of good character, who has already suffered greatly as a result of his act. This bears on the circumstances of the case itself and not the fact that Mr. Fox assumed high public office after the event in question. The holders of public offices will receive the same treatment under the law as the ordinary citizen, even though the consequences may be more injurious.

In the rather lengthy speech from which this is an excerpt, the Attorney General gave other reasons as well for his decision, including possible legal obstacles, the embarrassment of other parties, and the fact that no harm was done (*Legislature of Ontario Debates*, 1978: 51).

5. Even in *Panopticon* itself, Bentham writes: "Of the two, example and reformation, example is the greatest object; and that in the proportion of the number of the yet innocent to that of the convicted guilty" (1791:79n).

6. It is not clear whether Bentham believed that the warranted punishment should be determined by the harm to *all* potential victims or to each potential victim. The former seems likely (Bentham, 1780:16). However, there is no reason to accept this inegalitarian and indeed oppressive aspect of Bentham's theory, which would make the offender bear the full weight of the sum total of many lesser harms done to victims. Egalitarian solutions to this problem that do not affect the basic thrust of the approach will be found in Honderich (1976:202-206) and American Friends Service Committee (1971: Chapter 4).

7. Bentham distinguished between unofficial penalties ("Physical, moral and religious sanctions"), which he opposed taking into account as too uncertain, and matters of "sensibility", which he advocated taking into account so that the same pain could be inflicted even by different nominal punishments. Naturally, he believed that sensibility varied according to class, as well as sex and race (Bentham, 1780:21-35, 90). As the text indicates, this kind of reasoning is not as popular today as the unofficial penalty approach. For the purposes of my argument, I include both effects under "unofficial penalties."

8. Since writing this, there have been several final results reached in Québec concerning RCMP crimes. Only one of them resulted in a finding of guilty, and again an absolute discharge was granted on virtually the same reasoning as used five years earlier in the case of *Coutellier, Cobb, and Cormier*. See the case of *Blier* as reported in the *Winnipeg Free Press*, November 20, 1982, and the *Globe and Mail* of the same day.

9. For more extensive discussion of these two cases see: Commission d'enquête sur de operations Policieres en territoire quebécois (1981: Chapter 8); and Glasbeek and Mandel (1979).

Cases Cited
A. (1974), 26 C.C.C. (2d) 474 (Ont. H. Ct.)
Aylward (1978), 43 C.C.C. (2d) 455 (Ont. C.A.)
Atkinson, Ing, and Roberts (1978), 43 C.C.C. (2d) 342 (Ont. C.A.)
Blake (1978), 39 C.C.C. (2d) 138 (P.E.I. C.A.)
Breen (1982), 69 C.C.C. (2d) 554 (Nfld. C.A.)
Campbell (1981), 64 C.C.C. (2d) 336 (B.C. C.A.)
Cedras (1981), 61 C.C.C. (2d) 387 (Que. C.A.)
Coutellier, Cobb, and Cormier (unreported decision of the Cours des Sessions de la Paix, Montreal, Vincent, J. June 16, 1977)
Demeter and Whitmore (1976), 32 C.C.C. (2d) 379 (Ont. C.A.)
Doughty (1978), 40 C.C.C. (2d) 224 (P.E.I. C.A.)
Gamester (1978), 38 C.C.C. (2d) 548 (P.E.I. C.A.)
Gingera 1956, 1 C.C.C. 273 (Man. C.A.)
Hardy (1976), 29 C.C.C. (2d) 84 (Que. Sup. Ct.)
Harrison and Garrison (1978), 1 W.W.R. 162 (B.C. C.A.)
Hinch and Salanski (1968), 3 C.C.C. 39 (B.C. C.A.)
Ingram and Grimsdale (1977), 35 C.C.C. (2d) 376 (Ont. C.A.)
Johnson (1971), 5 C.C.C. (2d) 541 (N.S. C.A.)
Johnston and Tremayne (1970), 4 C.C.C. 64 (Ont. C.A.) *Kischel* (1979), 12 C.R. (3d) 97 (Ont. Co. Ct.)
Ko (1979), 11 C.R. (3d) 298 (B.C. C.A.)
Legare (No. 2) 48 C.C.C. (2d) (Que. C.A.)
MacArthur (1978), 39 C.C.C. (2d) (P.E.I. C.A.)
MacEachern (1978), 42 C.C.C. (2d) 189 (Ont. C.A.)
Maruska et al. (1981), 60 C.C.C. (2d) 438 (Que. Sup. Ct. Criminal Jurisdiction)
Maclean (1978), 7 C.R. (3d) S-3 (Ont. C.A)
McNamara et al. (No. 2), (1981), 56 C.C.C. 516 (Ont. C.A.) *Morrissette* and two others (1970), 1 C.C.C. (2d) 307 (Sask. C.A.)
Natrall (1972), 20 C.R.N.S. 265 (B.C. C.A.)
Paradis (1976), 38 C.C.C. (2d) 445 (Que. C.A.)
Parrot (unreported, May 7, 1979, H. Ct. Ont. reasons for sentence of *Evans*, C.J.O.)
Paterson (1963), (2 C.C.C.) 369 (B.C. C.A)
Pruner (1979), 8 C.R. (3d) S-8 (Ont. C.A.)
Rouse and McInroy (No.2), (1981), 59 C.C.C. (2d) 25 (B.C. C.A.)
Ruddock (1978), 39 C.C.C. (2d) 65 (N.S. C.A)
Sargeant (1974), 60 Cr.App. R. 74 (C.C.A.)
Sawchyn (1981), 60 C.C.C. (2d) 200 (Alta. C.A.)
Shanower (1972), 8 C.C.C. (2d) 527 (Ont. C.A.)
Stein (1974), 15 C.C.C. (2d) 376 (Ont. C.A.)
Vetrovec et al. (1980), 58 C.C.C. (2d) 537 (B.C. C.A.)
Warner, Urquhart, Martin, and Mullen (1946), 87 C.C.C. 13 (Ont. C.A.) approved in Lees (1979), 46 C.C.C. (2d) 385 (Sup. Ct. Can.)
Wells (1977), 7 C.R. (3d) S-17 (Alta. Dist. Ct.) *Wickham* (1978), 41 C.C.C. (2d)

42 (Ont. C.A.)
Willaert (1959), 105 C.C.C. 172 Ont. C.A.)
Wood (1975), 26 C.C.C. (2d) 100 (Alta. C.A.)
Wortzman (1979), 12 C.R. (3d) 115 (Ont. C.A.)
Zizzo et al., (1975), 23 C.C.C. (2d) (Ont. C.A.)

Defence of the North: The Native Economy and Land Claims
Geoffrey York

Elias Martin is a husky, mustachioed Cree who speaks quietly and slowly as he shivers in the chill October air of Northern Manitoba. Wearing a black T-shirt and jeans, he stands on a wooden doorstep, letting his eye wander over the small frame houses of Moose Lake, his home reserve. He is thinking about the violent youth gangs that are terrorizing the reserve's residents. "You have to live here to know the feeling," Elias Martin says. "People are scared. It affects the whole community."

A pot-holed gravel road stretches sixty kilometres through the barren bush of northwestern Manitoba before ending abruptly at the Moose Lake reserve and its adjoining Métis community. There is a hitchhiker on the road, a young transient Cree from Saskatchewan who sometimes travels to Moose Lake to visit his girlfriend. He does not like to stay very long — the reserve is too dangerous, too frightening, he says. There is a bad feeling at Moose Lake. So he sees his girlfriend briefly and then leaves.

It is the gangs and the constant violence that trouble the hitchhiker. Almost every weekend, the gangs are involved in beatings or brawls, and every night the people of Moose Lake have to barricade themselves into their houses, pushing chairs and logs against their doors and using ropes or chains to keep them shut. They know that the youth gangs sometimes break into houses at night, searching for liquor. "If they find some poor guy inside, they beat him up," Elias Martin says.

"A lot of people won't report crimes because they're afraid of the intimidation," says Staff-Sergeant Ove Larsen of the RCMP detachment at The Pas, the nearest town. Gang members who commit crimes are often permitted to roam freely on the reserve because witnesses are afraid to testify against them. In some cases, the RCMP persuade a witness to testify at a trial, but at the last minute, on the day of the trial, the witness backs out and refuses to testify. The RCMP have tried to persuade the Moose Lake band to establish a justice committee or a neighbourhood watch group to provide protection for the new people on the reserve. "But they are afraid to set that up because of fear of retaliation" Larsen says.

There are two rival gangs at Moose Lake, each with about two dozen Cree and Métis members, ranging in age from fourteen to thirty-five. They arm themselves with rocks, sticks, chains and knives. In a community with an unemployment rate of 85 percent and very few recreational facilities, the gangs are a lure for idle youths. "They have nothing else to do," Elias Martin explains.

The tragedy of Moose Lake is that the reserve was once a thriving, prosperous community. Located on the fertile soil of the Saskatchewan River delta, it was rich in wildlife — animals, fish and birds. Its hunting and trapping grounds were regarded as among the best in the province, and the band at Moose Lake was one of the most peaceful and self-sufficient in Manitoba. According to one study, commissioned by four Cree bands in the region, "crime and vandalism were practically nonexistent in 1960. The community prior to the flooding had no marked social problems but rather a high degree of coherence."

But in the early 1960s, thousands of hectares of wilderness — including about two-thirds of the land on the reserve — were submerged in water by the construction of the Grand Rapids hydro dam. Many reserve residents were forced to relocate to a new site, where the houses were jammed together on a small patch of land.

Before the hydro project, there were an estimated two thousand moose and large numbers of deer in the wilderness surrounding the Moose Lake reserve and the nearby Chemawawin reserve. About 380 moose were harvested every year. The ancestors of the Moose Lake and Chemawawin Indians had decided wisely when they chose the sites of their reserves in the 19th century. The Saskatchewan River delta was one of the last great breeding marshes for ducks and geese in North America, and its soil was rich enough to support grain and vegetable crops and a ranch of top-quality Hereford cattle. Even a successful muskrat ranch was established at Moose Lake. In the 1950s, the reserve and the surrounding region produced about $150,000 worth of muskrat pelts each year. Beavers and other fur-bearing animals were trapped in the wild, and the duck hunt brought in another $207,000 annually. There was a commercial fishery, and thousands of kilograms of whitefish were sold by band members every year.

But this traditional native economy was shattered by the hydro flooding of 1963 and 1964. Eighty million kilograms of cement were poured into the ground to create a massive dam twenty metres high, with dikes extending twelve kilometres on each side. Water levels on Cedar Lake were elevated by four metres, creating the fourth-largest lake in Manitoba. More than 2,200 square kilometres of delta land were intentionally flooded.

The cattle and muskrat ranches of Moose Lake were wiped out, the crops and gardens were destroyed, and the supply of moose fell sharply. After the flooding, Indian hunters often needed at least a week of hunting to find a single moose, and even then they sometimes returned empty-handed. "Moose populations are almost non-existent in the now deeply flooded area and [exist in] much fewer numbers in peripheral areas under shallow water," a provincial bureaucrat wrote in a 1969 report.

Incredibly, the Moose Lake band was given only $10,000 in cash compensation for the flooding. The band tried to sue the provincial government, but they were frustrated by procedural tactics that delayed the court cases.

Crime and alcoholism soon became a serious problem at Moose Lake. "Stress, anxiety and fear have been much in evidence since the flooding," a study of Moose Lake reported in 1978. Elias Martin, who works as an alcohol and drug counsellor at Moose Lake, now estimates that 90 percent of the community's adults are abusing alcohol or drugs. In 1986, alcohol helped spark a near-riot in which a number of band members were hospitalized and forty-one were arrested.

Jim Tobacco, chief of the Moose Lake band, says the crime rate on his reserve is one of the highest in Manitoba. "There's a very hostile attitude in the community. Our young people are always beating each other up. My people don't know who the hell they are. They live month to month, on welfare ... Our way of life and our resource base has been destroyed. We were promised benefits from the hydro project. Today we are poor and Manitoba Hydro is rich. The crime and violence, the gang warfare, are the price we pay for Hydro's vision of progress."

The impact of the flooding was even worse among the Cree people of Chemawawin, who lived nearby on the shores of Cedar Lake in the Saskatchewan River delta. Before the Grand Rapids hydro dam was built, they enjoyed the same abundant resources as the Moose Lake band and had a prosperous traditional economy of hunting, trapping, and fishing. Alcohol abuse was rare and crime was virtually unknown. "There are no apparent community problems," a provincial official reported in 1963. Another official said that the "thriving economy" was "the most striking aspect" of the reserve at Cedar Lake. The only people receiving welfare were single-parent families and disabled adults.

But all of that was radically altered by the Grand Rapids hydro project and the flooding. In the end, nearly the whole reserve disappeared under water, and the Cree were forced to relocate to a vastly inferior site about sixty kilometres southeast, on the opposite shore of Cedar Lake.

Manitoba Hydro had begun planning the Grand Rapids project in 1957, but the people of Chemawawin were not informed about it until the fall of 1960. The provincial government, acting on behalf of the Crown-owned hydro company, simply told the Cree residents of Cedar Lake that they would have to relocate within four years. The band was so isolated that it had virtually no experience in dealing with governments, and the Cree were not even told of their right to hire a lawyer. Moreover, the chief and most other band members spoke little English. Because the Cree had no legal counsel, it was relatively easy for the Manitoba government to persuade them to move. They were pressured into signing a final agreement in 1962.

The federal government made no effort to help the band. Using its powers under the Indian Act, the government simply expropriated the Chemawawin reserve and transferred the land to the province.

There is clear evidence that the federal and provincial governments were fully aware of the damage that the hydro dam would inflict on the people of Chemawawin and Moose Lake. In 1960, an official at Indian Affairs predicted that the flooding would cause the economic collapse of Chemawawin and Moose Lake bands. "Although a great deal of thought and effort has gone toward the selection of a new site for the bands concerned, the record does not indicate how or where these people are going to earn their living when their reserves have been flooded," the official wrote in an internal memorandum. "It is very doubtful if the wildlife resources will provide anything like the livelihood which has been available in the past and which was the primary reason the reserves were originally selected by these bands."

Provincial officials were privately forecasting that the hydro dam would cause a drastic decline in the populations of moose, waterfowl, and fish. "The economic values impaired would, no doubt, be greater than any compensation," one provincial memorandum warned. Later, a senior official admitted that he had seen a tragedy brewing as early as 1962, two years before the flooding. An environmental impact study, commissioned by the Manitoba government, confirmed that the flooding would cause serious damage—but its results were kept secret. In a confidential memo, a federal official warned Ottawa that "many of the resources from which the people derived a livelihood ... will be lost or seriously depleted for a number of years and in some cases, possibly forever."

Publicly, the Chemawawin Cree were given a completely different story. They were told that they would live in a modern town, with electric stoves, and a new highway to connect it to the south. In a formal letter of intent in 1962, a senior provincial bureaucrat promised that the Cree would not be hurt by the hydro development. "On behalf of the Manitoba government, we agree to take every step possible to maintain the income of the people of Chemawawin at the new site," the letter said. Premier Duff Roblin gave the Indians the same assurance in a letter in 1964. He told the band members that they "will in fact be able to earn as good a living as before and, we hope, a better living."

It soon became obvious that the government's assurances were just empty rhetoric. The Chemawawin band's new location, known as Easterville, was far removed from its traditional rich hunting and trapping areas. The site had been chosen by the Manitoba government primarily because it was closer to the south and would be cheaper to service. The wilderness surrounding the new site was almost entirely muskeg and swamp, and the reserve itself was covered with rock and gravel. Trees were sparse and stunted, leaving the reserve hot and dusty in the summer. James Waldram, an anthropologist who has documented the Easterville story, describes the site as "one of the most uninhabitable and depressing places one could imagine." Its nickname was "The Rock Pile."

Because the soil at Easterville was full of fractured limestone, the band was unable to dig pit latrines. Buckets had to be used for sewage, causing an increase in airborne bacteria, which led to serious infections among infants on the reserve. The poor sanitation also contaminated the water supply.

The band suffered a steep decline in its hunting and trapping, and there was a 93 percent reduction in the number of fish caught. As a result of the hydro dam and the flooding, Cedar Lake was choked with floating logs and debris, and the water level often fluctuated, so that it became dangerous to fish on the lake. Sometimes it took three separate trips before the Cree hunters could find a single moose.

By the late 1960s, alcohol abuse was spreading rapidly through the Easterville reserve. Vandalism had become common, and the children were often neglected. In 1966 a report commissioned by a federal-provincial committee concluded that the situation at Easterville was "desperate" and could soon become a "social disaster." Four years later, the commercial fishery on Cedar Lake was closed because mercury was leaching from the soil into the flooded areas — a common problem in hydro projects.

Manitoba Hydro, meanwhile, was boasting that the relocation of the Chemawawin band was a huge success because of the construction of new houses and schools at Easterville. In its public relations brochures, the corporation described Easterville in idyllic terms. "The brightly painted houses, nestled in a background of evergreens and birches, convey the impression of a lakeside summer resort."

The Cree sued the Manitoba government for breach of contract in 1970, but the government used a series of stalling tactics and legal maneuvers to prevent the case from going to court. As the community disintegrated, it became difficult for the band's lawyers to keep the case going, and the lawsuit eventually fell apart. By 1980, about 90 percent of the Cree were living on welfare, and a study found that mental depression was widespread among the people of Easterville.

Today, the Easterville Cree still occasionally travel across Cedar Lake to the old community of Chemawawin. They stare at the abandoned buildings. Sometimes, as they drift silently in their boats, they push an oar into the water and touch the submerged headstones of a flooded cemetery where their ancestors are buried.

In 1986, a consultant to the Easterville and Moose Lake bands said the people of Easterville had suffered "a profound trauma" as a result of the flooding and relocation. "There is certainly no evidence that the Chemawawin have recovered from the trauma of the move, the loss of their treaty lands and their resource base," the consulting firm of E.E. Hobbs and

Associates concluded. "Whatever wider benefits the Grand Rapids hydro project may have brought to Manitoba, for the Chemawawin Cree it has meant the destruction of their traditional way of life. Today the band has no viable economic base, few prospects for the future, a wide range of accelerating social problems and a diminished level of confidence and self-esteem, the inevitable outcome of the decline in the band's fortunes since the flooding."

Early in 1989, the Manitoba aboriginal justice inquiry heard the story of the hunters and fishermen who had lost their way of life. "We hope that when you come to write your report, you will cover not just the crimes of today but also the names of the guilty people who have done so much damage to our communities," Easterville chief Alpheus Brass told the judges.

The judges listened to a group of Easterville school children describe the effects of the flooding. "It hurts to see my community this way," said Waylon Munroe, a twelve-year-old student. "When people get bored they start to drink and to break into stores. Sometimes we fight each other. Teenagers commit suicide or try to escape by getting drunk, but I know that is not going to solve our problems."

The root cause of the Easterville tragedy was the government's refusal to let the band control its own future, Alpheus Brass told the inquiry. The lack of self-determination "was a poison poured into our community," he said.

Industrial development in native homelands is normally rationalized with the argument the projects are required for "the common good" or the "public interest." It is the same argument that is used to justify the expropriation of a farm or a cottage to make room for a highway or a transmission line. Yet, there are major differences between the expropriation of the property of an individual white landowner and the expropriation of traditional native hunting grounds.

First, a white landowner who loses his land can usually be adequately compensated with money. It is relatively simple for a farmer, for example, to use this money to purchase farmland somewhere else. A native community, in contrast, cannot maintain its way of life if its traditional homeland is gone. Historically, Indian bands have chosen to live in places where wildlife is abundant — but in the late 20th century it is often impossible for a dislocated Indian band to find a vacant site with adequate supplies of wildlife. The result, in many cases, is a life of welfare dependency.

Second, a white landowner has legal title to his land, which makes it easier for him to insist on compensation. But since reserve land is legally controlled by the federal government, Ottawa has the power to transfer Indian land to a provincial government or sell it to a corporation with only token compensation to the natives. In the past, this federal power has paved the way for quick transfers of Indian land to make room for hydro dams or other projects.

Third, a white landowner usually has experience in dealing with law-yers and bureaucrats, and he is aggressive in defending himself. But the residents of most native communities in remote areas of Canada are inexperienced in negotiating with governments. Language can also be a barrier.

Finally, white landowners will usually benefit from the industrial projects for which expropriations are conducted. By consuming the elec-tricity or minerals that are taken from the land, they are included in the "public interest" which profits from a development. But native people rarely gain any benefits from expropriations. They do not consume large amounts of electricity or other resources extracted from their land. The pattern is consistent: the power of expropriation is used against native people to the benefit of non-natives. Native people recognize that the "public interest" does not include them.

The Chipewyan Indians of northern Saskatchewan have been hunting and fishing on the wind-swept shores of the Wollaston Lake for hundreds of years. Their traditional hunting grounds stretched north to Hatchet Lake and the Cochrane River and almost to the present-day border of the Northwest Territories. Because of their isolation, their traditional econ-omy was undisturbed for centuries. And so the Chipewyan were unpre-pared for the sudden upheaval in their hunting territory in the early 1970s when the first uranium mine began its operations there on a massive scale.

Gulf Minerals Canada Ltd. had gained an exploration permit from the Saskatchewan government in 1968. Within a few months, the company discovered the Rabbit Lake ore body on the western side of Wollaston Lake, about thirty-five kilometres from the Chipewyan reserve, and began preparing the site for the start of production. No public hearings were held. Bulldozers roared, massive buildings sprang up, and roads and fences soon criss-crossed the hunting ground of the Chipewyan. In 1975, Gulf began extracting uranium from the site.

The Chipewyan, inexperienced in the strange world of provincial poli-tics, did not know how to fight the development. Instead they learned to endure the bulldozers and the fences, and they found new wilderness areas where they could hunt and trap. A few of them even found jobs at the mine.

Today, however, private companies and Crown corporations are plan-ning a dramatic expansion of the uranium industry in northern Saskatche-wan. Within a decade, there could be six mines on the western side of Wollaston Lake, bringing more turmoil into the lives of the native people who live at the Wollaston Lake reserve and the adjoining Métis commu-nity.

"Pretty near everybody doesn't like the mines," said Tony Dzeylion, a Chipewyan trapper whose trapline is just a few kilometres from the Rabbit Lake uranium mine. He watched his trapline fall into steep decline after the mine was constructed. "There's roads all over the place now. There's no trees because the bulldozers broke the trees. There's drilling all over the place. I've seen the beavers floating dead — they don't like the iron and the oil. There used to be lynx. Now there's no lynx at all. And the fox and the mink are gone too. If there's too strong uranium in the water, the fish are going to die."

The uranium mines of northern Saskatchewan have produced more that $2 billion in revenue and royalties for their corporate owners and the provincial government. Meanwhile, the Chipewyan and Métis people of Wollaston Lake have been suffering outbreaks of tuberculosis and hepatitis — a result of their deplorable housing conditions, severe overcrowding, lack of running water, and the decline of their traditional way of life. "Regardless of how productive they are at their traditional pursuits, they are finding it increasingly difficult to pursue this lifestyle in an area dotted by exploration camps, road building crews and mining activities," a consultant's report said in 1981.

Often there is a token attempt to consult native people before a major development proceeds, but in the case of northern Saskatchewan's uranium mines, consultation did not take place until after the fact. The Cluff Lake Board of Inquiry held public hearings into uranium mining in 1977 — two years after the Rabbit Lake mine began operating. The inquiry recommended the establishment of a nine-member Northern Development Board, including several native representatives, to regulate the uranium mines. In 1978, the provincial government established a "monitoring committee" to scrutinize the uranium industry. However, the Northern Development Board was never established, and the monitoring committee was abolished in 1982. Once more, in the face of new mining developments, the people of Wollaston Lake have been left with no official advocate and virtually no political power. In northern Saskatchewan, as in almost every region of Canada, the final authority has remained in the hands of non-native institutions.

Even the legislation that is supposed to protect the threatened land from environmental damage is of little help for the aboriginal people. The environment reports — thick volumes written in highly technical language — come pouring into the offices of the Chipewyan band councillors to satisfy the official requirements for environmental approval. But they pile up in stacks on the floor, unread, because the Indians cannot afford to hire a specialist to analyze the reports. In the history of Wollaston Lake band, only a handful of band members have ever completed high school, so for all practical purposes the environmental reports from the uranium companies are incomprehensible. And without money to hire experts, the Chipewyan cannot challenge the companies.

"The companies put a book on the table and away they go," says Jean Marie Tsannie, a Chipewyan band councillor at Wollaston Lake. "We don't have the education to go through all those environmental books. We can't do anything — they can start the mines without the permission of the people."

Individually, each uranium mine can satisfy the province's environmental requirements. But some experts are worried about the cumulative effect of six uranium mines in the same small corner of northeastern Saskatchewan. "Down the road, there could be a nasty surprise," says Sheila Swanson, a senior scientist at the Saskatchewan Research Council.

Already, testing has found high levels of ammonia in the effluent from the uranium mines in northern Saskatchewan. Ammonia can asphyxiate fish and damage their growth and reproduction, so there is a possibility that the ammonia could affect the fish in Wollaston Lake when the new mines are all operational. "One would suspect there could be problems," Swanson says.

But it is not only the fish that could be threatened by the environmental effects of the uranium mines. Dr. Dermot McLoughlin, a radiologist at Chedoke-McMaster Hospitals in Hamilton, Ontario, who has visited Wollaston to conduct preliminary work for the testing of wildlife in the region, believes that the moose and other animals in the area should be tested for radium and uranium. Some people have reported seeing moose drinking from the Rabbit Lake tailings pond, where uranium waste is dumped. "Because of the very high grade of uranium ore in that region, even if there are small amounts getting into the water and the wildlife it could eventually get into people's food," Dr. McLoughlin says.

Throughout the 1970s and 1980s, the native people of northern Saskatchewan voiced their opposition to the uranium mining. In 1977, for example, the chiefs of the northern Saskatchewan Indian bands told the Cluff Lake Board of Inquiry that they would oppose any expansion of the uranium mining industry until their hunting and fishing rights were guaranteed. Their opposition was ignored. By 1985, the people of Wollaston Lake had become so frustrated that they resorted to civil disobedience. They organized a blockade of traffic on the gravel road that links the Rabbit Lake uranium mine to its markets in the south. After blocking the road for three days, the Indians were faced with the threat of arrests by the RCMP. They ended the futile blockade and soon became resigned to their fate. Mary Ann Kkailther, a Chipewyan woman who helped organize the blockade in 1985, has given up her attempts to fight the uranium mining. "There's nothing we can do about it," she says.

When the uranium companies held meetings at Wollaston Lake in 1988 to describe their latest plans for new mines, the Chipewyan and Métis hardly bothered to register their opposition. "Everybody's heard the same thing over and over," says Terri Daniels, administrator for the Métis community at Wollaston Lake. "They knew it didn't matter what they said to the company. Sometimes I think that the companies think we're animals in the north. They don't ask the animals for permission, so why would they ask us?"

Once development has occurred, native people have no choice but to try to adapt to a new economy that has been imposed on them. Yet, it is difficult for Indians and Métis to gain employment in the mines or the hydro stations, which require highly trained staff for technical jobs. They are caught between the unfulfilled promise of the wage economy and the damaged traditions of the native subsistence economy.

Dennis Powder, a 27 year old Cree who lives at the Indian reserve of La Ronge in northern Saskatchewan, recalls the uranium- and gold-mining companies promising that half of their jobs would go to northerners. "I went to all the meetings for all the mines," he says. "I'm a welder, but I can't even get a job. They say I need more experience." In his bid for a mining job, Powder completed a one-year training course in welding. "All I got was congratulations," he says. Unable to find a job in the mines, he is now driving taxi in La Ronge for an average income of $23 per day. His brother took a six-week course in diamond drilling, but he too was unable to land a job in the mines.

Despite the promises made in the late 1970s, that at least 50 percent of their employees would be northerners, today the uranium companies acknowledge that only about 25 percent of the 1,500 employees at the existing uranium mines come from the north. And only about half of the northerners in the mines are native people. "People are asking what happened to all the jobs that were promised," says Mary Ann Kkailther.

For many people at Wollaston Lake, the cash income from a temporary job is attractive, but native people are usually given low-skill, low-status jobs and it isn't long before they return to the traplines and hunting grounds. William Hansen, a trapper at Wollaston Lake, worked at the Rabbit Lake uranium mine for several months in 1985. After a lifetime of moving freely on his trapline and on the lake, he found it difficult to adjust to the restrictions of a mining job. "We were in the same place all day. We're not used to that. It was very tough — shovelling rocks all day." Even the food was foreign to him. Accustomed to eating fish, he did not like the steak that was served to the miners. "A lot of us couldn't stand the grub. It was strange."

In 1981, a consultant's report commissioned by the federal and provincial governments to help plan the future of Wollaston Lake concluded that the native people "have not participated in the wealth generated by the mining activity." Seven years later, little had changed. A 1988 consultant's report said the employment created by the uranium mines had been "disappointing."

The havoc wreaked by hydro flooding and other forms of northern development has not been restricted to Indian and Métis communities in Manitoba and Saskatchewan. Throughout the 20th century, but especially after the Second World War, native communities have been assaulted by northern industrial development.

As non-native Canadians have sought greater prosperity by exploiting northern resources, aboriginal people have watched their traditional economy disintegrate in the wake of hydro dams, uranium mines, oil wells, logging operations, pulp mills, and mineral exploration. When the damage has come to public attention, it is usually presented as an isolated event, an unfortunate accidental side effect. Yet, the evidence shows it is neither an accident nor an isolated occurrence. And there is a clear pattern in almost every case — a pattern of official denials, lengthy delays in compensation, a weakened or destroyed native economy, mounting dependence on welfare, and a terrible toll of violence and anger in the affected communities.

In 1958, hydro dams flooded almost 1,600 hectares of the Whitedog reserve, damaging traplines at Whitedog and the nearby Grassy Narrows reserve in northern Ontario. Then, from 1962 to 1970, a pulp mill dumped 9,000 kilograms of mercury into the English-Wabigoon river system, poisoning the fish. Dozens of Ojibways at Grassy Narrows, who relied on fish as a staple in their diet, ended up with dangerous levels of mercury in their blood and symptoms of mercury poisoning such as tremors, tunnel vision, impaired hearing, and slow reflexes. For several years, politicians assured the Indians that their fears were exaggerated. The provincial government suppressed the results of the mercury tests. Warning signs were pulled down. But the Indians were eventually forced to stop fishing, and their commercial fishery was completely wiped out.

Alcoholism and crime, which had been minor problems at Grassy Narrows in the early 1960s, soon reached epidemic proportions. By the late 1970s, a survey found that two-thirds of the adults on the reserve were heavy drinkers, and half of the children in Grade 2 and Grade 3 were sniffing glue regularly. The suicide rate soared, and three-quarters of all deaths were caused by violence. Not until 1985 were the Ojibways compensated for the destruction of their way of life. The owners of the pulp mill agreed to pay $11.75 million in compensation, while the federal and provincial governments provided $4.92 million, and Ontario Hydro gave $1.5 million to the Whitedog band to compensate for the flooding.

The litany goes on. In 1952, the Carrier Indians of Cheslatta Lake in northern British Columbia saw their reserve disappear under water as a power dam was constructed to provide energy for a giant aluminum smelter at Kitamat. Their graveyards were flooded and the bones of their ancestors floated away. They lost fishing stations, trapping cabins and hunting trails. "Now my people depend on welfare and alcohol," the chief of the Cheslatta band said. A decade later, a dozen Sekani Indian villages in northern British Columbia were submerged under eighty metres of water when the W.A.C. Bennett Dam was constructed. Although the province made arrangements to help the white farmers who would be affected by the flooding, it ignored the 125 families in the Sekani band. A government report in 1962 quoted only one Indian. "By the time the water comes, I find some other place," the Indian was reported as saying. That seemed to satisfy the planners.

The federal government transferred the Sekani reserve into the possession of the province. The Sekani houses were burned down, the villages were bulldozed, and most of the Sekani were dumped into the territory of another Indian band. In the late 1960s, after several years of misery, the band migrated back to Ingenika Point, the only remaining habitable corner of their homeland. Because they did not officially have a reserve, the federal government gave them virtually nothing. They lived in one-room shacks made of logs salvaged from the hydro reservoir and carried buckets of water up a steep hill from the reservoir. The water soon became contaminated with salmonella. The Sekani became so desperate that they threatened to blockade the roads. "We're refugees on our own land," band chief Gordon Pierre said. In 1987, under pressure from the media, a provincial Cabinet minister flew to Ingenika Point and admitted that the living conditions were the worst he had ever seen in British Columbia. Eventually a morsel of compensation was provided — the houses were repaired and a deep well was drilled to provide drinking water.

In northern Quebec, a Cree band near the town of Chibougamau has been shunted from site to site since 1951 to make room for copper- and gold-mining and logging operations. The dislocation began when the Cree were uprooted because the sand on their island was required for the construction of a road to a mine. Every other piece of nearby land was owned by mining companies, so they had to move to a swampy point on a lake. In 1962, the band moved out of the swamp to a spot about two kilometres away and asked Ottawa to recognize this new site as a reserve. To save money, the department decided to merge the Cree with another band. They were told that they would not receive any federal assistance unless they joined the Mistassini band, about eighty kilometres from their traditional hunting grounds. They were warned that they should abandon their homes because their lake water was unfit to drink, and they were informed that a mining company had purchased and staked out the land on which the Cree had hunted for generations.

Seeing no alternative, the Cree reluctantly moved away. Their homes were torn down, and even the building where they held their religious services was demolished. They scattered into six isolated campsites, where they were regarded as squatters on provincial land. By 1986, they were living in one-room shacks with plastic sheets for roofs, and their children were falling ill because they had to drink contaminated water from stagnant lakes. Ottawa promised to establish a separate reserve for the band, but by 1988 the Cree were still landless because of delays in negotiations between the federal and provincial governments. "It's pathetic," a Quebec negotiator admitted. "They've been kicked around since the first prospector came in. Whenever they settled in at a lake, some prospector came in and found copper or gold."

For the past hundred years, governments have used the same strategies to deal with native people. James Waldram, an anthropologist who has studied hydro developments on Indian land in western Canada, points out the similarities between the Indian treaties of the 19th century and the wholesale removal of native communities to make way for resource development in the 20th century. The Indian treaties were negotiated in the 1870s to remove natives from the path of railways and agriculture, while the compensation agreements were negotiated in the 1960s and 1970s to move Indians away from modern industrial projects. Waldram points out that the 19th century treaties were often violated or disregarded by governments after they were signed. He warns that, in the same way, compensation agreements could be broken after the hydro projects have proceeded.

When the Indian treaties were signed a century ago, federal negotiators promised that the government would fulfill the treaties for "as long as the sun shines and the rivers flow." Ironically, as Waldram reminds us, many of the rivers are not flowing any more. They have been blocked by hydro dams.

The victimization of aboriginal people whose interests conflict with the goals of resource developers is not unique to Canada. The aboriginal people of Australia have seen their land expropriated for mining developments since the 1950s. In Norway, the Sami people chained themselves to a mountainside in 1980 in an effort to stop a hydro project that threatened to destroy their way of life. In the Amazon region of Brazil, thousands of indigenous people have suffered from oil exploration, hydro flooding, gold mining, logging, rubber extraction, sugar plantations, and cattle ranches. In the Philippines, hydro projects have jeopardized the ancestral lands of 85,00 tribal people. Large-scale logging operations in Malaysia have severely damaged the hunting and gathering economy of the nomadic Penan people.

In most countries, indigenous people were historically given the most barren and marginal land available. "These lands are now found to contain valuable minerals and resources," the World Council of Indigenous Peoples said in a report to an international conference in 1981. "Indigenous peoples are increasingly being seen as a nuisance to governments and transnational corporations. To promote corporate investments, the indigenous people must be removed or silenced to make room for mines, dams, plantations and factories. Indigenous nations today are suffering economically more than ever before and are not in control of sufficient resources to protect their interests and maintain their traditional forms of life." The world council summarized the problem in one brief sentence: "An Indian without land is a dead Indian."

Since the late 1960s, Canada's aboriginal people have begun to resist the destruction of their land. Their leaders have become better educated in the ways of the white man, and they have gained enough expertise and government funding to launch court challenges, hire consultants and lawyers, use the media, and organize blockades and demonstrations. As a result, governments have finally been forced to provide millions of dollars in compensation for hydro flooding. They have been compelled to establish training programs and job quotas to help native people get jobs at the sites of mining operations and hydro projects.

In 1966, when Manitoba announced plans for another massive hydro development in the north, native leaders were already aware of the damage inflicted on the Moose Lake and Chemawawin Cree by the Grand Rapids hydro dam. The new project, a diversion of water from the Churchill River into the Nelson River, would flood the homes of hundreds of Indians and Métis in the community of South Indian Lake. The project would also wreak havoc on the traplines of the Cree reserves of Nelson House, Cross Lake, Norway House, York Landing and Split Lake. The native people responded quickly by hiring lawyers to defend themselves. In the social climate of the late 1960s, public support for the Indians was widespread. Hearings were held in 1968 and 1969, and enormous crowds attended. A parade of native and non-native witnesses, ranging from scientists to homemakers, spoke out against the hydro project.

In 1969, the people of South Indian Lake went to court to seek an injunction to block the hydro project. The government immediately introduced legislation that would effectively kill the lawsuit and authorize the project to proceed. In the midst of the furious public debate that ensued, a provincial election was called, and the Conservative government was defeated by Ed Schreyer and the NDP. Ten weeks after his election, Schreyer announced that the project was being cancelled.

However, the premier soon unveiled a different version of the hydro project, in which half of the homes in South Indian Lake would still be flooded and hundreds of square kilometres of forests would be submerged. The NDP government became as obstinate as the previous government. Schreyer told the Indians that the project could not be halted because too much money had already been spent on it.

In 1972, the Indians went to court in another bid for an injunction, but they were severely hampered by a lack of money for legal expenses. When the province adopted a divide-and-conquer strategy, offering $1,000 in compensation to each trapper at South Indian Lake, many of the trappers, living in poverty, accepted the money. The lawsuit was abandoned in 1974. By then, the hydro project had been completed and the floodwaters were gradually rising. Fishing locations and traplines were destroyed. Most of the native residents were forced to abandon their homes and move to higher ground. As Schreyer himself admitted, the community of South Indian Lake was "slowly dying."

In 1979, a provincial inquiry concluded that the Manitoba government and Manitoba Hydro had adopted a stance of "confrontation, hostility and procrastination" as well as "a lack of frankness" in their dealings with the people of South Indian Lake and the other five native communities. The inquiry found that Manitoba Hydro knew it had no legal right to flood Indian lands. And it concluded that the provincial government had been in a conflict of interest because it had become an advocate for Manitoba Hydro at the expense of the native communities. South Indian Lake, which once had a thriving economy based on commercial fishing and trapping, today has an 85 percent unemployment rate. The floodwaters have brought mercury from the soil into the lake and the fish, posing a long-term threat to the health of the Indians, who now have high levels of mercury in their blood.

Unwilling to accept the position of victim, the five Cree bands affected by the hydro flooding had formed the Northern Flood Committee in 1974 to seek compensation. The Cree gained the support of the federal government and then negotiated a settlement with the province. The Northern Flood Agreement, signed in 1977, guaranteed compensation for damage to fishing and trapping. In the end, the bands obtained promises of compensation worth hundreds of millions of dollars from the provincial government, Manitoba Hydro, and the federal government. Their organized stand on the hydro project allowed the Cree bands to achieve a better outcome than the Moose Lake and Chemawawin Indians who suffered from the disastrous results of the Grand Rapids hydro project. But the bulk of the compensation was not provided until twenty years after the hydro project was launched and, as always, the money could never replace the land and the way of life that had been destroyed.

During the 1970s and 1980s, land claims became a crucial element in native resistance to industrial development as native people realized they needed a power base to help them control the pace of development in their traditional hunting and trapping territories. Successful land claims could give them the resources they needed to improve their economic future. The Cree of James Bay, led by Billy Diamond, and the Cree of Lubicon Lake, led by Bernard Ominayak, were among the most prominent of those who launched land claims to help protect their traditional territory. In both cases, the Cree bands were ignored in the early stages of industrial development. In both cases, they adopted a variety of imaginative tactics, eventually forcing government officials to pay attention to their demands.

The Cree of James Bay had never signed a treaty to surrender their land. Their hunting and trapping economy had survived for centuries because they saw the wilderness as a garden, a vast fertile land to be tended and harvested and protected. But in the spring of 1971, the Cree were shocked to hear a brief news item on the radio, announcing that the Quebec government was planning to flood their land to create the massive James Bay hydro project.

The government did not bother to consult the Cree. Indeed, the Cree were not even shown the details of the plan until nine months after the announcement. But the Indians were determined to resist the destruction of their territory. Led by Billy Diamond, the shrewd and aggressive chief of the Rupert House band, they organized their eight villages into a united front against Québec's $6 billion "Project of the Century." When the Cree were given a stack of government brochures on the project, they burned them in a gesture of defiance. To further dramatize their plight, Billy Diamond arranged for the Montréal media to tour the Cree villages. Then he turned to the courts, launching a legal challenge in a calculated bid to block the hydro project. Diamond told his followers that the Cree would "turn the white man's laws onto himself."

After seven months in the courtroom, the Cree emerged in 1973 with a temporary injunction to block the development. The injunction was suspended a week later, but the temporary Indian victory had shocked the provincial government into serious negotiations. By 1975, the Cree had negotiated Canada's first comprehensive land claim settlement. They received $150 million in compensation, along with extensive land rights for hunting, fishing, and trapping.

The Cree of Lubicon Lake, like the James Bay Cree, had never signed a treaty. They were overlooked when federal commissioners were negotiating treaties with Indian bands in northern Alberta in the 19th century. In 1939, after they petitioned for a reserve, Ottawa promised to provide one square mile for every band member. The reserve was officially approved and mapped in 1940, but the land was never transferred. Two years later, a federal official flew to Lubicon Lake and arbitrarily removed seventy-five people from the band's membership. Then he declared that the band was too small to warrant a reserve.

In 1980, dozens of oil companies began to bulldoze the band's hunting and trapping grounds. The forest was cleared to make room for pipelines, roads, oil wells, and trailer camps. One trapper woke up to find a road bulldozed to within three metres of his front door. Traplines were destroyed by slashing crews. Snare sticks and poles were chopped down. Trapping equipment was dug up and used as road markers. Indian trails were barred with "No Trespassing" signs. Hundreds of seismic lines were cut through the wilderness. "Hope this will not cause you any problems," one company said in a letter to a trapper at Lubicon Lake. The Indians were stunned. The oil companies and the provincial government were soon earning $1.3 million in daily revenue from four hundred oil wells in the Lubicon area. By 1989, an estimated $5 billion in oil revenue had been obtained from the Lubicon land.

Until the oil invasion, the Cree had maintained a life of self-sufficiency by hunting and trapping. Only 10 percent of the band members were on welfare. But in the early 1980s, as the oil companies roared into the Lubicon land, the native economy went into a steep decline. The Cree had taken an average of two hundred moose each year before the oil development, but they could find only three in 1984. The total value of hunting and trapping fell to one-tenth of its traditional levels. By the mid-1980s, an estimated 90 percent of the band members were dependent on welfare. There were twenty-two violent alcohol-related deaths among the Lubicon in an eighteen-month period. In 1987, more than forty band members fell sick with tuberculosis—a disease caused by overcrowding and inadequate diet.

After an investigation, The World Council of Churches warned of "genocidal consequences" among the Lubicon Cree. A federal investigator, former justice minister Davie Fulton, reached a similar conclusion. "Their need was urgent, their situation was desperate and worsening daily, and their efforts along the line of negotiation were producing no results," Fulton wrote in his report. But the Alberta government refused to halt the oil development or transfer any land to the Lubicon people.

Like their counterparts at James Bay, the Lubicon Cree tried to use the courts to protect their homeland. When they sought an injunction against the oil development, however, their request was denied. And when they used the courts to pursue their claim for a 234-square-kilometre reserve, they encountered nothing but delays.

The Lubicon band, on the brink of disintegration, declared that they would no longer recognize the authority of the Canadian court system. Led by their stubborn and tenacious chief, Bernard Ominayak, the Cree set up barricades on roads entering their land in October, 1988. For the first time, the oil companies were prevented from entering the area. Five days later, the RCMP tore down the barricades and arrested fifteen of the Indians. They also arrested a dozen Lubicon supporters, including two Quakers and two West Germans. But the blockade had succeeded in increasing the pressure on the provincial government. Two days later, the Alberta government agreed to provide a reserve of 204.5 square kilometres.

By early 1989, however, the Cree had reached a deadlock in their negotiations with the federal government for funding to help establish the new reserve. Oil wells continued to pump oil from the Lubicon land, and the fate of the Lubicon people was still uncertain.

As hydro dams and oil companies encroached on aboriginal land, native leaders realized that they could not gain control of their traditional homelands without filing land claims. The increasing number of land claims was also sparked by other factors: the arrival of a new generation of university-educated Indian leaders, the rise of native political consciousness, the cultural revival among aboriginal people, and their growing understanding of the differences between European and native concepts of land ownership. According to the native view, land must be controlled collectively by the community to ensure long-term stewardship of its resources. This view is incompatible with the European notion of private ownership, which often leads to short-term exploitation of the land.

In some cases, land claims were the result of honest disagreements over the interpretation of vaguely worded 19th-century treaties. Indian leaders tended to interpret the treaties broadly, looking at how the spirit of the treaties would have been understood by the chiefs who signed them. Government officials tended to take a narrow, legalistic view.

In many cases, oral promises were made to the Indians by the white officials who negotiated the treaties. These spoken promises were never recorded in the treaties, which had usually been drafted in advance. Yet, the Indian chiefs would never have signed the treaties without the oral promises. Land claims are a way of asserting the validity of those spoken promises, which were remembered by Indian elders and passed down by word of mouth to the current generation of Indian leaders.

Some treaties were arbitrarily extended to cover Indian bands that had never signed a treaty. In other cases, native people were simply cheated out of their land. Treaties were ignored, reserves were never created, and some white settlers stole land from Indian reserves. A number of treaty obligations, especially in the prairies, have never been fulfilled by the federal and provincial governments. Indian bands in Saskatchewan, for example, are still waiting for 1.1 million acres of land to which they are entitled under the treaties of the 1870s. In other cases, land grabs were authorized by official inquiries. In 1915, a commission in British Columbia allowed the government to take 47,000 acres of valuable land from Indian reserves and replace it with 87,000 acres of much poorer land. The Indians were not compensated for the land grab until the 1980s.

In some regions of Canada — including Labrador, Québec, British Columbia, and the Yukon and Northwest Territories — the land was never officially surrendered by treaty. The federal government, assuming that the Indians had no aboriginal title anywhere in those regions, allowed settlers and industrialists to invade the land. But the native people believe that they must have some legal right to the land they live on, since they have been using it since time immemorial. "Our interpretation is that we didn't give up any rights whatsoever," says William Erasmus, president of the Dene Nation in the Northwest Territories. "The only thing we did was that we acknowledged that other people were coming on to our land, so we had our hands open and said, 'Yes, we have lots of land; come on our land.' We didn't say, however, that we were going to give up our right to make our own decisions over our own lives, to have our institutions so that we can continue to survive as a unique people."

Indian land rights were confirmed as early as 1763, when King George III issued a Royal Proclamation declaring that the Indians should not be "molested or disturbed" in any of their homelands which were not specifically purchased by the Europeans. Unless the land was clearly ceded to the Europeans, it was reserved for the Indians.

A century later, the Nishga Indians of northwestern British Columbia were astonished to discover that the colonial government believed Indians had no right to their land. In the 1880s, the Nishgas took their case to the governor general, Lord Dufferin, who criticized the British Columbia government for suppressing their rights. But the province continued to insist that the Indian land rights had been extinguished. "We cannot understand it," Chief David McKay told a royal commission in 1887. "They have never bought it from us or our forefathers. They have never fought and conquered our people and taken the land that way ..."

The leaders of the Nishga Indians travelled to London in 1906 and 1909 to seek justice. They met Prime Minister Wilfred Laurier twice, and they created the Nishga Land Committee to lobby politicians and government officials. In 1915, the officials finally responded by giving the Nishgas a token land grant — an estimated 0.5 percent of the land in their former territory.

For fifty years, the Nishgas continued to fight. They submitted briefs to Parliament in 1926 and 1959. And in 1968 they hired Thomas Berger — a talented lawyer who later became head of the Mackenzie Valley Pipeline inquiry — to launch a court action affirming that the aboriginal title of the Nishgas had never been extinguished.

The political climate was poor. The weight of the federal government was tilted against the Indians. In a major policy paper in 1969, the government announced that aboriginal land claims and other aboriginal rights were too "general and undefined" to be accepted. Prime Minister Pierre Trudeau, who was strongly opposed to Indian land claims, summarized his government's position: "We say we won't recognize aboriginal rights. What can we do to redeem the past? If we think of restoring aboriginal rights to the Indians, well what about the French who were defeated at the Plains of Abraham? Shouldn't we restore rights to them?"

Nor was Trudeau willing to recognize Indian treaty rights. "We must be all equal under the laws and we must not sign treaties amongst ourselves," Trudeau said. "I don't think that we should encourage Indians to feel these treaties should last forever within Canada ... They should become Canadians as all other Canadians."

Indian leaders were fiercely opposed to Trudeau's vision of an assimilated culture. The Nishgas persisted with their court action and in 1973 the Supreme Court of Canada issued a landmark ruling. Six of the judges agreed that the ancestors of the Nishgas had aboriginal title to the land. Three of the six judges said that the aboriginal title had been extinguished in the 19th century, but the three remaining judges ruled that the aboriginal title continued to exist today.

The tie was broken by a seventh judge, who ruled against the Nishgas on a technicality. However, the Supreme Court of Canada decision had a dramatic effect on the federal government. For the first time, the concept of aboriginal title had been recognized by the highest court in the land. "Well, it looks like you've got more rights than I thought," Trudeau told an assembly of native groups.

Six months after the Supreme Court decision, the federal government revised its policy on aboriginal rights and announced that it was prepared to accept land claims from Indian groups in regions where no treaty had been signed. Since then, Canadian aboriginal groups have filed thirty-three comprehensive land claims in regions where native title had not previously been settled. In each case, they argued that they had never surrendered their land. Ottawa has begun negotiating six of these claims, and it has agreed to negotiate a further fifteen.

Several hundred Indian claims have been filed in Canada since the 1970s, but only a few dozen of these have been resolved. Most are specific claims, relating to an unfulfilled treaty promise or the loss of land from a reserve. Only one comprehensive claim — the James Bay land claim in northern Quebec — has produced a final settlement. In many cases, the government has simply rejected a claim outright — without explanation, without even producing a legal opinion to support the decision. When this happens, the courts are the only recourse for the Indian bands. Because of the time and money required for a court challenge, however, few Indian groups can afford to pursue this course of action.

Indian land claims are most strongly opposed in British Columbia, where for many decades the government refused to negotiate at all, arguing that settlements might bankrupt the province. Thomas Berger is among those who strongly criticized the B.C. policy. "Any government that, in the 1980s for political gain, seeks to turn the populace against the native people and their claims will occupy a lonely and unforgiving place in the history of our country," he wrote. In 1990, the British Columbia government finally promised to negotiate land claims, but its commitment to fulfill that promise was still unclear.

In the Northwest Territories, the federal government signed an agreement-in-principle with the leaders of 15,000 Dene and Métis people. The agreement would have provided about $500-million and about 180,000 square kilometres of land in a settlement of the Dene-Métis comprehensive land claim. But the deal collapsed in 1990 when the Dene and Métis refused to ratify it. They were concerned about a clause in the agreement which would have extinguished their aboriginal title to the land.

Another agreement-in-principle is still alive in the Yukon, where about 6,500 Indians negotiated a settlement that would give them $232-million and about 41,000 square kilometres of land — about nine percent of the total area of the Yukon. The Indians are guaranteed representation on a wildlife management board and a land-use planning board, and they would also gain rights to oil, gas, and other minerals in most of the land. It took fifteen years of negotiations to produce the agreement between the government and the thirteen Indian bands in the Yukon. By early 1991, the deal was not yet ratified.

The Bear Island Indians of Lake Temagami in northern Ontario have been less fortunate. Although they have never signed a treaty to surrender their land, in 1850, government negotiators persuaded an Indian leader from southern Ontario to sign a treaty on behalf of the band. For the equivalent of $25, the Bear Island Indians lost their land without even participating in or being aware of the surrender. The Indians ended up with a tiny reserve of only 2.5 square kilometres.

The federal government offered to give the Indians a much larger reserve in 1885, but the Ontario government refused to provide the land for the reserve. The Indians believe the province was already planning to sell the land to logging and mining companies.

The eight hundred members of the Bear Island band have been trying to negotiate a land claim settlement for more than 110 years. While the land claim was virtually ignored, an estimated $2.7 billion worth of timber and minerals have been extracted from the Indian homeland. In 1973, the band took drastic action, issuing a legal caution on 10,000 square kilometres of forests and lakes in its territory. The caution, based on the Indian claim of ownership of the land, effectively froze many kinds of development in the area. The Ontario government took the band to court, and in 1984 the Supreme Court of Ontario ruled against the Indians. The case was appealed. In early 1989, the Ontario Court of Appeal dealt a crushing blow to the concept of aboriginal rights. The court ruled that a government could extinguish aboriginal land title merely by declaring it extinguished — even if a proper treaty was never signed — and that the Crown could legally take Indian land without communicating with the Indians in the area. It also ruled that the Royal Proclamation of 1763 — with all its guarantees for Indian rights — was null and void as a result of another law, passed in 1774.

The Supreme Court of Canada will ultimately decide the fate of the question of aboriginal land title in Canada. Until then, a cloud of uncertainty lingers over the question of aboriginal land title in Canada and a growing number of native leaders are beginning to lose faith in the court system — the same system that was employed so skilfully by Billy Diamond and other leaders in the 1970s.

The recognition of native claims to a larger land base is crucial to the future of aboriginal self-government and economic development. Without land claim settlements, Indian reserves will be limited to their present size — too small, in most cases, to permit any realistic plan for economic development — and self-government will be a mere facade. "Without land, without resources, there is no self-sufficiency; and without being self-sufficient, there is no Indian government," the Association of Iroquois and Allied Nations said in 1983.

In the Cree villages of northern Québec, the James Bay Agreement was just the beginning of the fight for economic independence. In 1984, the James Bay Cree persuaded Ottawa to pass legislation giving them an unprecedented form of self-government. As the first Indians to be exempted from the Indian Act, they gained control of the planning and administration of almost all government services in the region, including health programs, economic development corporations, housing, education, and water and sewage services.

However, the federal government still retains some control over the annual flow of funds to the James Bay Cree. Throughout the 1970s and 1980s, they have been forced to fight for the money to which they are legally entitled, while funds have been delayed or withheld because of federal Treasury Board decisions. It took a deadly epidemic of gastroenteritis in 1980 to persuade Ottawa to begin providing the money required for proper water and sanitation services.

Even so, the James Bay and Northern Québec Agreement remains a model for comprehensive land claims and self-government. No other Indian band or tribal group in Canada has gained such a level of control over its own affairs.

In recent years, the federal government has backed away from the James Bay model of self-government, preferring to give Indian bands a set of diluted powers similar to those of municipalities. In 1986, for instance, the Sechelt band in British Columbia was given a mild form of municipal self-government. Other bands have been given "alternative funding arrangements" — a pale imitation of the principle of self-government.

In 1983, a special committee to the House of Commons recommended an amendment to the Constitution to entrench the right of Indians to self-government and urged Ottawa to settle Indian land claims as soon as possible. "Prospects for economic development would improve if the land base were expanded, claims were settled, and the control of resources on Indian lands were transferred to Indian First Nations," the committee said. "The assets now controlled by Indian governments are not sufficient to support those governments."

The committee also concluded that the federal Indian Act is "antiquated" and "completely unacceptable as a blueprint for the future." Oscar Lathlin, chief of The Pas band in northwestern Manitoba, agrees. He has watched the Indian Act cause frustrating delays in his band's business plans. When the band tried to lease parts of its land to car dealers and gas stations, almost two years passed before all the required approvals were received from the Indian Affairs minister. Because Indian bands are not considered to be legal entities, Lathlin had to get a loan guarantee from the Indian Affairs minister whenever his band wanted to borrow from a bank. "It's a heck of a way to do business," says Lathlin. "Compared to the average non-Indian businessman, we're at a disadvantage."

Because of the Indian Act and the restrictions it imposes, Indian bands are hampered by a great deal of legal uncertainty whenever they try to sign contracts, borrow money, purchase land, or launch lawsuits. They cannot even acquire legal title to the land they purchase. "The uncertainty permeates all dealings between bands and employees, suppliers, contractors, financial institutions and governments," a Halifax law firm said in a 1982 report. Even the Indian Affairs Department has admitted that the Indian Act "(o)ften leads to interminable technical complications to accomplish the simplest act."

Oscar Lathlin has helped his band to grow from a $250,000 annual budget in 1968 to a $17 million budget today, and his band controls $21 million in assets, including a 21,000-square-metre shopping mall. But he knows his people could be further advanced if they were not restricted by the regulations of the Indian Affairs Department. "It controls too much," the chief says. "The minister has such sweeping powers over Indian land and Indian people from the day you're born to the day you die." The Indian Affairs Department should be dissolved, he says, and native-controlled financial institutions should be created to help Indians gain access to capital.

Economic power, once obtained, can give Indian bands enough clout to protect their traditional economy from the ravages of industry. Lathlin is already planning for the day when his band will purchase 10 or 15 percent of the logging company in The Pas. That would allow the band to influence the company's cutting areas, in order to ensure the survival of hunting grounds and traplines. Until the Indians own a stake in the logging company, the loggers will simply ignore the hunters and trappers.

In his efforts to combine a modern economy with the traditional hunting and trapping economy of his people, Oscar Lathlin is challenging the conventional wisdom about northern economic development, which assumes that the native economy is doomed to failure. The Cluff Lake Board of Inquiry, which approved the expansion of northern Saskatchewan's uranium industry in 1977, was one of many official bodies that accepted the conventional view. "The intrusion of the twentieth century into all parts of Canada is inexorable and the accompanying force of industrial expansion in its diverse and sometimes subtle forms is irresistible," the inquiry concluded. "The important fact remains: the northerners are clearly moving toward a lifestyle which entails technology, modernity and industrialization."

Some observers, however, have questioned the value of this new lifestyle. Thomas Berger, who headed the Mackenzie Valley Pipeline Inquiry from 1974 to 1977, travelled to every village and settlement in the Mackenzie Valley and Western Arctic and listened to 283 days of testimony from 1,700 witnesses. Berger concluded that the traditional native economy must be preserved and strengthened — even if that means a delay for the inexorable march of resource exploitation in the north. "We have always undervalued northern native culture," he wrote, "and we have tended to underestimate the vitality of the native economy. We have been committed to the view that the economic future of the North lay in large-scale industrial development. We have generated, especially in northern business, an atmosphere of expectancy about industrial development. Although there has always been a native economy in the North, based on the bush and the barrens, we have for a decade or more followed policies by which it could only be weakened or even destroyed. We have assumed that the native economy is moribund and that the native people should therefore be induced to enter industrial wage employment."

The pipeline companies had told the Berger inquiry that hunting and fishing were relatively insignificant for northern native people. Yet, Berger's own eyes told him that the companies were wrong. Everywhere he travelled, he saw native people eating moose, caribou, muskox, dried whale meat, whitefish, trout, and arctic char. Testimony by native people and other experts confirmed that this food was still an important part of the diet and lifestyle of native northerners.

In their close relationship with the land, native people can be compared to Canada's family farmers, who have been stewards of the land for generations. The federal and provincial governments have always recognized the value of family farming: they have introduced dozens of programs to support agriculture and they have subsidized farmers and protected them from low prices and droughts. Commercial fishermen on the Atlantic and Pacific coasts have been supported by government programs and by extended unemployment insurance benefits in the off-season. Yet, native hunters and trappers have been told to abandon their lifestyle and make way for industrial development.

Berger warned that the unfettered growth of industrial development and resource exploitation in northern Canada will lead to unemployment, welfare dependency, alcoholism, sickness, crime, and violence among native people. "All of the evidence indicates that an increase in industrial wage employment and disposable income among the native people in the North brings with it a dramatic increase in violent deaths and injuries. I am persuaded that the incidence of these disorders is closely bound up with the rapid expansion of the industrial system and with its persistent intrusion into every part of the native people's lives."

He also concluded that the economic benefits of northern resource development are less than what some people assume. "The fact is that large-scale projects based on non-renewable resources have rarely provided permanent employment for any significant number of native people. There is abundant reason to doubt that a pipeline would provide meaningful and ongoing employment to many native people... The extension of the industrial system creates unemployment as well as employment."

Berger recommended a ten-year moratorium on the construction of the Mackenzie Valley pipeline. He also recommended steps to strengthen and modernize the traditional native economy. "Productivity must be improved and the native economy must be expanded so that more people can be gainfully employed in it," he said. The preservation and modernization of the native community would be cheaper than the massive cost of industrial development in the North. "Huge subsidies of the magnitude provided to the non-renewable resource industries would not be necessary."

Even before the Berger inquiry, northern native leaders such as George Erasmus of the Dene Nation were advocating steps to strengthen and modernize the traditional native economy. When the concept has been given a chance, it has worked. The government of the Northwest Territories, for example, has provided funds for outpost camps to support hunters and trappers. It has also helped pay the cost of airplane transportation for native people who participate in the traditional community hunt each fall.

In the past, Dene hunters from communities near Great Slave Lake would have to canoe hundreds of kilometres and trudge along dozens of portages to meet the caribou that migrate south in August and September. Then they would have to haul the meat back home. Now, with the air transportation subsidies, they can find the caribou more quickly and carry more meat back to their communities.

In northern Saskatchewan and Manitoba, as in other regions of Canada, provincial governments have invested huge sums of money in subsidies and tax breaks for uranium mines, hydro projects, and other forms of industrial development. Even a fraction of that money, invested in programs to support the traditional economy, could strengthen native communities immeasurably. "If any government paid as much attention to the traditional economy as they paid to these boom-town phenomenons—the mining exploration, the oil exploration — and if the same tax advantages and benefits went into it, we believe it would be very successful," Erasmus says.

Native leaders have lobbied for other policy changes to help support the traditional subsistence economy. For example, they have persuaded some oil and mining companies to give their employees rotating job duties and seasonal time off so that they can take part in hunting and trapping. "It's been reasonably successful," says Erasmus. "People can spend more time on the land, instead of this nonsense of only getting two weeks a year. Indigenous people can live in their own communities and follow their traditional economy and then get back into the organized work force for perhaps six weeks at a time."

The strengthening and modernization of the traditional native economy is becoming more crucial as new threats emerge. In the 1980s, a concerted effort by anti-trapping activists has led to a decline in European demand for furs, weakening the price of most furs caught by Canada's native people and sharply reducing their incomes. "Enthusiasts for animal rights have now joined the missionaries, bureaucrats and entrepreneurs in their rejection of the subsistence economy," Thomas Berger wrote in 1988.

There are other threats too. Sports hunters have invaded the traditional hunting grounds of Indian bands in many regions of Canada. Logging and mining roads have allowed sports hunters to drive their vehicles deep into native hunting territories. A study by Hugh Brody found that the sports hunters killed 3,625 moose in the hunting territories of seven Indian bands in northeastern British Columbia in a single year. In some of the traditional native hunting grounds, sports hunters have killed many more animals than the Indians have.

In Labrador, the Innu people are deafened by the supersonic roar of bombing practice runs and low-level training flights of military jets from a NATO base at Goose Bay. The intense noise has disrupted the migratory patterns of caribou, thus endangering the traditional Innu hunting economy. Geese, fish, and fur-bearing animals are also affected by the aircraft.

Provincial wildlife regulations are another threat to the native economy. A number of court decisions have upheld the right of Indians to hunt and fish freely , but the provinces have continued to enforce strict limits. Indians have traditionally hunted to build up a food supply for the winter and to provide food for children and elderly people who cannot hunt. Yet, they are charged when they exceed an arbitrary limit of fish or animals. Indian hunters in northern Manitoba, for example, have been fined and had their guns seized when they exceeded the provincial bag limit of six ducks a day. Others have been charged with hunting out of season, despite their treaty guarantees. Native fishermen have seen their nets seized because they did not obtain the required licences and permits. On the salmon rivers of British Columbia, Indians have come to blows with provincial fisheries officers who are determined to enforce fishing limits.

Industrial development, however, still presents the biggest danger to the aboriginal economy. But native leaders do not pretend that they can halt development forever. They simply want to achieve a balance between the native economy and the industrial economy.

The Cree of James Bay have accomplished the balancing act by purchasing an airline and establishing a canoe-building factory on their land to supplement their still-active economy of hunting and trapping. Hunters and trappers at James Bay are also supported by an Income Security Program, which the Québec government agreed to establish as part of the settlement with the James Bay Cree. The program guarantees a minimum cash income for full-time hunters and their families and an extra allowance for every day the hunter spends in the bush. The program pays for the cost of airplanes to fly the Cree hunters and trappers into remote areas where wildlife is plentiful. And it encourages them to remain active in the native economy even if there is a cyclical downturn in the supply of animals and birds.

Every other hydro project in Canada has led to a decline in the hunting by Indian people, but in northern Québec the Income Security Program has succeeded in strengthening the native economy. By 1981, there were nine hundred full-time Cree hunters at James Bay, compared to a total of fewer than six hundred in 1971. While every other hydro project in Canada has led to an increase in welfare dependency, the James Bay welfare caseload was actually reduced by two-thirds from 1971 to 1981. The Income Security Program is a model for other Indian communities across Canada. "Compared to unemployment or welfare, it is not only cheaper, but it enables people to remain productive, doing something that gives them a sense of achievement and personal worth," observed Richard Salisbury, an anthropologist who has studied the James Bay Cree.

The Cree of Lubicon Lake have a similar plan. They are proposing the creation of a $500,000 trust fund to support the income of their trappers, along with a wildlife management system to ensure the stability of the moose population. At the same time, they are planning an economic development project that would include a cattle farm, a vocational training centre, an eight-unit motel, a gravel pit and gravel-crushing operation, a concrete-making plant, a berry farm, a slaughter house, a gas station, and a grocery store. They are also hoping to establish a capital fund to provide money for the start-up of new businesses by Lubicon band members.

The Lubicon people are aiming to establish a diversified economy. "We'd like to keep hunting forever, if possible," Chief Bernard Ominayak says. "We're trying to preserve it as much as we can. But we're trying to balance everything, so that we're not dependent on just one thing."

To strike that difficult balance between the traditional economy and the modern economy, Canada's native people need to control their own land. In their vision of the future, the land is still the central element — just as it has been central to their way of life for centuries. Without a land base, they will be unable to modernize their economy, and their traditional way of life will be doomed. Land will always be the key to survival for aboriginal people. "Being an Indian means ... saying the land is an old friend your father knew, your grandfather knew, indeed your people have always known," Richard Nerysoo of Fort McPherson told the Berger inquiry. "If our land is destroyed, we too are destroyed. If your people ever take our land, you will be taking our life."

Child Custody Law and the Invisibility of Women's Work

Susan B. Boyd

Recent feminist approaches to law have moved beyond the earlier stance that identified the ways law oppressed women or reproduced the conditions of women's oppression. Rather than dismissing law as hopelessly "male," many feminists now argue that we must take careful account of the ways in which the legal system presents an avenue for feminist struggle and opportunities for women's resistance to domination in law and society (Brophy and Smart, 1985). This approach calls for a theoretical framework which takes a detailed and historically specific approach to analyzing the ways law has affected the status of women in different periods. In carefully examining the practical and ideological effects of law reform, we can approach an understanding of the utility and contradictions of various legal developments (Olsen, 1984).

One way to gain such an understanding is to try to determine which issues concerning women are best dealt with through gender neutral approaches often articulated through "rights" discourse, and which issues require approaches that recognize substantive differences between men and women. It is important to pay careful attention to the ideological components of various legal developments which are related to the material underpinnings of both women's subordination and law. Upon careful scrutiny, legal changes that seem to promote women's equality (for instance, joint custody, which supposedly enhances shared parenting) may not be as beneficial as one might think.

In this paper, I explore the difficulties for women inherent in current debates over joint custody and fathers' rights, and try to clarify the background and implications of the debates. I first examine the material bases, and ideological and practical aspects, of developments in child custody law in the 20th century, leading up to such recent phenomena as joint custody and the friendly parent rule. I conclude with suggestions for future law reform. I attempt to highlight the ways in which women's labour, particularly domestic labour around childcare, is structured and has been perceived in our society. I emphasize the role which law has played in this process, in an effort to untangle the current debates.

I focus on legal aspects of child custody rather than psychological literature and empirical studies about what works best for children and parents, because law has become an important reference point for child custody discussions and determinations, even though only a minority of cases reaches the courts.[1] The reported cases upon which I rely reflect only a minority of custody cases actually contested, and even then, only those ultimately reaching court and then attracting the attention of the case report editors. Despite the fact that they are not a statistically relevant sample, they do give us a picture of how judges evaluate male and female parenting behaviour, and they constitute the precedents most often referred to by practising lawyers, other judges, and possibly mediators. The legal system has an important status and represents a powerful ideological force in society, being "one of several ideological forms which combine to form and reproduce the ideological kernel of class hegemony" (Sumner, 1979:9). Thus, when social issues are taken up within the context of legal discourse, as child custody has been, the messages sent out by the law on that topic are imbued with special force. Due to the powerful ideology within the form of law itself — its mystical and mysterious quality — legal rules are particularly suited to telling us "what the world ought to be like, on the basis of illusions about what it is like" (Sumner, 1979:275-276).

Law represents more than a distillation of societal values or majoritarian power. It embodies not simply bourgeois economic ideology or even ideologies of fractions of the bourgeoisie or other classes, but also, to some extent, ideologies of minority groups and pressure groups, and various types of ideologies, such as ideologies of the family (Sumner, 1979:269). These ideologies may or may not reinforce ideologies related more directly to class. Feminists have extended this analysis of law as an arena of ideological formation and struggle in order to examine law's role in reproducing ideologies supportive of patriarchal relations. They have also argued, based on Antonio Gramsci's concept of counter-hegemony, that women's legal struggles are not futile or marginal to efforts to alter gender relations, but may be progressive in a dialectical fashion: "they may achieve some concrete improvements at the same time that they demonstrate experientially the partiality of law, its costs and delays, its mystified procedures and occasional flares of sheer brutality" (O'Brien and McIntyre, 1986:75). Women's struggles will, however, be structured and limited ultimately by relations of domination, such as patriarchal relations, and resistance to those relations (Macdonell, 1986). We can therefore examine family law with a view to discovering its connection with material realities of production and reproduction (Ursel, 1986) and the related struggles and development of ideologies within it.

The analysis in this paper is, however, limited to the extent that the familial ideologies reinforced by child custody law may be relevant primarily to the expectations held of white women. As Marlee Kline (1989) recently pointed out, ideologies of womanhood and motherhood concerning women of colour may well be quite different from those concerning white women. It is also possible that, whereas the law of child custody is of primary concern to white women in Canada, the law of child welfare may more fundamentally affect the relationships of First Nations women with their children.[2] Further work certainly remains to be done on the intersection between dominant white ideologies and other sets of ideological assumptions, the impact of these ideologies upon differing familial forms in Canada, and the relationship between child custody and child welfare laws.

Ideologies in Child Custody Law

In child custody law, feminists have reached a difficult conjuncture. In most modern custody legislation, mothers have lost any advantage they had under prior laws. Legal "reform" has been in the spirit of liberal feminist efforts in the 1970s to eliminate gender stereotyping in the legal system (Fineman, 1983), and has drawn on feminist criticisms of the problematic assumptions and ideologies concerning womanhood and parenting. As the reforms of the 1970s and early 1980s occurred, there quickly developed a "fathers' rights" movement — male-dominated groups that incorporate the rhetoric of feminist concerns about exclusive female responsibility for parenting in claiming "equal" paternal legal rights, often without arguing for equal responsibilities (Dawson, 1988; Lamb, 1987; NAWL, 1988). Fathers' rights movement claims fit well with the new child custody legislation, which makes no assumptions about which parent should receive custody, but obscures the problems that feminists increasingly identify with the new gender neutrality in child custody law. While women remain primarily responsible for domestic labour, including childcare, we confront a legal system which has difficulty in accommodating this gender specific fact. Judges tend to underrate the primary caregiving done by women and to overvalue any caregiving done by fathers.

I have argued elsewhere that this phenomenon results from an interplay between gender specific ideologies of the family that involve differential expectations of men and women as parents, and seemingly "gender neutral" ideologies implicated in the principles and discourses of equal rights that now prevail in family law (Boyd, 1989b). Under gender specific ideologies of the family, such as the ideology of motherhood, a higher standard of parenting is expected of women, so that if they work outside the home or otherwise deviate from that standard, they may diminish their motherly image. Expectations of fathers, on the other hand, are less onerous, so that any childcare done by fathers appears to be exemplary, even if it is less than that done by mothers.[3] In combination with these more traditional familial ideologies, the newer principle of equality increasingly prevalent in Canada with the *Charter of Rights and Freedoms* tends to obscure gender specific realities of family life. This can result in custody going to fathers, even if they have not been primary caregivers of children in the past. Female responsibility for the nurturing of children is devalued and rendered invisible by this process.

There has been a fairly rapid transition in child custody law from a "tender years" doctrine, which favoured those mothers who conformed to the expectations of middle-class womanly behaviour such as stay-at-home mothering, to a "best interests of the child" principle, which leaves the courts without guidelines in custody determinations (Fineman, 1988). The best interests principle used to be informed by the tender years presumption, but now is increasingly shaped by the vague equal rights discourse, within which factors such as the typical father's greater economic stability may influence judges in the granting of custody more than parent-child relations (Polikoff, 1983; Trudrung-Taylor, 1986). The transition to equal rights discourse in the area of child custody has paralleled changes in women's work patterns during the 20th century.

Changes in Women's Work and Child Custody Laws
Before 1970
Although urbanization and industrialization were on the rise at the end of the 19th century, Canada remained a predominantly rural society with two-thirds of its population living in rural areas (Prentice, 1988: 108-109). The majority of women lived in household units which produced many of the products needed for survival; at that time the family was predominantly a production rather than a consumption unit (Armstrong, 1987). Both husbands and wives worked hard to produce the family's requirements for survival, but women retained the extra load of bearing and rearing children. As children became old enough to work, fathers assumed a greater role in rearing and educating them, and there was often extra help in the form of relatives or a hired "girl" living in the household. "Nevertheless, women still bore primary responsibility for infants and for the children not well enough to work" (Armstrong, 1987:360-61).

Around this time, the legal system largely continued to favour paternal custody of legitimate children in those few custody cases that went to court, as it had done throughout the 19th century. There was, however, an increasing tendency to allow mothers to claim legal custody of *young* children, if the father was manifestly delinquent in some way (Backhouse, 1981). This tendency reflected the economic value which children held for fathers as they grew older, and the predominant role of mothers in the earlier years of children's lives. It also reflected an ongoing transition, connected with industrialization and urbanization, toward a perceived gulf between the personal domestic world of women and family and the developing public world from which women and children began to be excluded (Prentice, 1988:83). This transition was accompanied by an intensification of women's roles as mothers (Prentice, 1988:166).

By the 1920s, the tender years doctrine, upon which custody awards of young children to mothers were based, grew to take the form of a judicial preference for mothers, provided the woman seeking custody conformed to expectations of female purity. Mothers gained equal entitlement to custody in Ontario around 1925 (Abella, 1981), thereby diminishing more completely the previously absolute paternal legal authority over the family. This trend deepened when, in a 1933 Ontario case, the Court of Appeal stated that as a general rule children under seven years of age needed their mothers more than their fathers (Re Orr).

This change from a norm of paternal custody to a norm of equal parental rights qualified by a judicial assumption that the welfare of young children generally indicated maternal custody corresponded to pre-WWII changes in the family, as the family farm diminished even further and the demand grew for workers in urban industry (Armstrong, 1987:362).[4] The family had become smaller since the mid-19th century (Prentice, 1988:166) and now was less a productive unit and more exclusively a reproductive and consumption unit. As urbanization and industrialization opened up new job opportunities for women in various areas of Canada, fewer married women than men or single women sought employment, because they were tied to the household by childcare responsibilities. Women continued to do domestic labour in the home, some of which was arguably relieved by modern household conveniences (although standards were also becoming higher at this time) (Prentice, 1988:246). They also earned some cash income by taking in laundry, sewing or boarders, jobs which were compatible with childcare (Armstrong, 1987:363; Prentice, 1988:121-22). Since before WWI, mothers had become increasingly isolated in the home and more exclusively responsible for the happiness of the family and for childcare, with most men at work outside the home, older children at school, few accessible and affordable childcare facilities, and female domestics increasingly rejecting household service for work in industry (Armstrong, 1987:364-65). Childcare responsibilities also intensified at this time, as childcare became a more time-consuming, "scientific," and scrutinized activity (Prentice, 1988:217, 247-48). The tender years doctrine made some sense in this context and, significantly, did not prohibit fathers from obtaining custody when children grew older and were more independent.[5] The ideological implications of the tender years doctrine, however, were more complex, especially for those women who received its benefit at the expense of becoming increasingly confined in isolated households.

Although the divorce rate more than doubled between 1921 and 1936, relatively few divorces occurred in this period (Statistics Canada, 1983:59). Although companionate marriage was on the rise at this time, somewhat improving the legal status of women with regard to marriage and divorce, nonetheless women were encouraged to see themselves as carrying a special "duty, honour, and privilege to preserve family stability" (Prentice, 1988:255). For those mothers who did become involved in divorce, standards for their conduct were strict if they wished to obtain custody of their young children. Mothers were likely to obtain custody in those cases contested by husbands, but only if they had not been "at fault" in the marriage — if they had not deserted their family, committed adultery, or engaged in other "immoral" conduct. The tender years doctrine thus empowered women in some sense, but also restricted their choices in a way that reinforced their roles as domestic labourers (Olsen, 1984:15-16).

During the post-WWII years, some women who had entered the work-force during the "emergency" situation of the war, and especially younger women, retreated to the home in the wake of incentive programs and strong messages concerning motherhood (Prentice 1988:303-311). The tender years doctrine was part of that message, being a presumption that mothers should obtain custody on the basis of some *biological* or *natural* link with young children, and in particular daughters. It was more than a straightforward, common sense recognition that mothers are primary caregivers of children and so ought to receive custody, as the following quote from the 1955 Ontario Court of Appeal case, *Bell v. Bell*, shows:

> No father, no matter how well-intentioned or how solici-
> tous for the welfare of such a child, can take the full place
> of the mother. Instinctively, a little child, particularly a
> little girl, turns to her mother in her troubles, her doubts,
> and her fears. In that respect, nature seems to assert itself.
> The feminine touch means so much to a little girl; the
> frills and flounces and the ribbons in the matter of dress;
> the whispered consultations and confidences on matters
> which to the child's mind should only be discussed with
> Mother, the tender care, the soothing voice; all these
> things have a tremendous effect on the emotions of the
> child. This is nothing new; it is as old as human nature ...
> (344).

The tender years rule applied only to young children, implying that after age seven children required very little care, or at least different care, which could be orchestrated even by fathers. Male children in particular were viewed as needing increasingly little care by mothers. Even in 1977, after the tender years rule became a rule of "common sense" only,[6] judges continued to interpret it in this way: "Particularly in the case of a boy, the need for the mother lessens as the need for the father grows" (*Veighey*).

After the post-war period, various developments led to more and more women attempting to enter the work-force (Armstrong, 1987:368-89), although not all succeeded, and those who did often settled for part-time work and work in job ghettos. Women's labour force participation rates have doubled since the end of WWII, and today a majority of women want and need full-time work due to such factors as male unemployment, the failure of wages to keep pace with prices, the decreased economic saving of making things in the household to substitute for goods purchased in the market, and women's higher education. The rising rate of women in the labour force includes married women and women with children (Statistics Canada, 1986:4-5).[7]

Slow and often contradictory changes in child custody law away from presumptions favouring mothers and towards a more "neutral" principle of the best interests of the child occurred alongside these economic developments, and in conjunction with a rising divorce rate. Although the divorce rate held fairly constant during the 1950s, when the tender years doctrine reigned supreme, it began to rise again during the mid- and late 1960s, when the tender years doctrine still heavily influenced child custody law. The divorce rate soared during the 1970s (Statistics Canada, 1983:59), meaning that many more custody disputes occurred, although still only a minority were decided in court.

The 1970s

In the early 1970s, the Supreme Court of Canada acknowledged that the tender years doctrine was "merely" a rule of common sense rather than a legal presumption. This did not mean that the assumptions surrounding the tender years doctrine ceased to operate. Men who *petitioned* for divorce during the 1970s, however, had a 43 percent chance of being awarded custody (Statistics Canada, 1983). This is not to obscure the fact that women retained custody of children in 85.6 percent of divorces surveyed, but only to point out that in the minority of cases where fathers seemed to pursue custody sincerely (men were petitioners in approximately one-third of the cases), they had a better chance of obtaining it than is sometimes claimed. Fathers were not as prejudiced by child custody law in the 1970s as fathers' rights groups often argue; ideologies of the family were sufficiently strong that few fathers sincerely wanted custody (Weitzman, 1985:244). Also, when mothers were left with custody, "the father could be considered as the parent who fares better" at least in terms of time and expense (Statistics Canada, 1983:224), so that economic incentives for fathers to claim custody were not present.[8] Pressures on mothers to retain custody of children and pressures against fathers assuming the heavy responsibilities of childcare militated against paternal custody for most divorcing couples. More fathers did start to participate in childcare, however, and more attention was paid to them by the media and by the courts.

The cases reaching court in the 1970s demonstrated that ideologies of the family remained strong. The tender years doctrine, with its contradictory implications for women, prevailed in one form or another. Women who were employed, adulterous, or the instigators of marital breakdown were often viewed dimly by judges (Bradbrook, 1971). Fathers who tried to get involved with childcare, on the other hand, were often applauded. In the 1976 *Bolton* case, Justice McQuaid of the Prince Edward Island Supreme Court gave custody to a father, after noting that the primary responsibility for childcare fell on the mother during the marriage, *despite her employment,* and that the father's career had been "of primary and driving importance." Nevertheless, partly because the mother had left the children with the father temporarily while she sorted out her feelings about the marriage, during which time "he kept house as well as any man could be expected to," custody went to the father. The mother was blamed for having treated her "own interest as paramount to that of her children;" the father's work-orientation during the marriage was not viewed as negatively.

In addition, fathers who had mother "surrogates," such as grandmothers or new wives, were favoured for their ability to provide a "stable and secure environment" which resembled the nuclear family (*Morrow*). If a father could provide the preferred nuclear family environment for his children, complete with a stay-at-home surrogate mother, he might well be viewed as the preferred parent by judges. Mothers were, thus, to some degree regarded as fungible (Polikoff, 1983). "A 'good mother,' as Lord Denning said, means making and keeping a home for the children, with the father," and not leaving a marriage which was "by no means intolerable" (*Korteling*:22). If she did leave, she could be replaced by a surrogate mother who might even be preferable to the "deserting" mother in the eyes of a court.

If a mother took employment after divorce, and if the father could afford to hire a surrogate mother such as a housekeeper, paternal custody increasingly was viewed as acceptable during the 1970s. Thus, in the 1975 *Houston* case, Justice Pennell of the Ontario Supreme Court awarded custody to the father, whose business required him to travel, but who planned to hire a housekeeper, stating the following: "If the wife was in a position to devote herself entirely to looking after the children, as she is doing at the moment, I would be slow to remove them from their present environment" (86). Her alimony claim had failed, however, and so she had to go outside the home to work, putting her in the "same" position as the husband, who could afford to purchase a surrogate mother for the children while he was away.

Another phenomenon that emerged in the 1970s, as the tender years doctrine diminished in force and the visibility of women in the work-force increased, was a literature on fathers as "house-husbands" and their importance as parents (Drakich, 1989). Movies such as *Kramer v. Kramer* captured the public's imagination, prompting the image that most fathers now participated extensively in the care of young children, especially as callous women put their own interests first by entering the labour force — or worse still — leaving a marriage which seemed perfectly acceptable to outsiders' eyes. Around the same time, feminists argued for gender neutral family law legislation to remove stereotypical images of women, and some feminists advocated shared parenting as a solution to the domestic labour problem, as well as to the problem of how children internalize male and female behaviour patterns (Chodorow, 1978).

Judges who were confronted with the phenomenon of role reversal and house-husbands were not certain what to do. Judicial decisions awarding custody to house-husband fathers tended to denigrate the mother's participation in the work-force and to negate her status as a mother. In *Smith*, a 1978 British Columbian case, Judge Cashman gave custody to a father where "the normal role of the spouses had been reversed." The judge made it clear that the role reversal was a somewhat shocking aberration from the norm. He noted that the wife had been the more constantly employed spouse and seemed surprised that the husband, to the detriment of his own career, had followed her when she transferred to advance her position in the bank. He commented that even though the wife had ceased her employment shortly before the trial, she had clearly not been a mother to her children in the past and her "first interest is the pursuit of a career." This mother, in addition to being financially independent and paying for the matrimonial home, also had committed adultery and, even worse, did not plan marriage with the co-respondent. The point is not that the result in this particular case was necessarily wrong, but that the mother was evaluated by different standards from those applied to fathers who put careers first and committed adultery.

The 1980s

During the 1980s, some judges began to take for granted the ability of men to parent, too often without inquiring into their past "experience." This occurred as most legislation on child custody began to stress the best interests of the child as the paramount or sole relevant consideration (rather than parental conduct or assumptions about the inherent abilities of women to nurture) and as equality discourse began to prevail. Outraged comments by judges concerning female employment diminished, although implicit suggestions that employed women were inferior mothers continued (Boyd, 1989). The situation became more complicated to assess as competing ideologies interacted with one another and as guidelines, such as the tender years doctrine and spousal "fault," declined in acceptability. Expectations attached to traditional gender-based ideologies, for instance, a preference for maternal care of children, continued to influence some judges, but they were increasingly careful not to base their judgements explicitly on these preferences. Where a mother failed, however, to meet the expectations of traditional motherhood, judges were perhaps quicker to turn their gaze to the father as potential custodian because of the "ideology of equality" and assumptions that fathers were generally participating in childcare. One author argued that "there is no longer a maternal preference among judges, even on an informal basis" (McBean, 1987:189).

In the oft-cited *Roebuck* case, a 1983 decision of the Alberta Court of Appeal, Justice Kerans correctly noted that the 1955 *Bell* judgement (cited above) "confuses cultural traditions with human nature" and "traps women in a social role not necessarily of their choosing, while at the same time freeing men" (286). Kerans also correctly assessed the tender years principle as "part of subtle systemic sexual subordination." However, he overstated the case in saying the assumption "[t]hat the female human has some intrinsic capacity, not shared by the male, to deal effectively with infant children ... was once conventionally accepted but is now not only doubted but widely rejected." This assumption is still widely held and cannot be eliminated by judicial fiat. In addition, in rejecting the assumption that mothers are naturally suited to parenting young children, Kerans also ignored the *fact* that mothers continue to be primarily responsible for nurturing and are encouraged to do so by a subtle and systemic system of socialization and economic incentives, as well as by continuing social assumptions that they are naturally intended for the nurturing role. He thereby falsely assumed that a legal development (rejection of gendered stereotypes) had resulted in social changes to nurturing patterns. Although he noted that there currently exist several models of marriage, "traditional, modern or supra-modern," he failed to point out that the "supra-modern" marriage where "strenuous efforts are made to avoid *any* role distinction based upon sex" (287) represents a tiny minority of marriages. He adopted the modern "partnership" model of marriage and family law (286), without realizing its continuing gendered character and differential impact on women in economic areas (Duclos, 1987).

Kerans went on to apply his modern theory of marriage in a rather cavalier fashion to deny custody of the adopted daughter to a mother who was primary caregiver during the marriage (and who was unable to bear children), but who was now employed 9:00 to 5:00 and using daycare.[9] He preferred the offer of the father to raise the child on his parents' farm, with assistance from the paternal grandmother, and possibly from his prospective wife, as he planned to remarry. The father was applauded for his interest in childcare: "the learned trial judge did not find the father here to be any sort of radical; he did, however, find him to be, perhaps uniquely, willing to spend a great deal of time with his little daughter" (288).

Efforts by judges to adjust to "modern" and "supra-modern" marriages have tended to ignore the economic realities surrounding and constraining efforts to "share" parenting. This trend, in turn, sets the stage for the increasing acceptability of joint custody.

Domestic Labour and Constraints on Shared Parenting in the 1980s

The discourse of the professions favouring joint custody has not been based on reality. Imposing a legal norm or presumption of joint custody before shared parenting is a reality of current social relations between men and women does little to encourage male responsibility for childcare, yet gives a legal right to fathers based on a false assumption of fundamental change in parenting patterns.

Lynne Segal has pointed out that genuine shared parenting would require "gigantic economic restructuring" and that, in the meantime, economic, social, and political structures generally operate to discourage most men from participating meaningfully in child rearing, particularly of young children. In addition, even where shared parenting exists, as yet in a minority of families, it "cannot in itself overturn the power and status of men in wider economic, political and cultural spheres" (157). It does not, in itself, challenge the ideology of the private (and gendered) nature of caring work (159). There is ample evidence in Canada that when social services for the elderly are cut back, women tend to assume the responsibility for them in the home (Armstrong, 1984), just as they assume responsibility of young children in the home when childcare outside the home is limited or too expensive (Connelly and MacDonald, 1986:75-76).

These and other examples illustrate the fact that good intentions to share parenting and other nurturing roles are inhibited by structures surrounding and shaping the lives of family members. Women continue to work in sex-segregated jobs characterized as "women's work," still earn "women's wages" for these jobs, and are over-represented in part-time jobs which pay less and have fewer benefits than full-time jobs. Given these facts, we can understand mothers' "choices" to give up work for the sake of family responsibilities (Armstrong, 1987:371). This vicious circle, reinforced both by the fact that women have babies and qualify for maternity leave in Canada, and by the economic realities of women's work, dictates that women assume most primary caregiving of young children. Women, therefore, have more frequent work interruptions than men (Statistics Canada, 1986), and when a woman re-enters the work-force — due to strains on household budgets, the increasing lack of purchasing power of one person's income, or simply desire — she tends to take part-time work or jobs requiring fewer skills. "She gets women's work at women's wages" (Armstrong, 1987:371).

This scenario becomes more complex as increasing numbers of married women and women with children go into the work-force to supplement the family's income, especially as children grow older, but increasingly even when children are young (Statistics Canada, 1987:28-29). However, we cannot assume, as judges too often do, that when married women are in the work-force their husbands automatically share domestic labour, including childcare with them — though it does seem that fathers are more likely to assume some childcare responsibility than they are to assume responsibility for housework, especially housework that does not include use of a machine such as a vacuum cleaner (Luxton, 1986:45).

Canadian studies show that, although women and men are addressing the increasing need for women to earn money by readjusting patterns of responsibility for domestic labour, these patterns continue to be gendered (Eichler, 1988:172-175). While husbands of women with full-time employment work fewer hours in paid jobs than do husbands of full-time homemakers, the hours spent by all men on housework and childcare remain remarkably constant at an average of about one hour per day. When women have children, their domestic labour increases and remains primarily their responsibility regardless of their labour force participation

(Canadian Advisory Council, 1987:2-6). A recent study of 60 married city couples found that employed women are likely to spend twice as much time as their employed husbands with their children, as well as twice as much time peeling potatoes and picking up socks (*Globe and Mail*, 2 April, 1988; see Shaw, forthcoming). Some women try to balance a job and home life by creatively restructuring their lives in order to make money through home-based work, but usually in ways that remain compatible with their housework and childcare responsibilities (Mackenzie, 1986).

Many studies showing that domestic labour is still overwhelmingly assumed by women point out that women themselves are implicated in this phenomenon. This finding is not surprising, given that the strength of patriarchal relations within capitalism rests on the ability to purchase the consent of oppressed individuals within it. Susan Shaw and Meg Luxton found that women tend not to ask for help, reasoning that housework will be done better or more easily by themselves. This phenomenon is connected both to men's resistance to taking on domestic labour (Luxton, 1986:45) *and* to the fact that giving up responsibility for childcare means giving up a certain degree of power which women have had. In sharing parenting with fathers, mothers may in the short term "find themselves with less power in the home, the one place we were more likely to have power, while of course we are still undervalued and underpaid outside it" (Segal, 1987:157-58). In a related finding, mothers who shared custody of children with fathers experienced significant difficulty in adjusting to not having their children present and felt a sense of loss, even though two-thirds of them recognized that the increased free time gained was a benefit to them (Morris, 1988:25).

The resistance of men to sharing domestic labour should not be underestimated. In a 1981 study of working-class households in a mining town in northern Manitoba, Luxton found that there have been significant changes since her first study in the mid-70s. More women (though not all) in the 1980s expect to work outside the home and exert pressure on men and children to help with domestic labour. However, these women continued to organize the household, and their hours of domestic labour did not decrease in correspondence with increased hours of domestic labour assumed by men. Instead, men assumed domestic tasks performed simultaneously to the ones women performed, such as watching the children while mother made supper. This eased the stress on women, as they were not doing two jobs at once, but did not reduce the hours women spent on domestic labour. Men's adoption of childcare tasks also commonly created more work for women (Luxton, 1986:45).

Luxton did find that "[o]ne of the most significant transformations of men's involvement in domestic labour has been in the area of childcare. While most fathers have always spent some time with their children, particularly with older children, increasingly they are doing more of the day-to-day care-giving, especially with younger children" (46). More men went to the delivery room with their wives and "[m]en who were willing to attend the birth were subsequently more inclined to get up at night with the baby, to take over certain feedings and to be generally more involved with their small babies." Significantly, however, Luxton found that "women were still responsible for overall childcare. All twenty-five women said it was up to them to arrange daycare for their children when they worked outside the home. If the childcare arrangements fell through on any particular day, it was the woman who had to get time off work to stay home, although this can in part be explained by her lower pay and in part by his unavailability when underground" (1986:46). These latter two factors illustrate the inhibitions placed on shared parenting by economic structures and the nature of jobs (mining is still male-dominated).

Men are thus altering to some degree the nature of their parental relationship with children, so that it involves more one-to-one contact. However, this changing definition of paternal childcare must be understood within the perspective of continuing overwhelming female responsibility for organizing children's lives. Recent research indicates that although work is becoming less and less a central life interest for men, they are devoting more time to leisure activities — husbands spend significantly more leisure time outside the home than wives do, particularly in families with children (Stebbins, 1988:37-38). In addition, as Luxton points out, reorganization of domestic labour which does occur is being done on the level of individual households and has not involved collective organization in the public labour force that could result in structural changes in the conditions of labour (1986:51). Luxton also observed that ideologies of the family remain powerful and continue to play a central role in the way most people organize their interpersonal relationships and domestic lives (1986:50).

Research on domestic labour shows that judges and legislators who assume that increased visibility of women in the labour force indicates that men and women are sharing parenting "equally" are in large part mistaken. Participation in domestic labour such as childcare remains gendered, although the shape of those gendered relations is changing to some degree in some households. We are making changes within households which bode well for the breaking down of differentiated gender roles for men and women. Child custody law should not inhibit this trend by reinforcing restrictive gender-based ideologies such as the ideology of motherhood, incorporated in a tender years doctrine based in either "common sense" or law. We cannot return to that double-edged sword which, in giving women some power within the family and the law, nevertheless imprisoned women within strict behavioural standards.

Yet, proposed alternatives to the tender years doctrine, such as joint custody, may present a trap for women. In rejecting ideologies of motherhood, the discourse of equal rights embodied in joint custody denies the still gendered character of parenting. Ideologies of fatherhood, based on assumptions that patterns of gendered behaviour are changing more rapidly than in fact they are, can then superimpose inflated notions of the significance that paternal involvement has in child development (Drakich, 1989). However laudable equal rights discourse and ideologies of father-hood may be in the abstract in encouraging shared parenting and paternal involvement in child rearing, real changes are constrained ultimately by economic and social structures surrounding the family.

Joint Custody and Equal Rights in the 1980s

While erroneous public and judicial assumptions concerning the extent of shared parenting did not necessarily result in more custody awards to fathers during the 1970s (Statistics Canada, 1983:212), they did set the stage for the debates during recent years concerning joint custody. With the decline of gender-based guidelines for judges, such as the tender years doctrine, judges felt more at sea when making decisions and became more conscious of the arbitrariness of the adversarial system in divorce law (Fineman, 1983). At the same time, professionals in social work and mediation were paying increasing attention to defining the process of divorce as emotional rather than legal, criticizing the ability of the legal system to deal with divorce, stressing retention of the "family system" after family breakdown by restructuring it, and, correspondingly, advo-cating paternal involvement in children's lives after divorce as much as possible.[10] Judges and lawyers, who find custody cases difficult (Bradbrook, 1971:558), were more than happy to accept guidance from non-legal professionals and delegate authority to them where possible (Fineman, 1988).[11] Mediation and counselling rose in priority, with the interesting coincidence that most mediators and counsellors seem to favour joint custody (Irving and Benjamin, 1987). A finding in a recent Canadian study that, according to court records, maternal sole custody is a much less likely result when the case is mediated than when it is taken through the legal process verifies this trend (Richardson, 1988:35).

To what extent *are* fathers getting custody in Canada in the 1980s, and to what extent *has* joint custody caught on? Although the trend which prevailed in the 1970s continues, whereby the majority of fathers do not contest for custody seriously and mothers receive custody of most children by default, the numbers have shifted. Whereas mothers received custody in 85.6 percent of all cases during the 1970s, a more recent study prepared for the Department of Justice (Richardson, 1988) found that women received custody in 76.6 percent of cases in the divorce and family mediation study based in Saskatoon, Montreal, and St. John's, and in only 65.3 percent of the cases in the Winnipeg study. Fathers are not receiving sole custody more often; rather, where men show an interest in receiving custody, joint custody awards are arranged (Richardson, 1988:34-35).

Richardson's study showed that slightly less than half of the parents involved in joint custody arrangements in his Canadian sample had joint physical as well as joint legal custody. Another recent study of parents involved in voluntary (not court-ordered) co-parenting arrangements, most of which involved shared physical custody, reported a pronounced asymmetry of domestic roles prior to separation of the parents, and some asymmetry after: "Although most of the women were highly educated and usually held paid employment during the marriage, they had assumed the main responsibility for domestic labour" (Morris, 1989:15). Fathers tended to do more sharing of childcare than housework and the woman saw herself as coordinator of the family routines and obligations. After separation, while fathers had increased their level of involvement with their children, mothers more than fathers "expressed concern about their ex-spouse's standards being too low or too lax" (Morris, 1989:19). Mothers often resolved this concern by assuming more responsibility for coordinating the routines of the children, even when they were in the fathers' homes.[12] Even the children saw their mothers as more responsible than their fathers for organizing such things as medical and dental appointments, although transportation was shared (Morris, 1989:29). Cerise Morris does not make much of these findings — indeed she downplays any implication that mothers might be exploited by shared parenting. It does seem apparent, however, that the division of labour within even voluntary co-parenting arrangements is highly gendered and parallels to some degree the division of labour within marriage. While the children in Morris' study seemed to be thriving, this was achieved very often through extra effort by the mothers.

Morris concludes that assumptions of the nuclear family are being broken down through the shared parenting she found in her study. These assumptions may, however, simply be adjusting to the circumstance of parents of children living apart. When compared to Luxton's study of adaptations in the still very gender-divided households in Flin Flon, the continuities seem striking. The ideological privilege of the nuclear family may be breaking down to a limited degree in response to the exigencies of female employment, divorce and family breakdown, but it cannot do so beyond a certain point until the structures surrounding the family change too. Such change requires more than the creation of a legal system with presumptions of joint custody, which Morris just falls short of calling for (Morris, 1989:37).

In any case, shared parenting does not deal with the fact that many mothers do not have the "luxury" of experiencing such co-operation with a father. Lesbian mothers may provide male role models for their children (Gross, 1986:521-523) but are unlikely to seek out the biological father who provided the sperm for artificial insemination for this purpose unless he is already a friend of the family. For the half of female-headed lone-parent families that fall below the poverty line (Statistics Canada, 1983:2), the notion of shared childcare as a social goal or as a form of freedom is "sheer abstraction" (Uviller, 1978:119). Shared parenting as a policy objective is thus limited to some degree, in that it is a principle based on heterosexist, classist, and arguably racist assumptions of the nuclear family.[13]

The need for legal arrangements which support co-parenting after divorce is to some extent negated by Morris' research. It emerged from her study of co-parenting that only 64 percent of the couples who responded to her invitation to be in the study had a *legal* custody agreement. Of these, 70 percent had legally ordered maternal *sole* custody but were nonetheless participating in some form of co-parenting. None had paternal sole custody. More than one-third of the families, then, had made extra-legal, *de facto* arrangements for sharing parenting (Morris, 1988:14). This study confirms observations made elsewhere (Sevenhuijsen, 1986) that, where parents genuinely wish to arrange co-parenting, they will do so without legal presumptions in their favour. The high degree of satisfaction expressed by the parents and children in Morris' study reflects the voluntary nature of the arrangements she studied. Finally, to suggest that the legal system does not encourage co-parenting, consensual agreements, or paternal contact is to ignore several recent developments in Canadian law.

Legal Trends Towards Joint Custody in the 1980s

Contrary to the arguments of fathers' rights groups, recent legal developments related to custody, access, and enforcement encourage joint custody and paternal involvement with children, though not always through genuine "shared parenting." These developments appear under the cloak of the "best interests of the child" doctrine and through a combination of legislative and judicial initiatives. New federal divorce legislation and much provincial legislation on custody encourage mediation, and judges increasingly order that parents go to mediation before returning to court should a dispute arise in the future (*Charlton*). The new federal Divorce Act explicitly permits joint custody orders to be made, as do some provinces,[14] although none create a presumption in favour of joint custody as have many American states.[15]

The type of statute that permits joint custody as an option, as do our federal Divorce Act and the Ontario Children's Law Reform Act, can result in joint custody being ordered fairly extensively, even in inappropriate circumstances. These statutes have no directives or guidelines to restrict courts in awarding joint custody, so courts may do so in order to escape difficult decisions. For instance, joint custody may be awarded where parents are not in agreement, as has happened to a greater degree in recent years in Canada. Judges increasingly cast aside the earlier caution concerning joint custody manifested in 1979 by the Ontario Court of Appeal in the *Baker* and *Kruger* cases. Joint custody has been ordered despite one or both parents' unwillingness to try it. In the 1986 *Abbott* case, Justice Twaddle of the Manitoba Court of Appeal reasoned: "To say otherwise would encourage one parent to avoid the participation of the other in deciding questions as to their child's future by a mere statement that he or she was unwilling to share the responsibility" (171).[16] This view ignores the fact that most custodial mothers complain about the lack of participation of non-custodial fathers in childcare, rather than trying to prevent it. Mothers who do have concerns about paternal contact with children generally have good reasons, such as fear of abuse. This view also ignores the gendered impact of joint custody orders, and the inhibitions they place on the parent with primary physical custody of the children, usually the mother. Once a joint custody arrangement is in place, it becomes difficult for parents with primary physical custody to exercise discretion concerning their children (*Chauvin*) or to move to another geographical location (*Crawford; Smith; Derosier*).

Statutes allowing joint custody as an option are often accompanied by "friendly parent" provisions such as section 16 (10) of the Divorce Act, 1985, which directs courts to "give effect to the principle that a child of the marriage should have as much contact with each spouse as is consistent with the best interests of the child and, for that purpose, [to] take into consideration the willingness of the person for whom custody is sought to facilitate such contact." This provision has been aptly called "the silencer," since "women who seek to have access by the father blocked because of a past history of physical or sexual abuse, risk being labelled as 'uncoopera-tive' and stand to lose custody of their children" (Lamb, 1987:22). The negative evaluation of a mother which may occur under the friendly parent rule if she resists a joint custody arrangement is illustrated by an annotation to the *Parsons* case: "The fact that a spouse refuses to cooperate in the plan that best meets the needs of the children is evidence that the parent in question may be putting his/her own interests ahead of those of the children" (84-85). As Fineman (1988:765-766) points out, social work-ers' discourse tends to characterize a parent who seeks sole custody as having an illegitimate motivation and "[m]ediation advocates often char-acterize opposition to shared custody as pathological."

Recent legislative efforts in Ontario to enforce access rights are in line with the recent emphasis on retaining paternal involvement. This legisla-tion may seem innocuous and indeed laudatory at first glance. But in light of evidence in California that 70 percent of men without custody would prefer to see their children *less* often (Weitzman, 1985:258), and in Canada that women who are custodial parents identify as a major problem "that men do not always exercise their access rights or that they do so erratically and unpredictably" (Richardson, 1988:36), access enforcement legislation seems an unnecessary move. The majority of mothers want to encourage access by fathers unless it appears detrimental to children. This view accords with the fact that many women seem to favour the notion of joint custody, even when it takes a great deal of effort on their part to make it work (Morris, 1988).

Conclusion and Alternatives

Overall, then, initiatives to give parents equal rights to children via joint custody and other innovations are proceeding apace in Canada, despite rhetoric to the contrary. My argument has been that the 20th-century history of women's work in the home demonstrates continuing primary caregiving on the part of most women, despite significant changes in the configuration of family structures. The visibility of women in the labour force, however, has given rise to ideologies of equality, and the increased visibility of men as fathers has given rise to ideologies of fatherhood that express concern for paternal contact with children (Drakich, 1989; Holmes, 1987). As a result of these ideologies and a distaste for the assumptions behind the tender years doctrine on the part of feminists and fathers' rights groups (for different reasons), the legal system has increasingly emphasized shared parenting and paternal contact. Nonetheless, joint custody as a norm is unnecessary and indeed inefficient in enhancing genuine shared parenting, partly because it rewards a reality of shared parenting before it actually exists. Ironically, as Martha Fineman points out, the failures of divorced fathers (for instance, to visit children or pay support) are used as major arguments for giving men more control and power over children. This approach treats children as property in much the same way as the old paternal right to custody of legitimate children, only now the children can be divided equally. Fathers are thus empowered with rights over children without having to demonstrate any responsibility for their care (Fineman, 1988:740, 759).

The current conjuncture in child custody law, with various ideologies struggling with one another and emerging in contradictory fashions in custody decisions, illustrates the role of the law as a site of ideological formation and reproduction. The ideology of motherhood still appears in the form of the tender years (common sense) doctrine and in the form of assessments of employed or lesbian mothers, for instance, as not quite proper mothers (see Arnup, 1989; Gross, 1986). The ideology of liberal individualism accompanying advanced capitalism enhances a perception that individuals undifferentiated by gender can equally assume roles such as parents (Girdner, 1986) regardless of social structures, and is reinforced by "equality" guarantees in modern Canadian law.[17] Finally, the ideology of fatherhood, enhanced by *some* increased male participation in parenting and exaggerated due to the male domination of institutions like the media, combines with the ideology of liberal individualism to increase the appeal of joint custody which appears to encourage shared parenting and male involvement in childcare.

How feminists should cope with these legal reforms and proposals for reform is extremely problematic, given that it is difficult for women to criticize apparent willingness on the part of fathers to take responsibility for childcare, a request often made by feminists in the past. Any law which is intended to enhance the well-being of children is difficult for women to challenge publicly. In addition, although women seem less fond of joint custody than men, it is clearly not an anathema to many women (Richardson, 1988:35; Morris, 1988). We must pay attention to the reasons why women do not uniformly dislike joint custody, and why some adopt it *voluntarily* for the benefit of their children, while maintaining a critical stance towards trends to make joint custody a legal norm.

Where then should we turn to avoid the problems inherent in the discretion-laden "best interests of the child" principle, in the problematic assumptions inherent in the tender years doctrine, and in joint custody as a norm? Few feminists concerned about joint custody support a return to any form of maternal presumption. Many argue that a primary caregiver presumption would be better suited to both the interests of children and the current gendered dynamics of parenting (Smart and Sevenhuijsen, 1989). That presumption is based on a prediction that, in most instances, if parents must split up, children will be best served by retaining primary responsibility for their care in the hands of the parent who has demonstrated commitment to and expertise for this task in the past. It does not attempt to predict future parenting ability on the basis of good intentions expressed in court, economic status, adulterous conduct, or availability of a new partner, all of which can operate to deprive a child of the care of a mother who has been primary caregiver in the past. This deprivation seems to go against a child's best interests unless that caregiver has been truly unfit in terms of falling below a minimum standard. The primary caregiver presumption may prompt us towards more *genuine* shared parenting, both during cohabitation of parents and possibly afterwards. It can acknowledge the reality of continuing primary caregiving by women, reward those few men who are engaged in primary caregiving, and create incentives for more caregiving by men in the future. Neither does it preclude shared parenting arrangements being made voluntarily by parents who genuinely wish to cooperate in such an arrangement.

The primary caregiver presumption has been enunciated in three American state courts [18] and some of the principles underlying it have been applied, without formal adoption of the legal doctrine, by some Canadian courts.[19] For feminists, an important aspect of a primary caregiver presumption is its recognition of the labour which most mothers currently devote to childcare, which the gender neutral "equality" stance of most feminists in the 1970s tended to obscure. Until various structures surrounding families and parenting change, it is likely that men who gain custody of children will tend to delegate their parenting responsibilities to some degree to women such as grandmothers or new female partners. Giving custody to men as a means of radical change, or giving it to both men and women in the form of joint custody, does not challenge the wider social and economic structures that shape largely female responsibility for childcare.

While all parenting problems and legal problems associated with family breakdown cannot be solved by introducing a primary caregiver presumption, it may be a start. The primary caregiver presumption lends certainty to the area of law, gives judges a criterion that does not allow too much discretion to come into play, and allows them to predict the future on the basis of fact-finding concerning the past (Fineman, 1988:772). The primary caregiver presumption also lends enough certainty to the area that parties tend to litigate less and settle more (Neely, 1984). This too is important for primary caregivers because many mothers give up custody before even reaching the court due to economic pressures, which can be manipulated by a usually more financially comfortable father (Niman, 1987). Too often the flexibility of the "best interests of the child" principle allows factors not terribly relevant to parenting to militate against the possibility of a primary caregiver parent continuing to parent.

Neither should the primary caregiver presumption be viewed as depriving children of contact with one of their parents. Contact with "fit" secondary caregiver parents *is* important; although children's relationships with secondary caregivers differ from those with primary caregivers, they typically form strong attachments to both parents (Chambers, 1984:534). That contact actually has potential to increase in intensity through access (Aubert, 1979:148). Fathers who do continue to be committed to spending time with their children may exercise their access rights, although custodial mothers complain that relatively few fathers do so regularly (Richardson, 1988:36).

While no one envies the role of the access parent, the fact is that when a family splits up, unless the parents involved are very special people who cooperated in parenting before separation, it is unlikely that less skewed co-parenting is going to work. Morris notes that there was a "seeming tendency" in the parents she studied who were involved in post-separation shared parenting "for the fathers to have been, on the average, somewhat more involved in childcare than fathers in general are held to be" while spousal relationships were intact (Morris, 1988:17). Where this has not been the case, it may be difficult but not unrealistic to ask a father to carry on his contributions to parenting through access. As Fineman shows, joint custody holds out frequently unrealistic expectations characteristic of "fairy tales" to counter the supposed "horror story" of the beleaguered father deprived of contact with his children (Fineman, 1988:753). The quality of access time spent with children may in fact not differ significantly from Luxton's description of typical paternal childcare styles in intact families: "men 'babysat' their own children — something that women never did. The implication of this typical reference was that the children were the responsibility of the mother, and the father 'helped out' " (Luxton, 1986:46-47).

Strategies for altering socio-economic structures to be more conducive to wider participation in childcare by men and women have been canvassed in feminist literature. Compressed time options and flexible working hours have been found inadequate as strategies to ease the ability of workers to reconcile the demands of parenting and labour force participation (Canadian Advisory Council, 1987:7-8), partly because actual hours of work per week are not reduced. Childcare responsibilities of workers are one good reason for trade unions to argue for shorter hours of work per week, particularly when there is high unemployment (Luxton, 1987). Part-time work accompanied by pay and benefits proportional to those of full-time work would also improve the ability of fathers and mothers to continue involvement in the labour force, even with young children. When there are school-age children, problems of childcare before and after school hours would be eased through either adequately compensated part-time work or shorter hours of work per week, with those hours synchronized with those of school hours (Canadian Advisory Council, 1987:10). Legal provision of paternity leave *in addition to* maternity leave settlements would enhance the already existing trend for fathers to attend the birthing process and to engage in early childcare (Luxton, 1986). Finally, the struggle for adequate national childcare geared to various types of parental jobs, including shiftwork, is intimately connected with all of these proposals.

Only through struggle for social and legal change in these other areas that affect parenting can we create conditions which give incentives to men as well as women to engage in parenting. Until we have achieved a more genuine form of "equality" within families and within the social and economic structures shaping the decisions that individuals make concerning their families, putting a norm which assumes "equality" of parenting in our family law is a mistake.

Notes
Earlier versions of this paper were presented at the Clara Brett Martin Workshop Series, Faculty of Law, University of Toronto, 21 October 1988; and at a panel on Law and the Family co-sponsored by the Canadian Law and Society Association and the Conference on Critical Theory, Feminism and the Canadian Legal System, The Learned Societies, Windsor Ontario, 7 June 1988

1. In the 1970s only 15 percent of divorce cases where children were involved were contested (Statistics Canada, *Divorce* 219).
2. While this point seems likely to be true, it is in practice often difficult to determine from reported cases the racial identity of the parties.
3. How little fathers are expected to contribute, even now, to the care of young children in particular is illustrated by the *Wittal* case, which involved a wife who complained that when her truck-driver husband came in off the road he seemed bored and did not want to do things with her and/or the children. Judge Grotsky responded as follows: "Again, it must be remembered that in and prior to May of 1981 the children were only infants. There was not much he could do with them" (417).
4. Although urbanization and industrialization occurred in Canada more slowly than in England and New England, by 1921 only one-half of the population lived in rural areas, as compared to two-thirds in 1901 and four-fifths in 1851 (Prentice, 1988:108-109).
5. The tendency of courts to make "same-sex" custody awards where older children were involved, for instance awarding sons to fathers, makes sense in this light.
6. While lawyers make much of the transition from the tender years doctrine as a rule of law to a rule of common sense "only," this distinction is very legalistic and obscures the problematic assumptions behind even

a common sense assessment of the facts based on notions about women being more important to the early years of a child's life.

7. Statistics Canada reports between 1975 and 1983 the labour force participation rate of married women rose by almost 11 percentage points (from 41.6 percent to 52.3 percent, while the participation rate for women with children went from 42 percent to 57 percent). More recent data show that the labour force participation rate for women with a youngest child under the age of 3 is 53.9 percent in 1985 (up from 31.2 percent in 1975); for women with youngest child aged 3-5 years, 59.5 percent (up from 40 percent in 1975); for women with youngest child 6-15 years, 66.2 percent (up from 48.2 percent in 1975) (Statistics Canada, 1987:28).

8. There is an interesting correlation between the time when support orders began to be enforced more rigorously and the time when fathers began to claim custody more often. Custody cases sometimes show that when mothers with the children try to obtain support, fathers claim custody (See *Voegelin*).

9. In the 1988 *Klachefsky* case, the Manitoba Court of Appeal overruled a lower court decision giving custody to a father who could offer a new stay-at-home partner on the grounds that the child would not have to attend daycare. With this factor eliminated as an appropriate consideration, custody was granted to the mother who had been declared in the lower court to be the "better" parent. If it becomes unacceptable for judges to use daycare as a negative factor against working mothers, it is possible that primary caregiving in the past will be highlighted to a greater extent in custody decisions.

10. See Irving and Benjamin (1987) for an example of Canadian mediation literature.

11. Note that this attitude seems to run contrary to that of judges towards social workers and reports of the Official Guardian found in the early study by Bradbrook (1971): "All the judges seem resentful of those [social] workers who attempt to dictate to the judge what conclusions he should draw from the facts presented; this is regarded as an intrusion into the judge's right to adjudicate" (562). This study was conducted at an earlier stage than that discussed by Fineman. The judges did admit that they found custody to be an extremely difficult area, that they disliked hearing these cases, and that no guidelines were available (Fineman, 1988:558-59).

12. Two interesting quotes from mothers: "As his week is about to begin, I consult with him about *what* he has planned for our son ... I also remind him about the clothes he will need, the laundry, and anything else I think he needs to know." "Although he is a good father to the best of his ability. I don't trust his influence ... he's disorganized, sloppy and his house works in chaotic fashion ... I have to tell him to give our son a shampoo and wash his dirty socks." (qtd. in Morris, 1989:19). In *Kachefsky v. Brown* it was found that the mother had been primarily responsible for creating and making the joint custody arrangement work. Yet, she was not awarded physical custody at the first instance, when it became impossible for the joint

custody to continue due to her move for employment purposes. This decision was overruled by the Manitoba Court of Appeal.

13. Black families in the United States have been labelled as dysfunctional and pathological when measured against the ideal of the nuclear family (Zinn, 1989; Collins, 1989).

14. Orders for joint custody have always been implicitly permitted, in particular when the parents come to court asking for the court to ratify a prearranged joint custody agreement.

15. Note that California, one of the states which had a joint custody presumption, has now adopted more "neutral" legislation ("Impact of the New Divorce Law," San Francisco Chronicle, 2 September 1988, A14).

16. In Parsons v. Parsons, joint legal and physical custody was awarded despite the fact that the parents felt that a mediated joint custody agreement had not worked. The judge noted that the children wished the arrangement to continue, and hinted at almost a presumption in favour of joint custody when stating that the "parties have not satisfied me that ... joint custody has been a failure" (92). In Nurmi v. Nurmi, joint custody was ordered despite a mother's desire to retain final decision-making power after consulting with the father, and despite the judge's acknowledgement that the child should not spend 50 percent of his time with his father. (See also Kamimura). Other recent cases have placed great emphasis on fathers retaining decision-making power over children's lives even if joint custody is not explicitly ordered, for instance, through the mechanism of joint guardianship, which has the same practical effect as a joint legal custody order (Charlton; Hackett). Another recent trend is the refusal of courts to make explicit custody orders, resulting in de facto orders resembling joint custody (Abbott).

17. The Canadian Charter of Rights and Freedoms was argued by fathers in the Keyes case, and in the Harden case, where the father argued that the tender years doctrine violated the Charter by discriminating against him because of his sex. Both arguments were denied by the courts and custody was awarded to the mother, in the latter case with the court emphasizing the primary parenting of the mother.

18. (See Garska; Pikula; Pusey)

19. See Harden; Keyes; Grills; Menage; Qually; Hebb; Shaward; Perry; Atkinson.

Cases Cited

Abbott v. Taylor (1986), 2 R.F.L. 3d 163 (Man. C.A.)

Atkinson v. Atkinson (1987), 9 R.F.L. 3d 174 (B.C.S.C.)

Baker v. Baker (1979), 8 R.F.L. 2d 236 (Ont. C.A.)

Bell v. Bell [1955] Ontario Weekly Notes 341 (Ont. C.A.)

Bolton and Morningstar v. Bolton and Terry (1976), 26 R.F.L. 284 (P.E.I.S.C., Fam. Div.)

Charlton v. Charlton (1980), 15 R.F.L. 2d 220 (B.C.S.C.)

Chauvin v. Chauvin (1987), 6 R.F.L. 3d 403 (Ont. D.C)

Crawford v. Crawford (1985), 46 R.F.L. 2d 331 (P.E.I.S.C.)

Derosier v. Derosier (1987), 12 R.F.L. 3d 235 (Ont. D.C.)

Garska v. McCoy (1981), W. Va. 278 S.E. 2d 357 (W. Virg. S.C.A.)

Grills v. Grills (1982), 30 R.F.L. 2d 390 (Alta. Prov. Ct., Fam. Div.)

Hackett v. Hackett (1985), 43 R.F.L. 2d 5 (B.C.S.C.)

Harden v. Harden (1987), 6 R.F.L. 3d 147 (Sask. C.A.)

Hebb v. Hebb (1987), 76 N.S.R. 2d 102; 189 A.P.R. 102 (N.S.S.C.)

Houston v. Houston (1975), 21 R.F.L. 65 (Ont. S. C.)

Kamimura v. Squibb (Carruthers) (1988), 13 R.F.L. 3d 31 (B.C.S.C.)

Keyes v. Gordon (1985), 45 R.F.L. 2d 177 (N.S.C.A.)

Klachefsky v. Brown (1988), 12 R.F.L. 3d 280 (Man. C.A.)

Korteling v. Korteling and Buse (1974), 19 R.F.L. 21 (B.C.S.C)

Kruger v. Kruger (1979), 11 R.F.L. 2d 52 (Ont. C.A.)

Menage v. Hedges (1986), 8 R.F.L. 3d 22 (Ont. U.F.C)

Morrow v. Morrow (1976), 30 R.F.L. 204 (Sask. Q.B.)

Nurmi v. Nurmi (1988), 16 R.F.L. 3d 201 (Ont. U.F.C.)

Parsons v. Parsons (1985), 48 R.F.L. 2d 83 (Nfld. S.C.)

Perry v. Perry (1987), 75 N.B.R 2d 198; 188 A.P.R. 198 (N.B.Q.B.)

Pikula v. Pikula (1985), 374 N.W. 2d 705 (Minn. C.A.))

Pusey v. Pusey (1986), 12 Fam. Law Reporter 1584 (Utah Sup. Ct.)

Qually v. Qually (30 July 1987), Carter J. unreported, Payne's Digest 87-266 (Sask. Q.B.))

Re Orr, [1933] Ontario Reports 212 (Ont. C.A.)

Roebuck v. Roebuck (1983), 34 R.F.L. 2d 277 (Alta. C.A.)

Shaward v. Shaward (1987), 43 Man. R. 2d 111 (Man. Q.B.)

Smith v. Smith (1987), 7 R.F.L. 3d 206 (N.S. Fam. Ct.)

Smith v. Smith and Morrow (1978), 3 R.F.L. 2d 13 (B.C.S.C.)

Veighey v. Veighey (1977), 3 R.F.L. 2d 148 (Ont. S.C.-Div. Ct.)

Voegelin v. Voegelin (1980), 15 R.F.L. 2d 1 (Ont. Co. Ct.)

Wittal v. Himmelspach (1983), 36 R.F.L. 2d 413 (Sask. Q.B.)

Discussion

Each of the papers in this section, although focusing on diverse topics, paint a disturbing picture of the inequalities that exist in the structure and operation of the law. The recognition of unequal treatment of the poor, workers, aboriginal people and women is an important first step in developing a critical analysis of the operation of the law in Canada. In addition, some of the papers offer theoretical explanations of the specific laws being investigated. The value of examining unequal treatment within a theoretical approach is that it enables us to move beyond awareness of inequalities to the process of identifying the *source* of these inequalities. Using the theoretical insights offered in the Introduction, it will be argued that an understanding of the inequalities illustrated in this section can best be gained by examining where these groups are located within the relations of production and reproduction. That is, instead of locating the cause of differential treatment in the inclinations of specific individuals who possess power within society, the argument will be made that the practice and ideology of law must be situated within an economic and gendered structure in order to explain its operation. Using the four papers as examples, it will be shown that, in addition to an individual's class position, one's race and gender also serve to place a person within a specific location within this structure and, as a result, will affect that person's treatment within the legal system.

One of Marx's oft paraphrased statements is that "the ruling ideas are the ideas of the ruling class." This statement should not be interpreted to mean that an elite within society meet and determine what are acceptable ideas which should be promulgated to support their economic interests. Rather, it suggests that the impact of the mode and relations of production within a society affect all elements of that society, including the relative value that is attached to specific activities and to specific people. For example, Marxists have argued that the emphasis on individualism, competition and the linkage of prestige to wealth are all ideas that both reflect and support a capitalist economic system. If we extend Marx's quote to the arena of law, we should expect to find that a group's relationship to production (and reproduction) will influence how that group is treated within the legal system. Moreover, the actions of a group, even if they are illegal actions, will be differentially evaluated depending on how these actions are valued within the larger context of a system dominated by a particular economic structure.

Anatole France's satirical reference to the rich sleeping under bridges was meant to draw attention to the fact that, although laws are philosophically to be applied equally to everyone, some laws, by the very nature of the behaviour which they proscribe, apply to some classes more than others. That is, the rich are as likely to be found sleeping under bridges as the poor are likely to be found engaging in insider trading on the stock exchange! Charles Reasons, Lois Ross and Craig Patterson's paper provides an example of a set of laws that, in reality, apply to one class within society: those that own and control business. Nevertheless, using case histories and aggregate data, the authors present a convincing case that Canadian workplace health and safety laws provide little protection to workers. Through lax enforcement and minimal sanctions, employers are free to ignore health and safety provisions that were meant to reduce the hazards within the workplace, even though these law violations result in thousands of injuries and deaths each year. How is it that such harmful violations of the law are virtually ignored by the state and receive such little attention by the mass media? Using the premise stated earlier, it is necessary to examine the context of these harmful acts in order to understand the low priority they receive within the law. As Reasons, Ross and Patterson note, the injuries and deaths that occur in the workplace are seen as qualitatively different than assaults and homicides that take place on the street. Because the former take place within legitimate business activity, they are either defined as an unfortunate cost of industry or the result of worker carelessness. Even though many of these injuries were preventable, the fact that the costs of prevention may have even marginally affected the profit of the business somehow excuses or mitigates the violation of safety regulations. We have somehow come to accept the idea that there are a number of costs that must be tolerated in order for industry to thrive, whether these costs are massive pollution, a high incidence of industry related disease, or debilitating injuries and death. The ideological dictum is that the economic objectives linked to production should take priority: what is good for business is good for the country — even if it occasionally kills people.

Michael Mandel's investigation of Canadian sentencing practices illustrates another way in which the ideology associated with a capitalist economic system becomes filtered through the practice of law and how specific individuals, by virtue of their location within the system of production, are valued (and devalued) within the society. Mandel's evidence suggests that France's quote should be modified to note that even on those occasions when the rich are convicted of sleeping under the bridge, they will receive less severe penalties than the poor for this crime. Similar to Reasons and his colleagues, Mandel finds that there is little correspondence between the degree of harm caused by an illegal act and the severity of sanction the offender receives. Unlike the previous paper, however, where different laws applied to acts that had equivalent levels of harm (for example, homicide compared to a death producing act within the workplace), Mandel notes that a wide range of sanctions can be found even within identical types of crime. In addition to the legal variables (such as prior record) which were taken into account in determining the appropriate sentence, Mandel found that a number of extra-legal factors were used by the judiciary in assessing the "character" of the offender. While Mandel's finding that those in higher class positions were presumed to possess a better "moral character" might suggest an instrumentalist perspective, evidence is also presented that other factors, such as the offender's employment record and occupation, are significant in assessing character. It would seem that judges evaluate the social worth of an offender primarily on the nature of the offender's involvement in the economic system and where in the hierarchy of the economic system he or she is located. Thus, an individual on welfare would have less social value than a labourer, who in turn would have less social value than a manager or a senior level civil servant. This is consistent with the prevalent ideological view that one's worth stems from the nature of the work one engages in. Individuals receiving welfare are considered to be morally inferior and to have lesser "character" than individuals who are employed. As part of this ideology, it is also assumed that one's economic position is solely determined by an individual's effort. Thus, the judiciary rationalize giving more lenient sentences to individuals of high moral character on the grounds that crime is an aberration not consistent with their character and, as a result of this inconsistency, these offenders are presumed unlikely to engage in further crime. Given that judges have been given the power to use the moral character of the offender in determining the appropriate sentence to administer, it is not surprising that they would use it to justify giving lighter sentences to those in upper class positions.

Geoffrey York's review of the history of land claims by the aboriginal people of Canada, at first glance, appears to have little relationship to the issue of production. Rather, the history of aboriginal people has been one in which Indians and Métis have had, at best, a marginal relationship to the dynamics of capitalism. Until recently, their economic subsistence continued to be one of relying on traditional activities of hunting, trapping and fishing on areas set aside for them by the state. It is this very marginality, however, which can help to explain the state's cavalier approach to aboriginal groups on issues such as land entitlement. The state's approach to aboriginal people is a continuation of the colonial model first practised by Europeans in their settlement of Canada. In the expansion of the country, the state dealt with the "Indian problem" by making treaties that had the effect of isolating aboriginal people in areas considered to be of little economic value (that is, land with poor agricultural potential). With the emergence of industrial capitalism in the late 19th century, the colonial ideology of racism was maintained and adopted to legitimate state policies and economic exploitation. The indigenous peoples were kept at the periphery of industrial capitalism and defined as a "nuisance population" to be dealt with by marginalizing them socially, geographically, economically and politically. As part of this process, the state did not recognize aboriginal people as citizens of this country. Rather, the state took the role of a paternalistic overseer, with the responsibility of acting on behalf of the "best interests" of the indigenous population. For example, Indians were not considered juridical equals and did not receive the right to vote in federal elections until 1960. Within the framework of this racist ideology, the state could arbitrarily violate its own laws and expropriate lands for purposes of resource extraction and hydro-electric development when it best served the interests of capital accumulation. When the issue was one of the legal rights of natives versus corporate interests in mining, logging, oil, or cheap electrical power, the material interests related to production always took priority. The success of this racist ideology in legitimating the expropriation of native lands is evidenced by the fact that the Canadian mass media virtually ignored the actions. In turn, the public's response was one of ignorance or apathy. Since resource extraction offered employment to labourers and electrical development offered promises of cheaper energy to consumers, there was little difficulty in the state defining land expropriation as benefiting the entire country. As York notes, the expropriation of these lands was justified on the grounds of being in the "public interest" or for the "common good." Because of their marginal relationship to production, the native population was ignored in the equation of *who* was the public and *what* was the common good. The major beneficiaries of land expropriation were, in fact, corporations that profited from resource extraction and large scale industrial production that benefited from an abundant source of low cost energy.

The collusion of the state with corporate interests in land expropriation illustrates the absurdity of theoretically viewing the state as a neutral arbiter which functions to impartially resolve conflicts between different segments of the population. When a segment of the population has no power as a result of its marginal relationship to the means of production and no legitimacy as a political force because of a racist ideology, that group is relatively powerless in the legal arena when conflicts arise. Moreover, when the upheaval of native communities and the destruction of traditional means of subsistence lead to significant increases in alcoholism and a soaring crime rate, the racist ideology is again brought in to explain these phenomena. According to the conventional wisdom, the aboriginal "crime problem" exists not because aboriginal people have been victims of the arbitrary and sometimes illegal expropriation of their land. Rather, the linkage of crime to natives is almost exclusively debated within the context of the rate of criminal acts committed by natives and the racist ideology directs analysts to seek answers by looking for specific "traits" inherent within aboriginal people. The larger structural connection between natives and the state is ignored.

In the final paper in this section, Susan Boyd examines the practice of awarding child custody in the area of family law. Boyd's analysis furthers our theoretical discussion of the operation of law in two important ways. First, her linkage of the legal judgements surrounding child custody to the social position of women within society reveals that one's relationship to reproduction must also be considered when developing an explanation of the operation of law. Specifically, Boyd illustrates that historically — and to a significant degree currently — the structural division of labour which allocated to women the primary responsibility for reproductive labour and the ideology that supported this division have been the primary factors in the rationale used by the judiciary in awarding custody. Consistent with the socialist feminist premise that reproductive labour is as fundamental to society as productive labour, it should be expected that an allocation of reproductive labour within a patriarchal society will not only place women in subordinate positions within the productive and reproductive spheres, it will also be reflected in an ideology that permeates the court when the legal issue of whether the mother or the father is the "best parent" to provide care to the children of a dissolved marriage. This issue requires that the law make decisions which are connected to the basic assumptions related to the traditional structure of patriarchy: (1) that children of the marriage are the property of the father; and (2) that women are "naturally" suited to the task of raising children. Yet, when there is a dissolution of the marriage, the above assumptions produce a dilemma. If the children of the marriage are the property of the father (either literally or metaphorically) then, consistent with this view, the father should receive custody. If, however, the mother is seen as being "naturally" suited to providing the best care of the children, then the mother should receive custody.

This leads us to the second important feature of Boyd's work: the recognition that ideology is a dynamic constellation of values and beliefs, subject to significant changes related to shifts in the structure of production and reproduction. Her review of precedent setting court decisions in this area reveals that the manner in which the law resolves the issue of child custody cannot be understood without an awareness of the changes in the economic system and women's changing roles within the interdependent worlds of production and reproduction. Boyd's analysis of the relationship between the changes in the economic system and the changes in the ideological conceptions of familial rights and responsibilities, as reflected in the court decisions regarding custody, is a good illustration of the linkage between production and reproduction. As she points out, when the economic activities were centred around the home, the male head of the household had exclusive control over the family and was typically awarded custody of the children. With material changes in the relations of production and reproduction, changes in the ideology that supported a familial patriarchal system were necessitated. In the emerging system of industrial capitalism, a public world of wage labour (performed primarily by males) was separated from the private world of childcare and domestic labour (performed almost exclusively by women). The ideology that supported the separate spheres of work for men and women was reflected in the courts through the use of the "tender years doctrine," which presumed that women were "instinctively" better equipped to care for young children, while men were best suited to the world of productive labour. This legal guideline also signalled an erosion of the power of the individual patriarch, in that the courts were no longer willing to accept the view that the father had exclusive ownership of the children. This diminution of the individual patriarch's power, however, should not be taken as an indicator of the lessening of patriarchy. Rather, as Ursel (1984) has argued, it is a reflection of the change in the form of patriarchy to what is defined as "social patriarchy." In this form, women continue to be subordinated, but the subordination becomes increasingly supported and maintained by the state through a multitude of labour, family and welfare policies that promote women's proper role as wife and mother. By extension, the beneficiaries of social patriarchy are not just the male heads of the household, but also the state and capital, in that all of the labour required in the tasks associated with reproduction and the care of dependents is unpaid labour performed by women.

With the increase in the participation of women in the labour force, the court's reliance on the "natural" differences of the abilities of men and women in the care of children to justify custody decisions became less tenable. The tender years doctrine was replaced with a legal discourse of equal rights in which each parent is seen as being, in principle, equally capable of caring for the children. Boyd aptly illustrates, however, that the differential weight given to men who engage in *some* child care, the unwillingness to view women's participation in wage labour as equally acceptable to men's participation, and the refusal to acknowledge the structural incompatibilities between full time wage labour and traditional parenting, suggest that the current reliance on the principle of formal equality by the courts continues to be interpreted in a manner that is ideologically supportive of a patriarchal system.

One of the lessons that students of the law should learn from Boyd's analysis is that changes in the law that are often hailed as progressive reforms may, upon closer examination, have little or no effect in addressing fundamental inequalities. Although the criteria for awarding child custody have undergone significant changes within the last one hundred years, the ideology of patriarchy continues to influence the court. While, for example, some hailed the increase in joint custody decisions as an indication of the growing gender equality within Canadian society, Boyd's analysis of the success of joint custody leads to some skepticism on the gender neutrality of this practice. In the next section, the debates on social reform through law will be examined in more detail. As might be expected, the papers in this section will represent divergent positions on the strategies to adopt in using law as an instrument of change and on the more general question of the utility of law as an agent of reform.

Part Three

Change and Reform Through Law

Aboriginal Peoples and the Canadian Charter of Rights and Freedoms: Contradictions and Challenges

Aki-Kwe / Mary Ellen Turpel

> Whereas Canada is founded upon principles that recognize the supremacy of God and the rule of law...
> (Preamble to Part I, *Canadian Charter of Rights and Freedoms*).

> Your religion was written upon tables of stone by the iron finger of your God so that you could not forget. The Red Aboriginal people could never comprehend nor remember it. Our religion is the traditions of our ancestors — the dreams of our old men, given them in solemn hours of night by the Great Spirit; and the visitations of our sachems: and it is written in the hearts of our people (Chief Seattle to the Governor of Washington Territory, 1854).

> When anthropologists, government officials, and churchmen have argued that our ways have been lost to us, they are fulfilling one of their own tribal rituals — wish fulfilment.
> (Chief George Manuel, *The Fourth World*).

The contemporary world of aboriginal politics is inhabited by discussions about rights — the right to self-government, the right to title of land, the right to equality, the right to social services, and the right to practice spiritual beliefs. None of this is very new, nor is it surprising, given that non-aboriginal people have been writing on behalf of the "rights" of aboriginal people since the 16th century.

The earliest of these works were concerned primarily with how the colonial powers (Spain) should treat the "uncivilized" and savage peoples discovered in America (see, for instance de Las Casa, 1656 and de Victorio, 1917). Many would argue that there have been no real advances in "rights" for aboriginal people in America since the 16th century, but to seek advances in "rights" presupposes the acceptance of terminology. It strikes me that when aboriginal people discuss rights and borrow the rhetoric of human rights in contemporary struggle, we are using the paradigm of human rights, both nationally and internationally, as an instrument for the recognition of historic claims — and in many cases as the "only" resort. Is that really buying into the distinctly western and liberal vision of human rights concepts?

Underlying the use of human rights terminology is a plea for recognition of a different way of life, a different idea of community, of politics, of spirituality — ideas which have existed since time immemorial, but which have been cast as differences to be repressed and discouraged since colonization. In asking for recognition by another culture of the existence of your own, and for toleration of, and respect for, the practical difference that it brings with it, there seems to be something at stake which is larger than human rights, and certainly larger than the texts of particular documents which guarantee human rights, such as the *Canadian Charter of Rights and Freedoms*: a more basic request — the request to be recognized as peoples. I believe that from early colonization up to the present, no government or monarch has ever recognized aboriginal peoples as distinct peoples with cultures different from their own, in other words, as peoples whose ways of life should be tolerated and respected, even though certain customs may challenge the cultural assumptions of the newcomers.

I also believe that one reason for this, aside from the obvious one of the assertion of government power and the quest for economic dominance, is that aboriginal ways have been and still are presumed to be primitive, in the sense of "lesser" states of development. This presumption denies genuine differences by presuming that another culture is the same, just not quite as "civilized" yet. Hence, it is important for the colonial governments to take jurisdiction over aboriginal peoples in order to guide them to a more reasoned state where they can become just like them (it is not surprising that the church was usually the state's best ally).

No government has ever dealt with aboriginal peoples on an equal basis — without seeing us as means to an economic goal (settlement and development), as noble savages, the pagans without civilization, or as specimens for anthropological investigation and scientific collection.[1] Genuinely recognizing another people as another culture is more than recognizing rights of certain persons. It is not simply recognizing peoples of another colour, translated in European terms as "race," nor is it recognizing the presence of a minority because the minority is always defined by and in subordination to the majority. Placing the emphasis on race or minority (and consequently on rights) has the effect of covering over the differences at work to the majority's advantage. Aboriginal cultures are not simply different "races" — a difference explained in terms of biology (or colour): aboriginal cultures are the manifestations of a different human (collective) imagination.

To borrow the words of a non-aboriginal writer, [aboriginal] cultures "are oriented as wholes in different directions. They are travelling along different roads in pursuit of different ends, and these ends and these means in one society cannot be judged in terms of those of another society because essentially they are incommensurable ..." (Benedict, 1935). While it seems that, in the Canadian context, aboriginal peoples and non-aboriginal persons have some understanding and recognition of each other, it also seems that aboriginal peoples have been the ones who have had to suffer for tolerance (even by force and imprisonment).[2]

It is true that there have been treaties between aboriginal peoples and the British Crown. However, these do not amount, in my view, to a genuine recognition of diverse indigenous cultures; they were really Western-style (written in a highly legalistic form in most cases) methods to make way for progress, with "progress" defined according to the standards of the newcomers. After all, signing treaties was the British practice in almost all of the colonies, irrespective of cultural differences among those they "discovered" or "conquered." It is no wonder, then, that in studying the law of treaties, we quickly learn that, according to Anglo-Canadian legal standards, treaties (even before Confederation) are not seen as agreements between sovereign peoples or nations. When we inquire as to why treaties are not viewed as agreements between two (or more) sovereign peoples, we are generally led to the theory that aboriginal people (either at the time of treaty-making or now) were not sufficiently "civilized" and organized to qualify as "sovereign" peoples, or that they had already "lost" their sovereignty through some predestined and mysterious process (for example, by virtue of being "discovered").

Of course, there is no compelling reason, according to the doctrines and principles of international law, to view treaties between aboriginal peoples and the Crown as anything other than treaties between sovereigns, or *international* treaties. Nor does there seem to be any compelling reason for continuing to pretend that aboriginal peoples do not have distinct cultures, cultures which are deserving of recognition by the dominant (European) one which has been imposed in Canada. Why is it, then, that aboriginal peoples, and aboriginal claims, must be "fit-in" to the categories and concepts of a dominant culture, in some form of equivalence, in order to be acknowledged? There appears to be a contradiction at work in areas like human rights, that is, a contradiction between pretending, on the one hand to accept aboriginal peoples as distinct peoples and, on the other, of accepting something called aboriginal peoples' rights. This contradiction, which I explore briefly in the following pages, has led to a great deal of misunderstanding and has given the dominant culture (as represented by the government of Canada) plenty of scope in which to maneuvre, while avoiding a difference-based approach to aboriginal peoples as equals or as sovereigns.

"Aboriginal rights" is a category, primarily a category of law, in which most discussions about our historic claims and cultural differences are carried out in Canadian society. It is a category with severe limitations politically and legally — limitations which have been set, whether or not intentionally, by those who thought up the category — mostly non-aboriginal people. It is a realm in which discussions focusing on strange expressions like "title," "usufructory rights," "mere premises," "status," "referential incorporation," "extinguishment," and "existing" take on enormous significance, even though they do not seem to have anything to do with the everyday lives of aboriginal people. A frightening and frustrating thing about the centrality of these expressions is that they were thought up by the same non-aboriginal people that brought us the "rights" category; they seem incompatible with aboriginal ideas about land, family, social life, and spirituality. Yet, somehow, they are supposed to be helping us out, assisting in our struggle to continue to practice our cultures. Could it be that they just serve to limit the possibilities for genuine acknowledgement of the existence of aboriginal peoples as distinct cultures and political communities possessing the ability to live without external regulation and control?

I chose the first two quotations prefacing this article to illustrate the contradiction here. A *Charter* based on the supremacy of a foreign God and the (Anglo-American) rule of law just doesn't seem to be the kind of constitution that aboriginal peoples can get too excited about. Rather, it is the kind of constitution which we can get rather angry about because it has the effect of excluding aboriginal vision(s) and (diverse) views about the land and the society now called Canada. Clearly, as an historical document, it represents only one story of Canada — that is, the story of the colonialists. As a document held out to be the "supreme law of Canada" (according to Section 52 of the *Constitution Act*, 1982), it represents an act of ethnocentrism and domination, acknowledging at no point The Great Law of customary laws of the First Peoples of this territory (except unless through wish-fulfilment Section 35 is read in this way).[3]

Could aboriginal spirituality ever be represented by the likes of the preamble to the *Canadian Charter of Rights and Freedoms*? Do Chief Seattle's words render this impossible? Are we travelling along a different road, one which does not need formal written declarations to convince ourselves of what kinds of societies we are? Should we even try to do things this way? Who are we trying to please in doing so? Is it inevitable that aboriginal traditions and customs have to take the form of "rights" which are brought to courts, proven to exist, and then enforced? Is not the fundamental problem here the fact that everything has to be adjusted to fit the terms of the dominant system?

I view the problems of the aboriginal peoples — human rights area as further evidence of the fact that the dominant culture has never recognized aboriginal peoples as distinct peoples and cultures. I suppose that the exclusion or repression of the "aboriginal fact" of Canada in the present *Constitution Act* in a strange way bolsters the idea that aboriginal peoples are sovereign and distinct (yet entrapped) nations. Unless there was a conscious strategy of "ignore them and they'll go away," one would presume more ink would have been spilt on setting out the nature of the relationship between the Crown and the First Peoples of Canada; or at least on mentioning it more directly than in two perfunctory sections in the *Constitution Act*.

Larger questions loom over all of these problems. What does it mean for aboriginal peoples to advance claims enveloped in the rhetoric of human rights? While there is no question that there are serious human problems in aboriginal communities which seem to warrant redress as "human rights" violations, are such claims too piecemeal? Is there a difference between having discrete "rights" incrementally recognized, and being recognized as a people? What alternatives to rights-based claims are available? In the very pragmatic-oriented work of human rights lawyers and activists in Canada — a discourse about litigation strategies and legal doctrines — there hardly seems to be an opportunity to stop and consider these kinds of questions about aboriginal rights and the *Canadian Charter of Rights and Freedoms*. I wonder to what extent those who support struggles for the recognition of aboriginal rights have really considered these issues?

Generally, we have never really had to address these problems during the first five years of the *Charter* because we were too preoccupied with negotiations to recognize (both within the *Charter* and within another specific section of the *Constitution Act*) the "right to self-government."[4] When these negotiations failed miserably at the final meeting of the First Ministers in 1987 — a failure which was something of a foregone conclusion given that the aboriginal peoples were never seen as equal parties in the negotiation process from the beginning (instead we were given special "observer" status) — people returned to the *Charter* and the vague provision on the aboriginal rights in section 35 of the *Constitution Act, 1982* to consider legal challenges and claims based upon these provisions. It is my belief that questions regarding *which* forums and laws are especially urgent now. Such questions can hardly be avoided any longer, especially in light of the fact that aboriginal peoples are turning more to the *Charter* for recognition of their rights *vis-à-vis* the Canadian Crown, and perhaps more disturbingly, turning to the *Charter* to fight out internal battles in communities.

I would like to explore some of the layers of contradiction or conflict which are raised in the context of aboriginal peoples' claims and the *Charter*, and describe briefly an effort to meet one aspect of these contradictions which has been made by aboriginal women through the Native Women's Association of Canada. The views put forward here are my own, many of which have been developed in the course of advising the Native Women's Association of Canada on human rights matters in recent years. I have been greatly influenced in these questions by situations facing the Association and its constituents, and by both my mixed education and ancestry.[5] I do not propose to consider in any detail traditional and customary practices of specific aboriginal peoples, both for reasons of the limits of space here and because I have reservations about the extent to which knowledge about these matters can be transmitted in such a medium.[6]

The Origins of Human Rights

While it might seem obvious that human rights and the *Canadian Charter of Rights and Freedoms* are incompatible with aboriginal culture and traditions, it is helpful to trace the origin of the idea of human rights in the modern era in order to locate the differences here. The Anglo-American concept of rights was set out, for the most part, by two 17th century English political theorists, Thomas Hobbes (1651) and John Locke (1690). Locke is the more famous of the two on these matters. He developed a theory of "natural rights" — later "human" came to be substituted for "natural," after the recognition (post-Holocaust) that peoples are capable of barbaric actions in the name of what is "natural." Locke's theory of natural rights was based around his idea that every *man* (and emphasis should be on *man* because Locke is famous for his theory that society was naturally patriarchal) possesses a right to private property, or the right to own property. This right, he suggested, flowed from the fact that human beings are God's property ("God" as in the preamble to the *Canadian Charter*). He argued that people enter into "civil society" for the central, and negatively conceived, purpose of protecting their right to private property against random attack.

The idea of the absolute right to property, as an exclusive zone of ownership capable of being transmitted through the family (through males according to a doctrine called "primogenitor"), is the cornerstone of the idea of rights — the idea that there is a zone of absolute human right where the individual can do what he chooses: "The right is a loaded gun that the right holder may shoot at will in his corner of town" (Unger, 1986). It does not take much of a stretch of the imagination to see where slavery and the subordination of women found legitimacy in the Anglo-American tradition — with the absolute ownership of property, and autonomous domains, "naturally" rights will extend "even to another person's body" (Hobbes, 1651).

Although there is no pan-aboriginal culture of iron-clad system of beliefs, this notion of rights based on individual ownership is antithetical to the widely-shared understanding of creation and stewardship responsibilities of First Nations peoples for the land, or for Mother Earth.

Moreover, to my knowledge, there are no notions among aboriginal Nations of living together for the purposes of protecting an individual interest in property. Aboriginal life has been set out in stories handed down through generations and in customary laws sometimes represented by wampum belts, sacred pipes, medicine bundles, and rock paintings. For example, the teachings of the Four Directions is that life is based on four principles: trust, kindness, sharing and strength. While these are responsibilities which each person owes to others, they represent the larger function of social life, that is, to honour and respect Mother Earth. There is no equivalent of "rights" here because there is no equivalent to the ownership of private property. The collective or communal bases of aboriginal life does not really have a parallel to individual rights; they are incommensurable. To try to explain to an Elder that, under Canadian law, there are carefully worked-over doctrines pertaining to who owns every inch of the country, the sky, the ocean, and even the moon, would provoke disbelief and profound sadness.

The Structure of the *Canadian Charter*

Nevertheless, the Canadian human rights system, having been distanced in time and space somewhat from its origin and conceptual basis in the theories about the right to individual ownership to property, seems little less foreign, especially since so much is said of aboriginal matters in the context of human rights. Some writers even argue that, in Canada, the *Charter* recognized certain collective rights, such as aboriginal rights, and not merely individual rights. However, my reading of the law leads me to believe that the individual property basis of human rights is revealed clearly in the text of the *Canadian Charter*, as well as in recent cases which have been decided under the *Charter*. The language of the *Charter* refers to human rights enjoyed by "every citizen of Canada," "every individual," "any person," etc. The section of the *Charter* on enforcement applies to "[a]ny *one* whose rights or freedoms ... have been infringed," permitting them to apply to court for the order the court considers appropriate in the circumstances — almost always the singular subject.

The extent to which a human rights law set out in such individualist terms could ever either (i) be interpreted as including a collective understanding of rights, or (ii) lead to judges acknowledging that other peoples might not base their social relations on these individual "rights" notions, is highly questionable. There is nothing strong enough in the *Charter* to allow for either a collectivist idea of rights (or responsibilities), if such a theory is conceivable, or toleration of a community organized around collective values. When cases involving aboriginal peoples come before the courts, it is doubtful that different standards of legal analysis will be applied. Already the case law has taken a disturbing course from the viewpoint of aboriginal peoples.

With shades of private property notions in mind, the Supreme Court of Canada in the recent *Morgentaler* case on abortion suggested that "the rights guaranteed in the *Charter* erect around each individual, metaphorically speaking, an invisible fence over which the state will not be allowed to trespass. The role of the courts is to map out, piece by piece, the parameters of the fence."[7] In an earlier decision, one involving aboriginal persons, the Federal Court of Canada took the view that "in the absence of legal provisions to the contrary, the interests of individual persons will be deemed to have precedence over collective rights. In the absence of law to the contrary, this must be as true of Indian Canadians as of others."[8]

Even in the area of language rights — an area said to be a cornerstone of collective rights in the *Charter* — the Supreme Court of Canada in the recent case involving Québec's former *Bill 101* has indicated that this right is somehow both an individual and a collective one: "Language itself indicates a means by which a people may express its cultural identity. It is also the means by which the individual expresses his or her personal identity and sense of individuality."[9] How to go about reconciling these two aspects when they conflict is no easy task, and the Court gives little guidance here on its view of collective rights, except to say that the right to speak their language must be protected at law against the community's prohibition of it.

Even in the area of equality rights, as recognized in section 15 of the *Charter*, the text applies to "every individual." This provision has been interpreted by the courts not as a general recognition of the idea of equality (which, if read as "sameness," would be deeply disturbing to aboriginal people), but simply as a principle in relating to the application of given laws. In a recent equality case, the Supreme Court of Canada stated that section 15 "is not a general guarantee of equality, it does not provide for equality between individuals or groups within society in a general or abstract sense, nor does it impose on individuals or groups an obligation to accord equality treatment to others. *It is concerned with the application of the law.*"[10] The scope for aboriginal rights claims under section 15 is limited, even if such a course was seen as desirable by aboriginal leaders.

Moreover, we can begin to see the broader implications of these cases for aboriginal peoples or aboriginal claims. It is difficult to move in a certain direction as a people if individuals can challenge collective decisions based on infringement of their individual rights and if collective goals will not be understood or prioritized. Some people may view this as the triumph of democracy, but it makes the preservation of a different culture and the pursuit of collective political goals almost impossible.

In aboriginal communities where customary political and spiritual institutions are the guiding force (even alongside the imposed *Indian Act* system of Band Councils), such as the Haudenosaunee of the Iroquois Confederates, recourse to an individual-rights based law like the *Charter* could result in further weakening of the cultural identity of the community. This could take one of two forms: either a member of the community would challenge aboriginal laws based on individual rights protections in the *Charter* arguing that they have not been respected by their government (an internal challenge); or a non-aboriginal person could challenge the laws of an aboriginal government on the basis that they do not conform with *Charter* standards (an external challenge).

In the case of an external challenge, for example, on the basis of voting or candidacy rights where a non-aboriginal complainant argued that they could not vote or stand for elections in an aboriginal community because of cultural restrictions, the court would be given the authority to decide on an important part of the future of an aboriginal community. It would have to consider the protections of aboriginal rights in the *Charter* and weigh these against the individual right to vote recognized in section 3. Should Canadian courts (and non-aboriginal judges) have authority in these cases? Given the highly individualistic basis of the *Charter*, and of the history of human rights, would the collective aboriginal right stand a chance? I doubt it. As the Assembly of First Nations argued before the Parliamentary Committee on Aboriginal Affairs in 1982:

> [as] Indian people we cannot afford to have individual rights override collective rights. Our societies have never been structured that way, unlike yours, and that is where the clash comes ... If you isolate the individual rights from the collective rights, then you are heading down another path that is even more discriminatory ... The *Canadian Charter of Rights* is in conflict with our philosophy and culture ...[11]

The other possible challenge, the internal challenge, where a member of an aboriginal community felt dissatisfied with a particular course of action the aboriginal government was taking and turned to the *Charter* for the recognition of a right, is equally if not more worrisome. This kind of challenge would be a dangerous opening for a Canadian court to rule on individual versus collective rights *vis-a-vis* aboriginal peoples; it would also break down community methods of dispute-resolution and restoration. Here, the example of the *Indian Civil Rights Act*[12] in the United States is instructive. This act, based on the idea that protections for the *American Bill of Rights* should be extended to aboriginal communities, along with the establishment of tribal courts which would have the same function as American courts generally, has been greatly criticized by aboriginal people as imposing alien ways of life. As two noted scholars suggest:

> In philosophical terms, it is much easier to describe the impact of the ... Act. Traditional Indian society understood itself as a complex of responsibilities and duties. The [Act] merely transposed this belief into a society based on rights against government and eliminated any sense of responsibility that people might have felt for one another. Granted that many of the customs that made

> duties and responsibilities a serious matter of individual
> action had eroded badly in the decades since the tribes
> had agreed to move to the reservations, the impact of the
> [Act] was to make these responsibilities impossible to
> perform because the Act inserted the trial court as an
> institution between the people and their responsibilities.
> People did not have to confront one another before their
> community and resolve their problems; they had only to
> file suit in tribal court (Deloria and Lytle, 1984).

The lessons of the *American Indian Civil Rights Act* and of the establishment of tribal courts are important ones in light of the *Charter*. If internal disputes are brought before Canadian courts, it will seriously undermine the aboriginal system of government based on responsibility (like the Four Directions) and interpose a system of individual-based rights. It also has the effect of encouraging people to go outside the community, and outside of custom, to settle disputes in formal courts — instead of having to deal with a problem within a community.

This might sound like a hard line to take, especially when one considers the extent to which customs and traditional methods of governance and dispute-resolution have been dislodged in aboriginal communities after more than a century of life under the *Indian Act*. The experience of gender-based discrimination was employed as a technique of assimilation up until the 1985 amendments to the *Indian Act* (many see the gender-based discriminatory provisions as having continuing effect despite the amendments), and scarred many aboriginal communities as male-dominated Band councils frequently sided against women and with the Canadian government in the belief that to do otherwise would undermine the Crown's responsibility for aboriginal peoples.

As a consequence, women were forced to go outside the community to resolve the injustices of gender discrimination, so cases were brought under the *Canadian Bill of Rights* and eventually under the *United Nations Covenant on Civil and Political Rights*. Changes were made to the *Indian Act*, but many of the after-effects of gender discrimination still plague aboriginal communities, including problems associated with women returning to communities and being able to take up residence, educate their children, share in social services, and receive per capita payments from resource exploitation on aboriginal lands.

Communities have been slow to address questions related to the aftermath of gender discrimination in the *Indian Act*, and the mechanisms available to resolve disputes according to customary practices are not necessarily available. This places a great deal of pressure on aboriginal communities, which could lead to cases being taken to Canadian courts pursuant to the *Charter* for recognition of rights against aboriginal governments. As a result of concern over what this could lead to, in light of the individual-based notions of rights under Canadian law, and in light of lessons derived from the United States experience with the *Indian Civil Rights Act*, aboriginal women have been working on projects to encourage the development of First Nations laws in areas like "citizenship" and human rights and responsibilities — laws based, as far as possible, on inherent First Nation jurisdiction and customary practices.

An Alternative Approach: First Nations Human Rights and Responsibilities Laws

The Native Women's Association of Canada has addressed questions relating to gender discrimination in the *Indian Act* and related problems in aboriginal communities since the late 1970s. In 1985, when amendments to the *Indian Act* aimed at eliminating gender discrimination were finally passed, the Native Women's Association took the position that, while aboriginal women could support the end of unfair bias against women, they could not simply support the Federal government's efforts to "improve" the *Indian Act* and the extension of legislative control over the lives of aboriginal peoples through its paternalistic provisions. Consequently, the Association turned its attention to the development of a "First Nation Citizenship Code," or a model law which would address the issues of membership or citizenship in a First Nation, but would base its principles and jurisdiction not on Canadian law, but on the inherent jurisdiction of First Nations to regulate citizenship as practices since time immemorial.

The model code was distributed to every aboriginal community in Canada with a letter encouraging communities to take a First Nations approach to citizenship (and not an *Indian Act* approach) and to set up local mechanisms based, as much as possible, on customary principles for settling disputes, so that problems regarding citizenship could be addressed in the community itself and not in the Canadian courts. As it became clear that citizenship was not the only area of concern in communities (although the issue of Indian status was by far the most divisive), it was evident that some other efforts would need to be expended to discourage internal challenges of aboriginal government actions getting into Canadian courts under the *Charter*. In 1986, the Native Women's Association of Canada began to consider the development of another model law, parallel to the Citizenship Code, which would be a First Nations human rights and responsibilities law.

It appears that this Code (which at the time of writing is still in the draft stages) will be based on the inherent jurisdiction of First Nations to make laws for their peoples. It will include a very loosely and generously worded part on human rights and responsibilities, corresponding to the four groups of rights and responsibilities which come from the teachings of the Four Directions. Hence, there are the following responsibilities and rights:

(i) *kindness* — social rights
(ii) *honesty* — political and civil rights
(iii) *sharing* — economic rights, and

(iv)*strength* — cultural rights.

For example, the responsibility and rights category of strength/cultural rights would include provisions on the right to pursue traditional occupations, the right to education in aboriginal languages, the right to customary marriage and adoptions, the right to participate in ceremonies according to laws and traditions of the Nation, and, most importantly, the recognition of the fundamental importance of Elders and spiritual leaders in the preservation of ancestral and customary law and in the health and well-being of the community as a whole.

The provisions on the model law developed by the Native Women's Association on dispute-resolution provide options for a particular community to consider creating a law which fits within its customs and aspirations. These include mediation, the establishment of a Human Rights Committee, and a Council of Elders. Also included are options for setting up methods to deal with conflicts on a regional basis (for example, an Iroquois or Ojibway council of Elders). It is hoped that the work of the Association will contribute to the development of community laws and less formal community solutions to reduce the possibilities that individual members of the First Nations communities will have to go outside their communities (to foreign courts) for redress of grievances. It appears that the development of community codes is the best available solution to the problems in communities and to the threat of the (further) imposition of a Western individualistic human rights system on aboriginal communities.

Future Challenges

The work of the Native Women's Association of Canada really only addresses the problem of internal challenges based on the *Charter* by members of First Nations communities. It does not attempt to deal with other areas of concern, such as external challenges or claims brought by non-aboriginal peoples pursuant to the *Charter*, calling into question the collective basis of aboriginal communities.[13] Even claims brought by aboriginal communities against the Federal Government based on provisions of the *Charter* seem to present a dangerous opportunity for the court to take a restrictive view of collective-based community goals. Any case which presents a Canadian court with the opportunity to balance or weigh an individual right against a collective understanding of community will be an opportunity to delimit the recognition of aboriginal peoples as distinct cultures.

This is something quite different from dealing on an equal footing with aboriginal peoples about historic claims and cultural differences which have to be addressed and settled. These cases permit the court to say, "Yes, we do have jurisdiction over you, and we will decide what is best for you under Canadian law." It is not that different from the imposed system of rule under the *Indian Act*, except in the *Charter* cases, the court can cloak its decision in the rhetoric of democratic freedom, emancipation, multiculturalism and human rights for "all Canadians." The only way to really consider the political and cultural differences between aboriginal peoples and the Canadian state is through discussions which are quasi-international, so that the respective "sovereignty" of the parties will be respected.

Aboriginal peoples have been trying to pursue this (international) course during the past decade. The United Nations has established a special Working Group on Indigenous Populations to consider the human rights violations (really historic claims under international law) of indigenous peoples from around the globe. During the past seven years, there have been six meetings of the Working Group, and recently efforts have been directed at the development of a United Nations Declarations on Indigenous Rights. Although aboriginal peoples have been participating quite actively in this process of development of a United Nations Declaration, once again, we are really on the outside of the United Nations system. Nevertheless, certain States which are part of the United Nations structure have been willing to advocate for the recognition of indigenous rights in a declaration.[14]

The matters dealt with in the proceedings of the Working Group and in the Draft Declaration can hardly be ignored, especially when one considers the extent to which they are present in all areas of the globe. As one noted international scholar has suggested, "[t]he peoples of entrapped nations are a sleeping giant in the workings of power politics" (Falk, 1987). A cornerstone of an eventual declaration would have to be, from the aboriginal perspective, a recognition and explicit extension of self-determination to indigenous peoples under international law. There are persuasive arguments that, even without a specific declaration, international law already recognizes the right of all peoples (including aboriginal peoples) to self-determination.

Self-determination is something different than self-government, although it could include the latter. Self-government (which has been the pinnacle of all human rights discussions in the Canadian context) implies that aboriginal peoples were not previously able to govern themselves because they were not at an advanced enough stage of civilization, but can now take on some responsibility for their own affairs.[15] Very few people make a distinction between self-government and self-determination. In a recent (1988) report by the Canadian Bar Association Special Committee on Native Justice, the idea of self-government is used throughout without any distinction as to its historical context or political implications. On this point, aboriginal women in Canada, through the voice of the Native Women's Association, have again made their position in support of self-determination over self-government quite clear.[16]

In the international context, the draft declaration on indigenous rights is silent on the issue of self-determination. It contains many disturbing provisions on lesser notions like "autonomy ... in local affairs" and the "right to exist." While these might seem progressive in some situations where the very life of aboriginal people is systematically threatened on a daily basis, the provisions do not go far enough in recognizing aboriginal people as distinct cultures and political entities, equally as capable of governing and making decisions as European sovereigns, except with different political and cultural goals.

A great deal more work will have to be done in the next few years to ensure that the text of the draft declaration is one which will recognize indigenous people as legitimate, though different, governments and cultures. The only way to do this, in international law, is through a recognition of self-determination. Realizing this goal will require broad-based support from international society, manifested in the work of non-government organizations, women's movements, and sympathetic States. The Canadian government and Canadian people could do much to assist the international process if the government would simply recognize aboriginal peoples as distinct peoples with different but equally legitimate cultures and ways of life. This cannot be done through Canadian courts and in the rhetoric of Canadian human rights — it has to be done through a joint aboriginal-Canadian discussion process where, unlike the series of discussions held on Canadian constitutional amendments, aboriginal peoples are equal participants in the process, along with the Prime Minister and perhaps Provincial Premiers.

In the meantime, aboriginal women will continue to do what can be done to ensure that aboriginal communities are governed by customary laws and practices, through the development of First Nations laws, and through the political and spiritual voice of the Native Women's Association of Canada as guided by its Elders and affiliated women's organizations.

Notes

1. Here I am mindful of the rise of the museums of so-called "natural history" which were dedicated to the study of primitive peoples and the collection of cultural objects for display as curiosities. It was not only cultural or spiritual objects that were collected during the rise of the museum and curatorial science, but also human specimens. For example, see Harper (1986), or a recent article in *Harper's* magazine (March 1989) suggesting that the New York Museum of Natural History has the skeletal remains of 15,000 aboriginal persons in its collection, each carefully boxed and numbered.

2. For just a few examples, the prohibition of the potlatch under the *Indian Act*, the burning of the Longhouses of the Iroquois Confederacy at the turn of the century, and the convictions of the Innu in Labrador for protesting low-level military flights over their territory.

3. Aboriginal rights are mentioned only twice within the text of the *Constitution Act*, 1982. The first is in the *Charter*, in the Section 25 interpretative provision which provides (in part) that "[t]he guarantee in this Charter of certain rights and freedoms shall not be construed to abrogate or derogate from any aboriginal, treaty or other rights or freedoms that pertain to the aboriginal peoples of Canada ..."; the second is in Part II of the *Constitution Act* in Section 35 which recognized and affirms "existing

aboriginal and treaty rights."
4. Of course, not all aboriginal peoples participated in this process of negotiation. Many perceived it as a process designed to compromise historic claims and treaties in a document (the *Canadian Constitution*) which would suit the needs of the federal and provincial governments first, and aboriginal peoples second. Some people, such as the Mikmaq of Atlantic Canada, believe that the process was a violation of Canadian international human rights obligations. They have a complaint currently under consideration by the United Nations Human Rights Committee, CCPR/C/39/D/205/1986 (admissability decision released 25 July, 1990).
5. Mixed education meaning both formal legal training, and the significant teachings of my Grandmothers, Sisters, and the Lodge; and mixed ancestry — Cree and Anglo-Canadian, which seems to focus the mind on contradictions like those discussed in this article.
6. However, see "Our World According to Osennontion and Skonaganlehirá." *Canadian Woman Studies/Les Cahiers De La Femme* 10(2-3) (1989): 6 for valuable information on Iroquois customs and the idea of rights.
7. Madame Justice Wilson writing, *Morgentaler, Smoling and Scott* v. The Queen and Attorney General of Canada [1988] 1 S.C.R. 164.
8. Mr. Justice MacGuigan, *Boyer v. Canada*, [1986] 35 N.R. 305.
9. *Attorney General of Quebec & Brown and Ford & McKenna et al. v. La Chassure Brown's Inc.* [1988] 2 S.C.R. 8.
10. *Mr. Justice McIntyre, Law Society of British Columbia et al. v. Andrews et al.* [1989] 1 S.C.R. 143, emphasis added.
11. Minutes and Proceedings, House of Commons Standing Committee on Aboriginal Affairs, Evidence no. 58 (September 29, 1982).
12. U.S., *Statutes at Large*, 82:77.
13. Section 25 of the *Charter* mentioned in footnote 3 above is supposed to guard against such challenges, but it is difficult to predict whether the court will take a generous view in favour of collective rights, especially when everything else in the *Charter*, and in the history of human rights, seems to be directed to the protection of the individual from the community or government.
14. The Scandinavian states have been particularly supportive here.
15. The idea that aboriginal communities are not sufficiently advanced enough to control their own affairs is recognized in the *Indian Act*, where, under the provisions for Band Council control over financial decisions, a band can make laws for financial issues only when the Minister determines whether or not they have reached a sufficient stage of "development."
16. They have done so through a special declaration adopted unanimously at an Annual Meeting (Whitehorse, 1986).

The Potential of the Criminal Justice System to Promote Feminist Concerns

Laureen Snider

"Reducing Rapist's Jail Sentence Trivializes Attack, Women Say"
(*Toronto Star*, February 13, 1988, Pages 1 and 4).

"I have come to understand that political sophistication is not a luxury but an absolute necessity if even the best of intentions are not to wind up as inadvertent instruments of oppression" (Varda Burstyn, 1985:4).

"To transfer from dependence upon one man to reliance upon a male-dominated state is not liberation ... but merely the familiar dependence in a new form" (Veronica Strong-Boag, 1986:103).

While the alliance of feminism and the state has been steadily gaining strength over the last 20 years, recent research has documented the state's continuing tendency to ignore or denigrate the many crimes in which women are the primary victims (rape, "spousal" assault, the use of women in pornographic media industries, etc.) (Lea and Young, 1984; Chappell and Lewis, 1977; Brownmiller, 1975; Medea and Thompson, 1974; Chappell and Singer, 1977). Low conviction rates, atypical and discriminatory evidentiary requirements and the refusal of male-dominated criminal justice systems to prosecute men (who were often seen as legitimately controlling "their own" women through such crimes), impelled feminists to seek alternative remedies for these injustices. While some of the tactics tried to empower women through assertiveness, self defence training, consciousness raising and setting up women's hostels, shelters and clinics, others concentrated on increasing the responsiveness of the state, specifically the criminal justice system. Thus, we have seen many successful initiatives to rewrite the laws on rape, pornography and wife beating (Snider, 1985; Caringella-Macdonald, 1987; Marsh *et al.*, 1982). Such initiatives create criminal offences where none had existed before, make arrests, charges and convictions easier to obtain, and in some cases increase punishment. The aim was to use the state in order to widen the net of social control over (male) offenders — to punish more of them more severely for longer periods of time. This was an effort to use criminal law symbolically, to force the state to live up to its legitimizing myths of universalism and equality, to strengthen the women's movement by demonstrating that it had the official backing of the state, and to lessen the victimization of women by deterring potential offenders. While it does not appear that increasing punishment has, in fact, any deterrent effect (see summaries in Walker, 1985), attempts to use the state as an ally remain an integral part of feminist strategy.

The purpose of this paper is to argue that a strategy relying upon the criminal justice system is practically, theoretically and morally wrong. While the apparatus of government is too powerful to ignore, the criminal justice system is not a reliable ally. Entrusting more power to it means investing it with increased control over women's lives, control that is essentially invisible and unmonitored. It means giving over power which should be kept in feminist hands to a state bureaucracy with its own agenda — one which will not be consonant with feminist goals. From a moral perspective, strengthening the criminal justice system means encouraging inhumane and repressive solutions against populations already victimized by structural forces. Practically, such solutions play into the hands of those who are interested in increasing the level of social control over populations seen as problematic (the young, the poor, ethnic groups, women and "radicals" of all kinds). Politically, it facilitates superficial and individualistic analyses by representing the young, male, typically lower class criminal (the stereotypical defendant) as the prime and indeed the only villain. Victimizing women is not a class-specific phenomenon; punishing criminals is. Moreover, the criminal justice system's only documented success is in making those subjected to it more resentful, more dangerous, more economically marginal and more misogynous. Finally, from a theoretical perspective, attention is directed away from structural problems inherent in patriarchy and capitalism and towards reformist "solutions" which accept the present socio-economic system as a given.

This paper is divided into four parts: *Part I* recalls the history of expanding state control and the role feminist theory has played in this; *Part II* outlines the historical relations between the feminist movement and the state, showing what the results of feminist/state alliances have been; *Part III* looks at the connections between feminism and the state in modern times; and *Part IV* addresses the implications of the critique of criminalizing strategies for feminists. Strategies for empowerment which are in harmony with the goals of the feminist movement are set out in the conclusion.

I. The Expansion of Social Control

Debate about feminism, patriarchy and the state has been raging fiercely for the past decade. Much feminist work builds on Marxist literature which argues that states under capitalism act to facilitate accumulation by the owners and controllers of the means of production while simultaneously ensuring that legitimacy is maintained, in order to promote the continuance of the existing system of social and economic relations (O'Connor, 1973; Miliband, 1969; Panitch, 1977). To do this, then, states must sometimes go against the wishes of certain segments of the ruling class to prevent disorder, loss of legitimacy and rebellion by classes which have an unequal share of resources. Marxist theory, however, has seen the economic system of capitalism as the prime cause of all exploitation, failing to recognize that men of all classes have systematically dominated and exploited women. Patriarchy, defined as "a set of social relations which operates to control reproduction through the control of women both in their reproductive and productive labour" (Ursel, 1986:150), has been ignored as a theoretical and conceptual category (Hamilton, 1986a). Socialist feminist theories have attempted to correct this by focusing on the ways in which both class and gender reproduce patterns of dominance.

Historically, feminists argue, men-as-a-group secured economic, social and political control over women with the rise of agrarian societies, enshrining the principles whereby men had power over women and children, and ruling class males had power over all. Men of lower social orders, unable to wield influence politically or economically, nevertheless ruled the women and children of their social level (Burstyn, 1985). Ursel (1986) argues that, whereas in preclass, kin-based societies, communal patriarchy was the norm (production was subsumed to the needs of the reproductive, kin-based groups), with the emergence of class-structured societies (such as feudalism) familial patriarchy predominated. Production was de-centralized and the individual male patriarch maintained control over the household and women's access to resources. In the early stages of capitalism, familial patriarchy continued to predominate in that the family became the primary social institution for ensuring that attitudes appropriate to production and reproduction were learned.

With the growing centralization of production under capitalism, the system of familial patriarchy came under attack, since the labour of women and children was increasingly demanded outside the household. Factory owners wanted the labour of lower/working class women and children because of "super-profitability" (Burstyn, 1985:9); they were able to pay women and children even less than men, thus facilitating the extraction of surplus value. It is not surprising, then, that they no longer maintained that all women's activities should be confined to the familial sphere.

In the capitalist era, more and more of the actions, thoughts, feelings and behaviour of all classes and both genders have become subject to pressing, precise and intrusive control outside the family domain. Foucault (1979, 1969), E.P. Thompson (1966, 1975), Melossi (1980) and others have described the struggle waged in 18th and 19th century Europe to turn a work force accustomed to a high degree of self-determination and control over their productive and leisure behaviours into one which lived — worked, played, consumed and reproduced — under the aegis of stringent impersonal rules. As Melossi (1980) explained, workers had to be forced to endure the training process necessary to turn them from country labourers into disciplined factory workers. They submitted only when all alternative modes of survival — notably the subsistence economy — were closed off to them, leaving open only the unrewarding and dangerous avenues of vagrancy and crime. By the 20th century, this process was well advanced (Chan and Ericson, 1981; Cohen, 1979, 1985; Scull, 1981, 1977). Disciplinary institutions (the factory, school, workhouse, prison, hospital, etc.) were in place throughout civil society, overseen and guaranteed by an increasingly powerful and intrusive state apparatus in which the criminal law played an important part.

Family and welfare law have also been crucial parts of this transition, as state authority has been inserted ever deeper into areas formerly seen as "private," that is, controlled by the male family head (Donzelot, 1977; Lasch, 1979). The struggle of class versus gender interests, then, has led to a system of social patriarchy (Ursel, 1986:169-73). Patriarchy has not gone away; it has merely shifted its form. The state, rather than the individual male, increasingly controls the reproduction and labour of women. This shift has been actively encouraged by feminists who have attempted, since the earliest days of the movement, to use the authority of the state to challenge familial patriarchy.

Within this social theory, however, suspicion about the expansion of the state, and specifically about the potential of law to produce changes beneficial to less powerful classes, is deeply rooted. Lenin saw bourgeois law as inherently limited by the unequal relations on which it is founded, and useful therefore only as an arena for struggle and/or for political education (Bierne and Hunt, 1987:8). Picciotto (1982), Pashukanis (1978) and Balbus (1977, 1973) have argued that legal reform as a tactic merely redefines problems which are caused by an inherently exploitative economic structure into debates over individual rights. Understanding social problems in these terms, then, trivializes them and encourages the population to understand them in liberal terms, as issues of unequal rights allocation, demanding remedies to be found in the courts and not the streets. Such "solutions" direct attention away from the legal system's class bias, and obscure the fact that this system is based on a structure of exploitative relations of production that give rise to the very social problems it purports to solve. As Chambliss (1986:30) argues, legal reforms are state responses to conflicts created by the underlying contradictions themselves, and are therefore congenitally incapable of correcting them.

Within North American criminology, a variant of Marxist theory known as instrumentalism has long maintained that legal reform has no liberating or ameliorating potential within a capitalist order. And even if one resists this rationale at the level of theory (instrumentalism has been criticized for its epistemological and theoretical assumptions, as well as its naive, deterministic and functionalist conclusions), there are very few criminologists who dispute the conclusion that, at the empirical level, reform has not "worked" (cf. Martinson, 1974). Studies in areas from corporate crime to parole to legal aid (Mandel, 1986; Ericson, 1981; Ericson and Baranek, 1982; Lefcourt, 1971; Goff and Reasons, 1978) all point to the ineffectiveness of law. When law aims to empower the powerless (such as prisoners and welfare mothers), it fails because the intended beneficiaries lack the knowledge, power, time, ideological clout, access to the media and visibility to get the law enforced in ways which promote their interests (though lawyers, psychiatrists, social workers or other professionals who get an expanded state-financed clientele, often benefit). Conversely, when the aim is to control the powerful, laws fail because the targets, in this instance, corporations or merchants or state officials, have more than enough resources to block enforcement efforts (and the efforts are usually puny, anyway, for ideological and structural reasons).

Despite its oft-documented drawbacks, however, law has become the predominant weapon in the scenario of state expansion. Its ability to stigmatize and to convey symbolic messages about the social unacceptability of a particular behaviour has made law a favoured tool of reformers, while its invisibility, flexibility and coercive potential make it appealing to lawmakers and officials in the criminal justice system itself (police, crown attorneys, etc.). The fact that old laws are typically replaced with measures which embody the same values of control and order (Ericson, 1987:33) seems to be ignored by progressive groups. There is a widespread belief, hated by the Right and hailed by the Left, that the era following World War II has been marked by increasing permissiveness, symbolized by widespread and effective law reforms which have decriminalized abortion, legalized homosexuality, and the like. This is far from the truth.

The much vaunted liberalism of the 1960s, though important as ideology, was largely mythical in terms of legal change. Certainly it is true that affluence, the so-called youth rebellion of the sixties and a "new" middle class produced short-lived consensus on the need for restructuring and rationalizing some of the most authoritarian institutions and values of the past. However, as Hall (1980) and Melossi (1980) have pointed out, this occurred largely within interstices where tight disciplinary controls had already become obsolete. Hall (1980:14) explains this seeming liberalization as part of the shift in the micro-physics of power, a double taxonomy characterized by a move "towards stricter penalty and control, towards greater freedom and leniency." Some liberalizing may have occurred in Britain in homosexuality, divorce and abortion reform, but simultaneous tightening also occurred.

In Canada, the reform era of the sixties led to two mild reforms in criminal law: one which decriminalized private, consensual homosexual relations; and a second which allowed hospitals to set up medical committees to decide upon abortions, permitting them to take into consideration the psychological as well as the physical health of the woman. Prostitution laws were not changed, but courts held that prostitutes must engage in "pressing and persistent" advances to be guilty of a criminal offence. A Royal Commission Report in the early 1970s recommended the decriminalization of marijuana, but this never became law. While prison terms for possession of soft drugs have become less common, the maximum penalties in law remain unchanged. No massive trend to get the state out of bedrooms (or living rooms, bathrooms, etc) can be detected in such a record.[1]

The ironic truth is that, despite the widely held perception that Western democracies have become dangerously permissive, they have in fact experienced a continuous increase in control throughout the post-war period (Ratner and McMullen, 1983; Taylor, 1983). Throughout North America and Europe, control over what used to be called the dangerous classes has tightened, with incarceration rates skyrocketing and voluntary "treatment" programs increasingly transformed into compulsory detention. Even at the level of rhetoric, "rehabilitation" has been replaced by "just desserts," and *parens patriae* principles in juvenile systems have given way to "rights" frameworks. Reforms originally intended as ameliorating measures or alternatives to punitive control, such as parole or community service orders, become additions to existing systems as the net of social control continually gets wider (Ericson, 1987; Cohen, 1979, 1985; Chan and Ericson, 1981; Scull, 1977, 1981; Friedenberg, 1975).[2]

In Ontario in 1975-80, for example, there was a three-fold increase in the number of probation orders issued in proportion to the population, and in 1981 there was a similar increase in the number of community service orders added into the conditions of probation (Ericson, 1987:23-24). The number of police per citizen increased by over 50 percent between 1961 and 1975 in Canada, and the cost of the policing sector increased by a factor of 19 (Ericson, 1987:25). The situation is much more dramatic in the United States and Britain, where Right wing "law and order" governments have held power. The number of laws continues to grow (As Pound pointed out some years ago: "Of 100,000 persons arrested in Chicago in 1912, more than half were for violations of legal precepts which did not exist 25 years before") (Pound, 1930; cited in Hagan, 1986:47).

This "blind spasm of control" (Hall 1980:3) has not led to a society which is more just, humane or safe. Why, then, has the feminist movement turned to the state, and specifically to the criminal law, to secure improvements in the position of women? As the next section documents, it is certainly not because the movement has found the state a reliable ally in the past.

II. Women and the Criminal Justice System

To understand why the feminist movement has sought remedies in state action, one must look at the history of the movement. Urbanization and industrialization have reconfigured the terrain in which women operated. Although women had few rights under kin-based familial patriarchy, they were an integral part of an extended family and community network which provided them with an essential role, a secure status and various social and religious supports. With the industrial revolution, traditional support systems vanished, leaving working class women utterly dependent upon men who were less bound by traditional familial responsibilities, and who were unable to extract from employers a wage which would support one person, let alone a family. When women, in desperation, turned to the wage economy, they were usually paid one-third to one-half of the male wage.

Middle and upper class women were affected too, albeit in quite different ways. As more and more of their traditional responsibilities were taken over by professionals or alleviated by machines, their leisure time expanded. Often equipped with a basic education, told they embodied morality and goodness, yet denied basic political and social rights, they came to feel increasingly confined. At the same time, the contradictions between the hypothetical "special" role women were supposed to embody and the conditions to which working class women were subjected was perceived by more and more. Thus, the first wave of feminism came to be dominated by middle and upper class women, and focused upon achieving changes which would benefit their "social inferiors." This factor was crucial in shaping the direction the movement would eventually take. Temperance and prohibition, universal suffrage and education, day nurseries for the children of working women, and special courts for juveniles were all part of this process.

Once they entered the public sphere, women faced virulent opposition from all sides. At first, although isolated individuals might have been sympathetic, virtually all formal institutions — the church, educators, the nascent media, the legal profession and industrialists — opposed the concept of women's rights, and the specific reforms women sought. Faced with such opposition, feminist leaders increasingly predicated their right to be involved on their "special qualities" as women. Thus, it was argued that women *qua* women were more moral than men and had an obligation to help resolve issues relating to the welfare and upbringing of future generations. The expertise associated with their role as mothers, nurturers and protectors of the race became the dominant ideological weapon they employed against those who accused them of being unwomanly and of involving themselves in affairs of state which were none of their business. This argument allowed feminists to gain both tactical and strategic advantage.

Unfortunately for feminism as a movement, this strategy was not without costs. It helped set the stage for excluding all but single childless women from fulltime professional positions in the business world. Once the particular goals that had brought them into the public sphere were achieved, women were required, by their own rhetoric, to retreat to look after their own children, homes and husbands. Their "special mission" had been achieved. Indeed, this is what happened. Until the late sixties, when the modern feminist movement was forged out of a somewhat different set of contradictions, married women were expected to stay out of the labour force, except when their services were explicitly required by special circumstances (such as the absence of men during the two World Wars).

More immediately, the emphasis on women's special attributes strengthened the elitism which had always been present in the movement. The majority of working class and poor women never had the option of being dependent upon affluent males, and thus were always forced to seek wage labour, at least part-time, in addition to being wives and mothers. While some reforms may have benefited them (for example, those specifying maximum hours or improving working conditions), their need to earn a fair wage was largely ignored. The social relations of capitalism must be forced to take into account the imperatives of reproduction; thus, when feminists defined such issues as secondary or irrelevant and stopped struggling for universal daycare and maternity leave, the exigencies of profit maximization and patriarchy ensured that the status quo would remain unchanged. Allowing women to fulfill their roles as mothers and nurturers was increasingly the dominant goal, not making it easier for them to operate outside the home or in the absence of a male household head. As privileged women continued to set the tone of the movement, the stage was set for an increasing reliance on the state. Women of this class believed in the benevolence of the state while working class women, who were more likely to have seen its coercive side, generally lacked such blind faith.

Thus, we see the women's movement in the 19th and early 20th centuries calling for ever greater state control through criminal law. Its increasing involvement with the "purity" movement, its fight for laws against alcohol and prostitution, for compulsory sterilization of those deemed unfit (such as the mentally ill and retarded), and for the institutionalization of all deemed not to fit middle class morality became the dominant foci. In the area of prostitution, for example, the threat of venereal disease combined with religious precepts, secured widespread support for measures to "rescue" the prostitute by criminalizing her occupation. Many middle and upper class feminists of the day, wives and mothers themselves, were terrified by the public health menace posed by prostitutes. In much of North America, prostitution was widely tolerated, especially in the frontier cities and ports, until late in the 19th century, for it was seen as providing a necessary sexual outlet for men. In the United Kingdom, the Contagious Diseases Acts were passed in 1866 and 1869, requiring prostitutes to register with the police and be examined for venereal disease

(Walkowitz, 1980). This public health approach set the stage for an alliance with the essentially conservative eugenics movement, which was directed against the massive fertility and disease spreading capacity believed to characterize the lower orders (Garland, 1986:130-60).

On this continent, concern about white slavery and venereal disease combined with widespread fears about the stability of the social order, the growth of cities and multinationals and the influx of non Anglo-Saxon immigrants to fuel the criminalization movement. Laws such as the 1892 *Criminal Code* amendment (Canada) were passed with the aim of protecting virtuous women, rescuing fallen ones, tending to the health of both and punishing the males profiting from the sex trade (McLaren and Lowman, 1988; Cassel, 1987; Backhouse, 1985). However, the near-universal result of such laws was to legitimize the detention and incarceration of hundreds of lower class women who had few alternate ways of earning a living; to provide law enforcement officers with a new group of powerless people they could manipulate; and to lock up a very small number of lower class men whose race or class made them vulnerable (McLaren and Lowman, 1988; Bland 1985; Musheno and Seeley, 1986; Rafter, 1985; Backhouse, 1985; Rosen, 1982; Daly and Chesney-Lind, 1988). The situation would have been even more calamitous if the 19th century criminal justice system had been as large and powerful as it is now. Because most cities of the time contained large populations of prostitutes who would take up all the time, space and money available for law enforcement or medical examinations if the law was fully enforced against prostitution, police used it selectively, as a weapon. Tacit understandings grew up, and deals were made whereby prostitutes could avoid arrest if they provided favours—not necessarily in kind, as information, money or even deference were all common coin. The most affluent prostitutes, usually those catering to the better class of men, were largely exempt from arrest, as were their clients. The bulk of enforcement efforts and control fell on the young woman, and on the lower and working class streetwalker.

Many similar measures followed. Reformatories were founded to rescue criminal women from the inadequate and often filthy facilities, typically tucked into a corner of men's prisons, that had been used to incarcerate them throughout the 19th century (Cooper, 1987; Rafter, 1983). A majority of the women put into these institutions (81.4 percent in one study) were incarcerated for offences such as appearing drunk and disorderly on the street, visiting saloons or engaging in "promiscuous" conduct (Rafter, 1983:224). Such offences, of course, were not enforced only against women. But as Rafter (1983:291) says: "Men simply were not sentenced to state prisons for promiscuity or saloon visiting." While it is difficult to demonstrate that they would not have been locked up if special reformatories had not been built (there remains the possibility that they would have merely been crowded into the existing male prisons), we do know that an expansion in the number of women incarcerated followed the construction of reformatories (Rafter, 1983). It seems fair to conclude, therefore, that they represented another extension of control over the lives and the value systems of poor and working class women. There is no evidence that the institutions fulfilled any of their humane objectives, since even those who were won over by the wardens had to return to the same overwhelming poverty, the same exploitation and starvation level wages that they had fled.

The processing of delinquents provides another example of the alliance between feminists and the state against working class women. By the late 19th century, middle class children were, by and large, sheltered and protected. Working class children, on the other hand, laboured in agriculture, domestic service, mines and retail shops and engaged in street trading of all kinds. Their leisure was generally free of adult supervision and revolved around the street. The same social forces that pushed working class men and women into cities produced a population of youngsters with no adult authority or control. Humane concerns for their welfare co-existed with self-interested fears that these children would become criminals and/or revolutionaries, either upsetting the status quo or preying on the affluent classes. Juvenile criminals were then subjected to the same courts and prisons as adults, and it was felt these conditions provided "schools" for aspiring criminals. The physical conditions to which they were subjected, and the high level of abuse were problems upon which the humanitarian wing of reformers (including the feminist movement) concentrated. In addition, there were economic issues, since no one was available to teach the boys their proper role as breadwinners or to inculcate in them the self-discipline necessary to engage in wage labour. And girls not only did not learn the feminine virtues and skills necessary for their role as homemakers and nurturers of the next generation, they were also subjected to severe sexual exploitation and physical abuse. The survival of children of both sexes, moreover, was put in jeopardy by the conditions in which they were forced to live (Chunn, 1988; Platt, 1969; Sutherland, 1976; Rooke and Schnell, 1983).

This led to the passage of laws providing compulsory education on the one hand, and special legal arrangements for juvenile offenders on the other. Despite concerns that education would serve to perpetuate and legitimize the existing relations of production (Katz, 1968; McNeil, 1986; West, 1984), it opened the door to knowledge, upward mobility and even revolutionary philosophy for many working and lower class children; it has had, in other words, many positive consequences. It is much more difficult to argue positive effects from reforms in the criminal justice system. First, these reforms led to an increase in the number of juveniles arrested and processed (for a review of these studies, see: Hagan, 1980). Second, and more important for our purposes, the effect on girls was disproportionately severe. Although studies have found that girls committed far fewer crimes, and their offences were far less serious, the juvenile courts treated them more severely than they did boys (Chesney-Lind, 1987; Chunn, 1988). Between 1899 and 1909 in Chicago, for example, half of all girls convicted, but only one-fifth of all boys, were sent to reformatories. In Milwaukee, twice as many girls were sentenced to training schools as boys, and in Honolulu they were three times as likely to receive this most severe of sanctions (Chesney-Lind and Sheldon, 1988). Once incarcerated, they were detained on average five times as long, for offences that would have been dismissed had they been laid against boys, such as uncontrollability or promiscuity (Chunn, 1988; Chesney-Lind and Sheldon, 1988). Parents, more specifically mothers, were also hit by these laws, in that a frequent "solution" for unruly youth who were not suitable for incarceration was to take them away by putting them out for adoption. In Toronto, for example, the Juvenile Court processed 1542 adoptions between 1920 and 1928 (Chunn, 1988). Women who were unwilling to play the role of mother in the manner required by the state authorities or those who lacked a respectable husband were especially vulnerable.

Laws on chastity and abortion and laws allowing welfare agencies, schools, courts and jails to lock up, sterilize or institutionalize all who did not conform to the puritan values of the upper middle class became the order of the day. Middle class female reformers were too naive to envisage the uses to which such laws would be put. Moreover, they benefited directly from the orgy of law passing, since they were often the professionals and custodians hired (albeit for wages far inferior to males) to staff the state/welfare/juvenile systems thus created (Garland, 1985; Cohen and Scull, 1983). As Morrison (1976:73) has summarized:

> By seeing poverty and crime as based IN the victim ... the women's movement could ... concentrate on the presumed defects in the victim and condemn the ... impoverished environment while, at the same time, ignoring the ... continuing impact of victimizing social forces. Moreover, such an ideology helped middle class women in the feminist movement to reconcile the preservation of their own class interest in maintaining the status quo with the urgings of a humanitarian conscience.

In the workplace itself, the logic of capitalist social relations necessitated the exploitation of every section of the working class population, including female and child labour. The result of this was twofold. First, it challenged the system of familial patriarchy (discussed earlier) in that working class men could no longer directly control their wives and children. Because wives and children were increasingly drawn into the labour force outside the home, husbands also lost control over the labour power which had previously serviced them. Second, the social and physical dislocation produced by this stage of capitalism led, as is well known, to horrendous social conditions (Marcus, 1974). Thousands of men, women and children were forced to live in disease ridden hovels, lacking clean water and even the most rudimentary sanitation facilities. Fears that women would be unable to produce future generations of labourers co-existed with the aforementioned fear that new generations would be too unhealthy and too lacking in proper work habits, in discipline, industriousness and piety, to be utilized if they did survive. Moreover, there was a real danger of plague, and plagues traditionally pay scant heed to class boundaries. Overlaying all of this was the fear of revolution. All of these concerns fed the wave of workplace reforms that developed throughout the late 19th and early 20th century.

Every industrialized country took some initiatives to regulate workplace conditions during this period. Typically, laws were passed requiring guards to be placed on machinery, setting levels of ventilation, restricting the length of the working day and week, and specifying the conditions under which women and children could be hired (Carson, 1979; Tucker, 1987; Ursel, 1986). In the province of Ontario, for example, the Factories Act (1984), the Shops Act (1888), the Mines Act (1890) and the Wages Act (1886) and Workmen's Compensation Act (1886) were the first of a series of provincial laws regulating labour (later supplemented by federal legislation).

Here once again, the results were somewhat different than proponents envisaged. Feminists had originally wanted women and children out of the factories, but this was impossible given the fact that the wages paid working men were too low to sustain a family. As a result, they focused upon protecting the health and moral purity of women workers. Perhaps this was all that would have been achievable in any case, since protective legislation was fiercely resisted by the capitalist class, which saw it as a major interference with property rights. The laws that were finally passed would have provided only a bare minimum of protection for either gender if they had been properly enforced. As it turned out, the sections of the law requiring companies to install facilities to minimize fraternization between the sexes, and to provide separate washrooms for women, were enforced at the expense of provisions regulating the far more crucial and life threatening workplace hazards (Ursel, 1987; Tucker, 1987). In a sense, then, feminist attempts to use law to improve the condition of women labourers backfired to the detriment of both men and women.

Thus, where women attempted to use law to secure control over their conditions of employment outside the home, they were largely unsuccessful. Inside the home, their efforts were successful but counterproductive. Essentially, they helped the state gain entry into and control over the house, lives and bodies of poor and working class women. As we saw, the women most vulnerable to increased state controls were those in homes lacking a male patriarch — widowed, divorced or abandoned mothers of all social classes — or those where the male was deemed inadequate in his job as husband/father/controller, such as wives of alcoholics. The degree to which women measured up to middle class standards on childrearing, health, housekeeping and sexual morality was gauged, and when they were found wanting, their children frequently were taken away from them (without or in some cases with their consent) (Strong-Boag, 1986; Rothman, 1971, 1980; Platt, 1969). The strategy of using criminal law, then, was counterproductive both to women *qua* women (as a gender), and to women in the working and lower classes.

This does not mean, however, that the first wave of feminism accomplished nothing. Securing the public rights of citizenship for women, such as the right to vote and to own property, were of pivotal significance for they provided the foundation upon which modern feminism could build. Where our 19th century sisters struggled for universalistic reforms which conferred basic rights, they achieved great victories; where they sought increased state control through criminalization, they damaged the lives of those they sought to help. The warning enunciated by Burstyn (1985:15-16) still applies:

> The logic of state processes invariably favours political agendas and methods that reinforce capitalist and patriarchal social relations ... We must be extremely selective about the kind of power that we confer on the state in our name.

III. Modern Feminism and The State

Has this changed? Modern feminism has attempted to improve women's lives through initiatives on such issues as battering and rape, which strike at the foundations of gender relations. Battering, a type of assault, has long been a criminal offence. Theoretically, the option also exists for a woman to sue for civil damage (Patterson, 1979), but this is a totally unrealistic "solution" for practical (most women have neither the power nor the money to launch successful suits) and ideological (the legal system has never been predisposed to accept or award damages to women under such conditions) reasons. Moreover, when committed within the family context, assault has been largely ignored by the criminal justice system. Police are reluctant to press charges; prosecutors encourage women to drop charges if made; justices of the peace dislike taking a woman's uncorroborated word as a basis on which to initiate criminal prosecution; and judges are loathe to hand out severe penalties (Macleod, 1980; Dutton, 1984; Patterson, 1979; Dobash and Dobash, 1975). Part of this reluctance relates to the widespread tendency of justice personnel to treat offences which occur between acquaintances or within a family less seriously than they do "stranger offences" (Silberman, 1980). However, it is also bound up with patriarchal attitudes among male criminal justice officials; attitudes which specify that men have a right if not a duty to exercise authority over women and children, and predispose them to look upon women with suspicion and distrust.

Fierce lobbying and educative efforts by feminists have resulted in the appointment of "crisis teams" or domestic assault response squads, typically composed of some combination of male and female police and social workers, to respond to domestic dispute calls. Such teams usually have some training in counselling, and may attempt to remove the batterer from the home. Typically, arrest is not the foremost of the arsenal of weapons at their disposal. In some jurisdictions, such as the province of Ontario, police discretion has been removed: police are required to bring charges, and Crown prosecutors to pursue them (Ontario, 1982:12). Results are mixed. One American study found that future incidents declined when husbands were arrested rather than advised or warned (Sherman and Berk, 1984). But in Ontario, the first two people to go to jail under the "get tough" policy were both female victims. They had refused to testify against their batterers and found themselves doing time for contempt of court (*Toronto Star*, August 10, 1986:A8).

Morgan (1981) studied the development of the shelter movement in the United States. Between 1974 and 1979, she points out, the Law Enforcement Assistance Administration (LEAA) funded 35 shelters and launched a multitude of police crisis training programs. Morgan is not convinced, however, that this represents a victory for battered women. She points out that the LEAA at that time needed a new mandate to demonstrate its utility and organizational efficiency, but could not afford to arrest and incarcerate all men who assaulted their wives (since estimates tell us this would mean charging one of every ten men) (Dobash and Dobash, 1975; Macleod, 1980). The strategy, therefore, was to minimize costs to the system while controlling the political and ideological agenda of family disputes.

The motivations of the agency would not bother us here, however, if the results had substantially aided the victims. Unfortunately, this does not appear to be the case. The use of the criminal justice system to deal with family violence, first of all, exacerbated existing class biases. Lower class (especially black) batterers ended up serving time, while middle and upper class offenders, if charged, were diverted into private treatment facilities and clinics (Morgan, 1981:29-30). Lower class victims also received treatment that differed from their middle class counterparts, as they were most likely to end up in state run services where the prevailing philosophy was to view the poor or working class family as basically inadequate. Such agencies are also more likely to focus on individual pathologies, ignoring the social and structural conditions which force women to remain in abusive relationships. These psychological approaches tend to blur the distinction between victims and victimizer, often blaming the woman for her situation. Morgan argues that the purpose of the criminal justice system is "the identification, sanctioning and punishment of ... deviant segments of the working class," to ensure "the continuous production and reproduction of labour power for capital (1981:27). As she summarizes the situation: "Reforms developed within the criminal justice system ... reestablish gender domination, social control and class domination under other guises" (1981:26).

Attempts to use criminal law to find a solution to the problem of rape have not fared better. Reforms in rape laws have been more extensively evaluated than almost any other feminist initiative. These laws were among the earliest targets of second wave feminists, who pointed out that rape was traditionally a crime committed by men against men in which the female was a mere vehicle, a piece of property whose value had been lowered. The special emphasis in rape laws on the defiling of the virgin thus became understandable, since loss of virginity defrauded the male who "owned" her (father or guardian) by lessening her worth as a bride. The exclusion of married women from rape laws (to the point where they were sometimes deemed legally responsible for the rape having occurred) (Brownmiller, 1975), and the lack of legal protection for wives became clear, since it could not be seen as a crime for a man to rape a woman who was already his own property.

The feminist literature attacked the basic precepts of the Anglo-American legal system — the assumptions of universality and equality — with assertions that rape laws embodied the prejudices and fears of the dominant male group. Rape's special rules of evidence, whereby corroboration of a woman's testimony and proof of her chaste character were required, exemplified male distrust (Medea and Thompson, 1974; Russell, 1975). Assaults which humiliated and terrorized women were written off by the legal system as jokes or male prerogatives. Studies documenting the suspicion and hostility of police toward rape victims showed that 50 percent and more of all reported sexual attacks were classified by police as unfounded (Brookbank, 1982; Clark and Lewis, 1977; Neufeld and Bogaard, 1977). (An unfounded incident is so classified when the investigating officers deem that no crime has occurred.) This, plus the relatively light sentences meted out for rape, created a dissatisfied, vocal, embarrassing and increasingly powerful constituency calling for legal change and undermining the legitimacy of the existing law.

Several characteristics of typical rape laws made efforts to secure convictions particularly problematic. First, laws frequently contained provisions requiring victims to prove they had not consented to the act. Typical of this is the Canadian doctrine of recent complaint, which enabled a judge to advise the jury that the time lapse between the commission and the reporting of an offence allowed them to "draw conclusions adverse to a complainant" (MacDonald, 1982b:6). Corroboration requirements also reflected suspicion of the victim's credibility. The victim's previous sexual activity was deemed legally relevant; the inference being that women with a "sexual past," who had given consent to intercourse with one man, had thereby given consent to all. Or, it could be interpreted to signify that the consent of the unchaste woman was not necessary. The result of this was low conviction rates for rape (Clark and Lewis, 1977:56; Canada, 1978:12; Marsh *et al.*, 1982; Caringella-MacDonald, 1987), and high rates of nonreporting (Canada, 1984).

Reformers have tried to correct the evidentiary problems and emphasize the violence of the act more than its sexual nature. Thus, feminists attempted to redefine rape as sexual assault; criminalize all non-consensual touching, from fondling a breast to anal intercourse; and broaden the definition of the offence to include sexual assaults involving two males or a husband and wife. Looking at specific objectives, they wanted to increase the number of original complaints (thereby decreasing the high rates of non-reporting), diminish the high attrition rates in prosecution, increase arrest, prosecution and conviction rates and provide more access and greater protection for victims, with the overall result being greater justice for the victims (Caringella-Macdonald, 1985:6-7).

Evaluations of the effectiveness of reforms have produced mixed conclusions. Laws have been changed in a fair percentage of states— and federally— through the Sexual Assault Act, Bill C-127— in the U.S. and all of Canada. One of the earliest evaluations, done by Marsh *et al.* (1982) on the 1975 Michigan law, used before and after crime data supplemented by in-depth interviews with system officials (judges, prosecutors, defence attorneys and police), as well as rape crisis centre personnel, in six of Michigan's thirteen counties. The crime statistics showed an increase in the hoped for direction — more sexual assaults were reported, and more arrests and convictions registered. Although these trends began before the law was changed, Marsh *et al.* nonetheless argue that the data show the law was having the desired effect. Turning to the subjective evidence, the bulk of those interviewed also thought that the new laws made it easier for victims to testify and increased the likelihood of convicting defendants. Overall, the Marsh study concludes that specific procedural changes in case processing were attained, but that changes in attitudes about "serious" and "trivial" assaults, and real versus spurious victims were not. Violent stranger rapes against respectable women were still treated as the only really serious sexual assaults.

The data are not without limitations; both the objective and the subjective evidence are suspect. First, crime statistics are a notoriously misleading index in a field where, it is estimated, up to 90 percent of the offences are never reported (Chambers and Millar, 1987; Canada, 1982; Clark and Lewis, 1977). Second, the interview data must be viewed with suspicion, because they come from those with the highest stake in the court system, those whose jobs, income, self-esteem and identity depend on making laws work. However, this is not to say that these results must be totally discounted. While not necessarily an accurate reflection of the overall effects of the reform of this law, the perceptions of key actors are still important. Perceptions do have real social effects, as sociologists have known for some time, and some of these will be helpful to the feminist cause. For example, the fact that all rape crisis staff thought the reforms increased the chances of securing conviction in court could lead them to encourage more victims to press charges. Other perceptions, however, may counteract this. For example, the belief that reforms had gone too far, and that defendants were now being unjustly convicted may lead officials to act in ways which redress this balance, thus nullifying the reforms.

However, later studies in the United States, Canada and the United

Kingdom were less optimistic. Victim credibility and consent are still key factors in the decision-making process, and prejudice against women — specifically against those who challenge patriarchy by their style of life (women living without male "protectors," women who hitchhike or associate with more than one man, native, ethnic or poor women) — is unchanged. Sexual history is still being used on the informal level, in deciding whether or not a complaint is serious enough to justify prosecution, even where it cannot be mentioned in court (Loh, 1980, 1981; Caringella-MacDonald, 1987). Caringella-MacDonald's (1987:21-22) survey of the effectiveness of rape law reform concludes that there has been "overall, no change in unfounding or clearance rates or in the rates of conviction." Furthermore, even at the courtroom level, the most visible component of the reform process, judicial discretion, is more likely to be exercised in favour of the offender than the victim (Canada, 1985).[3]

The most recent review article concludes there are only two areas in which rape law revisions have had a demonstrable effect: increasing conviction rates and lessening crime attrition ("limited success" here); and reducing the subjective trauma experienced by the victim at the hands of the criminal justice process (Berger *et al.*, 1988:333-39).

It is not clear that even these changes, minimal as they are, have been brought by alterations in the criminal law. Nor is it obvious that this was the most efficient and humane avenue to use. It makes just as much sense to see changes in the attitudes and behaviour around rape as resulting from the ideological victories, the different attitudes to women, that years of feminist struggle have secured. Given increased pressure, courts would have been hard pressed to maintain their most visible misogynist practices even under the original legislation. And it is certainly no accident that the least visible parts of the process are the ones that have remained least changed.

IV. Theoretical Considerations

Marsh *et al.* (1982:6) and Handler (1978) have both pointed out that legal change is meant to work on two levels: the symbolic and the instrumental. The symbolic level refers to the state's sending a signal on behalf of a "popular consensus" about the moral status of a particular act. In the case of criminalization, the message to be conveyed is that this particular act is abhorrent. The assumptions embodied are consensus/pluralist ones, but Marxist and feminist groups have also accepted symbolic change as a goal of law reform. Unfortunately, we know very little about whether law, specifically criminal law, is the most efficient or effective vehicle to change social attitudes. In fact, we have no evidence that it is in any sense independent of changes in the balance of power, and the allied activities of lobby groups.

We know a little more about instrumental legal changes, those with tangible procedural and behavioral goals, especially where these have been unsuccessful (the reported outcome of the majority of studies). We know that formal legal change seldom gets down to the informal level, to the day-to-day operation of the criminal justice system, the level at which real decision-making occurs. Most issues are negotiated informally, with the formal law acting at best as a guide (Marsh *et al.*, 1982:6). Indeed, many would argue that the meanings assigned and the operational definitions developed by officials reflect their own personal and organizational needs (particularly the latter) far more than they reflect written law. Laws are subjective constructions: "due process is *for* crime control," as McBarnet (1981) and Ericson and Baranek (1982) have said. As Silbey (1985:19) points out, in many areas, the desired outcomes are determined, and then the appropriate legal categories invoked.

Handler (1978) argues, nonetheless, that instrumental goals can be accomplished under certain circumstances: the legal change must specify procedures to be followed; it must be easily monitored; it must be technically simple; and it must reduce organizational discretion. Ekland-Olson and Martin (1988:371-75) isolate three principles which they see as related to unsuccessful law reform. Reforms will be most difficult to accomplish when they are directed at systems which are normatively and structurally isolated; when they threaten the existing authority structure and power of the target organization; and when interpersonal antagonisms among the main players are high. Marsh *et al.* (1982:115) sum up conditions for successful law reform as follows:

> Ideally, if constituencies are to succeed, they must design reforms whose costs to the organization do not outweigh the benefits; they must establish and maintain legitimacy; and finally ... they must remain organized and committed long enough to monitor and augment the system's compliance with the reform.

Thus, achieving successful legal change, change which fulfills the expectations of the group seeking it, is quite a challenge in any institutional area. And feminist groups have several impediments which others seeking changes in the criminal law (those wanting higher penalties for drunk drivers or cocaine users, for example) do not have. They are outsiders, and they are ideologically at odds with many basic assumptions. Reforms which aim at empowering women must challenge structures of patriarchy, question the status quo which reflects male values, and undermine the quest to keep women down both literally and figuratively (MacKinnon, 1983).

All of this makes comprehensible the failure of feminists to successfully enlist the criminal justice system as an ally. Where women are mobilized and vocal, the state can be forced to respond; and passing laws to tighten up social control is congruent with both its interests and its history. Feminists do not determine, however, the mobilization or enforcement of the law. Once the external pressure stops and attention shifts to other issues, normal patterns within the criminal justice system will reassert themselves. And these patterns will reflect the need of the criminal justice system to maintain itself, to process cases efficiently (according to its own definitions of the "going rate"), to focus upon "real" crimes, and to act in ways which are congruent with dominant structural forces in the society. In operational terms, this means it will tend to target lower and working class people, resist feminism and support the status quo of economic, social and familial relations.

To bring about the kind of changes feminism demands requires shifting the distribution of wealth and power from men as a class to women and children as a class. This would, of course, require a massive series of reforms, from the provision of equal pay for work of equal value and universal daycare, to egalitarian property rights. Men as a group and capitalists as a class, both of which have benefited enormously from the free labour, deference and subservience of women, will be loathe to see any change in the status quo. (And women committed to the present system for ideological, economic or psychological reasons will also resist.) This kind of change, a basic redistribution of power, will be the most difficult to achieve through the criminal law, as Handler (1978) and others have pointed out. Thus, it is very much in the interest of the state to dilute the influence of feminism. Diversion (shifting attention to more peripheral, less threatening issues), containment/cooptation and repression are all tactics which can and will be used; indeed the willingness of Western regimes to respond to feminist cries for criminalization, be it laws against pornography or against rape, illustrates such tactics (Burstyn, 1985:26). Criminalizing more behaviour, and thereby encouraging the state to step up control and repression, in order to advance a movement whose basic aims are to lessen oppression, seems a strange strategy as well as an ineffective and counterproductive one. As Burstyn (1985:15) has said: "We cannot use the controlling, punitive and top-down structure of the state to mend and reweave the delicate fabric of sexual life."

Conclusion

Finally, I would like to explore routes out of this impasse. It has been argued throughout that the criminal justice system is a dead end; does this mean that feminists should just put up with the victimization, the pain, the powerlessness and the injustices to which women are presently subjected? The tendency of theory, especially critical social theory, to paralyse action and thereby reinforce the status quo, has been noted before (Cohen, 1985; Giddens, 1976, 1981; Sumner, 1981), and needs to be avoided. Let us take a brief look, then, at strategies which appear to offer the potential for humanitarian and non-oppressive social change.

The feminist movement itself provides the most striking examples of successful strategies. This does not mean it has won all its battles, chosen the best tactics at all times or come close to achieving its goals. But the ability of a minority of relatively powerless women in virtually every country in the developed world to secure a hearing, to get their items on the agenda, and to publicize their concerns has been of major importance. It has led to remarkable changes in all institutional spheres. Assaults on male dominance of language forms, challenges to established religions, documentation of the virtual absence of women at the top levels of government and business, and a major re-evaluation of what has passed for conventional knowledge in the major disciplines in the university, all of these are examples of its impact. That successes have been most conspicuous, thus far, for middle class white women in first world countries was perhaps inevitable, but the movement has not ended there. More and more women are returning to school and careers, divorcing husbands who refuse to share household labour or who seek to control their activities, and challenging double standards in personal relationships, on the job and elsewhere. Women are crowding into professions and business in unprecedented numbers.

While results are not easy to document, it does appear that initiatives such as consciousness raising groups have been successful at the ideological level in helping women free themselves psychologically and physically from the patterns of submission, dependence and guilt which have hitherto controlled their behaviour. Organizational responses to women's needs, such as rape crisis centres or shelters for battered women (especially those controlled by feminists) have provided women in crisis with safe places of refuge. As well, the opportunities opened up by feminist struggle in the marketplace have given many women the opportunity to escape oppressive conditions and seek financial independence.

I do not want to exaggerate the successes — they are partial and incomplete; the best programs are threatened by the dangers of state control and cooptation or they are starved for funds; native women, immigrants and lower class women have not shared equally in the advances; and the dangers of regression and backlash are great. However, they do illustrate the potential of what Sumner (1981) has called "rights struggles" to challenge democratic governments which are premised on the ideal of equal rights for all. To be successful, such initiatives must be fought on all institutional fronts and at all levels, as feminism has been. They cannot rely on the legal system to initiate change, and certainly not upon the criminal justice system.

However, because the legal system is basic to capitalist relations, successful movements do at some point have to challenge the structures of civil and criminal law. The strategy which appears to have the most potential can be summed up, in Brickey and Comack's (1987:106-7) phrase, as a "jurisprudence of insurgency." Since law is part of a social formation which generates its own internal contradictions, resistance to it will determine which of these contradictions can be built upon to first weaken and then transform the existing structure. This requires feminists not to strengthen the present system of oppression by calling for more of the same, but to use law against itself, to challenge it, to seek legal changes which redefine the system of social relations which keep women and lower/working class groups under control. The aim, then, is to "use existing tension in the system to push the contradictions that arise from the structures of capitalism" (Brickey and Comack, 1987:105).

This does not mean criminalizing a broader range of behaviours. It is no accident that the successes of the feminist movement were not achieved by strengthening criminal law. Civil law has been useful in entrenching changes won by struggle on the ideological, social and economic levels. Changes such as the Married Women's Property Act passed in Canada in 1872, which gave women control of wages they earned during marriage, or the 1859 provision which allowed married women to retain control of property they inherited (rather than having it become automatically the property of the husband) are basic to any movement. Repealing laws — criminal or non-criminal — which stand in the way is also essential. However, as argued elsewhere (Snider, 1985, 1986), the predominant role of criminal law is to coerce and contain, which makes it an inappropriate site for achieving social transformation (see also Daly, 1989). Successful reforms, those which have been the basis for ameliorative social change, share certain characteristics. They must have the potential on the ideological level to be viewed as rights rather than privileges. They need to benefit a broad range of social classes to garner the power needed to secure both law passage and enforcement. Ideally, they should be susceptible to "institutionalization" — that is, institutions should be founded to maintain and administer the reform in question. Doing this creates middle class jobs within state bureaucracies, thus providing a powerful group of people with a vested interest in the continued existence of the reform who have a position within the state machinery from which to fight (Snider, 1986:230-32).

To summarize, then, feminism should fight for universalistic rights, rights which apply to all women, whatever their class. Privileged women may need these rights less (although the expression that every woman is just "one man away from welfare" is still surprisingly valid); however, their ability to identify with the reform will be crucial, politically and ideologically, for preserving and extending it. The right to reproductive choice, maternity leave, equal wages and universal daycare are examples of reforms worth fighting for, building upon the right to vote and own property secured by the first wave of feminism.

Such changes require adjustments in the structures of capitalism, thereby forcing the system to confront the principles of equality and democracy which it espouses. In this sense, then, they build upon the contradictions of capitalism, testing the relative autonomy of the state from the economic structure (Jessop, 1982; Thompson, 1975, 1980). Institutions dedicated to social control — and the complex of organizations which comprise the criminal justice system in a modern state provide an example of this — do not have the Janus-like potential to build on their contradictions that characterize the institutions dedicated to health care, for example, or education. This apparent paradox can be explained by looking at the dual nature of law. Some laws, those embodied in civil statutes or enabling documents such as constitutions, are aimed at creating social space and enlarging rights; others, on the contrary, take away behavioral and attitudinal alternatives and foreclose social space. Laws embedded in criminal codes exemplify the latter, because they set out to stigmatize, exclude and punish. This they do well. However, the nature and purpose of criminal law mean that the potential to go beyond this function is severely limited, with the results that were documented above.

In addition, feminism should fight for ideological change, a transformation in the ways that men and women conceive of women's "place" in the society. Although it is not clear whether changes in dominant ideologies can occur independent of structural change, it is obvious that both transformations are necessary. Changing ideas which make men feel they have a right to assault women is every bit as important as providing battered women with the economic opportunities and political power to free themselves from such men. Moreover, it is ideological change which allows the victims, and their sons and daughters, to see that it is not part of "woman's role" to serve as an outlet for male aggression. Moves by feminist groups to provide shelter and advice for such women and their families have also been useful on the individual level (although, one would like to think these initiatives will be much less necessary over the long term, if macro-level changes are secured). All of these struggles have much more potential, on every level of analysis, than getting the police to come and throw batterers in jail, thereby making victims more dependent (albeit on the state), more impoverished and more vulnerable — and setting the stage for an increase in social control which is sure to ensnare victims along with victimizers.

Overall, then, the feminist movement needs to fight for an environment which is free of sexism. This means creating social orders, organizations and families which are truly "person-enhancing." What this would mean in concrete terms is not yet entirely clear; nor does it need to be, as constructing utopias can merely distract us from the job at hand. However, the humanistic goals of the movement have always emphasized the importance of allowing both men and women to reach their potential of promoting cooperation over competition, and of preventing the victimization of the weak by the strong. To achieve this, feminists must aim at collective empowerment in all forms.

This paper has argued that the criminal justice system is not an ally the feminist movement can reliably use to achieve humanistic and liberating goals. Structurally, states in capitalist societies benefit by the existing patterns of class and gender dominance; tactically, feminists cannot control the writing of the laws, nor the uses to which they are put after they are passed. The historical record of the initiatives of the recent and distant past, and their near-universal failure to achieve the goals envisaged, is striking. The major consequence has been to increase state control over lower and working class women as well as men, to the benefit of neither. We need to put much more effort into developing strategies which build on the successes of the feminist movement, strategies which have the potential to further the genuine humanitarian objectives of feminism.

Notes

1. It is true that challenges to established authority structures, and to the relations they promoted, did lead to the acceptance of ideas and practices which conservative forces in the sixties and thereafter have found threatening. For example, unmarried couples began to live together, unwed mothers stopped routinely giving up their children and the birth control pill was invented and legalized. None of these changes, however, were the result of decriminalization. Canada was "liberalized," to the degree this has occurred, in spite rather than because of reforms in the criminal law.

2. Seemingly permissive progressive reforms which turn out upon analysis to represent only a shifting modality of control have been documented within a wide range of institutional sites, including the legal system, prisons, mental hospitals and the medical system (Cohen, 1985; Chan and Ericson, 1981; Greenwood and Young, 1980; Scull, 1981). It is likely that such changes were for the benefit of the middle classes, who wanted the freedoms in the consumptive and reproductive spheres which capitalist ideology promised. However, while the substitution of control by professionals for control by police, where it occurred, may have meant less repression for these classes, it may well have had the opposite effect for working and underclass populations, and for young people. These groups are much more likely to be targeted as clients by state professionals since they are heavily scrutinized, and they are much less likely to have sufficient resources, ideological or otherwise, to resist such "help."

3. See also the Chambers and Millar (1987:61-65) study of 196 incidents of sexual assault recorded by the police in Glasgow and Edinburgh over a fifteen month period in 1980-81.

Considering the Impact of the Battered Women's Movement on the State: The Example of Manitoba
Jane Ursel

In the past 15 years the women's movement, particularly the battered women's movement, has challenged the criminal justice and social service system on its historic response or lack of response in wife abuse cases. As a result of this concerted lobbying effort by women across Canada, governments have begun to respond and a variety of new programs and policies have been implemented. In the wake of this new level of activity by the federal and some provincial governments, a debate has arisen within the women's community about the costs and benefits of increased government involvement in this issue. On one side of the debate are women who view the increased involvement of the state as having the positive outcome of increasing services to battered women and their children and increasing penalties for battering.[1] On the other side of the debate are women who argue that increased involvement of mainstream institutions results in cooptation, distortion and depoliticization of the issue (Barnsley, 1985; Currie, 1990; Snider, 1989).

This particular debate reflects a larger one within the women's movement concerning the state and patriarchy and issues pertaining to the formulation of realistic and progressive strategies for feminists in their approach to the state.

> One of the key questions for a specifically feminist approach to the state is the extent to which the state is autonomous from, or is itself one of the structures and relations of masculine dominance. In other words, is the state in its current form irretrievably an institution of men's power? Or is it a form of power in society which is

contested and malleable (Randall, 1988:10)?

This larger debate poses a number of questions which are critical to feminist politics and strategies. Are there issues in which there is a potential convergence of the state's interests and women's interests? If so, can reforms then be progressive and worth working for? What criteria do we use to distinguish a progressive from a cooptive reform? These are critical questions which need to be dealt with both theoretically and empirically. The following discussion represents an attempt to begin to grapple with these questions.

In the *first* part of the discussion, I will briefly outline two alternative feminist perspectives on the state and patriarchy and the different conclusions they lead to in terms of understanding the impact of state involvement in the wife abuse issue. In the *second* section, I will provide a brief history of changes introduced in the criminal justice and social service systems. The *final* section will include an analysis of data on the outcome of these changes.

I. Divergent Feminist Perspectives on the State

While all feminists agree that the history of women is a history of subordination due to the persistence of patriarchal roles, rules and regulations, not all feminists are in agreement about how these rules operate and perpetuate themselves over time. Recently, the question of patriarchy and its perpetuation has centred around the state, its legislation and its role in perpetuating gender inequality. There has been a dramatic growth in feminist theorizing on the state in the last five years. However, despite the diversity, when it comes to practice there are basically two schools of thought. The first includes those writers who perceive the state "in its current form irretrievably an institution of men's power," eliminating any possibility of issues in which there could be a convergence of state and women's interests (MacKinnon, 1987, 1989; Barnsley, 1985). The second school of thought includes those who perceive a contradiction in the operation of patriarchy within the state, creating a contested terrain and the possibility of a convergence of state and women's interests on particular issues (Eisenstein, 1981; Ursel, 1988). The purpose of this section of the paper is to examine the relation between these particular theoretical perspectives on the state and their policy and practice implications for people working in the field of wife abuse.

The first perspective, most frequently articulated by radical feminists, flows from an analysis whose primary focus is on the consistency of patriarchy over time. While this approach does not deny historical specificity, the attention is directed to the consistency of the effect of patriarchy. "Feminists do not argue that it means the same to women to be on the bottom of a feudal regime, a capitalist regime, and a socialist regime; the commonality argued is that despite real changes, bottom is bottom" (MacKinnon, 1982: 523). The radical feminists' focus on effect pulls them away from process. Thus, while their works may acknowledge history, typically they do not use it. The clearest expression of this tendency is MacKinnon's rejection of historical materialism as male-stream method (MacKinnon, 1982:525).

MacKinnon's emphasis upon effect results in an approach to the state and patriarchy not unlike Gertrude Stein's description of a rose. For Stein, a rose is a rose is a rose. For MacKinnon, patriarchy is patriarchy is patriarchy, and the state is patriarchal. Whatever variations may exist in the operations, interests or processes of patriarchy, they pale in comparison to its effect. There is little to be learned from the process, the lesson lies in the effect. MacKinnon states that sex is eroticized dominance, law is the medium for making male dominance both invisible and legitimate, and the state is patriarchal. The state, she maintains, is the realm of male dominance. She allows for no autonomy, relative or otherwise, of the state from patriarchy (MacKinnon, 1989).

Given an interpretation of the state as inherently, monolithically and irretrievably patriarchal, it is understandable why feminists who subscribe to this perspective of the state would view its involvement in a feminist issue as corrupting, coopting and depoliticizing. The policy implications are clear: whatever the state touches reinforces patriarchy even if, perhaps, it wears a benevolent face. In the case of wife abuse policies and programs in Canada, this position has been articulated by Snider (1990), Barnsley (1985), Price (1988) and Currie (1990), who focus on the negative impact of state involvement.

With regard to the criminalization of wife abuse, Snider maintains that:

> ... a strategy relying upon the criminal justice system is practically, theoretically and morally wrong. While the apparatus of government is too powerful to ignore, the criminal justice system is not a reliable ally. Entrusting more power to it means investing it with increased control over women's lives, control that is essentially invisible and unmonitored (Snider, 1990:142-143).

Barnsley introduces the concept of institutionalization:

> ... as a short-hand term for what happens to women's issues when the women's movement succeeds in getting the state and its various institutions to respond ... the process by which the state takes on women's issues, redefines them and compromises them, often beyond recognition (Barnsley, 1988:18).

Barnsley (1988:20) also provides a comprehensive list of the negative consequences of state involvement in wife abuse:

1. "compromising of feminist services and organizational structures."

2. "undermining of the base of the women's movement."

3. "professionalization and bureaucratization of feminist work."

4. "redefinition of women's experience so women's issues can be absorbed into traditional frameworks and dominant ideology and rendered invisible again."

5. "governments choosing to fund non-feminist and even `anti-feminist' church groups and social service agencies which support the values of the `majority'."

6. "governments and other agencies succeed in arguing that transition house workers must have professional credentials rather than valuing workers' life experience."

7. "the trend towards generalist, institution-based "victim services"."

The primary difficulty with analyses which announce the failure of the battered women's movement (Currie 1990:88)[2] is that their criteria for success or failure is measured in terms of the state's impact on the movement. It is presumed that the battered women's movement has had little impact on the state (Snider, 1989; Barnsley, 1988). Thus, in the assessment of impact, no one is looking at the possibility of change within the system and, what is most disturbing, no one is looking at its impact on battered women.

A search for an alternative to the above critiques stems from a conviction that the battered women's movement should have as its primary criterion of success or failure the circumstance or predicament of battered women. One must develop a means of determining whether a battered woman or a woman at risk has more options and supports available to her today than was the case prior to state involvement. This, it seems, should be at least as important a measure of success or failure as observations on the impact of the state upon the movement. A second factor which must be considered in the overall assessment of success or failure is the extent to which the battered women's movement affected the state, that is, the criminal justice system and the social service system upon which its major lobbying efforts were concentrated. Finally, a search for an alternative to the above perspective on the state is motivated by what seems to be a poverty of strategic options which flow from an analysis which speaks only to the problem of cooptation in reform and not to the potential for reform. Such an analysis presents an overly deterministic model of the state, allowing no room for social agency and change.

In this regard, both Barnsley and Snider advance a conception of the state that centres on its one dimensional patriarchal character and its omnipotent effect:

> The ideology in which we are all trained gives the state
> and its institutions the tools and the responsibility to
> respond to the demands of the women's movement in
> such a way as to contain any threats to dominant interests
> (Barnsley 1988:20).

This concept of an overly deterministic state which can coopt all social movements is simply not a concept verified by history. It is also a concept which begs the question of what should feminists do while waiting for the revolution?

While one can certainly agree with the above authors that it is dangerous to underestimate the "enemy" (patriarchal power in the state), I would also maintain that it is equally unwise to overestimate the "enemy." The former case, we are warned, leads to cooptation at best, complicity at worst. In the latter case, however, we should be aware that overdetermination leads to strategic confusion or paralysis at best, and internicine destructiveness at worst.

The assertion that "state involvement is bad," or that "from a moral perspective, such initiatives encourage inhumane and repressive solutions" (Snider 1989:2), transforms strategic issues into moral axioms. The debate shifts from assessments of when and how it is appropriate to involve the state to moral assessments of the political motives of women and agencies according to their degree of involvement with the state. Women who work in the state are by definition bad, complicit individuals; women who work with the state are certainly suspect; and women who have college degrees or are otherwise credentialed are understood to have a mainstream (anti-feminist) approach (Barnsley 1988:20) to the problem.[3] These divisions, which have been identified by a number of authors (Currie, 1990; Barnsley, 1988), are far more than academic and have led to destructive splits within the community of service workers, including organized lobbying efforts to block the development of particular services.

While interagency conflict is the most troubling consequence of the moral axioms implicit in an overdeterministic model of the state, poor strategy is another consequence. The definition of the state as the enemy results in the failure to grasp opportunities which present themselves, as well as a failure to recognize allies within the state. For many feminists, the concept of allies within the state is a contradiction in terms. However, the work of Franzway, Court and Connell (1989) suggests that one should not ignore the reality of women who work within the state and the fact that many of these women are feminists. They introduce the concept of "femocrats" to identify feminists who were specifically recruited into the bureaucracy to translate feminist social/political demands into social policy. Their analysis of the role of these women in bureaucracy is loaded with strategic implications for feminists lobbying the state.

While it is unrealistic to assume that a consensus can be reached among feminists concerning the most effective strategies for change, it is to be hoped that differences in strategies can be recognized as such and not become the basis for identifying large numbers of women and agencies as the enemy (that is, guilt by association with the state). Redirecting the criteria of success or failure from the exclusive question of "what is the impact of the state on the movement?" to include "what is the impact of the movement and the state on the options available to battered women?" should help to move the debate out of the murky waters of moralizing onto a clearer ground for assessing strategies.

To this end, the second school of thought on the state and its relation to patriarchy offers a more promising framework. This approach views the state as less monolithic, identifies contradictions in the operation of patriarchy within the state, and sees possibilities for convergence of state interests with women's interests on some issues. Pursuing this alternative does not ignore the fact that, when the state becomes involved, changes to organizations and services will occur. However, it does take issue with the conclusion that the costs of state involvement outweigh the benefits, and the implication within that conclusion that the overall effect of reform is cooptation.

This alternative perspective is articulated by Eisenstein (1984), who adopts a "dual systems" conceptualization of women's oppression in capitalist society, that is, Eisenstein sees capitalism and patriarchy as separate though interdependent systems. She identifies contradictions between the organization and interests of capitalism and patriarchy, and within these contradictions identifies opportunities for feminist political action. Building on Eisenstein's concept, I undertook an earlier research project in which I studied state intervention in, and structuring of, patriarchal relations through an analysis of one hundred years of family, labour and welfare legislation in Canada.

In "The State and the Maintenance of Patriarchy" (1988), I argued that the restructuring of productive relations associated with Canada's transition from an agrarian to an industrial society involved a restructuring of reproductive relations as well. I suggested that this restructuring involved a transition from a decentralized, familial patriarchal system characterized by the particular subordination of individual women to a male head of household (husband/father) to the generalized subordination of women through centralized social patriarchal structures embedded in the political/economic institutions of the day.

As a result of this emphasis on history and process, rather than seeing patriarchy "is patriarchy is patriarchy," I argued that the power relations and dynamics of familial patriarchy are significantly different than the emergent patterns of social patriarchy. I argued, in fact, that the state became directly involved in the dismantling of particular familial patriarchal relations in order to facilitate a better fit between production and reproduction in the new economic order.

Old rules of patriarchal domination which were necessary or tolerable under the old pronatalist familial patriarchal system became obsolete and/or impediments to the new social order. In these cases, the state did act to undo the old relations because it had become in the interests of state, as well as to women, to do so. In short, the perpetuation of the old relations had become costly to the state, as well as women. Under these circumstances, I would argue, history has indicated that it is possible to introduce truly progressive reforms and to use the power of the state to do so. Some of the better known examples are the Married Women's Property Act introduced throughout Canada in the 1860s to 1870s, and the Maintenance Enforcement Act introduced throughout Canada in the 1970s. In both of these cases, the state was primarily motivated by the need to minimize the number of dependents upon the public purse. However, this motivation coincided well with women's desire to have the right to own their own property, keep their own wage and, in the case of Maintenance Enforcement, have the father of their children contribute to the costs of raising their children. One need not argue that the state and women have the same interest (since this is extremely unlikely), but only that they have a shared interest in dismantling laws, practices and conventions of an old patriarchal order which have always been costly to women and, over time, became costly to the state.

It is in this context that a consideration of state involvement in the issue of wife abuse can be assessed most strategically. Is wife abuse a vestige of the old familial patriarchal system in which the patriarch had ultimate control over the lives and well being of his family members? Does the state have any interest or reap any benefit, in the current social economic order, in the perpetuation of this pattern of individualized dominance? Does the perpetuation of wife abuse present costs to the state and the social system today?

If it can be established that wife abuse serves no useful function in the current social patriarchal order, and if it can be further established that it is, in fact, costly to the state, both in terms of social costs and political legitimacy, then it seems we have a set of circumstances in which state interests can be seen to coincide with the interests of women. Under such circumstances in the past, this has led to the introduction of decidedly progressive reforms.

What will be argued here is that, as a result of the active and aggressive lobbying of women across Canada for over a decade, it has now become evident to the state that the perpetuation of wife abuse is costly, both in terms of the social costs of the sustained victimization of large segments of the population and in terms of the political costs (legitimacy of the state). I suggest that it can be argued — and defended — that in the late 20th century there are no economic and/or structural interests of the state in the perpetuation of wife abuse.

If these are, in fact, reasonable arguments then it follows that it is a reasonable, indeed, a preferred strategy for the women's movement to use the full force of the state, its money, its legal apparatus and its political legitimacy to provide more support and more options to battered women and women at risk to escape such violence.

In taking the position that it is possible under certain circumstances to use the power of the state to achieve progressive reform, the remainder of the discussion will examine state response to wife abuse in the province of Manitoba over the past seven years. In assessing the impact of state involvement, primary consideration will be given to the following questions:

1) Has there been a significant, measurable change in the state's response to wife abuse in the criminal justice and social service system? and
2) What does this mean for battered women?

II. The System's Response to the Battered Women's Movement[4]

Prior to looking at the Manitoba data in detail, it is worth noting that Manitoba is merely a specific example of a more generalized trend throughout the country toward increased state involvement in the issue of wife abuse. James Browning reported in 1984 that there were 160 shelters in Canada and 24 treatment programs for batterers. Four years later, the National Clearing House reported that the number of shelters across the country had increased to 392 and the number of treatment programs had increased to 114. In addition, in 1985 the federal government announced a $40 million commitment over five years to address the issue of family violence. Half of this fund was to be allocated to finance wife abuse shelter facilities through Project Haven, a CMHC program. Thus, while the analysis of changes within Manitoba is specific to that province, it is also indicative of a broader national phenomenon.

The starting point of this analysis is the first major systemic response, which occurred in Manitoba in 1983. In that year, the Attorney General of Manitoba directed police to lay charges in all reported cases of spouse abuse when there were reasonable and probable grounds that an assault had taken place. Prior to this directive, wife abuse cases were treated differently from general assault cases, in that the victim usually had to request that charges be laid against her assailant. The directive required that in wife abuse cases, as in general assault cases, decisions to charge were to be based solely on evidence rather than on the requests of the victim. This directive is taken as a starting point because it had the effect of making wife abuse a publicly visible and calculable problem.

Several factors become apparent when one examines the data collected in Manitoba over the past seven years. First, major systemic changes have been introduced - these will be measured in terms of new programs, new policies and new expenditures. Second, changes in the criminal justice system and the social service system have not occurred in isolation of one another, nor at the expense of the social service system (as suggested by

Currie, 1990:90 and Barnsley, 1988:20). Finally, there is no indication that government services are replacing or overtaking community-based, nongovernmental organizations and agencies (again as suggested by Currie, 1990:91 and Barnsley, 1988:20).

In proceeding with the analysis of changes in Manitoba over the past seven years, it is helpful to identify the changes as occurring in three phases, with significant resistance occurring at each phase. It will be suggested that, at each point, resistance became a trigger for new developments, which characterized subsequent phases and pushed the process of systemic change forward. These three stages of change are as follows: *Phase I 1983-1984*, in which the greatest innovations occurred in the criminal justice system; *Phase II 1985-87*, in which the greatest innovations were in the social service system; and *Phase III 1988-90*, in which changes in the social service and criminal justice systems are concurrent. Furthermore, an attempt will be made to show how developments within one system became the catalyst for change in the other system, thus reinforcing the momentum for change. The analysis will proceed by outlining a history of the change process within and between the criminal justice system and social service system, beginning with the initial change, the source of resistance and the "resolution" within each stage.

Phase I 1983-84

This is the period that marks the state's first formal entry into the issue of wife abuse. The critical event was the new directive on charging policy issued by the Attorney General in February of 1983.[5] A key related event was the funding of a provincial committee on wife abuse in the fiscal year 1982-83. Both of these developments were a response to escalating lobbying by women's groups in the province.

The new directive had the most dramatic short term impact on the system and produced the strongest "change back"[6] reaction by the system. Suddenly, 1,136 wife abusers were charged by the police and RCMP (see Table I), and at least two thirds of them were making their way to court. Aware from the beginning that there would be resistance from criminal justice personnel, the provincial Wife Abuse Committee lobbied the Attorney General to set up a separate court with designated Crown Attorneys to handle domestic assault cases.

As a result of this foresight, the government's first response to resistance within the system was to set up a separate court. In November 1983, a court was set aside two days a week to handle the increased volume of wife abuse cases. The court was designated to handle the not guilty pleas (which were considered to be the more difficult cases and would require the most sympathetic and experienced court personnel).

Despite this move, the bulk of the cases landing in court were guilty pleas and the more autonomous staff of the criminal justice system, judges and defence lawyers, spoke out against the new directive in the Spring of 1984.[7] A number of judges and defence lawyers denounced the new policy as a failure, asserting that it clogged up the criminal courts with what were essentially "family counselling issues."

The strong "change back" reaction was, however, successfully countered by the concurrent social service funding of wife abuse services. While the funding was extremely low, it did provide salaries for women committed to wife abuse services who could carry on a more sustained lobbying effort to counteract the resistance in the system. As part of this funding, a report was prepared and submitted to the Attorney General's office within days of the public condemnation of the directive by defence lawyers and some judges. The report documented overwhelming public support of the new directive and provided an analysis of court processing of wife abuse cases which indicated that these cases varied little in attrition (that is, stays, dismissed for want of prosecution or discharges) from the processing of general assault cases (Ursel, 1986).

Thus, while the changes within the criminal justice system were most vulnerable to "change back" pressures, the modest state commitment to wife abuse services and the increasing social acceptance of this issue as a serious social problem served to support and sustain the initial steps towards a new criminal justice policy.

During this first phase, a momentum was building within the women's community to press for increased funding of wife abuse services. In the fiscal year 1981-82, the total sum of state support for wife abuse services was $51,800, providing small grants to a shelter in Winnipeg and a crisis centre in Thompson. By the end of this phase, state funding had increased to $315,800 in grants for five different community-based wife abuse services as well as a $100,000 commitment to a public awareness campaign on wife abuse. Thus, in the 1983-84 phase, the primary resistance to change came from within the criminal justice system, and the primary support for the government to stick with the new directive came from the battered women's movement and the community at large.

Phase II 1985–87

This stage is characterized by a general adjustment within the systems (criminal justice and social service) to the fact that wife abuse had become a reality to be dealt with. During this phase, we see the development of supporting services and policies, the creation of an office to coordinate wife abuse programs within the state, and a growing conflict between the state and the Manitoba Committee on Wife Abuse over ownership of the issue.

i. Developments in the Criminal Justice System

Within the criminal justice system, four initiatives were introduced: 1) police recruit training on the issue of wife abuse in 1986; 2) growth of batterers' treatment groups; 3) the Women's Advocacy Program in 1986; and 4) court policy on reluctant witnesses in 1987. All of these initiatives were developed in conjunction with, or because of, initiatives in the social service system. All were designed to help the criminal justice system deal more effectively with wife abuse cases, but they did not introduce any further changes in the structure or procedure for processing wife abuse cases.

Police recruit training and batterers' treatment groups are self-explanatory. At the beginning of this phase, there was no formal agreement between the social service system and the police academy. At the end of this phase, wife abuse training was built into the curriculum for recruits and the government wife abuse office was negotiating a curriculum for in-service training for active officers. With regard to batterers' treatment groups, at the beginning of this stage there were three programs in the province; one run out of probation services and two non-funded programs operating in community-based agencies. At the end of this period, there were four probation services programs and a new community-based program called *Evolve* funded to run treatment groups for batterers, as well as separate groups for women and children. *Evolve* was also mandated to provide training for agencies and individuals planning to operate such groups. In addition, a joint province-native agency proposal was submitted to Health and Welfare Canada to start up a Native Family Violence Program similar to *Evolve* but responsive to the specific needs of aboriginal people.

The Women's Advocacy Program (WAP) was initiated by the provincial wife abuse office as a service specifically for women whose partners had been charged with wife abuse. Its mandate was to support victims, to provide a bridge between the social service and criminal justice system, and to facilitate the operation of the criminal justice system. The program consists of a lawyer and two counsellors who provide women with legal information about their partner's case, criminal justice procedures and their role as a witness, as well as counselling and referral to a range of social services. The service functions to sensitize the criminal justice system to the needs and interest of the victim, as well as to absorb a great deal of the court personnel's frustration in dealing with the complexities of wife abuse cases.[8] In addition to providing the victim with information, counselling, referral and support during court attendance, they also provide pre-sentence reports so the judge can duly consider the women's interests in determining sentencing. This program has resulted in greater victim/ witness cooperation in the processing of wife abuse cases (see Table IV).

Even with additional support, victims of wife abuse typically express a great deal of anxiety and ambiguity about their role as witnesses in court. In response to this problem, the prosecutions' office of the Attorney General issued policy guidelines in May of 1987 to ensure reluctant witnesses were not doubly victimized by charges of contempt of court when they refused to testify. The guidelines directed all crowns to refer a woman requesting that charges be dropped to the Women's Advocacy Program. There was a recognition that treating all persons before the court equally in these cases would only perpetuate inequalities because women/

victims were at a serious power disadvantage in their families and in society at large. The processing of wife abuse cases was not to be treated as just the same as general assaults. The victim/witness in wife abuse cases should receive special supports (WAP) and special considerations as a result of their specifically disadvantaged position relative to men.

The impact of these initiatives were: first, charges increased over time (see Table I); second, court attrition was reduced and more appropriate sentencing began to emerge (see Table III); and third, judicial and legal criticism of the charging directive ceased. The fourth impact was that public monitoring of wife abuse sentencing via press reporters in court led to greater public scrutiny and criticism of judges and/or crown attorneys whose behaviour was seen to fail to support the intent of the directive. Finally, defence lawyers learned how to work the system, knowing informally which judges were less sympathetic to the directive and shopping around via remands until they could get their client in a "friendly" court.

ii. Developments in the Social Service System

During the second stage of development, the major systemic changes occurred within the social service departments. These developments included:

1. A dramatic increase in funding for wife abuse programs, from $300 thousand at the end of the first stage to $1.739 million by the end of the second phase.

2. An increase in community-based wife abuse services throughout the province, from five programs at the end of the first phase to 23 programs at the end of the second phase, including ten shelters, a number of non residential programs and second stage facilities.

3. The creation of an office within the government to coordinate the development of and administer the funding to wife abuse services.

The creation of the government office precipitated a polarization of wife abuse workers and agencies with divergent views on the desirability of state involvement. While *ad hoc* and reactive involvement by the state was considered a necessary cost of getting state funding, the move to proactive, developmental involvement signalled by the creation of the government wife abuse office was perceived as a real threat by some.

The Manitoba Committee on Wife Abuse became the focal point for individuals and agencies who perceived state involvement with great suspicion and saw the government wife abuse office as the enemy. There are as many interpretations of the source of the conflict as there were actors involved, however, my reading of it was a resistance to government moving from the role of passive to active participant.

The drama of the second period reflected the rapid growth of services and the extreme polarization over the issue of state involvement. The consequence was the conflict-ridden birth of a network of wife abuse services throughout the province. This period of inter-agency conflict offers an interesting test of the two theories of state conduct we are considering. The first theory, which sees no convergence of state and women's interests on this issue, would suggest that the intense conflict within and between agencies would provide an ideal opportunity for the state to withdraw from any program or financial commitments to the issue. The second perspective, which suggests a potential convergence of state and women's interest in confronting the problem of wife abuse, would suggest that, despite the "divide and conquer" option available to the state, it would continue its commitment because wife abuse had become costly to the state as well.

The latter scenario prevailed, although there were clearly casualties of the conflict (the first were the "femocrats" who staffed the wife abuse office[9] and the second was the Committee itself which literally imploded a year later).[10] Despite these casualties, the momentum for growth was sustained by the legitimacy of the issue within the community at large, the energy and commitment of the wife abuse workers and lobbyists, and the weight of statistical evidence on the prevalence of the problem being generated from the criminal justice system.

During this conflict-ridden process, significant policy and program changes were introduced into the social service system itself. These changes were initiated within social service departments to facilitate the growth of community-based wife abuse services. They included:

1) A government policy supporting the use of provincial social housing projects by agencies funded to provide second stage housing and support programs.

2) A change in the regulations to the Social Assistance Act to provide one-tier (provincial) per diems to shelters within a two-tier welfare system.[11]

3) The introduction of fee waiver grants to ensure that no shelter suffers financially for housing a woman who does not qualify for per diem payments from social assistance.

4) An arrangement with the Department of Housing to provide a facility and operating grants to agencies funded to provide shelter services.

5) The establishment of the first native-run wife abuse program and the first immigrant family violence service.

6) An $800 thousand dollar training program was negotiated between the Department of Employment Services and Economic Security and the wife

abuse government office to train 20 "grass roots" local women as wife abuse counsellors. The program paid wages and expenses for the women for two years of in-service and in- class training.[12]

While the growth was rapid and the process was volatile, the state consistently supported the principle that wife abuse services be provided by community-based wife abuse committees and agencies. This principle was the key policy battle championed by the "femocrats" within the bureaucracy. To their credit, they saw the policy well-entrenched before they were removed from their positions.

Only one internal government program was established in addition to the administrative staff, and that was the Women's Advocacy Program. Thus, the entry of the government in the social service sector served primarily to increase the number of community-based services and increase the voice of immigrant and native women in the design of such services. It is interesting to note the differences in the reactions to change that occurred in the first and second phases. In the first phase, the focus for change was the criminal justice system and the major "change back" pressure came from within the system. In the second phase, the focus for change was the social service system and the major "change back" pressure came from outside of the system, from elements within the battered women's movement, whose primary concern was loss of ownership of the issue.

Phase III 1988–1990

In this phase, which is ongoing, what appears to be happening is a process of legitimation and normalization of the changes which were introduced in the criminal justice and social service systems. The rapidity of change in both systems left a lot of work unfinished. Problems and issues that have been identified as a result of five or six years of experience in the two systems are now on the agenda to be addressed. The distinguishing feature of this phase is an absence of "change back" pressures, indicative of a general acceptance of the issue within the two systems and a greater acceptance of the state as an actor by lobbyists and service providers outside of government.

Because the overwhelming majority of services are offered by community-based programs, government activity in the social services is largely limited to funding and facilitating those services. The unfinished business in this field concerned the development of an adequate funding formula for the large number of new services in the province. The government response was to mount a province-wide consultation process known as the "Women's Initiative" with a dual focus on services to battered women and women's economic needs. The consultation report recommended a number of changes in funding which resulted in increased provincial expenditures on wife abuse services. The provincial budget increased from $1.7 million in 1987/88 to $4.3 million in 1989/90.[13]

The other key recommendation contained in the report suggested a major public awareness campaign with a strong message that wife abuse is a crime. This is the only development which received any resistance during this phase. The resistance came from outside of government from individuals and agencies who have remained suspicious of any state initiatives in the area of wife abuse.

Because wife abuse initiatives are largely internal to the criminal justice system, there are more systemic changes and developments to enumerate. One of the outcomes of wife abuse being a high profile issue in the community and a high priority issue in government was a new interest in the monitoring of wife abuse court cases. This monitoring was made possible by the high level of media interest and frequent press coverage of wife abuse court cases. When judges or crown attorneys are perceived as failing to live up to the intent of government policy, there is widespread publicity resulting in both public and systemic censuring of inappropriate behaviour.[14] Also, the number of Crown appeals have increased as the public and the Department of Justice have become more demanding about the appropriateness of sentences.

In addition to substantial public monitoring, the existence of services to victims provides advocates for women who have not been well served by the system. Complaints about failures in the system are made by wife abuse agencies to the police, the crown attorneys, judges and the Minister of Justice. A particularly valuable source on the operation of the system is the staff of the Women's Advocacy Program, who work very closely with all of the components of the criminal justice system — police, crown attorneys, judges and probation officers.

This intensive monitoring of the process has made the various offices of the criminal justice system anxious to develop better response systems. The Winnipeg Police Department has now developed a curriculum on wife abuse for active police officers as well as recruits. The Judicial Education Committee, the Crown Attorney's Educational Committee and the Manitoba Law Society have all sponsored symposiums and workshops on court processing of wife abuse cases, with wife abuse workers and, on occasion, wife abuse survivors invited to make presentations.

As a result of the cooperation of supportive members within the system, identification of trouble spots and high case attrition not subject to public scrutiny has led to the launching of a case tracking project. The domestic assault tracking project is a joint federal-provincial initiative designed to track 100 percent of all wife abuse cases which occur within a designated six months in three sites in the province. All cases will be followed through the system from the initial call to the police through to completion of correctional intervention. The goal of the project is to get more information on processes not open to public scrutiny (that is, police decision-making at the incident, plea bargaining in the Crown's office, and so on). It is hoped that this information will assist in developing policies and procedures for a better response system.

In addition to studying the system, the courts undertook some restructuring to create a single court in which all wife abuse cases from preliminary hearing to sentencing are heard. This specialization was designed to limit defence lawyers' ability to shop around for a "sympathetic" court, as well as to ensure a team of specially trained crown attorneys and experienced judges to staff the court. This court became operational in the fall of 1990.

At the beginning of this discussion, I argued that a comprehensive assessment of the success or failure of the battered women's movement must go beyond an analysis of the impact of the state on the movement, and must consider the impact of the movement on the state and, most important, the impact of the movement and the state on options and services for battered women. From the above brief history, I would suggest that there is sufficient evidence to conclude that the battered women's movement did have an impact on the state, specifically the criminal justice and social service systems' response to wife abuse. In the final section of the paper, I will present the data that I have collected as measures of change within the system as a means of assessing the actual or potential impact of these changes on battered women or women at risk.

III. Considering the Evidence
i. Assessing the Change in the Criminal Justice System

As a result of the new directive, a greater number of wife abuse cases resulted in arrests than in the past. Although pre-directive records do not specify domestic assault charges, we can estimate the increase in domestic cases by the dramatic increase in assault charges after the new directive was introduced. In 1983, the year the directive was issued, 3,673 assault charges were laid as opposed to 2,458 in 1982. This increase is more than double that experienced between 1981 and 1982. Since 1983, police and RCMP data indicate that the number of persons being charged in wife abuse cases has risen slowly but steadily. Table I indicates the total number of arrests in Winnipeg and by the RCMP outside of Winnipeg each year for the past seven years.

In addition to knowing the numbers of individuals charged, the analysis of police data provides us with some information on the accused. Table II indicates some of the more salient statistics about the offenders. As is well known, the overwhelming majority of persons arrested in cases identified as "domestics" are men in a marital or couple relationship with the victim. Of particular interest is the age of the assailants, over 70% are under the age of 40. This suggests that these men have 20 to 30 years more of relationships ahead of them and, if the cycle is not broken, this will mean 20 to 30 more years of victimization of their partners. Another important factor is the number of children involved in these relationships; on average 60% of these cases have dependent children in the home. This raises serious concerns about the lessons these children are learning and the potential for perpetuating the inter-generational cycle of violence (Sinclair, 1985; Carlson, 1984).

Table I
Number of Persons Charged with (Spousal) Assault
in Manitoba 1983, 1984, 1985, 1986, 1987, 1988 and 1989.

	Winnipeg		**RCMP Manitoba**		
Year	**No. of Offenders**	**% Male**	**No. of Offenders**	**% Male**	**Total**
1983	629	96%	507	94%	1,136
1984	640	98%	699	92%	1,339
1985	859	95%	793	95%	1,652
1986	957	95%	629	96%	1,586
1987	922	94%	698	94%	1,620
1988	990	95%	803	94%	1,793
Total	4,977		4,129		9,126

When we consider the socio-economic characteristics of the accused, we see that their education and employment level is below the national average. In short, they are no exception to the general pattern in Canada that people of low socio-economic status are more likely to be apprehended by the police. This pattern has been invoked by Snider (1990) as one reason why women should not look to the state and the criminal justice system for support. She states that such intervention is repressive because it only reinforces the class biases in the system. However, it is important to consider that, in the overwhelming majority of cases (75%), it is the victim who makes the call to the police. If low income women do not have any other form of recourse to save themselves and their children, should such intervention be denied them because it reflects a general bias in our society? We know that when people have other alternatives available to them, they will choose those alternatives rather than the police. However, for poor and working class women who do not have family, friends and/ or lawyers who can assist them, they must rely, like it or not, on the police to protect them. Surely it is a very distorted sense of justice that would deny these women and their children such protection.

A final important observation about the accused is the very high rate of prior records (PR) these individuals have. On average, 70% of the individuals arrested have prior records, with a very significant number having records for assault, either domestic or general. This provides

Table II
Domestic Assault Statistics Information
on the Accused, Winnipeg 1983 - 1987

Year	1983	1984	1985	1986	1987
Sample size	373	393	522	336	253
1) **Sex**	%	%	%	%	%
Male	95	97	94	97	97
Female	5	3	6	3	3
2) **Age**					
18-30	46	48	50	52	57
31-40	30	31	29	28	26
41 +	22	21	20	20	17
3) Married	60	58	67	69	58
Other	40	42	33	31	42
4) **Children**					
Yes	60	60	55	58	57
No	40	40	45	42	43
5) **Education**					
<High School	69	67.4	75.1	70.4	57.0
High School	25	19.8	19.9	24.2	25.0
>High School	5	3.3	5.0	5.4	2.4
6) **Employment Status**					
Employed	52.3	54.1	53.5	55.7	55.7
Unemployed	34.5	29.8	27.6	26.2	23.0
Welfare	13.2	15.1	18.9	16.1	15.0
7) **Prior Record**					
Yes	65	72	70	73	77
No	34	28	30	27	23
8) **Pr Type**					
Domestic	44	55	34	18	16
General	20	17	29	27	18
Other	36	27	37	55	66
9) Pr since 1983	-	-	15	12	9

some fairly compelling evidence that the persons arrested have a history of violence and are dangerous. Of particular interest in these statistics is the declining percentage of prior records for "domestic" assaults after 1984. Items 8 and 9 in Table II (PR domestic and PR domestic since 1983) both show a decline over time. The most optimistic interpretation of this data would be that the arrest policy was reducing the rate of recidivism in wife assault cases. While there are some studies that suggest this pattern (Sherman and Berk 1984; Jaffe, Wolfes, Telford and Austin 1985), more detailed follow-up studies would be necessary to confirm that this is the case in Winnipeg.

Table III
Processing of Domestic Assault Cases In the
Winnipeg Criminal Justice System 1983 - 1987

Year	1983	1984	1985	1986	1987
Sample size	373	393	522	336	253
% Cases Stayed	33%	32%	31%	28%	32%
# Cases Proceed To Court	250	268	360	242	172
Court Attrition*	19%	4%	6%	8%	-
% Sentenced	48%	64%	63%	64%	-
Most Frequent Disposition**					
Cond. Discharge	12%	13%	14%	18%	14%
Probation +	9	10	8	20	20
Suspended Sent.	9	11	11	19	20
Jail	2	5	4	8	7
Fine	9	7	8	7	12
Counselling on Final Disposition	9%	16%	11%	19%	32%
Type of Counselling					
Alcohol	-	55%	55%	41%	47%
Batterers		7	5	46	20
Other		38	40	13	34

* Includes all cases of Dismissed for Want of Prosecution, Discharge, Absolute Discharge and Acquittal.
** Based on the first, most serious charge dealt with.

While we know that the directive has changed the arrest rate, the next question about change in the criminal justice system is the issue of crown attorney and court processing. In the previous section, resistance from some judges and lawyers to the directive in the initial phase of change was identified. However, Table III suggests that court processing changed over time, most importantly, in terms of the rate and type of sentencing. The highest attrition rate occurs in the crown attorney's office, where on average one-third of the cases are stayed. If, however, the case makes it to court, the overwhelming majority emerge with a finding of guilt and a sentence. Table III indicates that the court attrition rate dropped dramatically, from 19 percent in 1983 to 4 percent the following year. As a result, the number of persons sentenced increased from 48 to 64 percent in the same year.

With regard to the type of sentencing, there is a growing concern about what constitutes an appropriate sentence or sanction for the crime of wife abuse. Fining assailants is seen to provide little useful intervention and could be construed as little more than extracting a levy for abuse. The victim's expressed wishes, as well as the opinion of workers in the field, suggest that sentences which mandate counselling are necessary to break the cycle of violence. Three sentences most likely to provide for monitoring, protection for the victim and/or counselling are: probation $+^{15}$ (which increased from 9 percent to 20 percent); jail sentences (which also increased from 2 percent to 7 percent); and counselling as an order on final disposition (which increased from 9 percent to 32 percent between 1983 and 1987). Dispositions which provide for ongoing monitoring and counselling interventions have been actively promoted by wife abuse workers and advocates. The sentencing patterns identified in Table III suggest that this lobbying has been effective.

The intent of the changes introduced in the criminal justice system over the past seven years was to provide wife abuse victims with more protection and to make the court more sensitive to their needs. The higher arrest rate indicates an effort on the part of police departments to provide greater protection, while the changing pattern of sentencing suggests an attempt by the courts to be more sensitive to women's needs. An important measure of the outcome of these efforts is the increasing rate of victim cooperation with the criminal justice system over the past seven years. Table IV provides some measure of this development in the consistently declining rate of court Dismissals For Want Of Prosecution (DFWOP's), as well as the reduction in the crown attorney's reports citing "victim reluctance" as reason for stay.

While it is not being suggested that all of the problems within the system are solved or that victims are always treated well by the system, it can be argued that real changes with beneficial results for women have been introduced. While these changes are not enough, they do provide evidence that the system is moving in the right direction. In this regard, perhaps the greatest success of the battered women's movement is the level of legitimacy this issue has acquired in the public eye. This legitimacy has led to the high level of public monitoring of the system, which has created the political will to proceed with the Tracking Project and the new Family Violence Court. Both of these recent developments will be a critical force in ensuring that the changes continue, and that they continue in the right direction.

Table IV
Victim Witness Cooperation in Wife Abuse Cases
in Winnipeg 1983–87 as Measured by Stays of Proceedings
and Court Dismissals for Want of Prosecution (DFWOP)

Year	Total # Charged	Sample Size	% DFWOP	% Stayed	Victim/Reluctance* as reason for Stay
1983	629	373	18%	33%	95%
1984	640	393	6%	32%	85%
1985	859	522	9%	31%	30%
1986	957	336	5%	28%	34%**
1987	922	253	1%	32%	18%

* This category includes "refused to testify" as recorded by Crown and "left town." Please note the high rates in 1983-84 were probably a function of the data collection procedure. In these two years the question "reason for stay" was open-ended. In subsequent years, Crowns were provided with a detailed breakdown of reasons for stay.

** In 1986 the Women's Advocacy Program was introduced resulting in the significant reduction in victim reluctance in the 1987 data. For reasons yet to be determined this has not resulted in a concurrent reduction in the stay rate.

II. Assessing Change in the Social Service System

In assessing change in the social service system, there are really only two statistical measures available: the number of programs the government funds and the amount of funding provided. Table V indicates consistent growth in both areas. The number of community-based wife abuse services increased from 2 in 1982 to 25 in 1990, and government expenditure increased from $52 thousand to over $4 million in the same time period. Since the government's role is largely limited to that of funder, all the other measures of impact lie within the service agencies themselves.

The increased number of community-based agencies and the increased funding they receive led to the development of a broader

Table V

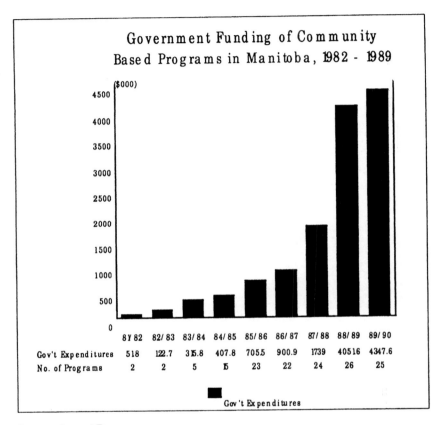

Government Funding of Community Based Programs in Manitoba, 1982 - 1989

	81/82	82/83	83/84	84/85	85/86	86/87	87/88	88/89	89/90
Gov't Expenditures	51.8	122.7	315.8	407.8	705.5	900.9	1739	4051.6	4347.6
No. of Programs	2	2	5	15	23	22	24	26	25

Gov't Expenditures

Source: Annual Reports
- Department of Community Services and Department of
Employment Services and Economic Security, 1981 - 1988.
- Department of Family Services and Department of Housing,
1988/89 - 1989/90.
- Department of Housing, 1986 -1990.

network of services. While many services have concentrated on crisis response, 24-hour crisis lines and shelters, there are also second stage programs and non-residential counselling programs to support women and children in the intermediate and longer term process of restructuring their lives. In addition, as the funding for services improves, the community-based agencies are less plagued with staff turnover, allowing them more time and energy to devote to program development. In recent years, shelters have put a great deal of energy into developing programs for children in their facilities. Most agencies are now reporting an increase in the variety and quality of the services they offer. Unfortunately, the only data available at this time indicating the utilization rate of these services is shelter data. Table VI identifies the growing number of women and children accommodated in shelters between 1985 and 1989, the period of most substantially increased funding.

Conclusion

The purpose of this discussion has been to introduce new criteria into a literature which is currently assessing the success or failure of the battered women's movement. The existing assessments have focused on the impact of state involvement on the movement itself. In contrast, it has been suggested here that a consideration of the impact of the movement on the state is an equally important criterion. Furthermore, it has been suggested that an assessment of the impact of the movement and the state on the supports and options available to battered women should be the ultimate criterion.

With regard to the first criterion, the impact of the movement on the state, the discussion has identified both a history and a statistical summary of changes which have been introduced in the criminal justice and social service systems as a result of the battered women's movement. With regard to the second criterion, the impact of these changes on battered women, the measures are less obvious. It has been demonstrated that, as a result of state involvement, the number of services for wife abuse victims increased ten fold from 1982 to 1990. It has also been demonstrated that the growth of government expenditures has experienced an even more dramatic increase during a decade when fiscal restraint was the dominant feature of state management.

On the basis of this quantitative evidence, one could conclude that battered women and women at risk are better off today, as a result of state involvement, than they were ten years ago. However, critics of state involvement suggest that the most important measure is qualitative. Are the services being run by "bona fide" feminist agencies? Concerns expressed about ownership of the issue cuts to the quick of feminist politics. Does one group of women — the founders of the battered women's movement — who share a specific analysis of patriarchy, a specific political agenda, as well as a specific class and racial background, have the "ownership" of an issue which destroys the health and life of many different women of different class and racial backgrounds, who have many different political perspectives and many different views of patriarchy? Can a single issue political movement realistically expect to be anything more than a movement for reform of that issue? And, as the momentum for reform accelerates, involving many more women and many different perspectives, by what criteria

Table VI

Number of Abused Women and Their Children Accomodated in
Wife Abuse Shelters — 1985, 1986/87, 1987/88, 1988/89.

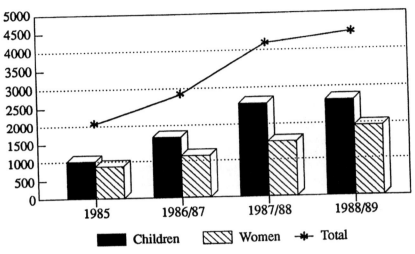

Sources: Manitoba Department of Community Services Annual Reports 1985-1988
Manitoba Department of Family Services Annual Report 1988/1989

do we conclude the movement has failed?

The involvement of the state does change things. The increased funding has resulted in more agencies becoming involved and these agencies are more heterogeneous. While none of the original services have been replaced and all are still operating (with the exception of the Manitoba Committee on Wife Abuse), new agencies with new approaches have entered the field of service delivery.

Examples of this diversity are the development of an immigrant women's program and a number of native services (a shelter, a provincial crisis line and a non-residential counselling program). In addition, shelters have been developed in small, rural, religiously conservative communities. While the key actors in these new agencies have not had an historical connection to the battered women's movement, must we conclude that they are anti-feminist?

If we find that, as a community broader than the women's movement becomes empowered to act on this issue, and in taking ownership uses a language and philosophy fitting to their own community, is it fair to conclude that the issue has been coopted? Broad societal legitimation of an issue does mean that feminists lose *exclusive* ownership of the issue. However, the recognition by the larger community that wife abuse is a prevalent problem should be taken as a measure of success of the movement.

In the case of Manitoba, it is perhaps more accurate to talk about the wife abuse issue as being democratized rather than coopted. It is true that not all actors and agencies in the field will share the analysis of patriarchy common to the founders of the battered women's movement. However, the work they do does serve to increase the supports and options for women and children escaping violent homes and assists them in establishing secure, independent living alternatives. In the absence of state involvement, there would have been many fewer agencies involved, although they would undoubtedly have been more explicity feminist in ideology. In making the choice between many services providing substantive material supports and few services of a more homogeneous feminist substance, it can be argued that, in the former, the material benefits outweigh the ideological in these very real life and death situations.

In conclusion, the different assessments of the "success" of the battered women's movement reflect different strategic approaches to the state based on different theoretical understandings of the patriarchal character of the state. The first theoretical perspective reviewed in this paper perceives the state as fundamentally and irretrievably patriarchal. The policy implications of this perspective are to approach the state apprehensively, with the expectation that whatever the state touches will be turned to patriarchal purposes. The practice which follows from this policy is the vigilant guarding of the feminist ownership of the issue, which leads to placing a value and emphasis on feminist homogeneity in services and, thus, to an ensuing attitude of caution and distrust of heterogeneity in services. This has often resulted in bitter divisions and rivalries between agencies and among service deliverers.

The alternative view of the "success" of the battered women's movement which is presented in this paper is based on a different criterion of success which flows from a different theoretical analysis of the state. The alternative theoretical perspective perceives contradictions in the dynamic of patriarchy in the state. It is argued that these contradictions create a contested terrain and the possibility of a convergence of state and women's interests on particular issues. The policy implications of this alternative perspective are to approach the state strategically, to select issues in which a potential for convergence of interests do exist, and then to involve the state as much as possible in working towards those changes. The practice which flows from this policy promotes a proliferation of resources and services, rather than the protection of ownership of the issue. The practice seeks to involve as many actors in as many ways as possible to confront the crime in all of its different locations and manifestations. This perspective is outward-looking in both its criteria of success (that is, "how has the movement had an impact upon the state and the women at risk?") and in its strategies for change.

Strategic decisions to consciously and carefully use the state should be informed by an assessment of state interest in particular patriarchal structures or functions. Not all issues are as amenable to useful state involvement as wife abuse. It goes without saying, however, that feminist strategies to use the power of the state, its laws, its money and/or its legitimacy, must always include ongoing monitoring and lobbying to ensure progressive reform.

Notes

1. This position is less likely to be found in the academic literature, but is frequently articulated by workers and lobbyists in the wife abuse field. This perspective is most frequently voiced in the public media in order to encourage/pressure governments to increase funding and support for agencies assisting battered women and their children. For example, see: "Government Funding for Shelters for Abused Women Warmly Welcomed in Thompson," *Thompson Times*, June 26, 1987; "Abuse Group Seeks Funds and Recognition," *Winnipeg Free Press*, August 2, 1987; and "Province to Fund Women's Shelters," *Brandon Sun*, June 24, 1987.

2. "As a public discourse, wife battery has been transformed from a critique of patriarchal power to demands for protection from male power ... The demand for re-distribution of social power, which can only result from radical social change and which underscored the early women's movement, has been translated into demands for expansion of current institutions. To argue that this *failure* merely reflects the general *failure* of a liberal approach is oversimplistic ..." (Currie, 1990:88-89, emphasis added).

3. I am puzzled by the frequency with which feminist academics perceive the presence of college educated or credentialed staff in a wife abuse service as evidence that these services have become mainstream. Many of the women who currently are applying as volunteers and/or paid staff in shelters are students or graduates of Women's Studies programs.

4. This section of the paper focuses on the legal and social service response resulting from the new political and social visibility of wife abuse in the province of Manitoba. The major sources of data are as follows: Spouse Abuse Statistics, Winnipeg Police Department 1983-1989, RCMP quarterly reports 1983-1989, an analysis of a selective sample of 1,877 wife abuse cases processed within the City of Winnipeg 1983-1987, and program and expenditure data from the Department of Family Services 1983-1989. The history of the process of change within the criminal justice and social service systems is based upon my involvement with the process in the position of Provincial Co-ordinator of Wife Abuse Services, 1985-1987.

5. The RCMP issued a similar directive on charging in domestic assaults

in 1982. Ontario and other provinces issued similar directives throughout the period 1982 to 1984.

6. The term "change back" is used to refer to pressure to return to the status quo. It is a term introduced by Harriet Goldhor Lerner in her book *The Dance of Anger.*

7. *Winnipeg Free Press,* May 17, 18, 19, 22 30 and June 30, 1984.

8. The extreme ambivalence of the victim towards her assailant, which is part of the cycle of violence, often confronts police and crown attorneys as an impediment to the fulfillment of their work role (that is, getting a conviction). The reluctant witness/victim is a frequent source of frustration for court personnel. By separating out the advocacy role from the prosecutorial role, the Women's Advocacy Program plays an important function in absorbing this frustration. They provide a sympathetic and supportive environment in which women as victims can work out their decisions concerning their role in court and their willingness or disinclination to testify.

9. Franzway, Court and Connell provide an interesting discussion of the process and the outcome of community-based feminists concentrating their attacks on the state on "femocrats," in their book *Staking a Claim:* of staff and all of the volunteers resigned. Several months later, the government decided to terminate their funding.

11. A two-tier welfare system designates local municipalities as responsible for social assistance for the first three months and is based on the presumption that local authorities are the best judge of the eligibility of applicants for temporary assistance. In practice, this has resulted in local authorities being much more rigid gate keepers because their resources are so much more limited than those of the province. In the case of women seeking shelter, their stay is paid through a per diem rate provided by social assistance. However, in small communities, the reluctance of local authorities to assume such expenses meant that when a woman was deemed ineligible for social assistance, either the shelter had to absorb the costs themselves or the woman was discouraged from going to the shelter. The introduction of a one tier system (that is, provincial responsibility for per diem rates) eliminated this substantial barrier to equitable service for women.

12. The training package provided by the provincial government program *New Careers* reports that nineteen women were recruited and thirteen graduated. Ten are still working in wife abuse and one graduate has gone on to university to obtain a social work degree and another entered law school.

13. The expenditures listed only include funds provided to community-based, non-governmental services. These funds include expenditures in the Departments of Housing and Family Services and in social assistance per diem payments.

14. Some examples of the press coverage of wife abuse cases in court are: "Days of Terror Net Suspended Term," *Winnipeg Sun,* December 18,

1987; "Wife Abuser's Jail Sentence to be Appealed," *Winnipeg Free Press*, February 8, 1990; "Woman Terrified of Husband — Out of Jail in 8 Weeks," *Winnipeg Sun*, February 7, 1990; "Justice — More or Less — Two Cases Point Out Vast Gap in Sentencing," *Winnipeg Sun*, February 16, 1990.

15. Probation + refers to any disposition in which probation is given as the sentence or in addition to other sanctions. For example, 1 year suspended sentence and 1 year supervised probation.

Law, Ideology and Social Change: An Analysis of the Role of Law in the Construction of Corporate Crime

Neil C. Sargent

This paper starts from the premise that little has been achieved in the way of theoretical advancement in Canadian corporate crime research since Goff and Reasons' (1978) study, *Corporate Crime in Canada*, first appeared.[1] This is all the more surprising since the last several years have witnessed a veritable explosion of interest in theories of the state and law on the part of critical criminologists in Canada.[2] Yet, with apparently few exceptions (see Snider, 1987, 1990; Smandych, 1986), most critically-informed research on corporate crime in Canada remains locked in an instrumentalist embrace which views the failure of the criminal justice system to respond to corporate crime as a transparent reflection of ruling class interests (Casey, 1985).

In this paper, I attempt to develop a critical analysis of corporate crime[3] which avoids the reductionism of such instrumentalist analyses. The object of the exercise is not simply to elaborate a more refined theoretical model to explain the well-documented failure of the criminal justice system to control corporate crime (although I would argue that this is a worthwhile aim in itself). Rather, theory is important because it informs praxis. Consequently, one of the primary aims of this attempt to re-examine the theoretical nature of the relationship between law, class and corporate crime is to identify potential emancipatory legal and political strategies which could lead to greater accountability on the part of corporate offenders for their illegal actions.

The first part of the paper, therefore, critically examines the conception of law and the state underpinning most instrumentalist accounts of corporate crime. The next three parts of the paper explore the ideological dimensions of law and the complex role of law as a site of ideological struggle over the social meanings attached to corporate crime. The last part of the paper then looks at implications for praxis and the possibility of a constructive engagement with criminal law. Drawing on feminist experience with criminal law reform in the area of domestic violence, it is argued that criminalization should not be looked upon as a panacea in forcing the state to address the problem of corporate crime, and that critical attention should be given to exploring other progressive avenues for legal and political struggle which are capable of identifying and empowering the social interests in need of protection through the law.

Unpacking Instrumentalist Accounts of Corporate Crime

Much recent research into corporate crime in Canada has tended to adopt an instrumental Marxist perspective to account for the prevalence of corporate crime and the failure of the criminal justice system to respond to this phenomenon (Goff and Reasons, 1978; Snider, 1978, 1982; Glasbeek, 1984; Casey, 1985). Implicit in these accounts of corporate crime is a theory of law and the state as essentially passive agencies that can be captured by dominant class interests and used to maintain and consolidate their dominant economic position. Emphasis is placed on the superior resources of powerful corporate interests in defining legislation that is designed to regulate unlawful corporate behaviour as being non-criminal in nature (Snider, 1982; Reasons, Ross and Patterson, 1986; Glasbeek, 1984). Similarly, the interpenetration of personnel between the state bureaucracy and the private sector is viewed as a reflection of the susceptibility of regulatory enforcement agencies to "capture" by the corporate interests they are required to regulate (Goff and Reasons, 1978; Snider, 1978, 1982). The mass media are also credited with playing an important role in downplaying the social and economic costs associated with corporate crime, and thereby creating a political climate in which far fewer resources are allocated towards controlling illegal corporate behaviour than are devoted towards "managing" street crime (Goff and Reasons, 1978; Snider, 1978).

The strengths of this model are important to keep in mind. By stressing the importance of agency, instrumentalism places concepts such as power, class and capitalism at the centre of any analysis of the social function of law and legal institutions. Law is not seen simply as a meta-social structure which merely reflects evolving social values or needs (Gordon, 1984). By contrast, liberal reform theorists, offering competing accounts of the relative immunity accorded to corporate offenders under the Criminal Code and regulatory statutes, tend to leave out of their accounts the considerable empirical evidence which indicates that powerful corporate interests are often able to influence the law-making process in such a way as to limit the scope and effectiveness of laws designed to control corporate criminal behaviour (Stone, 1975; Law Reform Commission of Canada,

1976, 1985).

Yet, it is also important to recognize the theoretical weaknesses of instrumentalist analyses of corporate crime. Although emphasizing the importance of agency to an understanding of the legal process, the instrumentalist model focuses only on elite agency, and leaves out of its analysis any account of the way in which law may also operate as a rallying point for opposition to ruling class dominance (Thompson, 1975; Brickey and Comack, 1987). Attempts to reconstruct the social character of law through such instrumentalist analyses tend to disregard any sense of historical contingency or struggle associated with the law-making or law-enforcement processes (Carson, 1974, 1980; Smandych, 1986; Brickey and Comack, 1987; McMullan, 1987).

In addition, the theoretical and empirical adequacy of the concepts of class and state used in most instrumentalist analyses is open to question. Thus, Smandych (1986) notes that the instrumentalist conception of class creates a "false impression" of ruling class unity, and is therefore incapable of accounting for intra-class conflict within the capitalist class. Similarly, the instrumentalist conception of the state as a captive agent of the capitalist class fails to account for the legitimation function of the state within advanced capitalism (Mahon, 1980; Smandych, 1986). Rather than simply acting as the agent of the dominant class, the state must also be responsive to pressures "from below" in order to maintain the social conditions that are necessary for continued capitalist accumulation. Indeed, it is precisely the state's ability to transcend the particular interests of individual capitalists which is "crucial in order for it to be able to protect the long-run interests of the capitalist class as a whole" (Smandych, 1986:55; McMullan, 1987).

At the same time, the instrumentalist conceptualization of law as an essentially repressive tool which can be manipulated at will by dominant class members to maintain their privileged class position can also be criticized for precluding any analysis of the contradictory way in which law mediates class relations within capitalist society (Picciotto, 1979; Bierne and Quinney, 1982; Brickey and Comack, 1987). As Picciotto (1979) points out, most instrumentalist theorists tend to uncritically assume the externality of class to law. Class bias and inequality in the legal system are seen as resulting from external factors such as the class background of judges and legislators, and the ability of capitalists to influence the law-making process, rather than inhering in the legal form itself. Concomitantly, the internal form of legal norms and legal discourse are assumed to be purely contingent. Law is thus viewed "from the outside," so to speak, as an infinitely malleable agency which can be molded in an indeterminate number of ways to serve a variety of ideological or instrumental purposes.

Recent work by neo-Marxist and feminist theorists on law has tended to cast doubt on the validity of such instrumentalist assumptions concerning the uncontradictory way in which law reflects dominant class interests or reinforces capitalist or patriarchal ideologies (Bierne and Quinney, 1982;

Hunt, 1985; Brickey and Comack, 1987; Gavigan, 1988; Bartholomew and Boyd, 1989a). As Bierne and Quinney note: "There is much evidence to demonstrate that dominant classes are unable to manipulate legal institutions and legal doctrine consistently, without contradiction and without political opposition" (Bierne and Quinney, 1982: 11). As a result, much recent critical theorizing on law has been directed towards developing more sophisticated models to explain the consensual nature of law, particularly the ways in which law functions to reproduce ideologies supporting patriarchal and capitalist relations of production, even in the face of evidence of the differential application of law in practice (Bierne and Quinney, 1982; Gavigan, 1988; Bartholomew and Boyd, 1989a).

This new emphasis, in turn, has led to increased interest in the concept of ideology on the part of many neo-Marxist and feminist theorists, and on the role of law as an institutional site for the production and dissemination of ideologies that serve to sustain or reproduce consent for unequal and exploitative class, race and gender relations within capitalism (Hunt, 1985; Gavigan, 1988; Boyd, 1989a). Indeed, the pervasive ideological role of law in both defining the way in which social relations are lived and experienced, and the manner in which social and political conflicts are identified and resolved, is seen as central to an understanding of the way in which law contributes to the reproduction of capitalist and patriarchal hegemony within liberal-democratic societies (Hunt, 1985; Gavigan, 1988).

The Ideological Dimensions of Law

Gavigan (1988) notes that exploring the ideological dimensions of law involves two separate levels of inquiry which are intimately connected. One level of inquiry involves exploring the extent to which the conduct and values of legal actors (judges, legislators, police officers, parole officers, prosecuting lawyers and regulatory enforcement officers) are informed by ideologies which have their source outside law, but which become encoded within legislation and legal doctrine in such a way as to become virtually unquestioned and therefore unassailable. In this sense, law represents a powerful discursive medium or site in which ideologies are articulated and disseminated. As Gordon (1984:109) observes, the peculiar power of law is rooted not so much in its ability to command obedience through fear of legal sanctions, but rather in its ability to "persuade people that the world described in its images and categories is the only attainable world in which a sane person would want to live."

A second level of inquiry suggested by Gavigan (1988) requires an investigation of the ideological dimension of legal rules and legal discourse. This, in turn, implies a recognition that the language of law (its concepts, sources of knowledge and formal modes of reasoning) constitutes a powerful form of discourse that is imbued with codes of meaning which operate to privilege certain accounts of the nature of social ordering or power relations, while rendering other readings invisible or unthinkable. Hunt (1985:15), for example, points out that law plays an important ideological role in individualizing and decontextualizing the experience of social relations under capitalism: "It is by transforming the human subject into a legal subject that law influences the way in which participants experience and perceive their relations with others." This ideological effect does not occur only in an abstract legal realm, but is part of the lived experience of social actors (Althusser, 1971; Hunt, 1985). In an important sense, therefore, the experience of social actors is constructed and given social and political meaning through legal discourse and legal categories.

At the same time, we should be alert to the connections between the ideological dimensions of law and those of other social institutions. Law does not operate in a vacuum, isolated from other sites of ideological discourses and practices (Sumner, 1979). But law does play a special role within the liberal state as the idealized expression of power relations and of understandings about the nature of social ordering. Moreover, the recognition that legal ideology is constitutive of social reality and shapes the experience of social actors is important to an understanding of the contradictory character of law. In particular, it helps to account for the fact that exposing the class-biased or race-biased or gender-biased character of the operation of the law in practice does not necessarily weaken either law's claim to popular legitimacy or the moral hegemony of the concept of legality itself (Sargent, 1989).[4]

Law as an Arena of Struggle

This two-dimensional conception of legal ideology opens up a more fruitful line of theoretical inquiry than is possible within most instrumentalist accounts of law. Instead of viewing legal ideology in terms of false consciousness, as a mystifying agent that obscures the "real" nature of social relations under capitalism, law is viewed as being constitutive of social relations, in the sense that it is implicated as a site of ideological discourses and practices through which meanings of the social world are constructed, contested and disseminated.

This approach, in turn, has implications for theorizing the potentiality of law as an agency of social transformation. Emphasizing the dynamic character of law as a site of ideological struggle opens up the possibility of a constructive engagement with law in a way that avoids the reductionism of most instrumentalist and structural Marxist analyses (Sumner, 1981; Brickey and Comack, 1987; Bartholomew and Boyd, 1989a). Thus, Hall and Scraton argue:

> There is no historical guarantee that capital must prevail, and no certainty that it can prevail on its own terms, outside the limits imposed by contestation and struggle. The outcomes of particular struggles, sometimes waged within and about the law, sometimes against it, will have real and pertinent effects on how particular historical

> struggles develop. Law, in this sense, is constitutive of
> (i.e., it creates) the very conditions of historical develop-
> ment and struggle, and does not merely reflect them
> (1981:493).

A related debate concerning the potential of legal rights discourse in effecting social transformation has taken place among feminist legal theorists. Here again, the thrust of the debate has been between those feminist theorists who adopt a determinist or reductionist view of law (Clark and Lewis, 1977; Rifkin, 1980) and those who adopt a more histori- cally specific and theoretically more contextualized approach (Minow, 1985; Gavigan, 1986, 1989). Thus, Gavigan (1986) argues that the ideologi- cal content of legal rights to equality and freedom of the person should not be taken as predetermined by the requirements of patriarchy or the needs of the capitalist mode of production, but may take on different meanings and content at different historical conjunctures, depending on the organi- zation of social relations and the balance of social forces in any society.

It follows from this that a critical engagement with law should seek to contest the limits of the social meanings encompassed within the forms of legal discourse and the content of legal doctrine. This strategy necessarily involves looking at the complex and varied ways in which the ideological dimensions of legal discourse, legal doctrines, and legal institutions inter- sect in order to determine where and how reform efforts should best be targeted.

At the same time, it is important to be aware of the strategic limits of relying on legal reform alone in seeking to achieve fundamental social reordering. As Picciotto (1979) points out, relying on law as an agent for social change involves using a two-edged sword. In significant ways, law represents a powerful mode of discourse that operates to shape the form through which progressive legal and political struggles take place (Pic- ciotto, 1979; Brickey and Comack, 1987). Consequently, there is a danger that the ideological assumptions hidden in bourgeois legal rights dis- course will have a tendency to channel and emasculate rights struggles and other progressive legal reform strategies that rely on law alone (Picciotto, 1979).

Nevertheless, we should be hesitant about writing off this form of political struggle altogether. As Brickey and Comack (1987) observe, legal rights discourse represents an increasingly important mode of political discourse within liberal democratic states. Despite its bourgeois character, therefore, "rights discourse at the least offers the potential of facilitating the mobilization of political action among subordinate groups" (Brickey and Comack, 1987:103). Moreover, feminist experience with law has shown that legal rights struggles can be used assertively, not only to strike down existing laws that formally discriminate against women, but also as an arena in which to elaborate an alternative, radical vision of equal rights that is capable of addressing the systemic nature of social inequalities

(MacKinnon, 1990).

Feminist experience with legal rights struggles also leads to the observation that little is gained, either theoretically or in terms of praxis, from trying to distinguish between the courts as a site of political struggle and the legislative arena (see Fudge, 1990). From this perspective, engaging in progressive reform strategies, whether through *Charter* litigation or through political lobbying efforts designed to achieve legislative or regulatory reform, should be viewed tactically as different forms of political action, rather than as being theoretically or practically distinct. At issue, therefore, is the tactical question of what is the best forum in which to pursue a political goal, rather than whether to engage with law at all. Adopting a theoretical position that seeks to predetermine the limits of what can be accomplished through the judicial arena risks being left behind by the course of events, and forgoes an opportunity of setting the agenda for political action, which is one of the primary strategic goals of any form of political struggle.

This is not to say that all forms of political action involving law and the state are equal, or that framing political demands in terms of legal rights claims does not carry a risk of individualizing the issues at stake and thereby defusing their political significance. In practice, this means that legal reform strategies must be coupled with political struggles outside the legal arena which are aimed at mobilizing collective political action and provoking a response from the state that addresses collective interests (Brickey and Comack, 1987). Additionally, any political engagement with law must be conscious of the different levels at which the ideological assumptions underpinning the discourse and practice of law interact. Otherwise, reform efforts that seek to achieve only instrumental changes in the content or administration of law are likely to undermine the realization of substantive social change.

Law, Ideology and the Construction of Corporate Crime

The significance of this reconceptualization of the ideological dimensions of law to the study of corporate crime is that it permits a more sophisticated analysis of the relationship between law, state and crime than is possible within an instrumentalist framework. Rather than viewing the definition of crime as simply a reflection of the needs of capitalism or of the power of the ruling class to influence the law-making process, it becomes possible to conceive of the definition of criminality in more dynamic terms, as an arena of struggle in which competing ideologies and conceptions of social order are in contention (Sargent, 1989).

This perspective represents a significant departure from the theoretical assumptions underlying much of the current debate over the use of criminal sanctions against regulatory violators. Much of the critical literature on corporate crime has concentrated on establishing that there is no real difference in terms of harm or culpability between regulatory violations committed by corporate offenders and ordinary street crimes (Goff and Reasons, 1978; Snider, 1978, 1982; Glasbeek and Rowland, 1979; Glasbeek, 1984; Reasons, Ross and Paterson, 1986). Thus, in an influential article, Glasbeek and Rowland (1979) have demonstrated that in legal theory there is no reason why existing *Criminal Code* offences such as manslaughter or criminal negligence could not be used against corporate employers where employees are injured or killed as a result of the employer's negligent or reckless violation of mandatory safety standards.[5] Failure to utilize criminal sanctions in such circumstances, according to Glasbeek, proves the inherent class bias of the legal system and its willingness to permit "harm-causing conduct when it is closely related to private profit-making" (Glasbeek, 1984:429).

The strategic assumption underlying this form of critique is that, by exposing the falsity of liberal claims regarding equality before the law, the whole rickety edifice of liberal legalism will start to crack, rather like the walls of Jericho. This strategy simultaneously implies a considerable faith in the effectiveness of legal ideology in shaping popular consciousness about the nature of social and political relations under capitalism, at the same time as it seeks to dismiss law's ideological effect as a myth.

Missing from this type of account, however, is any explanation of the way in which legal ideology works in shaping public attitudes about the nature of corporate crime, not only on the part of legal actors such as lawyers, judges and the police, but also on the part of the victims of corporate crime and the general public. This is not self-evident. Rather, what needs to be explored is precisely the manner in which the juridic distinction between "crimes" and regulatory offences both relies upon and simultaneously affirms popularly held assumptions about the sanctity of the market in such a way as to reinforce popular consent for the differential treatment of corporate and street crime.

As Olsen (1983) points out, the idea of the market as a private, autonomous sphere in which social relations are governed by voluntary agreements between sovereign individuals, rather than by formal legal norms, represents a crucial component of liberal ideology within Western liberal democracies. Implicit within this discourse of private ordering through the market is a conception of social actors as juridically autonomous beings who are treated as formal equivalents in the eyes of the law. Consequently, any social or economic inequalities between individuals or social groups that persist within the market are seen as being the result of private choice, and therefore as not justifying state intervention.

Far from challenging this conception of the market as an autonomous, self-regulating sphere, the proliferation of regulatory legislation in areas such as occupational health and safety and environmental protection indirectly reinforces this discourse. Glasbeek (1986) points out that underlying the regulation of occupational health and safety in Ontario lies a laissez-faire ideology according to which the enforcement of regulatory standards ultimately rests upon the threshold of voluntary compliance within the marketplace, rather than on the threat of externally imposed legal sanctions. Criminal sanctions are, therefore, seen as a last resort to back up negotiated compliance strategies which represent the primary enforcement mechanisms of the regulators (Carson, 1970; Gunningham, 1984; Hawkins, 1984; Snider, 1990).

At first glance, it is easy to account for the failure to utilize penal sanctions against corporate violators as a result of a process of regulatory capture, whereby the regulatory agencies are coopted by the very industries they are required to regulate (Reasons, Ross and Patterson, 1981; Braithwaite, 1984; Mahon, 1980). And there is little question that the informal political pressures brought to bear on regulators, the absence of countervailing pressures by other interested groups, and the closeness of the ongoing relationship between regulator and regulated industry tends to bear out this thesis to a considerable degree (Goff and Reasons, 1978; Braithwaite, 1984; Snider, 1990). At the same time, however, the ideological significance of the public/private distinction as a contributing factor in shaping regulatory attitudes towards enforcement should not be underestimated.[6]

In attempting to articulate a progressive strategy to counter the differential treatment of corporate and street crime, it is important to avoid the temptation to portray the public/private distinction as an historically unchanging ideological discourse that is invoked by the liberal state to legitimize the oppressive exercise of private power through the market. Instead, this dichotomy should be seen as part of the ideological terrain of liberalism, which plays an important role in shaping the experience of social and economic relations, even on the part of oppressed groups. "Public" and "private" are thus socially and historically constituted concepts, the scope and political significance of which are contested and can vary at different times and in different social and political contexts (Fudge, 1987).[7] Thus, the public/private distinction represents a powerful form of political discourse that is also relied on, for example, by the labour movement in resisting state efforts to legislate striking workers back to work or to limit the right to picket. In fact, the well-justified suspicion on the part of organized labour towards judicial or legislative interference with the collective bargaining process relies, at heart, on a similar discourse about the limits of state intervention into the private sphere of the market (see Glasbeek, 1986:4; Kahn-Freund, 1969).

An obvious parallel can be drawn with that other private and ostensibly unregulated sphere, the domestic realm of the family and reproduction, although in this sphere social relations are assumed to be based on affective or status claims, rather than on contract.[8] Nevertheless, in this arena, too, the articulation of a distinction between "public" and "private" realms has (at least, arguably, until recently) provided the ideological foundation underlying the differential treatment of sexual assault and other forms of domestic violence directed against women and children within the family, as compared with the treatment of sexual assault and other crimes of violence between strangers (Silberman, 1980).

It follows from the use of this parallel that we should not deny the potential significance of political struggles centered on law in challenging the tenets of prevailing ideological discourses. The definition of criminality remains a crucial site of ideological struggle over the social meanings attached to phenomena such as workplace or domestic violence. The success of the feminist movement in politicizing the issue of domestic violence has been both a causative factor and at the same time a consequence of demands for legal reforms aimed at reducing police discretion and changing prosecutorial policies over when to initiate criminal proceedings in wife battering cases (McLeod, 1987; McGillivray, 1987; but see Hilton, 1989; Snider, 1989). Such demands, in turn, are premised on the assumption that the criminal law does play an important symbolic role in defining or demarcating the limits of the public and the private, and the limits and form of state intervention into the "private" sphere.

In a similar fashion, efforts to utilize criminal sanctions against corporate offenders also rely on the symbolic potential of criminal law in challenging popular understandings about the nature of corporate crime. What is at stake in the current debate, therefore, is less the instrumental effectiveness of criminal sanctions in deterring harmful corporate behaviour, as it is the way in which certain forms of social behaviour are characterized by the legal system. By continuing to treat corporate violations of environmental standards, occupational health and safety laws and minimum wage legislation as regulatory issues rather than "true crimes," the criminal justice system implicitly reinforces the ideology of the market as an autonomous, self-regulating sphere which should remain outside the purview of the criminal law. By analogy, the differential treatment of domestic assault from other types of assaults both reflects and simultaneously affirms the sanctity of the private realm of the family, which has been identified as playing a central ideological role in the oppression of women (MacKinnon, 1983a; O'Donovan, 1985). Extending the reach of criminal law into the private sphere of the family and the market, therefore, has an important ideological significance with regard to meanings about the nature of social relations, independently of its direct instrumental effects in reducing the degree of violence in the workplace or in the home.

Before hitching our wagon to this particular star, however, it is important to be aware of the limits of a strategy of relying on the criminal law alone in changing social attitudes towards corporate crime. Here again, the experience with domestic violence offers a useful parallel. Changes in the prosecutorial policies of police and crown attorneys with respect to domestic violence have sometimes led to Kafkaesque results, with women charged and convicted with contempt of court when they have refused to give evidence against their abusive partners.[9]

This absurd outcome needs to be understood in the light of the formal, abstract character of the criminal trial process, which has the effect of factoring out the unequal power relations that characterize an abusive domestic relationship, thereby decontextualizing the issues that are brought before the court. The transfer of domestic assault cases from the private, hidden realm of the family to the public gaze of the criminal law is accompanied by a redefinition of both the issues at stake and also the participants involved in a way that fundamentally alters both the way in which the facts of the case are experienced by the participants, and also the way in which the participants themselves are constructed by the legal system (see McBarnett, 1981). Thus, the adversarial nature of the trial process as a contest about different interpretations of legally constructed "facts" between the accused, on the one hand, and the Crown, on the other, has the effect of marginalizing the experience of the victim/witness. In this dichotomous world of the courtroom, there is no obvious room for a third protagonist, whose understanding of the issues at stake and interest in the outcome of the trial process may be informed by very different concerns than those of the Crown (McGillivray, 1987). Consequently, the victims of the abuse become marginalized by the trial process, rather than being empowered. This process of decontextualization also accounts for the way in which witnesses who are reluctant to testify against their abusive partners are forced to choose between imprisonment for contempt, and testifying in court and risking retaliation (McGillivray, 1987; Sheehy, 1987). While this parallel cannot be extended to the arena of corporate crime without obvious qualifications,[10] it remains true that the ideological assumptions embedded in the form of trial and in legal conceptions of responsibility do have the effect of decontextualizing the issues brought before the court and recontextualizing them in terms recognizable to the legal gaze. Perhaps most conspicuously, the corporate organization itself is reconstituted through the legal gaze into the form of an individual moral actor for the purpose of fitting the corporate persona into the discourse of criminal law conceptions of responsibility and sanctioning (Sargent, 1989). Once again, the concerns of the victims become marginal to the major legal issues involved in the trial, which centre around questions of whether the legal "rights" of the accused corporation have been infringed upon, or whether the corporation had the necessary *mens rea* to commit the offence charged.

The practical implications of this form of juridic discourse in anthropo-morphizing the corporation can be seen very clearly in the Supreme Court Decision in *Hunter et al. v. Southam, Inc.* (1984), 14 C.C.C. (3d) 97. The case arose out of an inquiry under section 8 of the federal *Combines Investigation Act* following the simultaneous closure of several newspapers in various Canadian cities by rival newspaper groups, in circumstances which left each newspaper group in sole possession of the only major newspaper in each regional market. Acting under the power conferred under s.10 (3) of the Act, the Director of Investigation and Research authorized several combines investigations officers to enter and seize documents and other articles held at the business offices of the Edmonton Journal. This action was challenged by Southam Inc., the corporate owner of the paper, on the grounds that the wide powers conferred under s.10 (3) — which required only the authorizing officer's reasonable belief that evidence relative to an inquiry carried out under the Act may be found at the premises to be searched — violated its right to be secure against unreasonable search and seizure under s.8 of the *Charter*. After lengthy court proceedings, the Supreme Court of Canada upheld the unanimous decision of the Alberta Court of Appeal (*Southam Inc. v. Hunter* (1983), 147 D.L.R. (3d) 420, 3 C.C.C. (3d) 497), holding that the powers of investigation and search under section 10 of the *Combines Investigation Act* contravened s.8 of the *Charter*, and thus were of no force or effect.

In striking down the offending provisions of s.10 (3) of the *Combines Act*, the Supreme Court endorsed a broad, purposive interpretation of s.8 of the *Charter*, stressing that its aim is to protect individuals from unjustified state intrusions on their privacy.

In considering the validity of the powers of investigation and search under s. 10 (3) of the *Combines Act*, the Supreme Court held that the minimum criteria for authorizing entry, search and seizure under s. 10 (3) fell below the minimum standard required to protect the individual's right to freedom from unreasonable state intrusion (and for this purpose "individual" includes corporations). In view of the criminal nature of the proceedings under the *Combines Act*, the Court held that reasonable and proper grounds for belief that an offence under the Act has been committed, and that evidence relevant to the offence is likely to be found at the premises to be searched, must be established, upon oath, before such authorization should be given. In effect, therefore, the Court imposed the same conditions as are required for issuance of a search warrant under s.443 of the *Criminal Code*, notwithstanding the Minister's argument that combines offences require specialized techniques for detection and suppression.

This decision was hailed by civil libertarians as a victory for the rights of all accused persons in criminal proceedings. But the context in which the decision was handed down is crucial to an understanding of its ideological significance in terms of the control of corporate crime. The effect of the decision, as business commentators immediately pointed out (Thompson, 1985), was to negate the pro-active enforcement powers of the Director of Investigation and Research under the Act.[11] Given the low visibility of most offences under the *Combines Act*, which in turn means that few offences are likely to be reported by victims — contrary to most forms of street crime (Braithwaite and Geis, 1982) — and the insistence by the courts on "hard" evidence to sustain a conviction under section 32 of the Act, the need for pro-active investigatory powers on the part of enforcement officers is apparent (Sargent, 1989). In striking down the investigation and search powers of the Director in the name of the individual's right to protection from unreasonable search and seizure, the Supreme Court's decision underscores the tension that exists between the ideological assumptions underlying the individualist orientation of the criminal justice system and its ability to respond to corporate crime (Sargent, 1989).[12]

On the other hand, in *C.E. Jamieson & Co. (Dominion) Ltd. v. Attorney-General of Canada et al.* (1987), 37 C.C.C. (3d) 193, the search and seizure powers of inspectors under s.22 of the federal *Food and Drugs Act* were held to be unconstitutional by the trial division of the Federal Court on the grounds that they violated s.8 of the *Charter*, since they were exercisable in the context of a criminal proceeding (see also *Re Ontario Chrysler (1977) Ltd. and Rush et al.* (1987), 39 D.L.R. (4th) 100 (Ontario High Court of Justice).

Perhaps even more fundamental is the ideological significance of the requirement of *mens rea* as the cornerstone of the subjectivist model of criminal responsibility enshrined in the *Criminal Code*. The relevance of this legal concept to the debate over corporate crime lies not so much in its practical or instrumental significance as an obstacle to imposing corporate liability, as in its ideological importance as a means of articulating the juridic distinction between so-called "true crimes" and mere regulatory or public welfare offences. Thus, in *R. v. City of Sault Ste. Marie* (1978), 40 C.C.C. (2d) 353, Dickson J. distinguished between "true crimes" and regulatory or public welfare offences in the following terms:

> The doctrine of the guilty mind expressed in terms of intention or recklessness, but not negligence, is at the foundation of the law of crimes. In the case of true crimes there is a presumption that a person should not be held liable for the wrongfulness of his act if that act is without *mens rea*.

Dickson J. contrasted such "true crimes" with public welfare offences:

> ... which are not criminal in any real sense, but are prohibited in the public interest ... Although enforced as penal laws through the utilization of the machinery of the criminal law, the offences are in substance of a civil nature and might well be regarded as a branch of administrative law to which traditional principles of criminal law have but limited application. They relate to such everyday matters as traffic infractions, sales of impure food, violations of liquor laws, and the like (at p. 357).

Such everyday matters as pollution, workplace safety and consumer protection are, of course, precisely the types of offences with which corporate offenders are most frequently charged. Moreover, such everyday offences often result in the creation of more severe risks to life, health, safety or the environment than many offences found in the *Criminal Code*. Nevertheless, by articulating a distinction between "true crimes" and mere regulatory or public welfare offences, which are conceived of as being less morally opprobrious, and therefore involving less social stigma, this juridic concept contributes to the creation of a legal double standard in which enforcement of regulatory offences is continually subordinated to the enforcement of conventional *Criminal Code* offences by the police, crown prosecutors and the judiciary (Sargent, 1989).

The point being made is not that criminal sanctions can never be imposed effectively against corporate offenders. Clearly, this is not the case.[13] Rather, the point is that it is important to explore the complex ways in which the ideological assumptions underlying the form and content of criminal law intersect with the ideology of the market as a private self-regulating sphere in such a way as to reinforce the creation of a separate realm of regulation in which corporate offenders remain relatively immune from criminal sanctions, regardless of the degree of harm resulting from their illegal behaviour or the degree of culpability exhibited by the corporate offender (Sargent, 1989).

Implications For Praxis: Towards a Policy of Constructive Engagement with Law?

It follows from the preceding discussion that there is room within a critical analysis of corporate crime for a more constructive engagement with law. This is not to say that critical commentators on corporate crime in Canada have in the past ignored the role of law in their accounts of the failure of the criminal justice system to respond to corporate crime — on the contrary. But the theoretical assumptions underlying these accounts of corporate crime have been informed by a very reductionist view of the relationship between law, the state and class interests; one which has tended to preclude the possibility that law could be used for progressive social ends.

Paradoxically, though, reliance on criminal law remains a central part of the prescriptive program of most instrumentalist theorists, who advocate the use of criminal law as a means of exploiting the contradictions inherent in liberal ideology, and at the same time mobilizing collective political action around the issues of corporate crime (Glasbeek and Rowland, 1979; Glasbeek, 1984; Reasons, Ross and Patterson, 1986; Snider, 1990).

Yet, relying on criminal law also involves costs. Any attempt at constructive engagement with criminal law over the definition and control of corporate crime necessarily involves according a degree of legitimacy to the law and the criminal justice system as agencies for progressive social change, which ignores the historical evidence that the criminal justice system has largely been used as a mechanism for extending state control over socially marginalized groups (Snider, 1989). Moreover, as feminist experience with criminal law reform has shown, lobbying for changes in legislation and in police prosecution policies also involves a risk of ceding control to these agencies over the way in which the problem is defined (McGillivray, 1987; Snider, 1989; Hilton, 1989). Consequently, attention may be diverted away from a structural analysis of capitalism or patriarchy towards a focus on constructing male batterers or corporate criminals as isolated offenders in need of treatment, rather than as examples of a more deep-seated problem concerning social attitudes towards violence or other forms of deliberately inflicted harm (Snider, 1989; Hilton, 1989).

The strategic issue of retaining control over the way in which the social problem is defined may have particular significance in the context of workplace violence, for example. It is arguable that reliance on the criminal law to stigmatize employers in isolated cases would be less empowering to employees than collective efforts to gain more control over workplace safety through the collective bargaining process. The use of criminal law would not be precluded by this approach; but would not be regarded as the instrument of first resort. On the other hand, the criminal justice system may be preferable as an agency of first resort in the context of environmental crimes, in view of the lack of any equivalent collective forum through which the public victims of pollution can take control over the issue or impose organizational constraints on corporate polluters.

Regardless of these strategic considerations, the criminal law still remains a very potent site for challenging the implicit immunity accorded to many corporate offenders through the regulatory process. This can be seen from the widespread media attention focused on the well-known Ford Pinto trial in the United States. Even though the prosecution was ultimately unsuccessful in obtaining a conviction against Ford, the trial played an important role in politicizing the issue of corporate responsibility for dangerous products in a manner that would have been much less likely had the corporation merely been prosecuted for a regulatory violation (Cullen, Maakestad and Cavender, 1984).[14] Consequently, despite its inbuilt tendency towards disempowering victims and decontextualizing the facts of the case, the very public character of the trial process allows it to be appropriated as a politically visible forum in which conceptions of social and political relations can be contested.

Nevertheless, it is important that political campaigns organized around the issue of corporate crime should not be confined to isolated cases. Such campaigns, important though they are, are unlikely to be effective in securing long term changes in law enforcement practice without corresponding changes in the attitudes of law enforcement agents. This, in turn, implies the need for more control over the exercise of discretion by crown prosecutors and regulatory officials over when to lay criminal charges against corporate offenders. Otherwise, there is a danger that the reduction of political pressure following any particular well-publicized case will simply result in the restoration of the status quo.

At the same time, we should be aware of the limits of focusing on criminal law alone in winning the battle against corporate crime. Despite their highly visible nature, criminal prosecutions are likely to remain peripheral to the everyday business of regulatory inspection and negotiated compliance. Therefore, altering the attitudes towards compliance on the part of regulatory officials is at least as important as providing more effective enforcement tools for regulatory officials and crown prosecutors to use once the regulatory compliance process has failed.

This means, in practice, that any legal reform efforts at the level of criminal law must be coupled with wider political struggles aimed at changing the enforcement approach of regulatory officials, and also empowering the client groups whose interests need protection. To use the analogy of domestic violence again, in the long run it is important to focus political efforts at state action designed to increase the choices open to women in deciding when to leave a violent relationship, rather than to rely primarily on a strategy of criminalization and prosecution. Despite its symbolic significance in stigmatizing male violence, a strategy of criminalization ultimately reinforces the view of women as victims. By definition, the use of criminal law implies reliance on state agencies, in this case the police, to protect women's right to freedom from domestic violence, rather than focusing on alternative strategies aimed at empowering women themselves (see Hilton, 1989).

In the same way, defining the corporate crime "problem" as primarily one of insufficient sanctions imposed against corporate offenders has the effect of shifting the focus of political action away from the organized struggles by workers, consumers, feminists or visible minorities, to the role of the state enforcement agencies themselves. This has the effect of reinforcing the perception of these social groups as victims of capitalist greed and inadequate state action, rather than as active political agents whose demands for improved material conditions have succeeded in placing the issue of regulation on the political agenda.

Yet, as Snider (1987) notes, social conditions such as health standards, life expectancy, working conditions (for women as well as men) and product safety have been improved through such struggles, despite the fact that "state action has been minimal, obstructive, and more often supportive of corporate crime than the reverse" (Snider, 1987:56). This paradox results, in part, from the ability of progressive social movements to appropriate the discourse of rights and to frame political demands in terms of a claim of right (for example, a "right" to a ten hour day; a "right" to a vote; a "right" to a clean environment; a "right" to a safe and smoke-free workplace; a "right" to equal pay for work of equal value; a "right" to freedom from discrimination; and a "right" to freedom of reproductive choice).

At the level of political praxis, utilizing rights discourse to articulate claims for state action involves a significant shift in the way in which the interests at stake in the corporate crime debate are articulated. Indeed, the debate itself is radically changed. Instead of focusing on the need for state intervention and policing to control undesirable corporate conduct, the focus shifts towards defining certain socially desired goals in terms of positive rights, which can be enforced by the individuals or groups who possess the rights through the courts or through administrative agencies such as federal and provincial human rights tribunals (Swaigen and Woods, 1981; Schrecker, 1989).

Not only does this shift in the form of the debate have the effect of positively empowering those social groups whose interests can be protected through rights claims, it also has the subsidiary effect of altering the terms of political discourse around the limits of state intervention in the market. The ideological justification for state intervention in the market to protect the rights of individual citizens or groups to employment equity or freedom from discrimination, for example, rests on very different grounds than the exercise of its coercive powers through the criminal law to regulate private industry in "the public interest." In the latter case, the onus clearly lies on the state to justify its intrusion into the private sphere of the market in terms of an overarching but undefined public interest. Consequently, there is always room for the corporations who are subject to regulation to challenge the limits of state authority through the courts. In the former case, state intervention is restricted to protecting the "rights" of discrete individuals or groups, even if the form of intervention mandates certain forms of behaviour on the part of the corporate sector, with the threat of civil or administrative sanctions behind it.

Constructing the debate over regulation in terms of rights discourse obviously has some costs. For every rights claim that is articulated in progressive terms, it is equally possible to articulate a countervailing and regressive claim of right. The debate over abortion that pits women's "right" to reproductive choice against the "right" of the fetus clearly bears this out.

On the other hand, at present, rights discourse tends to be claimed exclusively by the corporate sector as a weapon to resist state attempts at effective regulation. Appropriating rights discourse as the basis for regulatory intervention could turn out to be a powerful ideological weapon in favour of more effective enforcement. Moreover, by framing the justification for regulation in terms of rights claims, the state's direct role in enforcement would become subordinate to that of the individuals or groups whose rights are protected by the legislation. This would not preclude the use of penal sanctions where a deliberate pattern of regulatory violations is established. But, as occurs at present under human rights legislation, reliance on criminal prosecution would not be the enforcement instrument of first resort. In view of the conspicuous lack of success by state enforcement agencies in ensuring compliance with regulatory standards through the use of criminal prosecutions, the need to consider alternative progressive strategies for regulatory enforcement is apparent (Schrecker, 1989).

Conclusion

In summary, I have argued that a strategy of criminalization is not a panacea to the problem of inadequate regulatory enforcement of corporate crime. Despite its symbolic importance in stigmatizing corporate violators as criminals, the practical utility of criminal sanctions in controlling corporate crime is limited by ideological factors embedded within the form and the content of criminal law which influence the attitudes towards enforcement on the part of crown prosecutors and regulatory officials. In order to operationalize a strategy of criminalization, therefore, it is crucial to develop progressive legal and political strategies aimed at controlling the exercise of prosecutorial discretion and challenging the dominant ideological assumptions underlying the present two-tiered structure of criminal law and the associated conception of the market as a private self-regulating sphere.

At the same time, feminist experience with criminal law reform in the areas of domestic violence and sexual assault poses questions about the potential effectiveness of the criminal law in achieving meaningful social change in attitudes towards violence against women (Snider, 1989; Hilton, 1989). This skepticism has led some feminists to advocate less reliance on criminal law and greater reliance on legal and political strategies that are designed to empower women as individual and collective political actors, rather than simply strengthening existing state enforcement agencies that have traditionally been antithetical to women's interests (Snider, 1989; Hilton, 1989).

Despite its earlier start, critical engagement with criminal law reform in the area of corporate crime has been even less "successful" than feminist struggles over such issues as domestic violence and sexual assault. It seems appropriate, therefore, to learn from this experience and to try to develop alternative strategies for the control of corporate crime that are less heavily dependent on state enforcement agencies.

Notes

I would like to thank Susan Boyd, Elizabeth Comack and an anonymous reviewer for their constructive suggestions and comments in writing this paper.

1. Alongside Goff and Reasons' study of the *Combines Investigation Act* should be added Laureen Snider's theoretical explorations of corporate crime research (see especially: Snider, 1978, 1979 and 1982).
2. A good indication of the breadth and strength of the recent literature can be found in several recent edited sets of essays published by Canadian critical criminologists (see especially: Fleming, 1985; Brickey and Comack, 1986; Boyd, 1986; MacLean, 1986; Ratner and McMullan, 1987; Caputo *et al.*, 1989).
3. The definition of corporate crime utilized in the present study is based on that developed by Kramer (1984:18):

> By the concept of "corporate crime" then, we wish to focus attention on criminal acts (of omission or commission) which are the result of deliberate decision making (or culpable negligence) by persons who occupy structural positions within the organization as corporate executives or managers. These decisions are

organizational in that they are organizationally based — made in accordance with the operative goals (primarily corporate profit), standard operating procedures and cultural norms of the organization — and are intended to benefit the corporation itself.

This definition stresses the organizational nature of corporate crime and serves to differentiate corporate crime from what Clinard and Quinney (1973:190) have referred to as "occupational crime" namely, "offences committed by individuals for themselves in the course of their occupations and the offences of employees against their employers."

4. The recent report of the Royal Commission on the Donald Marshall prosecution illustrates this point. Despite the fact that the whole of the Nova Scotia justice system has been exposed as racist in its treatment of Native Canadians and blacks, the concept of "justice" itself has not been implicated by this or exposed as a sham. In fact, by ascribing the "denial of justice" to Donald Marshall to racial biases on the part of legal actors within the Nova Scotia justice system, the whole report represents an affirmation of the concepts of legality and equal justice. In other words, the report admits that racism may permeate the legal system through the attitudes and behaviour of legal actors, but does not admit that there is anything inherently racist within the concept of justice itself.

5. A recent case that illustrates Glasbeek and Rowland's argument was reported in the *Globe and Mail* (June 3, 1988: A1). The case involved the prosecution of both the president of a one-person trucking company and the driver of the truck for criminal negligence causing death in respect of their deliberate failure to repair the faulty brakes on the truck, which resulted in an accident in which two innocent persons were killed. Both the president of the company and the driver were sentenced to five years in jail.

6. The continuing significance of this laissez-faire approach to health and safety in the workplace is evident in the dispute over incentive bonus payments to underground workers which led to the closing of the Cominco zinc mine in Kimberley B.C. (see the *Globe and Mail*, February 1, 1990: B1). In November 1989 Cominco broke with industry practice by refusing to pay an incentive bonus to its underground workers, resulting in a drop in ore production to one-third of the previous rate. Through the bonus scheme, which was paid separately from the union wage structure negotiated under the collective agreement, workers were expected to trade a lower standard of safety for an increase in salary, which could result in a doubling of take-home pay. Effectively, therefore, the incentive bonus scheme resulted in a two-tier set of safety standards at the mine: the formal standards applicable to hard rock mining under provincial occupational health and safety legislation, and the *de-facto* (lower) standards applicable under the incentive bonus scheme. According to the *Globe and Mail* article, the dispute arose from the company's attempt to unilaterally change the terms on which the bonus was paid, rather than from a concern with safety

standards on the part of the union.

7. As Olsen (1983) points out, the public/private distinction takes on different meanings and has very different social and political significance according to whether one is talking of the family or the economy. Within feminist discourse, for example, the market is referred to as part of the "public" realm; while Marxist and liberal theory rely on a shared conception of the market and the family as being part of a "private" realm of civil society that is separated from the public realm of the state and politics.

8. Klein (1985) points out, however, that in the area of family law such assumptions are increasingly giving way to a new set of assumptions based on liberal individualism and personal choice (see also Boyd, 1989a). The recent litigation over surrogate mothering contracts in New Jersey in the famous Baby "M" trial involved radically opposed conceptions of the social basis of mothering and reproduction, and of the role of contract as an appropriate social ordering device in the private sphere of reproduction. See *In the Matter of BABY "M", a pseudonym for an actual person*, 525 A. 2d. 1128 (1987) (trial decision, per Sorkow J.); *In the Matter of BABY "M", a pseudonym for an actual person*, 537 A. 2d. 1227 (1988) (appeal decision, per Willnetz, C.J.).

9. Snider (1989) cites an article in the *Toronto Star* observing that the first two people to go to jail under Ontario's "get tough" policy on wife battering were both women who refused to give evidence against their husbands and were jailed for contempt (*Toronto Star*, August 10, 1986: A8). See also McGillivray (1987), who discusses the implementation of Saskatchewan's "No-Drop" policy on wife abuse.

10. While in no way similar to the situation of an abused woman locked in a dependency relationship with an abusive partner, the victims of corporate crime may also be intimidated into refusing to give evidence against a corporation for violation of emission standards or health and safety regulations, for example, where the corporation is the major employer in a one-industry town. Being a whistle-blower can be a very risky proposition.

11. In this respect, the Supreme Court's decision was consistent with earlier Supreme Court rulings that had rendered many of the most serious offences under the Act, such as the merger provisions, effectively unenforceable (see: Goff and Reasons, 1978). In 1986, the Conservative government furthered this process by enacting significant revisions to the *Combines Act*, aimed at decriminalizing its enforcement provisions and replacing them with an administrative enforcement mechanism (see Stanbury, 1986-87).

12. By contrast to the Supreme Court's insistence on procedural protection for corporate offenders in criminal proceedings (*Hunter et al. v. Southam Inc.* (1984), 14 C.C.C. (3d) 97, *supra*, text at footnote 11.), several decisions by lower courts have held that the requirement of a warrant does not apply to administrative powers of inspection under administrative or regulatory statutes, even where prosecution may follow from the results of the

inspection, see *R. v. Rao* (1984), 12 C.C.C. (3d) 97 (Ontario Court of Appeal); *Re Belgoma Transportation Ltd. and Director of Employment Standards* (1985), 20 D.L.R. (4th) 156 (Ontario Court of Appeal); *Bertram S. Miller Ltd. v. The Queen* (1986), 31 D.L.R. (4th) 210 (Federal Court of Appeal). In *R. v. Rao* (1984), 12 C.C.C. (3d) 97, at 112) Martin J.A. stated: "In my view ... a clear distinction must be drawn between a general power to enter private premises without a warrant to search for contraband or evidence of crime and a power conferred on designated officials to enter premises for inspection and audit purposes and to seize records, samples or products in relation to businesses and activities subject to government regulation."
13. see Glasbeek (1984), *supra*, text at fn. 5.12.
14. See also the decision to lay criminal charges against the corporate owners of the Herald of Free Enterprise, the ominously named ferry that capsized in Zeebrugge harbour in Belgium in 1987, killing 193 passengers and crew, after the cargo doors on the car deck were not closed before leaving harbour (*Globe and Mail* January 26, 1990: B1). Like the Ford Pinto prosecution in the United States, this represents the first such corporate homicide trial in the United Kingdom. The Exxon Valdez disaster is another case in point.

Discussion

For some social scientists, the adequacy of a theory is determined primarily by its ability to explain the phenomenon under question, such that the practical application or utility of a theory is often given scant attention. From a socialist feminist framework, however, the ultimate value of theory is based on the degree to which it can inform the actions we take to bring about change. Borrowing the concept of *praxis* from Marx, the position taken by socialist feminists is that there is an integral interdependence between the process of developing knowledge through theorizing and investigating social patterns, and the process of applying this knowledge in developing strategies for social change. From this perspective, the true test of a theory is the extent to which it can provide insights into identifying those avenues of change that are most likely to alter the conditions of inequality that exist in society and, just as importantly, those avenues that are unlikely to produce meaningful change. Moreover, the lessons learned from the relative success or failure of different strategies should be used to examine the theoretical premises upon which they were based and thereby improve the theory's adequacy. The four authors in this section have taken on the issue of examining the feasibility of engaging in social change through law. While all of the papers start from a common position that legal and political systems have the potential to reduce inequality, there are substantial differences in their prescriptions as to which strategies to pursue to effect change.

Mary Ellen Turpel's discussion of aboriginal people and the law frames the issue of law and social transformation in its broadest context. As Canadians, we pride ourselves on the democratic nature of our system. In particular, the entrenchment of the *Charter of Rights and Freedoms* in 1982 was heralded by many as further evidence of the country's commitment to the rights and freedoms of its citizens. As Turpel notes, however, the particular form that those rights take is inherently limited. "Bourgeois" rights emerged out of a particular historical context, that is, they originated from the premise that every man (sic) possesses a right to private property and to the protection of that property (including, in some cases, the ownership of other human beings, such as women and slaves). Moreover, they are clearly intended as *individual* rights. From this perspective, the question becomes: to what extent can bourgeois rights — as enshrined in the *Charter* — be used as a vehicle for the realization of aboriginal autonomy?

As noted by Turpel, there is no equivalent in aboriginal traditions of ownership of private property, and the idea of "individual" rights is inimical to the community-based nature of aboriginal life. Given the inherent limitations of rights discourse, Turpel argues that strategies which rely on current Canadian law, and the *Charter* in particular, become suspect. To the extent that the *Charter* enshrines individual as opposed to collective rights, and that internal and external challenges or claims based upon the *Charter* will work to erode the jurisdiction of First Nations people to realize community-based collective goals, then it will only impede attempts by aboriginal peoples to achieve self-determination. In response, therefore, Turpel argues that the solution lies in the recognition of aboriginal peoples as sovereign nations which possess their own distinct culture and way of life.

Similar to Turpel, a Marxist analysis of law suggests that the legal and political philosophy of individual rights acts as *the* ideological premise supporting an economic system which is based upon the individualization of human beings in their relationship to the market and to each other. Given the significant ideological role which rights discourse occupies in a capitalist society, can the demand for recognition of a sovereign aboriginal nation within the existing Canadian nation state become a reality?

In an earlier article (Brickey and Comack, 1987), we argued that a "jurisprudence of insurgency" necessitates pushing the rule of law to its full limit and extent. Given the inherent tensions and contradictions built into a legal system that champions individual equality while simultaneously ignoring collective and structured inequality, the area of collective rights was suggested as a potentially powerful weapon of social transformation. At the same time, however, given the role of the Canadian state in maintaining hegemonic control, it could be argued that such attempts to realize collective rights will be met with strong resistance by the state. Turpel's reference to court decisions on the relative priority of individual and collective rights illustrates this resistance. In addition, even when subordinate groups have some degree of economic and political power (for example, labour unions), they have had little success in having their collective rights recognized (see: for example, Glasbeek, 1987). More significantly, as the events of Oka, Quebec in the summer of 1990 illustrated, the state (both federally and provincially) has been unwilling to acknowledge the claim for autonomy by aboriginal peoples, regardless of the validity of their claims. While the state was prepared to concede that the town of Oka was wrong in its attempt to use Mohawk land for the extension of a private golf course, it broke off negotiations when the natives linked the specific problem to the larger issue of sovereignty. Indeed, the same Premier of Quebec who argued that Bill 178 was justifiable on the grounds of protecting collective language rights rejected the claim of aboriginal autonomy by stating that all Canadians are subject to the same set of laws. It would appear, therefore, that if aboriginal self-determination is to become a reality, a general "crisis of legitimacy" would be required. The massive mobilization of native groups and their supporters in Canada in their show of solidarity with the Mohawks may represent the seeds of such a crisis.

The remaining three papers in this section all deal with a common issue: the value of using the criminal law as an avenue for progressive change within society. The authors, while claiming a common theoretical perspective, present a full range of positions on this issue: from rejection of the criminal law as an avenue of change — to limited acceptance, with caveats, of the value of the criminal law — to an empirical example that is used to illustrate the potential of criminal law as an instrument of change. Since Laureen Snider and Jane Ursel both address the issue of criminal law in the area of feminist concerns, the different strategies advocated by these two authors will be examined first. This will be followed by a discussion of Neil Sargent's assessment of the value of criminal law in the area of corporate crime.

Laureen Snider views the criminal law as an arena where the state gains more control over the lives of its citizens, especially the economically marginalized. Her argument that engaging the state through criminal law has had either no effect or negative effects is documented by her reference to both historical examples where women have come under greater control of the state through the criminal law, and contemporary examples where "progressive" legal change brought about by lobbying from feminist groups has failed to improve the life conditions of women.

Snider's indictment of the attempts to form an alliance between the feminist movement and the state is similar to the structural Marxist perspective, which views the state as a relatively autonomous entity that serves to support the long-term interests of capital through the legitimation of the existing system. Following this view, since all legal reforms will benefit the long-term class and patriarchal interests within the existing relations of production and reproduction, any changes in the law are unlikely to produce meaningful change for women or other groups that are in a subordinate position. Nevertheless, while Snider advances the argument that the feminist movement is mistaken in attempting to enlist the criminal justice system as an ally in producing reforms, in her final section she does suggest that, in order to achieve change, it is necessary to engage the state through the expansion of women's rights, reforms in civil law, and the provision of broader institutional supports for women. In this respect, the issue is not *whether* legal battles should be fought, but *which* legal battles will have the potential to produce meaningful change.

One is hard pressed not to agree with Snider that the criminal law provides a powerful mechanism for the reproduction of class, race and gender divisions, and that efforts at criminal law reform have had a poor track record. Yet, the question remains as to whether the criminal law should be "taken on" as a progressive legal struggle. In this regard, given the brutal and pervasive consequences of the inequality that characterizes much of the criminal law, to what extent can progressive strategies actually afford to exclude this most oppressive arm of the law? Moreover, from the point of view of the feminist engagement with the state over issues such as wife battering, it could be argued that, while the long-run solution to the issue lies in the empowerment of women-as-a-group in society, there is also the more short-run imperative of putting a stop to the violence that battered women encounter at the hands of their abusive partners. With the knowledge that, every year in Canada, one in ten women are battered and approximately one hundred women are killed by their male partners, this issue has to be viewed, in a very real sense, as a "life and death" matter.

In this respect, there is a need to distinguish between long-term and short-term objectives that could be simultaneously advanced to work toward social transformation. On the one hand, the kinds of structural changes advocated by Snider need to be pushed and aimed for. At the same time, short-term strategies could be framed which would have as their objective the partial amelioration of current injustices within the criminal law. Even limited success in the latter area could provide benefits for those groups in the most powerless and vulnerable positions. If one accepts this strategy of short-term and long-term objectives, then the issue of using the criminal law as a locus of progressive change becomes an empirical one: is it possible to implement reforms that improve the more immediate life conditions of subordinate groups?

It is in this context that we can locate Jane Ursel's work. Ursel's paper represents an empirical investigation of the value of using criminal law as an area of reform. Her analysis suggests that, at least in the area of wife abuse, it is possible to work with the state in improving the life conditions of women through changes in the operation of criminal law. Ursel takes the position that, while the state may not share the interests of the feminist movement, there are historical moments that arise in which the state's interests and women's interests overlap, and it is to the advantage of women to both recognize these instances and to seize the initiative in pushing for change when these overlapping interests are present. Her specific assertion that wife abuse is a vestige of familial patriarchy that is costly to the state (both economically and in terms of legitimacy) is used to give a context to the willingness of the state to work with feminists in improving the criminal justice system's response to the plight of battered women. By noting the contradiction of wife abuse within a state that is structurally and ideologically committed to social patriarchy, Ursel's account of the success of the feminist movement in this area strikes a plausible chord. That is, under a system of familial patriarchy, where the individual patriarch had total control of women and children, the act of hitting one's wife fell within the domain of "acceptable behaviour." However, with the move to social patriarchy and the attendant decrease in the power of the individual patriarch, a space has opened up whereby the legitimacy of this form of violence can be challenged.

Although Ursel's analysis may seem at odds with Snider's views on legal change, there are similarities which should be noted. In her discussion of the conditions which will increase the likelihood of successful legal reform, Snider emphasizes the necessity of advocating changes that specify procedures to be followed, can easily be monitored, and have the effect of reducing organizational discretion within the system. A review of Ursel's chronological description of the initiatives taken to alter the system's response to wife abuse reveals specific examples of the conditions that Snider describes. These include: the development of a separate court to process wife abuse cases, the creation of a Women's Advocacy Program, directives issued to crown attorneys and police officers which had the effect of reducing discretion, and the consistent monitoring of the justice initiatives by the media.

While Ursel's analysis presents a convincing case that reform is possible within the criminal law, and suggests that we should look to other areas of law where the state's interests may coincide with the desire for progressive change, a more difficult issue that follows from her analysis is: what strategies should be used and to what extent is change possible under those conditions in which the area of reform being advocated is one where the state has no vested interest in supporting change? Such an area of reform is the topic taken up by Neil Sargent in his paper on the efficacy of using the criminal law to control corporate crime.

Sargent notes that, in a manner analogous to feminist efforts to use the criminal law to control sexual assault and domestic violence, there have been attempts to hold corporations accountable within the criminal law. The results, however, indicate that the ability to control corporate crime has been less successful than the impact on sexual assault and domestic violence. Sargent's account for this lack of success is that, unlike the example of wife abuse described by Ursel, it is not in the state's interest to treat harmful conduct by corporations as a crime. He argues that earlier instrumental Marxist accounts of corporate crime failed to recognize the ability of the state to ideologically justify the contradictions of treating equally harmful forms of behaviour as qualitatively different. Sargent claims that, because of this ideological support, legal reform in this area will demand more than data collected by social scientists which demonstrate the harmful consequences of corporate crime. Rather, any attempt to define specific corporate behaviour as criminal must, to be successful, challenge the ideological view that there is a strong relationship between a healthy economy the degree to which it is left unfettered by the state, even if the consequence of this "market freedom" leads to the injuries and deaths described by Reasons, Ross and Patterson. Sargent aptly describes how this ideology pervades the language of law (in the juridic distinction between crimes and regulatory offences), the moral assessment and stigma associated with the law violators (criminals versus offenders of civil law), and the low priority given to those corporate law violations that are within the criminal law (aggressively prosecuting "real" criminals versus corporate offenders).

By theoretically identifying ideology as a crucial component of the problem to be addressed, Sargent suggests that the strategies of change to be used in the area of corporate crime be selected with an emphasis on the capability of those strategies to unravel the ideological web that masks the existing inequalities. Instead of rejecting any specific avenue of reform, he notes that this struggle will be most effective if concurrent reforms in the political and legal arenas are attempted. While pessimistic about the use of the criminal law as the major thrust of reform, Sargent acknowledges that there are instances, such as the Ford Pinto trial, where criminal law can be effective in highlighting the ideological contradictions within the law. He insists, however, that the collective efforts of labour unions to increase the safety of workers and the use of rights discourse to hold corporations more accountable have even greater potential in placing restrictions on corporate crime.

While all of the papers in this section have, in varying degrees, attempted to link their strategies for change to a critical theoretical conception of the state and law, there is still much disagreement on how one translates Marxist and socialist feminist theories into practice. Based on the positions advocated by the different authors, it would be a difficult task to find common ground in explicating a recipe for change. Part of this divergence should be expected, however, given the different problems of inequality being addressed. That is, there is no reason to expect that similar strategies would be equally successful when dealing with issues that range from increasing the collective rights of aboriginal peoples to controlling corporate crime. Indeed, a theory of the state that links a group's power to its location within the productive and reproductive system would suggest that markedly different strategies would be required in the process of social change, depending on the degree of change being sought and the impact of this change on the existing productive and reproductive relations. It is in this context that the reader should assess the different arguments advanced in the four papers.

Conclusion

Future Directions in the Sociology of Law

Future Directions in the Sociology of Law

In the Introduction, we indicated that the Marxist approach to understanding the law-society relationship has been at the forefront of the "sociological movement in law." As that movement has proceeded, work within the area has been continually altered and reformulated. Indeed, if one compares this book to the first Canadian edited book within the sociology of law (Greenaway and Brickey, 1978), the growth in theoretical sophistication and the greater breadth of issues covered is immediately apparent. We also indicated in the Introduction that, throughout the 1980s, Marxist theorizing on law was gradually reformulated, in large part, in response to the challenge of the feminist movement. In the endeavour to capture the interconnection of class and gender inequalities as they are reflected and reproduced by law, sociologists of law have increasingly been drawn to a socialist feminist framework to inform their theory and research. As with any area of study, however, this process of development is never complete. As work in the sociology of law continues, new lines of inquiry emerge. In this concluding section, our aim is to sketch out two specific directions which merit further attention by sociologists of law. These relate, on the one hand, to the issue of race, in particular, to the situation of aboriginal peoples and their struggles with the Canadian state and, on the other, to the need for more comparative analyses on the law-society relationship.

The Neglect of Race Issues

As was noted in the Introduction, sociological analysis does not take place in a vacuum. The events that capture the attention of the larger society often, directly or indirectly, influence what sociologists study and the theoretical perspective they adopt in their explanation of these events. In addition, the life experiences of researchers (including their class location, gender and race) often shape how they view the world and what issues they consider to be of significance for study. There is a "double edged sword" quality to this relationship between sociological analysis and the larger society. It is valuable in that it sensitizes us to examine issues such as inequality that are defined as problems within the larger structure, but it can also have the capacity to blind us to significant issues if these issues are effectively hidden by the cultural myths and misconceptions that are embedded in the dominant ideology of that society. Sociologists, and social scientists generally, have no special immunity from these cultural myths, even when they are theoretically sensitive to the pervasive impact ideology can have in shaping our views of the world. There is nothing fixed or immutable, however, about the ideological blinders that focus our attention on some elements of the social world and lead us to ignore other elements. Indeed, we would argue that one of the most important tasks of sociological analysis is, through theoretical and empirical work, to adjust — if not remove — these blinders.

In this regard, one of the basic premises to emerge from feminism has been that women have been rendered invisible by codified knowledge (Spender, 1980 and 1981). Historically, the producers of knowledge have all been male. They have produced theories and analyses and proceeded to check with one another as to their accuracy. Over time, each of the academic disciplines has developed its own canon, that is, a body of knowledge considered essential to a full understanding of the discipline, its claims and its major findings. That canon, and the views of the world reflected by it, are both very much male-defined and male-centered. Moreover, women have not only been excluded as producers of knowledge, they have also been missing as research subjects. One implication of this exclusion is that scientific studies have tended to generalize what they have learned from the study of men to the lives of women. When women are considered, they tend to be measured against male norms and standards (Gilligan, 1982). In response, one of the tasks of feminist scholarship has been to develop knowledge that is *women-centered*, knowledge that is about and for women.

As evidenced throughout this book, feminism has had a dramatic impact on the nature of the sociological enterprise. The proliferation of literature on women and the law in the last decade has gone a long way to rectify the history of neglecting women's experiences and to improve our theoretical approach to law. Following this, it could be suggested that there are some important lessons to be learned from examining the impact of feminism on the sociology of law. In particular, we would argue that it is time to apply these lessons to other segments of society that have traditionally been neglected by sociologists of law, especially the recognition of racism as a significant influence within Canadian law and the awareness of the unique problems faced by racial groups in their subordination by the state through law.

While it is too early to know whether the events that have come to be known as "Canada's Indian Summer" will mark the beginning of a new level of political struggles by aboriginal groups, the public attention given to these events should lead sociologists of law to reflect on the woeful lack of attention that has been paid to aboriginal issues in law specifically, and the more general inattention to the state's use of racism within the legal system. This inattention includes not only the absence of theorizing on the ways in which the state has incorporated racist practices within the law; there has also been a paucity of empirical work on the effects of race on a group's experiences within the legal system. Indeed, it is easier for sociologists teaching in the area to find material on the emergence of vagrancy statutes in 14th century England than on the Canadian state policy of sending aboriginal children to residential schools in the 20th century — a policy that aboriginal people have labelled "cultural genocide."

The theoretical and empirical work that is necessary must be sensitive to a number of issues. First, the experiences of different racial groups within Canada are significantly varied to alert sociologists to avoid the error of conceptualizing race as a unidimensional variable within a larger theoretical framework. When, for example, one compares the life experiences of Chinese Canadians since the mid-19th century to the experiences of aboriginal people, marked differences can be found. Just as the experiences of women differ depending upon their class location, the experiences of different racial groups must be examined in the context of their relationship to the economic infrastructure. More research is needed on the different state policies that have been enacted to "deal" with different racial groups within the country and how these state policies are connected to the capitalist economy. While history informs us that racist practices preceded the emergence of capitalism, the papers by York, Turpel and Calliste suggest that capital and the state continued these practices and transformed them to fit the requirements of the accumulation process. Second, sociologists must remain sensitive to the fact that race is a *social* category. As a social category, race has been used as a powerful ideological construct to justify the systemic subordination of a group.

In sum, while much work has been done in specifying the nature of the interconnection between class and gender, it is necessary to turn our attention to how race fits into this dynamic. Although it is premature to speculate what a theory of law that included race as well as class and gender within its explanatory framework would look like, it is incumbent upon researchers in the sociology of law who investigate the issue of race to be sensitive to the work that has been conducted by Marxists and socialist feminists in identifying the role of the state within capitalism and the use of the legal system to materially and ideologically support the productive and reproductive relations within that system. Thus, while it is important to document specific laws and state practices that subordinate racial groups, it is also necessary to move beyond documentation if we are to understand *why* these practices emerged and, in many instances, continue to exist. This theoretical and empirical work should be established as a priority within Canadian sociology of law.

A Call for Comparative Historical Research

Another focus of research that has received little attention within the sociology of law in Canada is the area of comparative historical studies (Laxer, 1989). By comparative historical studies, we mean the systematic examination of the operation of law over time in two or more countries in order to better understand how the law functions within different economic and state systems. This is an essential task for a fully mature sociology of law that operates from a theoretical framework in which priority is given to different state formations and their relationship to forces of production and reproduction.

An adequate investigation of the relationship between capitalism and law requires that studies be conducted in such a way that variation in those elements that make up capitalism (for example, the concentration of capital, the degree of organization of the working class, and the degree of participation of women in production) be investigated in order to determine what impact these variations have on the structure and operation of the legal system. This is an example of what Wayne Taylor (1990) refers to as "variation design." There is more than one method that facilitates studying the variation in economic forms. Heeding Marx's methodological advice to focus on economic and social forces within an historical framework, much of the best empirical work has used historical analysis to examine the variation of capitalism and patriarchy and the effects of this variation on law and state policy. As a number of the papers in this book illustrate, by investigating the historical changes in law that correspond to changes in capitalism and patriarchy, sociologists can examine the linkages between these phenomena.

There are issues that arise, however, that cannot be adequately addressed by restricting the analysis to investigations of historical changes within one social formation. Since the state is often the unit of analysis, confining research to one country often represents the equivalent of a case study, with all of the attendant limitations in generalizing the findings of this one case to other cases. To increase the confidence in the theoretical linkages between law, economy and the state, comparative studies need to be undertaken. Examples of comparative studies within the sociology of law include Glendon's (1981) examination of the relationship between family law and economic structure, Scull's (1984) research into the declining use of prisons and other total institutions in capitalist countries, and Tigar and Levy's (1977) historical analysis of the changing form of law that accompanied the emergence and development of capitalism in Europe. It should be noted, however, that research which compares legislation between states will not significantly contribute to our knowledge if the comparison is done in a manner that ignores the historical circumstances within each country that have resulted in specific legislative and policy initiatives. Scull's (1984) research, for example, suffers from the failure to historically specify the political and economic forces within each country that facilitated or hindered the process of decarceration. As a result, Scull is at a loss to account for the differences in the rate of incarceration that he found between capitalist states. Nevertheless, although all of the above studies contain flaws, the theoretical arguments presented in them are strengthened by their ability to reveal patterns that existed in more than one country.

In addition to studying other countries to expand beyond a case study approach, it is sometimes necessary to engage in comparative research to obtain information that will bear on specific theoretical concerns. This is often the case, for example, when there is little variation within one country to adequately examine a range of conditions. If we are interested in studying the degree to which working class organization (defined as degree of unionization and political party involvement) affects state intervention in creating and enforcing rigorous workplace health and safety regulations, it would not be possible to restrict our analysis to Canada, given the limited historical variability in the percentage of the population that is unionized. Rather, it would be necessary to examine countries that exhibit a wide range of working class organization and compare their respective workplace health and safety laws. Similarly, to explore the thesis that the strength and form of patriarchy in a society will be the predominant influence shaping the content and enforcement of sexual assault legislation requires a selection of countries that differ on the dimension of patriarchy.

To date, there has been little comparative work done in the sociology of law in Canada. While this is perhaps understandable, given the relatively recent resurgence of interest in this area, the development of a sociology of law will be severely limited if we confine our research to a case study approach. Since there are elements of the operation of law which are provincially controlled, it is possible to conduct some comparative work by, for example, comparing police and court operations between provinces within the country. Most significant civil and criminal legislation, however, falls within the federal jurisdiction and investigation of this legislation will demand comparative historical work that examines other state systems. John Myles' recent statements on the importance of comparative studies to social science in Canada is equally applicable to the specific area of the sociology of law:

> (T)he whole point of the movement towards the development of a truly *Canadian* sociology since the '70s (has been) to develop a social science that would allow Canadians to understand their own history and institutions so as to transform them ... the study of Canadian society in isolation, no matter how scholarly and rigorous, is simply not up to the task ... In sum, Canadian sociology must always be comparative since a sociology of Canadian society is impossible otherwise (Myles, 1989:7).

In conclusion, the two issues which have been raised are likely to be the subject of future analysis and debate in the sociology of law. As the "sociological movement in law" proceeds, we can also expect other salient issues to capture the attention of social analysts. Needless to say, as the papers within this collection demonstrate, the sociology of law has become a most challenging and stimulating area in which to work.

Bibliography

Abella, Rosalie Silberman. 1981. "Family Law in Ontario: Changing assumptions." *Ottawa Law Review*. 13: 1-22.

Aiton, G. 1961. "The Selling of Paupers by Public Auction in Sussex Parish." *New Brunswick Historical Society Collection*.

American Friends Service Committee. 1971. *Struggle for Justice*. New York: Hill and Wang.

Anthias, F. and N. Yuval-Davis. 1983. "Contextualizing Feminism—Gender, ethnic and class divisions." *Feminist Review*. 15: 62-75.

Arat-Koc, S. 1989. "In the Privacy of Our Own Home: Foreign domestic workers as a solution to the crisis in the domestic sphere in Canada." *Studies in Political Economy*. (Spring) 29: 33-58.

Armstrong, Pat. 1984. *Labour Pains: Women's Work in Crisis*. Toronto: Women's Press.

Armstrong, Pat. 1987. "Women's Work: Women's Wages." In Greta Hoffmann (ed.), *Women and Men: Interdisciplinary Readings on Gender*. Toronto: Fitzhenry and Whiteside, p. 354.

Armstrong, Pat and Hugh Armstrong. 1984. *The Double Ghetto: Canadian Women and Their Segregated Work*. Toronto: McClelland.

Armstrong, Pat and Hugh Armstrong. 1985. "Beyond Sexless Class and Classless Sex: Towards feminist Marxism." *Feminist Marxism or Marxist Feminism: A Debate*. Toronto: Garamond Press, p. 1-37.

Arnopoulos, S. 1979. *Problems of Immigrant Women in the Canadian Labour Force*. Ottawa: Canadian Advisory Council on the Status of Women.

Arnup, Katherine. 1989. "'Mothers Just Like Others': Lesbians, divorce, and child custody in Canada." *Canadian Journal of Women and the Law*. 3(1): 18-32.

Asch, Michael. 1984. *Home and Native Land: Aboriginal Rights and the Canadian Constitution*. Toronto: Methuen.

Ashford, Nicholas. 1976. *Crisis In The Workplace: Occupational Disease and Injury*. Cambridge, MA.: MIT Press.

Aubert, Anna-Marie. 1979. *Divorce in Canada*. Toronto: Academic.

Augier, F., S. Gordon, D. Hall and M. Reckford. 1960. *The Making of the West Indies*.

Trinidad: Longman.

Avery, D. 1975. "Continental European Immigrant Workers in Canada, 1896-1919: From 'stalwart peasants' to 'radical proletariat'." *Canadian Review of Sociology and Anthropology*. 12(1): 53-61.

Backhouse, Constance B. 1981. "Shifting Patterns in Nineteenth-Century Canadian Custody Law." In David H. Flaherty (ed.), *Essays in the History of Canadian Law*. Vol. 1. Toronto: Osgoode Society, pp. 212-248.

Backhouse, Constance B. 1985. "19th Century Canadian Prostitution Law: Reflection of a discriminatory society." *Social History*. 387: 390-393.

Balbus, Isaac D. 1971. "Ruling Elite Theory vs. Marxist Class Analysis." *Monthly Review*. 23: 36-46.

Balbus, Isaac D. 1973. *Dialectics of Repression*. New York: Russell Sage Foundation.

Balbus, Isaac D. 1977. "Commodity Form and Legal Form: An essay on the 'relative autonomy' of the law." *Law and Society Review*. 11.

Barber, M. 1980. "The Women Ontario Welcomed: Immigrant domestics for Ontario homes, 1870-1930." *Ontario History*. 72: 148-72.

Barnett, Harold. C. 1981. "Corporate Capitalism, Corporate Crime." *Crime and Delinquency*. 27: 4-23.

Barnsley, Jan. 1985. *Feminist Action, Institutional Reaction: Responses to Wife Assault*. Vancouver: Women's Research Centre.

Barnsley, Jan. 1988. "Feminist Action, Institutional Reaction." *Resources for Feminist Research*. 17(3): 18-21

Bartholomew, Amy and Susan Boyd. 1989. "Towards a Political Economy of Law." In Wallace Clement and Glen Williams (eds.), *The New Canadian Political Economy*. Montreal: McGill Queen's Press.

Becker, Howard. 1963. *Outsiders*. New York: The Free Press.

Beckford, G. 1972 *Persistent Poverty: Underdevelopment in Plantation Economies of the Third World*. New York: Oxford University Press.

Beirne, Piers. 1979. "Empiricism and the Critique of Marxism on Law and Crime." *Social Problems*. 26: 373-85.

Beirne, Piers and Alan Hunt. 1987. "Law and the Constitution of Soviet Society: The case of Comrade Lenin." Unpublished paper.

Beirne, Piers and Richard Quinney, (eds.). 1982. *Marxism and Law*. New York: John Wiley and Sons.

Bell-Robertson, Brady and Craig Boydell. 1972. "Crime in Canada: A distributional analysis." In Craig Boydell *et al. Deviant Behaviour and Societal Reaction*. Toronto:

Holt Rinehart and Winston, pp. 93-116.

Benedict, Ruth. 1935. *Patterns of Culture*. Boston, New York: Houghton Miflin.

Bentham, Jeremy. 1775. "Principles of Penal Law." In J. Bowring (ed.), *The Works of Jeremy Bentham*. Vol. I. New York: Russell and Russell.

Bentham, Jeremy. 1780. "An Introduction to the Principles of Morals and Legislation." In J. Bowring (ed.), *The Works of Jeremy Bentham*. Vol. I. New York: Russell and Russell.

Berger R., P. Searles and W. Neuman. 1988. "The Dimensions of Rape Reform Legislation." *Law and Society Review*. 22(2): 329-57.

Berger, T. 1977. *Northern Frontier, Northern Homeland*. Ottawa: Department of Supply and Services.

Berger, T. 1988. "Introduction to the Revised Edition." *Northern Frontier, Northern Homeland*. Vancouver: Douglas and McIntyre.

Beyer, M.A. (ed.). 1978. *Violence in Canada*. Toronto: Methuen.

Bland, L. 1985. "In the Name of Protection: The policing of women in the first world war." In Julia Brophy and Carol Smart, *Women In Law*. Boston: Routledge and Kegan Paul, pp. 23-49.

Bled, Y. 1965. "La Condition des Domestiques Antillaises á Montréal." Masters thesis. University of Montreal.

Bliss, Michael. 1973. "Another Anti-Trust Tradition: Canadian anti-combines policy, 1889-1910." *Business History Review*. 57: 177-78.

Bodsworth, F. 1955. "What's Behind the Immigration Wrangle?" *Maclean's Magazine*. May 14, p. 127.

Bograd, M. 1984. "Family Systems Approach to Wife Battering: A feminist critique." *American Journal of Orthopsychiatry*. 58: 558-568.

Bonacich, E. 1972. "A Theory of Ethnic Antagonism: The split labor market." *American Sociological Review*. 37: 547-59.

Bonacich, E. 1975. "Abolition, the Extension of Slavery, and the Position of Free Blacks: A study of split labor markets in the United States, 1830-1863." *American Journal of Sociology*. 81(3): 601-28.

Bonacich, E. 1976. "Advanced Capitalism and Black/White Relations in the United States: A split labor market interpretation." *American Sociological Review*. 41: 34-51.

Boyd, Neil (ed.). 1986. *The Social Dimensions of Law*. Scarborough: Prentice-Hall.

Boyd, Susan B. 1989a. "Child Custody, Ideologies and Employment." *Canadian Journal of Women and the Law*. 3(1): 111-113.

Boyd, Susan B. 1989b. "From Gender Specificity to Gender Neutrality? Ideologies in Canadian child custody law." In C. Smart and S. Sevenjuijsen (eds.), *Child Custody and the Politics of Gender*. London: Routledge, pp. 126-157.

Bradbrook, Adrian. 1971. "An Empirical Study of the Attitudes of the Judges of the Supreme Court of Ontario Regarding the Workings of the Present Child Custody Adjudication Laws." *Canadian Bar Review*. 49: 557-576.

Bradbury, B. 1982. "The Fragmented Family: Family strategies in the face of death, illness, and poverty, Montreal, 1860-1885." In J. Parr (ed.), *Childhood and Family in Canadian History*. Toronto: McClelland and Stewart.

Braithwaite, John. 1979. *Inequality, Crime and Public Policy*. London: Routledge and Keegan Paul.

Braithwaite, John. 1984. *Corporate Crime in the Pharmaceutical Industry*. London: Routledge and Kegan Paul.

Braithwaite, John and G. Geis. 1982. "On Theory and Action for Corporate Crime Control." *Crime and Delinquency*. 28: 292.

Brand, D. 1984. "A Working Paper on Black Women in Toronto: Gender, race and class." *Fireweed*. (Summer/Fall) 19: 26-43.

Brickey, Stephen and Elizabeth Comack (eds.). 1986. *The Social Basis of Law: Critical Readings in the Sociology of Law*. First Edition. Toronto: Garamond Press.

Brickey, Stephen and Elizabeth Comack. 1987. "The Role of Law In Social Transformation: Is a jurisprudence of insurgency possible?" *Canadian Journal Of Law And Society*. 2: 97-120.

Brody, H. 1981. *Maps and Dreams: Indians and the British Columbia Frontier*. Vancouver: Douglas and McIntyre.

Brody, S.R. 1976. *The Effectiveness of Sentencing: A Review of the Literature*. London: HMSO.

Brookbank, C. 1982. *Sexual Assault: Proposed Canadian Law 1981 - Preliminary Findings*. Draft Report to the Federal Department of Justice. Ottawa, February.

Brophy, Julia and Carol Smart (eds.). 1985. *Women in Law: Explorations in Law, Family and Sexuality*. London: Routledge.

Brown, R. and R. Cook, 1974. *Canada 1896-1921*. Toronto: McClelland and Stewart.

Browning, James. 1984. *Stopping the Violence: Canadian Programmes for Assaulting Men*. Ottawa: Health and Welfare Canada.

Brownmiller, S. 1975. *Against Our Will: Men, Women and Rape*. New York: Simon and Shuster.

Bruner, A. 1979. "The Genesis of Ontario's Human Rights Legislation: A study in law reform." *University of Toronto Faculty of Law Review*. 37(2): 234-55.

Bullen, J. 1986. "Hidden Workers: Child Labour and the Family Economy in Late Nineteenth Century Urban Ontario." *Labour/Le Travail*. 18: 163-187.

Burawoy, M. 1976. "The Functions and the Reproduction of Migrant Labor: Comparative material from Southern Africa and the United States." *American Journal of Sociology*. 81(5): 1050-1087.

Burstyn, Varda. 1985. "Political Precedents and Moral Crusades: Women, sex and the state." In Varda Burstyn (ed.), *Women Against Censorship*. Vancouver: Douglas and McIntyre, pp. 4-32.

Burstyn, Varda and Dorothy Smith. 1985. *Women, Class, Family and The State*. Toronto: Garamond Press.

Callender, C. 1965. "The Development of Capital Market Institutions in Jamaica." *Social and Economic Studies*. 14: 3.

Calliste, Agnes. 1987. "Sleeping Car Porters in Canada: An ethnically submerged split labour market." *Canadian Ethnic Studies*. 19(1).

Calliste, Agnes. 1988. "Blacks on Canadian Railways." *Canadian Ethnic Studies*. 20(2).

Cameron, J. 1943. "The Law Relating to Immigration." L.L.M. thesis. University of Toronto.

Canada. Department of the Interior. *Annual Report*. 1906-1917.

Canada. 1978. *Statistics of Crime and Other Offences*. 1973. Ottawa: Statistics Canada.

Canada. 1982. *Minutes of Proceedings and Evidence of the Standing Committee on Justice and Legal Affairs Respecting Bill C-53*. Ottawa: House of Commons, Issues # 77 to 106.

Canada. 1984. Solicitor General, *Bulletin on Reported and Unreported Crimes*. Canadian Urban Victimization Survey: 1-4.

Canada. 1985. Department of Justice, *Sexual Assault Legislation In Canada: An Evaluation*. Reports 1 and 2. Ottawa: Policy, Programs and Research Branch, Department of Justice, July.

Canada. Department of Citizenship and Immigration. *Annual Report*. 1918-1931, 1922-1931.

Canada. Department of Immigration and Colonization. *Annual Report*. 1950-52, 1953, 1954, 1955-61.

Canada. Department of Mines and Resources. *Annual Report*. 1945-49.

Canada. Employment and Immigration. "Foreign Domestic Movement: 1985 Statistical Highlights."

Canada. Employment and Immigration. "Foreign Domestic Movement Statistical

Review, 1986." (July 1987).

Canada. Employment and Immigration. "Foreign Domestic Movement Statistical Highlight Report, 1987." (December 1988).

The Canada Year Book 1915. Ottawa, 1916.

Canadian Advisory Council on the Status of Women. *Integration and Participation: Women's Work in the Home and in the Labour Force.* Ottawa: CACSW, 1987.

Canadian Bar Association. 1988. *Aboriginal Rights in Canada: An Agenda for Action.*

Caputo, T.C., M. Kennedy, C.E. Reasons and A. Brannigan (eds.). 1989. *Law and Society: A Critical Perspective.* Toronto: Harcourt Brace Jovanovich.

Caringella-MacDonald, Susan. 1987. "Marxist and Feminist Interpretations on the Aftermath of Rape Reforms." *Contemporary Crises.* 12(4).

Carlen, Pat and Anne Worrall. 1987. *Gender, Crime and Justice.* Milton Keynes: Open University Press.

Carlson, B. 1984. "Children's Observations of Interparental Violence." In Albert Roberts (ed.). *Battered Women and Their Families.* New York: Spring Publishers, pp. 147-167.

Carrothers, W.A. 1938. *Oriental Standards of Living.* Part II of *The Japanese Canadians.* By C.H. Young and H. Reid. Toronto: University of Toronto Press.

Carson, William G. 1970. "White Collar Crime and the Enforcement of Factory Legislation." *British Journal of Criminology.* 10: 383.

Carson, William G. 1974. "Symbolic and Instrumental Dimensions of Early Factory Legislation: A case study in the social origins of criminal law." In R. Hood (ed.), *Crime, Criminology and Public Policy.* London: Heinemann.

Carson, William G. 1980. "The Institutionalization of Ambiguity: Early British Factory Acts." In E. Stotland and G. Geis (eds.), *White-Collar Crime: Theory and Research.* Beverly Hills: Sage Publications.

Casey, John. 1985. "Corporate Crime and the State: Canada in the 1980s." In Thomas Fleming (ed.), *The New Criminologies in Canada.* Toronto: Oxford University Press.

Cassel, J. 1987. *The Secret Plague: Venereal Disease In Canada 1838-1939.* University of Toronto Press.

Castells, M. 1975. "Immigrant Workers and Class Struggles in Advanced Capitalism: The Western European experience." *Politics and Society.* 5(1).

Chalmers, L. and P. Smith. 1988. "Wife Battering: Psychological, social and physical isolation and counteracting strategies." In A. Tigar McLaren (ed.), *Gender and Society: Creating a Canadian Women's Sociology.* Toronto: Copp Clark Pitman, pp. 221-44.

Chambers, David L. 1984. "Rethinking the Substantive Rules for Custody Disputes in Divorce." *Michigan Law School*. 83: 477-569.

Chambers G. and A. Millar. 1987. "Proving Sexual Assault." In Carlen and Worrall (eds.), *Gender, Crime and Justice*. Milton Keynes: Open University.

Chambliss, William. 1964. "A Sociological Analysis of the Law of Vagrancy." *Social Problems*. (Summer) 12: 67-77.

Chambliss, William (ed.). 1975a. *Criminal Law in Action*. Santa Barbara, California: Hamilton.

Chambliss, William. 1975b. "Toward a Political Economy of Crime" *Theory and Society*. (Summer) 2(2): 149-70.

Chambliss, William. 1986. "On Lawmaking." In S. Brickey and E. Comack (eds.), *The Social Basis of Law: Critical Readings in the Sociology of Law*. Toronto: Garamond Press, pp. 26-51.

Chan, Anthony B. 1983. *Gold Mountain: The Chinese in the New World*. Vancouver: New Star Books.

Chan, J. and R.V. Ericson. 1981. *Decarceration and The Economy of Penal Reform*. Research Report. Centre of Criminology, University of Toronto.

Chapman, T.L. 1979. "The Anti-drug Crusade in Western Canada, 1885-1925." In D.J Bercusson and L. Knafla (eds.), *Law and Society in Canada in Historical Perspective*. University of Calgary, Studies in History Vol. 2.

Chappell, D. *et al.* 1977. "A Comparative Study of Forcible Rape Offences Known to the Police in Boston and Los Angeles." In D. Chappell and S. Singer (eds.) *Forcible Rape*. New York: Columbia University Press.

Chappell, D. and Susan Singer. 1977. "Rape in New York City." In *Forcible Rape*. New York: Columbia University Press.

Chappell, D. and Susan Singer (eds.). 1977. *Forcible Rape*. New York: Columbia University Press.

Cheng, T. 1931. *Oriental Immigration in Canada*. Shanghai: The Commercial Press.

Chesney-Lind, Meda. 1987. "Female Offenders: Paternalism re-examined." In L. Crites and W. Hepperle (eds.) *Women, The Courts and Equality*. Newbury Park: Sage Publications, pp. 115-39.

Chesney-Lind, Meda. 1988. "Girls and Status Offences: Is juvenile justice still sexist?." *Criminal Justice Abstracts*. (March) 20(1): 144-65.

Chesney-Lind, Meda and R.A. Shelden. 1988. "Issues in the Institutionalization of Girls." Paper presented at American Society of Criminology Meetings, Chicago. Nov. 9-12.

Child, A. 1978. "The Ryerson Tradition in Western Canada, 1871-1906." In N.

McDonald and A. Chaiton (eds.), Egerton Ryerson and His Times. Toronto: MacMillan and Company.

Chodorow, Nancy. 1978. The Reproduction of Mothering: Psychoanalysis and the Sociology of Gender. Berkeley: University of California Press.

Chodos, R. 1977. The Caribbean Connection. Toronto: James Lorimer.

Chunn, D.E. 1988. "Boys Will be Men, Girls Will be Mothers: The legal regulation of childhood in Toronto and Vancouver, 1920-45." Paper presented at Canadian Sociology and Anthropology Meetings, June 1-4.

Cicourel, Aron. 1968. The Social Organization of Juvenile Justice. New York: John Wiley and Sons.

Clairmont, D. and D. Magill. 1970. Nova Scotian Blacks: An Historical and Structural Overview. Halifax: Institute of Public Affairs, Dalhousie University.

Clark, Lorenne and Debra Lewis. 1977. Rape: The Price of Coercive Sexuality. Toronto: The Women's Press.

Clarke, A. 1967. The Meeting Point. Toronto: Macmillan.

Clinard, M.B. and Richard Quinney. 1973. Criminal Behaviour Systems: A Typology. New York: Holt, Rinehart and Winston.

Cockerill, R.W. 1981. "Probation Effectiveness in Alberta." Canadian Journal of Criminology. 17: 284.

Cohen, Gerald A. 1978. Karl Marx's Theory of History: A Defence. Princeton University Press.

Cohen, Stanley. 1979. "The Punitive City: Notes on the dispersal of social control." Contemporary Crises. 3: 339-363.

Cohen, Stanley. 1985. Visions of Social Control. Oxford: Basil Blackwell, Polity Press.

Collins, Patricia. 1989. "A Comparison of Two Works on Black Family Life." Signs. 14(4): 875-84.

Comack, Elizabeth. 1987. "Women Defendants and the `Battered Wife Syndrome': A plea for the sociological imagination." Crown Counsel's Review. 5 (11 and 12).

Connelly, M.P. 1976. "Canadian Women as a Reserve Army of Labour." PhD. dissertation, University of Toronto.

Connelly, M.P. 1977. "Women workers and the family wage in Canada." In Hoiberg (ed.), Women and the World of Work. New York: Plenum Press.

Connelly, M.P. and M. MacDonald. 1986. "Women's Work: Domestic and wage labour in a Nova Scotia community." In Roberta Hamilton and Michele Barrett (eds.), The Politics of Diversity: Feminism, Marxism and Nationalism. Montreal: Book Center, pp. 53-80.

Cooper, S.D. 1987. "The Evolution of the Federal Women's Prison." In E. Adelberg and C. Currie (eds.), *Too Few To Count*. Vancouver.: Press Gang, pp. 127-145.

Corbett, D.C. 1957. *Canada Immigration Policy: A Critique*. Toronto: University of Toronto Press.

Craven, Paul. 1980. *'An Impartial Umpire': Industrial Relations and the Canadian State, 1900-1911*. Toronto: University of Toronto Press.

Craven, Paul and T. Traves. 1979. "The Class Politics of the National Policy." *Journal of Canadian Studies*. 14(3): 14-38.

Cross, Michael S. (ed.). 1974. *The Workingman in the Nineteenth Century*. Toronto: University of Toronto Press.

Cross, Michael and Gregory Kealey (eds.). 1982. *Canada's Age of Industry, 1849-1896: Readings in Social History, Volume 3*. Toronto: McLelland and Stewart.

Cullen, F., W. Maakestad and G. Cavender. 1984. "The Ford Pinto Case and Beyond: Corporate crime, moral boundaries and the criminal sanction." In Ellen Hochstedler (ed.), *Corporations As Criminals*. Beverly Hills: Sage Publications.

Currie, Dawn. 1986. "Transformation of Juvenile Justice." In Brian MacLean (ed.), *The Political Economy of Crime*. Scarborough: Prentice-Hall.

Currie, Dawn. 1990. "Battered Women and the State: From the failure of theory to a theory of failure." *Journal of Human Justice*. (Spring) 1(2): 77-96.

Daly, Kathleen. 1987. "Structure and Practice of Familial-Based Justice in a Criminal Court." *Law and Society Review*. 21(2): 268-89.

Daly, Kathleen. 1989. "Criminal Justice Ideologies and Practices in Different Voices: Some feminist questions about justice." *International Journal of Sociology of Law*. 17(1): 1-18.

Daly, Kathleen and Meda Chesney-Lind. 1988. "Feminism and Criminology." *Justice Quarterly*. 5(4):497-538.

Damas and Smith Ltd. 1981. "Wollaston Lake: Community planning study." Toronto.

Danner, Mona. 1989. "Socialist Feminism: A brief introduction." *The Critical Criminologist*. 1(3): 1-2.

Das Gupta, T. 1986. *Learning From Our History*. Toronto: Cross-Cultural Communication Centre.

Davey, Ian. 1975. "School Reform and School Attendance: The Hamilton central school, 1853-1861." In M. Katz and P. Mattingly, (eds.), *Education and Social Change*. New York University Press.

Davey, Ian. 1978. "The Rhythm of Work and the Rhythm of School." In N. McDonald and A. Chaiton (eds.), *Egerton Ryerson and His Times*. Toronto: MacMillan and Company.

Davis, Angela. 1983. *Woman, Race and Class*. New York: Vintage Books.

Dawson, Brettel. 1988. "Fathers' Rights Groups: When rights wrong women." *Broadside*. 9(8): 6-7.

de Las Casa, Bartolomé. 1656. *The Fears of the Indians* (tr. Phillips)

De Mause, L. (ed.). 1975. "The evolution of childhood." In *The History of Childhood*. New York: Harper and Row.

de Victorio, Francisci. 1917. *De Indis et de Iure Belli*. (tr. Nys).

Deloitte, Haskins and Sells. 1988. "Economic Development Strategic Plan." Report for the Visions North Community Futures Committee, Saskatoon.

Deloria V. and Lytle C. 1984. *The Nations Within: The Past and Future of American Indian Sovereignty*. New York: Pantheon.

Dickinson, J. 1986. "From Poor Law to Social Insurance: The periodization of state intervention in the reproduction process." In J. Dickinson and B. Russell (eds.), *Family, Economy and State*. Toronto: Garamond Press.

Dickinson, J. and B. Russell (eds.). 1986. *Family, Economy and State*. Toronto: Garamond Press.

Diebel, L. 1973. "Black Women in White Canada: The lonely life." *Chatelaine*. (March), pp. 38-39, 84, 86-88.

Dobash R.E. and R. Dobash. 1975. *Violence Against Wives: A Case Against the Patriarchy*. New York: Free Press.

Dodge, Bernadine. 1988. "More Sinned Against: Women and the law in 19th century Ontario." Unpublished paper, Trent University Archives, Peterborough, Ontario.

Doern, G.B. 1977. "The Political Economy of Regulating Occupational Health: The Ham and Beaudry reports." *Canadian Public Administration*.

Domhoff, Wm. 1970. *The Higher Circles*. New York: Random House.

Donzelot, J. 1977. *The Policing of Families* (trans. R. Hurley). New York: Pantheon Books.

Drakich, Janice. 1989. "In Search of the Better Parent: The social construction of ideologies of fatherhood." *Canadian Journal of Women in the Law*. 3(1): 69-87.

Dubinsky, Karen. 1987. "R.E.A.L. Women — Really Dangerous." *Canadian Dimension*. (October) 21(6): 4-7.

Duclos, Nitya. 1987. "Breaking the Dependency Circle: The Family Law Act

Reconsidered." *University of Toronto Faculty of Law Review*. 45: 1-36.

Durkheim, Emile. 1964. *The Division of Labor in Society*. New York: The Free Press.

Dutton, D. 1984. *The Criminal Justice System's Response to Wife Assault*. Ottawa: Programs Branch User Report #26, Ministry of the Solicitor General, Secretariat.

Edwards, Susan. 1987. "Prostitutes, Victims of Law, Social Policy and Organized Crime." In Pat Carlen and Anne Worrell (eds.), *Gender, Crime and Justice*. Milton Keynes: Open University Press, pp. 43-57.

Eichler, Margrit. 1988. *Families in Canada Today*. 2nd ed. Toronto: Gage.

Eisenstein, Zillah. 1979. "Developing a Theory of Capitalist Patriarchy and Socialist Feminism." In Zillah Eisenstein (ed.), *Capitalist Patriarchy and the Case for Socialist Feminism*. New York: Monthly Review Press, pp. 5-41.

Eisenstein, Zillah. 1981. *The Radical Future of Liberal Feminism*. New York: Longman.

Eisenstein, Zillah. 1984. *Feminism and Sexual Equality*. New York: Monthly Review Press.

Eisenstein, Zillah. 1988. *The Female Body and the Law*. Berkeley: University of California Press.

Ekland-Olson S. and S. Martin. 1988. "Organizational Compliance with Court Ordered Reform." *Law and Society Review*. 22(2): 359-83.

Ericson, Richard V. 1981. *Making Crime: A Study of Police Detective Work*. Toronto: Butterworth.

Ericson, Richard V. 1982. *Reproducing Order: A Study of Police Detective Work*. Toronto: Butterworth.

Ericson, Richard V. 1987. "The State and Criminal Justice Reform." in R. Ratner and J. McMullan (eds.), *State Control: Criminal Justice Politics in Canada*. Vancouver: University of British Columbia Press, pp. 21-38.

Ericson, Richard V. and Patricia M. Baranek. 1982. *The Ordering of Justice*. Toronto: University of Toronto Press.

Falk. 1986. "Promise of Natural Communities." In Thompson (ed.), *The Rights of Indigenous Peoples in International Law*. University of Saskatchewan Native Law Centre.

Fattah, Ezzat A. 1976. "Deterrence: A Review of the Literature." In Law and Reform Commission of Canada, *Fear and Punishment*. Ottawa: Minister of Supply and Services Canada.

Fergusson, C.B. 1966. "The West Indies and the Atlantic Provinces: Background of the present relationship." In *The West Indies and the Atlantic Provinces of Canada*. Halifax: Institute of Public Affairs, Dalhousie University.

Ferns, H. and B. Ostry. 1955. *The Age of Mackenzie King*. Toronto: Lorimer.

Findlay, S. 1988. "Feminist Struggles with the Canadian State: 1966-1988." *Resources for Feminist Research*. 17(3).

Fineman, Martha. 1983. "Implementing Equality: Ideology, contradiction and social change: A study of rhetoric and result in the regulation of the consequences of divorce." *Wisconsin Law Review*, pp. 789-886.

Fineman, Martha. 1988. "Dominant Discourse, Professional Language, and Legal Change in Child Custody Decisionmaking." *Harvard Law Review*, 101(4): 727-74.

Finklehor, Gelles, R.G. Hotaling and M. Straus (eds.). 1983. *The Dark Side of Families*. Beverly Hills: Sage Publications.

Fleming, Thomas (ed.). 1985. *The New Criminologies in Canada*. Toronto: Oxford University Press.

Foucault, M. 1979. *Discipline and Punish: The Birth of the Prison*. New York: Pantheon Books.

Franzway, S., D. Court and R.W. Connell. 1989. *Staking a Claim: Feminism, Bureaucracy and the State*. Cambridge: Polity Press.

Fraser, D. 1966. "The West Indies and Canada: The present relationship." In *The West Indies and the Atlantic Provinces of Canada*. Halifax: Institute of Public Affairs, Dalhousie University, pp. 33-41.

Frenette, J. 1985. *The History of the Chibougamau Crees*. Chibougamau, Quebec: Cree Indian Centre of Chibougamau.

Frideres, J. 1983. *Native People in Canada: Contemporary Conflicts*. Toronto: Prentice-Hall.

Friedenberg, E. 1975. *The Disposal of Liberty and Other Industrial Wastes*. New York: Doubleday.

Friedman, Lawrence. 1977. *Law and Society: An Introduction*. New Jersey: Prentice Hall.

Fudge, Judith. 1987. "The Public/Private Distinction: The possibilities of and limits to the use of Charter litigation to further feminist struggles." *Osgoode Hall Law Journal*. 25: 485.

Fudge, Judith. 1990. "The Violence of Abstraction: what do we mean by law and social transformation?" *Canadian Journal of Law and Society*. 5: 47-69.

Galliher, G.H. and F. Walker. 1978. "The Politics of Systematic Research Error: The case of the Federal Bureau of Narcotics as a moral entrepreneur." *Crime and Social Justice*. 29-33.

Garland, David. 1976. *Punishment and Welfare*. London: Gower Books.

Gavigan, Shelley. 1986. "Women and Abortion in Canada: What's law got to do with it?" In Meg Luxton and Heather Jon Maroney (eds.), *Feminism and Political Economy: Women in Canada.* Toronto: Methuen.

Gavigan, Shelley. 1988. "Law, Gender and Ideology." In Bayevsky (ed.), *Legal Theory Meets Legal Practice.* Toronto: Academic Printing and Publishing.

Gavigan, Shelley. 1989/90. "Petit Treason in Eighteenth Century England: Women's inequality before the law." *Canadian Journal of Women and the Law.* 3(2).

Gendreau, Paul. 1979. "Norms and Recidivism for First Incarcerates: Implications for programming." *Canadian Journal of Criminology.* 21: 416.

Gerth, Hans and C. Wright Mills. 1974. *From Max Weber: Essays in Sociology.* New York: Oxford University Press.

Giddens, Anthony. 1976. *New Rules of Sociological Method.* New York: Basic Books.

Giddens, Anthony. 1981. *The Class Structure of Advanced Societies.* Second Edition. London: Hutchinson.

Gidney, R.D. 1975. "Elementary Education in Upper Canada: A reassessment." In M. Katz and P. Mattingly (eds.), *Education and Social Change.* New York University Press.

Gilligan, Carol. 1982. *In a Different Voice.* Cambridge, MA: Harvard University Press.

Girdner, L. 1986. "Child Custody Determination: Ideological dimensions of a social problem." In Seidman and Rappaport (eds.), *Redefining Social Problems.* New York: Plenum, pp. 165-83.

Glasbeek, Harry. 1984. "Why Corporate Deviance is Not Treated as a Crime: The need to make 'profits' a dirty word." *Osgoode Hall Law Journal,* 22: 393.

Glasbeek, Harry. 1986. "The Maiming and Killing of Workers: The one-sided nature of risk taking in capitalism." *Jurisprudence Centre Working Papers.* Ottawa: Department of Law, Carleton University.

Glasbeek, Harry J. and Michael Mandel. 1979. "The Crime and Punishment of Jean-Claude Parrot." *Canadian Forum.* 21(10).

Glasbeek, Harry and Susan Rowland. 1979. "Are Injuring and Killing at Work Crimes?" *Osgoode Hall Law Journal.* 17: 506.

Glendon, Mary Ann. 1981. *The New Family and the New Property.* Toronto: Butterworths.

Goff, Colin H. and Charles E. Reasons. 1978. *Corporate Crime in Canada: A Critical Analysis of Anti-Combines Legislation.* Scarborough, Ontario: Prentice-Hall.

Gold, David, Clarence Y. Lo and Erik Wright. 1975. "Recent Developments in Marxist Theories of the Capitalist State." *Monthly Review.* 27: 29-51.

Goldstick, Miles. 1987. *Wollaston: People Resisting Genocide*. Montreal: Black Rose Books.

Goodard, J. 1988. "Forked Tongues." *Saturday Night*. February, pp. 38-45.

Gordon, R. 1984. "Critical Legal Histories." *Stanford Law Review*. 36.

Graff, H.J. 1976. "Respected and Profitable Labour: Literacy, jobs and the working class in the nineteenth century." In G. Kealey and P. Warrian (eds.), *Essays in Canadian Working Class History*. Toronto: McClelland and Stewart, pp. 58-82.

Graff, H.J. 1978. "The Reality Behind the Rhetoric: The social and economic meanings of literacy in the mid-nineteenth century: The example of literacy and criminality." In N. McDonald and A. Chaiton (eds.), *Egerton Ryerson and His Times*. Toronto: Macmillan.

Gramsci, Antonio. 1971. *Selections from the Prison Notebooks*. New York: International Publishers.

Green, A. 1976. *Immigration and the Postwar Canadian Economy*. Toronto: Macmillan.

Green, M. 1979. "The History of Canadian Narcotics Control." *University of Toronto Faculty of Law Review*. 37: 42-79.

Greenaway, Wm. and S. Brickey. 1978. *Law and Social Control in Canada*. Toronto: Prentice Hall.

Greenberg, David F. (ed.). 1981. *Crime and Capitalism: Readings in Marxist Criminology*. Palo Alto, California: Mayfield Publishers.

Greenwood, Victoria and Jock Young. 1980. "Ghettos of Freedom: An examination of permissiveness." National Deviancy Conference. *Permissiveness and Control*. New York: Barnes and Noble.

Griffiths, C. and S. Verdun-Jones. 1989. *Canadian Criminal Justice*. Toronto: Butterworths.

Gross, Wendy L. 1986. "Judging Best Interests of the Child: Child custody and the homosexual parent." *Canadian Journal of Women in the Law*. 1(2): 505-31.

Gunningham, N. 1984. *Safeguarding the Worker*. Sydney: Law Book Co. Ltd.

Haddad J. and S. Milton. 1986. "The Construction of Gender Roles in Social Policy." *Canadian Woman Studies/Les Cahiers De La Femme*. 7(4).

Hagan, John. 1978. "Explaining Official Delinquency: A spatial study of class, conflict and control." *The Sociological Quarterly*. 19: 386.

Hagan, John. 1980. "The Legislation of Crime and Delinquency: A review of theory, method and research." *Law and Society Review*. (Spring) 14(3): 603-629.

Hagan, John. 1986. "New Legal Scholarship: problems and prospects." *Canadian Journal of Law and Society*. 1(1): 35-57.

Hagan, John and Jeffrey Leon. 1977. "Rediscovering Delinquency: social history, political ideology and the sociology of law." *Social Problems*. 42: 587-98.

Hagan, John, J. Simpson and A. R. Gillis. 1979. "Feminist Scholarship, Relational and Instrumental Control: A power theory of gender and delinquency." *British Journal of Sociology*. (September) 39(3): 301-336.

Hall, S. 1980. *Drifting into a Law and Order Society*. London: The Cobden Trust.

Hall, S. and P. Scraton. 1981. "Law, Class and Control." In M. Fitzgerald *et al.* (eds.), *Crime and Society: Readings in Theory and History*. London: Routledge and Kegan Paul.

Hamilton, Roberta. 1986. "The Collusion with Patriarchy: A psychoanalytic account." In Roberta Hamilton and Michele Barrett (eds.), *The Politics of Diversity*. Montreal: Book Center, pp. 385-97.

Hamilton, Roberta. 1986a. "Working at Home." In Roberta Hamilton and Michele Barret (eds.), *The Politics of Diversity*. Montreal: Book Center, pp. 139-53.

Hamilton, Roberta and Michele Barret (eds.). 1986. *The Politics of Diversity*. Montreal: Book Center.

Handelman, D. 1964. "West Indian Associations in Montreal." Masters thesis. McGill University.

Handler, J. 1978. *Social Movement and the Legal System: Theory of Law Reform and Social Change*. New York: Academic Press.

Hartmann, Heidi. 1981. "The Unhappy Marriage of Marxism and Feminism: Towards a more progressive union." In L. Sargent (ed.), *Women and the Revolution*. Boston: South End Press.

Hawkins, F. 1972. *Canada and Immigration: Public Policy and Public Concern*. Montreal: McGill-Queen's University Press.

Hawkins, K. 1984. *Environment and Enforcement: Regulation and the Social Definition of Pollution*. Oxford: Clarendon.

Henry, F. 1968. "The West Indian Domestic Scheme in Canada." *Social and Economic Studies*. 17(1): 83-91.

Henry, K. 1981. *Black Politics in Toronto Since World War I*. Toronto: The Multicultural Society History of Ontario.

Heron, Craig and Brian Palmer. 1980. "Through the Prism and the Strike: Industrial conflict in Southern Ontario, 1901-1904." In P. Grayson (ed.), *Class, State Ideology and Change*. Toronto: Holt, Rinehart and Winston, pp. 47-71.

Hilton, Z. 1989. "One in Ten: The struggle and disempowerment of the battered women's movement." *Canadian Journal of Family Law*. 7: 313.

Hobbes, Thomas. 1651. *Leviathan*. Oxford: Basil Blackwell, 1946.

Hobbs, E.E. and Associates. "The Grand Rapids Hydro Development and the Devastation of the Cree." Final Report, 1986.

Hogarth, John. 1971. *Sentencing as a Human Process.* University of Toronto Press.

Hoiberg, A. (ed.). 1980. *Women and The World of Work.* New York: Plenum Press.

Holmes, Oliver W. 1881. *The Common Law: Lecture II.* Boston: Little, Brown and Company.

Holmes, Sheila M. 1987. "Imposed Joint Legal Custody: Children's best interests or parental rights?" *University Of Toronto Faculty of Law Review.* 45(2): 300-323.

Honderich, Ted. 1976. *Punishment: The Supposed Justifications.* Revised Edition. Harmondsworth: Penguin Books.

Hood, Richard and R. Sparks. 1970. *Key Issues in Criminology.* New York: McGraw-Hill.

hooks, Bell. 1981. *Ain't I a Woman?.* Boston: South End Press.

Hopkins, Andrew. 1979. "Pressure Groups and the Law." *Contemporary Crises* 4: 421-22.

Houston, S. 1975. "Victorian Origins of Juvenile Delinquency: A Canadian experience." In M. Katz and P. Mattingly (eds.), *Education and Social Change.* New York University Press.

Houston, S. 1978. "School Reform and Education: The issue of compulsory schooling." In N. McDonald and A. Chaiton (eds.), *Egerton Ryerson and His Times.* Toronto: Macmillan, pp. 254-276.

Houston, S. 1982. "The `Waifs and Strays' of a Late Victorian City: Juvenile Delinquents in Toronto." In J. Parr (ed.). *Childhood and the Family in Canadian History.* Toronto: McClelland and Stewart, pp. 129-142.

Houston, S. and A. Prentice (eds.). 1975. *Family, School and Society in Nineteenth Century Canada.* Toronto: Oxford University Press.

Hunt, Alan. 1976. "Law, State and Class Struggle." *Marxism Today.* 20(6): 178-87.

Hunt, Alan. 1978. *The Sociological Movement in Law.* London: MacMillan.

Hunt, Alan. 1985. "The Ideology of Law: Advances and problems in recent applications of the concept of ideology to the analysis of law." *Law and Society Review.* 19(11).

Hurl, Lorna. 1981. *An Analysis of Social Welfare Policy: A case study of the development of child welfare policies and programmes in Manitoba, 1870-1924.* M.S.W. thesis. University of Manitoba.

Hurl, Lorna. 1988. "Restricting Child Factory Labour in Late Nineteenth Century

Ontario." *Labour/Le Travail*. (Spring) 21: 87-121.

Iacovetta, F. 1986. "'Primitive Villagers and Uneducated Girls: Canada recruits domestics from Italy, 1951-52." *Canadian Woman Studies*. 7(4): 14-18.

Irving, Howard and Michael Benjamin. 1987. *Family Mediation: Theory and Practice or Dispute Resolution*. Toronto: Carswell.

Jaffe, P., D. Wolfe, A. Telford and G. Austin. 1986. "The Impact of Police Charges in Incidents of Wife Abuse." *Journal of Family Violence*. 1(1): 37-49.

Jaggar, Allison and Paula Rothenberg (eds). 1984. *Feminist Frameworks: Alternative Accounts of Relations between Men and Women*. Second Edition. New York: McGraw-Hill.

Jamieson, Stuart M. 1968. *Times of Trouble: Labour Unrest and Industrial Conflict in Canada, 1900-1966*. Ottawa: Information Canada.

Jankovic, I. 1978. "Social Class and Criminal Sentencing." *Crime and Social Justice*. 10(9).

Jessop, Bob. 1977. "Recent Theories of the Capitalist State." *Cambridge Journal of Economics*. 1: 353-73.

Jessop, Bob. 1982. *The Capitalist State: Marxist Theories and Methods*. London: Martin-Robertson.

Johnson, L. 1974. "The Political Economy of Ontario Women in the Nineteenth Century." In J. Acton et al. (eds.), *Women at Work*. Toronto: Women's Press.

Kahn-Freund, O. 1969. "Labour Law and Public Opinion." In Vilhelm Aubert (ed.), *Sociology of Law: Selected Readings*. London: Penguin Books.

Katz, Michail. 1968. *The Ironies of Early School Reforms*. Cambridge, MA: Harvard University Press.

Katz, M. and P. Mattingly (eds.). 1975. *Education and Social Change*. New York University Press.

Kealey, Gregory S. (ed.). 1973. *Canada Investigates Industrialism*. University of Toronto Press.

Kealey, Gregory S. (ed.). 1980. *Toronto Workers' Response to Industrial Capitalism, 1867-1892*. University of Toronto Press.

Kealey, Gregory S. and Bryan D. Palmer. 1981. "The Bonds of Unity: The Knights of Labor in Ontario, 1880-1900." *Histoire Sociale/ Social History*. 14: 369-411.

Kealey, Gregory S. and Peter Warrian (eds.). 1976. *Essays in Canadian Working Class History*. Toronto: McClelland and Stewart.

Kealey, Linda. 1974. "Introduction." In J. Acton et al. (eds.), *Women at Work*. Toronto: Canadian Women's Educational Press.

Kealey, Linda. 1978. *A Not Unreasonable Claim: Women and Reform in Canada, 1880s-1920s*. University of Toronto Press.

Kelso, J.J. 1911. *Early History of Humane and Children's Aid Movement*. Toronto: King's Printer.

Kerbo, Harold R. and Richard Della Fave. 1979. "The Empirical Side of the Power Elite Debate: An assessment and critique of recent research." *Sociological Quarterly*. 20: 5-22.

King, V. 1958. "Calypso in Canada." *Canadian Welfare*. (November): 173-183.

Klein, S.S. 1985. "Individualism, Liberalism and the New Family." *University of Toronto Faculty of Law Review*. 43: 116.

Klein, Alice and Wayne Roberts. 1974. "Besieged Innocence: The problem and the problems of working women — Toronto, 1896-1914." In J. Acton, *et al*. (eds.), *Working Women*. Toronto: Canadian Women's Educational Press.

Kline, Marlee. 1989. "Race, Racism and Feminist Legal Theory." *Harvard Women's Law Journal*. 12: 115-150.

Klockars, Carl B. 1979. "The Contemporary Crisis of Marxist Criminology." *Criminology*. 16: 477-515.

Kramer, R.C. 1984. "Corporate Criminality: The development of an idea." In Hochstedler (ed.). *Corporations As Criminals*. Beverly Hills: Sage Publications.

Kruttschnitt, Candace. 1981. "Social Status and Sentence of Female Offenders." *Law and Society Review*. 15: 247.

Lamb, Louise. 1987. "Involuntary Joint Custody." *Herizons*. (January/February) 20.

Lamming, G. 1961. "The West Indians: Our loneliest immigrants." *McLean's Magazine*, Nov. 4, pp. 27(52): 54-56.

Lasche, Christopher. 1979. *Haven In a Heartless World: The Family Besieged*. New York: Basic Books.

Law Reform Commission of Canada. 1976. *Criminal Responsibility for Group Action*. Working Paper 16. Ottawa: Supply and Services.

Law Reform Commission of Canada. 1985. *Sentencing in Environmental Cases*. Ottawa: Supply and Services.

Laxer, Gordon. 1989. "The Schizophrenic Character of Canadian Political Economy." *Canadian Review of Sociology and Anthropology*. (February) 26(1): 178-92.

Lea J. and J. Young. 1984. *What Is To Be Done About Law and Order?* Harmondsworth, Middlesex: Penguin Books.

Leah, R. 1980. "Immigrant Women — Double Victims — A Study of Working Class Immigrant Women in the Canadian Labour Force." A paper presented at the

Annual Meeting of the Canadian Sociology and Anthropology Association, Montreal, 1980.

Leah, R. and G. Morgan. 1979. "Immigrant Women Fight Back: The case of the seven Jamaican women." *Resources for Feminist Research*. Pt. 2 (November). 8(3): 23-24.

Lefcourt, R. 1971. "Lawyers for the Poor Can't Win." In R. Lefcourt (ed.), *Law Against the People*. New York: Vintage Books.

Lerner, Harriet Goldhor. 1985. *The Dance of Anger*. New York: Harper and Row.

Leslie, G. 1974. "Domestic Service in Canada, 1880-1929." In Acton, *et al.* (eds.), *Women at Work: Ontario, 1850-1930*. Toronto: Canadian Women's Educational Press.

Levens, B. and D. Dutton. 1977. "Domestic Crisis Intervention: Citizen's requests for service and the Vancouver Police Department's response." Vancouver.

Levitt K. and A. McIntyre. 1967. *Canada-West Indies Economic Relations*. Montreal: The Centre for Developing Area Studies, McGill University, pp. 90-101.

Lewis, G. 1968. *The Growth of the Modern West Indies*. New York: Modern Reader Paperbacks.

Li, Peter S. 1979. "A Historical Approach to Ethnic Stratification: the case of the Chinese in Canada, 1858-1930." *Canadian Review of Sociology and Anthropology*. 16: 320-32.

Li, Peter S. 1980. "Immigration Laws and Family Patterns: Some demographic changes among Chinese families in Canada, 1885-1971." *Canadian Ethnic Studies*. 12(1): 58-73.

Locke. J. 1690. *Two Treaties on Civil Government*. London: G. Routledge and Sons, 1884.

Loh, N. 1980. "The Impact of Common Law and Reform Rape Statutes of Prosecution: An empirical study." *University of Washington Law Review*. 55.

Loh, N. 1981. "What has Reform on Rape Legislation Wrought: A truth in criminal labelling." *Journal of Social Science*. 3: 2-52.

Lorentson, Edith and E. Woolner. 1950. "Fifty Years of Labour Legislation in Canada." *Labour Gazette*. 50(4): 1412-39.

Lowe, Graham. 1979. "The Rise of Modern Management in Canada." *Canadian Dimension*. 14(3): 32-38.

Luxton, Meg. 1980. *More Than a Labour of Love: Three Generations of Women's Work in the Home*. Toronto: Women's Press.

Luxton, Meg. 1986. "Two Hands for the Clock: Changing patterns in the gendered division of labour in the home." In R. Hamilton and M. Barrett (eds.), *The Politics of Diversity*. Montreal: Book Center, pp. 35-52.

Luxton, Meg. 1987. "Time for Myself: Women's work and the 'fight for shorter hours'." In H. Maroney and M. Luxton (eds.), *Feminism and the Political Economy: Women's Work, Women's Struggles.* Toronto: Methuen, pp. 167-178.

Luxton, Meg and Harriet Rosenberg. 1986. *Through the Kitchen Window: The Politics of Home and Family.* Toronto: Garamond Press.

Macdonald, D. 1982a. *Sexual Offences: Comparative Study on the Present Law Bill C-127, The Report of The Law Reform Commission.* Ottawa: Law Government Division, Research Branch, Library of Parliament, September 20, 1982.

MacDonald, D. 1982b. *The Doctrine of Recent Complaint.* Ottawa: Law and Government, Research Branch, Library of Parliament. March 8, 1982.

MacDonald, D. 1982c. *The Evolution of Bill C-127.* Ottawa: Law Government Division, Research Branch, Library of Parliament. September. 14, 1982.

Macdonell, D. 1986. *Theories of Discourse: An Introduction.* Oxford: Basil Blackwell.

Mackenzie, Suzanne. 1986. "Women's Responses to Economic Restructuring: Changing gender, changing space." In Roberta Hamilton and Michele Barrett (eds.), *The Politics of Diversity.* Montreal: Book Center, pp. 81-100.

MacKinnon, Catherine A. 1982. "Feminism, Marxism, Method and the State: An agenda for theory." *Signs.* 7(3): 515-44.

MacKinnon, Catherine A. 1983. "Feminism, Marxism, Method and the State: Toward a feminist jurisprudence." *Signs.* 8(4): 635-658.

MacKinnon, Catherine A. 1987. *Feminism Unmodified: Discourses on Life and Law.* Cambridge, MA: Harvard University Press.

MacKinnon, Catherine A. 1989. *Toward a Feminist Theory of the State.* Cambridge, MA: Harvard University Press.

MacKinnon, Catherine A. 1990. "Breaking New Ground." *Leaf Lines.* 3(2):1.

MacLean, Brian (ed.). 1986. *The Political Economy of Crime: Readings for a Critical Criminology.* Scarborough: Prentice-Hall.

Mahon, R. 1980. "Regulatory Agencies: Captive agents or hegemonic apparatuses?" In P. Grayson (ed.), *Class, State, Ideology and Change: Marxist Perspectives on Canada.* Toronto: Holt, Rinehart and Winston.

Mandel, Michael. 1986. "Democracy, Class and Canadian Sentencing Law." In S. Brickey and E. Comack (eds.). *The Social Basis of Law.* Toronto: Garamond Press.

Marcus, S. 1974. *Engels, Manchester and the Working Class.* New York: Vintage.

Marglin, S. 1974. "What do Bosses Do? The Origins of Hierarchy in Capitalist Production." *Review of Radical Political Economy.* 6(2): 33-60.

Marsh, J., A. Geist and N. Caplan. 1982. *Rape and the Limits of Reform.* Boston: Auburn House.

Marshall, R. 1965. *The Negro and Organized Labor*. New York: John Wiley.

Martin, L. and K. Segrave. 1985. *The Servant Problem: Domestic Workers in North America*. Jefferson, NC: McFarland Publishers.

Martinson, R. 1974. "What Works? Questions and answers about prison reform." *The Public Interest*. (Spring) 35: 22-54.

Marx, Karl. 1976. *Capital: A Critique of Political Economy*, Volume I. B. Fowkes (trans.). Harmondsworth: Penguin Books.

Marx, Karl. 1977. "Preface to a Contribution to the Critique of Political Economy." In D. McLellan (ed.), *Karl Marx: Selected Writings*. Oxford University Press, pp. 388-91.

Marx, Karl and Fredrich Engels. 1975. *The Communist Manifesto*. Great Britain: C. Nickolls.

McBarnett, D.J. 1981. *Conviction: Law, the State and the Construction of Justice*. London: MacMillan Press.

McBean, Jean. 1987. "The Myth of Maternal Preference in Child Custody Cases." In Sheilah Martin and Kathleen E. Mahoney (eds.). *Equality and Judicial Neutrality*. Calgary: Carswell, pp. 184-192.

McCormack, A. Ross 1977. *Reformers, Rebels and Revolutionaries: the Western Canadian Radical Movement, 1899-1919*. University of Toronto Press.

McCormick, Albert E. Jr. 1979. "Dominant Class Interests and the Emergence of Antitrust Legislation." *Contemporary Crises*. 3: 399-417.

McDonald, N. and A. Chaiton. (eds.). 1978. *Egerton Ryerson and His Times*. Toronto: Macmillan.

McGillivray, A. 1987. "Battered Women: Definition, models and prosecutorial policy." *Canadian Journal of Family Law*. 6: 15.

McLaren, Angus and Arlene McLaren. 1986. *The Bedroom and the State*. Toronto: McClelland and Stewart.

McLaren, J. and J. Lowman. 1988. "Prostitution Law Experiment in Canada, 1982-1920: Unravelling myth and reality." Paper presented at Canadian Law and Society Association, Windsor, June.

McLeod, Linda. 1980. *Wife Battering in Canada: The Vicious Circle*. Ottawa: Minister of Supply and Services Canada.

McLeod, Linda. 1987. *Battered But Not Beaten: Preventing Wife Battering in Canada*. Ottawa: Canadian Advisory Council on the Status of Women.

McMullan, John. 1987. "Epilogue: Law, justice, and the state." In Ratner and McMullan (eds.), *State Control: Criminal Justice Politics in Canada*. Vancouver:

University of British Columbia Press.

McNeil, L. 1986. *Contradiction of Control: School Structure and School Knowledge.* London: Routledge and Kegan Paul.

Medea, A. and K. Thompson. 1974. *Against Rape.* New York: Farrar, Strauss and Giroux.

Melossi, D. 1980. "Strategies of Social Control in Capitalism: A comment on recent work." *Contemporary Crises.* 4: 381-402.

Middleton, N. 1971. *When Family Failed.* London: Gallancz.

Miles, R. 1982. *Racism and Migrant Labour.* London: Routledge and Kegan Paul.

Miliband, Ralph. 1969. *The State in Capitalist Society: The Analysis of the Western System of Power.* London: Basic Books.

Minge-Kalman, W. 1978. "The Industrial Revolution and the European Family: The institutionalization of childhood as a market for family labour." *Comparative Studies in Society and History.* (September). 20: 8-68.

Minow, M. 1985. "Forming under Everything that Grows: Toward a history of family law." *Wisconsin Law Review*, p. 819.

Mitchell, Julliet. 1971. *Women's Estate.* New York: Pantheon Books.

Mitchelson, Wendy. 1987. "Early Women's Organizations and Social Reform: Prelude to the welfare state." In A. Moscovitch and J. Albert (eds.), *The Benevolent State.* Toronto: Garamond Press, pp. 77-95.

Moore, D. 1985. *Don Moore: An Autobiography.* Toronto: Williams-Wallace.

Morgan, P. 1981. "From Battered Wife to Program Client: The state's shaping of social problems." *Kapitalistate.* 9: 17-41.

Morris, Cerise. 1988. *The Politics and Experience of Co-Parenting: An Exploratory Study of Shared Custody in Canada.* The CRIAW Papers, No. 20. Ottawa: Canadian Research Institute for the Advancement of Women.

Morrison, T.R. 1975. "Their Proper Sphere: Feminism, the family, and child-centred social reform in Ontario, 1875-1900." *Ontario History.* 67: 45-63.

Munro, J.A. 1971. "British Columbia and the `Chinese Evil': Canada's first anti-Asiatic law." *Journal of Canadian Studies.* 6(4): 42-51.

Musheno, M. and K. Seeley. 1986. "Prostitution Policy and the Women's Movement." *Contemporary Crises.* 10: 237-55.

Myers, G. 1972. *A History of Canadian Wealth.* Toronto: James Lorimer.

Myles, John. 1989. "Introduction: Understanding Canada: Comparative political economy perspectives." *Canadian Review of Sociology and Antrhropology.* (February) 26(1): 1-9.

Nash, E. 1960. "Trading Problems of the British West Indies." In Cumper (ed.), *The Economy of the West Indies.* Kingston: United Printers, pp. 223-42.

National Association of Women and the Law (NAWL). 1988. "Fathers' Rights, Mandatory Mediation: The equality backlash in family law." Special Issue of *Jurisfemme.* 8(3).

Neely, Richard. 1984. "The Primary Caretaker Parent Rule: Child custody and the dynamics of greed." *Yale Law and Policy Review.* 3: 168-185.

Neufeld, S. and B.V. Bogaard. 1977. *Characteristics of Rape.* Vancouver: Vancouver Rape Relief.

Newman, D. 1966. *Conviction: The Determination of Guilt or Innocence Without Trial.* Boston: Little Brown.

Niman, Harold. "The Price of Custody." Annual Institute of the Ontario Branch of the Canadian Bar Association, Toronto, Feb 6. 1987.

Northrup, H. 1944. *Organized Labor and the Negro.* New York: Harper and Brothers.

O'Brien, Mary and Sheila McIntyre. 1986. "Patriarchal Hegemony and Legal Education." *Canadian Journal of Women and the Law.* 2(1): 1-19.

O'Conner, James. 1973a. *The Fiscal Crisis of the State.* New York: St. Martin's.

O'Connor, James. 1973b. "Summary of the Theory of the Fiscal Crisis." *Kapitalistate.* 1(1): 79-83.

O'Donovan, K. 1985. *Sexual Divisions in Law.* London: Weidenfeld and Nicholson.

Offe, Clause. 1975. "The Theory of the Capitalist State and the Problem of Policy Formation." In L. Lindberg *et al.* (eds.), *Stress and Contradictions in Modern Capitalism.* Lexington: Lexington Books.

Olsen, Fran E. 1983. "The Family and the Market: A study of ideology and legal reform." *Harvard Law Review.* 96: 1497.

Olsen, Fran E. 1984. "The Politics of Family Law." *Law and Inequality.* 2(1): 69-95.

Olsen, Gregg. 1984. "Women in Nineteenth-Century Canadian Industry: A Comparative Approach." Masters thesis. University of Windsor.

Ontario, Legislative Assembly. 1982. *First Report on Family Violence: Wife Battering.* Toronto: Standing Committee on Social Development, September.

Ostry, B. 1960. "Conservatives, Liberals and Labour in the 1870s." *Canadian Historical Review.* 41: 93-127.

"Our World According to Osennontion and Skonaganlehirá." *Canadian Woman Studies/Les Cahiers De La Femme.* 10(2-3): 6.

Palmer, Bryan D. 1979. *A Culture of Conflict: Skilled Workers and Industrial Capitalism in Hamilton, Ontario, 1860-1914.* Montreal: McGill-Queens University Press.

Palmer, Bryan D. 1983. *Working Class Experience: The Rise and Reconstitution of Canadian Labour 1800-1980.* Toronto: Butterworth.

Panitch, Leo. 1977a. "The Role and Nature of the Canadian State." In L. Panitch (ed.), *The Canadian State: Political Economy and Political Power.* Toronto: University of Toronto Press, pp. 3-27.

Panitch, Leo (ed.). 1977b. *The Canadian State: Political Economy and Political Power.* Toronto: University of Toronto Press.

Parr, J. 1980. *Labouring Children.* London: Croom Helm.

Parr, J. (ed.). 1982. *Childhood and Family in Canadian History.* Toronto: McClelland and Stewart.

Parsons, Talcott. 1980. "The Law and Social Control." In Wm. Evan (ed.), *The Sociology of Law: A Social-Structural Perspective.* New York: The Free Press, pp. 60-68.

Pashukanis, E.B. 1978. *Law and Marxism.* London: Ink Links.

Patterson, E. 1979. "How the Legal System Responds to Battered Women." In E.M. Moore (ed.), *Battered Women.* Beverly Hills: Sage Publications.

Pearce, Frank. 1976. *Crimes of the Powerful.* London: Pluto Press.

Pentland, H.C. 1950. "The Role of Capital in Canadian Economic Development before 1875." *The Canadian Journal of Economics and Political Science.* 16(4): 457-74.

Pentland, H.C. 1981. *Labour and Capital in Canada 1650-1860.* Toronto: James Lorimer and Company.

Phillips, Paul A. 1967. *No Power Greater: A Century of Labour in British Columbia.* Vancouver: B.C. Federation of Labour.

Phizacklea, A. (ed.). 1983. *One Way Ticket: Migration and Female Labour.* London: Routledge and Kegan Paul.

Picciotto, S. 1979 and 1982. "The Theory of the State, Class Struggle and the Rule of Law." In B. Fine *et al.* (eds.), *Capitalism and the Rule of Law.* London: Hutchinson. Also in P. Beirne and R. Quinney (eds.), 1982. *Marxism and the Law.* New York: John Wiley.

Piliavin, S. and S. Briar. 1964. "Police Encounters with Juveniles" *American Journal of Sociology.* 70: 206-14.

Platt, Anthony. 1969. *The Child Savers: The Invention of Delinquency.* Chicago: University of Chicago Press.

Platt, Anthony. 1974. "Prospects for a Radical Criminology in the United States." *Crime and Social Justice.* 1: 2-10.

Polan, D. 1982. "Toward a Theory of Law and Patriarchy." In Kairy (ed.), *The*

Politics of Law. New York: Pantheon.

Polikoff, Nancy D. 1983. "Gender and Child-Custody Determinations: Exploding the myths." In I. Diamond (ed.), *Families, Politics, and Public Policy: A Feminist Dialogue on Women and the State*. New York: Longman, pp. 183-202.

Portes, A. 1978. "Migration and Underdevelopment." *Politics and Society*. 8(1): 1-48.

Potter, H. 1949. "The Occupational Adjustment of Montreal Negroes 1941-48." Masters thesis. McGill University.

Poulantzas, Nicos. 1973. *Political Power and Social Classes*. London: New Left Books.

Poulantzas, Nicos. 1975. *Classes in Contemporary Capitalism*. London: New Left Books.

Poulantzas, Nicos. 1978. *State Power and Socialism*. London: New Left Books.

Pound, R. 1930. *Criminal Justice in America*. New York: De Capo Press.

Prentice, Alison. 1975. "Education and the Metaphor of the Family: The Upper Canadian example." In M. Katz and P. Mattingly (eds.), *Education and Social Change*. New York University Press.

Prentice, Alison, Paula Bourne, Gail Cuthbert Brandt, Beth Light, Wendy Mitchinson and Naomi Black. 1988. *Canadian Women: A History*. Toronto: Harcourt.

Price, Lisa A. 1988. *Women's Interests: Feminist Activism and Institutional Change*. Vancouver: Women's Research Centre.

Purich, D. 1986. *Our Land: Native Rights in Canada*. Toronto: James Lorimer and Co.

Quinney, Richard. 1975. "Crime Control in a Capitalist Society." In I. Taylor, P. Walton and J. Young (eds.). *Critical Criminology*. London: Routledge and Kegan Paul, pp. 181-202.

Quinney, Richard. 1977. *Class, State and Crime: On the Theory and Practice of Criminal Justice*. New York: David McKay.

Rafter, Nicole. 1983. "Chastising the Unchaste: Social control functions of women's reformatory, 1894-1931." In S. Cohen and A. Scull (eds.), *Social Control and the State*. Oxford: Martin Robertson.

Rafter, Nicole. 1985. *Partial Justice*. Boston: Northeastern University Press.

Ramirez, J. 1983-1984. "Good Enough to Stay." *Currents*. 1: 17-19.

Randall, M. 1988. "Feminism and the State: Questions for theory and practice." *Resources for Feminist Research*. 17(3): 10-6.

Ratner, Robert. 1987. "Rethinking the Sociology of Crime and Justice." In R. Ratner and J. McMullan (eds.), *State Control: Criminal Justice Politics in Canada*. Vancouver: University of British Columbia Press.

Ratner, Robert and John McMullan. 1983. "Social Control and the Rise of the `Exceptionalist State' in Britain, the United States and Canada." *Crime and Social Justice.* (Summer): 31-43.

Ratner, Robert and John McMullan (eds.). 1987. *State Control: Criminal Justice Politics in Canada.* Vancouver: University of British Columbia Press.

Ravetz, J. 1977. "The Political Economy of Risk." *New Scientist.* 8 (September).

Reasons, Charles, Lois Ross and Craig Patterson. 1981. *Assault on the Worker: Occupational Health and Safety in Canada.* Toronto: Butterworths.

Reasons, Charles, Lois Ross and Craig Patterson. 1986. "Your Money or Your Life: Workers' Health in Canada." In S. Brickey and E. Comack (eds.), First Edition. *The Social Basis of Law.* Toronto: Garamond Press.

Reiman, Jeffrey. 1981. "The Crisis of Liberalism." *Crime and Social Justice.* Summer: 36-38.

Reiman, Jeffrey. 1984. *The Rich Get Richer and the Poor Get Prison* Second edition. New York: John Wiley and Sons.

Report of the Special Committee on Indian Self-Government in Canada. Ottawa: Queen's Printer, 1983.

Reschenthaler, G. 1979. *Occupational Health and Safety in Canada: The Economics and Three Case Studies.* Montreal: Institute for Research on Public Policy.

Richardson, C. James. 1988. *Court-based Divorce Mediation in Four Canadian Cities: An Overview of Research Results.* Ottawa: Minister of Supply and Services Canada.

Rifkin, J. 1980 and 1982. "Towards a Theory of Law and Patriarchy." In P. Beirne and R. Quinney (eds.), *Marxism and the Law.* New York: Wiley. Also in *Harvard Women's Law Journal.* 3(83) 1980.

Rinehart, James. 1975. *The Tyranny of Work.* Ontario: Longman.

Robin, M. 1972. *The Rush for Spoils: The Company Province, 1871-1933.* Toronto: McClelland and Stewart.

Rock, Paul. 1983a. "The Status and Roles of Criminology and Its Institutional Relations with Public Policy and Practice." Paper presented to the Ninth International Congress on Criminology, Panel 1.

Rock, Paul. 1983b. "Victims — Policy in Canada: The emergence of the justice for victims of crime initiative." Paper written for the 33rd International Course in Criminology: Victims of Crime, February, 1983.

Rogerson, Carol. 1988. "Winning the Battle, Losing the War: The plight of the custodial mother after judgement." In Margaret E. Hughes and E. Diane Pask (eds.), *National Themes in Family Law.* Toronto: Carswell, pp. 21-54.

Rollins, J. 1985. *Between Women: Domestics and Their Employers.* Philadelphia:

Temple University Press.

Rooke, P. and R.L. Schnell. 1982a. "Guttersnipes and Charity Children: Nineteenth century child rescue in the Atlantic provinces." *Studies in Canadian History: A Canadian Perspective.*

Rooke, P. and R.L. Schnell. 1982b. "Childhood and Charity in 19th Century British North America." *Social History.* 15(May): 157-179.

Rooke, P. and R.L. Schnell. 1983. *Discarding the Asylum: From Child Rescue to the Welfare State in English-Canada, 1800-1950.* Lanham, MD: University Press of America.

Rosen, R. 1982. *The Lost Sisterhood: Prostitution in America: 1900-1918.* Baltimore: John Hopkins University Press.

Rothenberg, P. (ed.). 1988. *Racism and Sexism: An Integrated Study.* New York: St. Martin's Press.

Rothman, David. 1971. *The Discovery of the Asylum.* Toronto: Little Brown.

Rothman, David. 1980. *Conscience and Convenience: The Asylum and Its Alternatives in Progressive America.* Boston: Little Brown.

Rudin, Bradley. 1972. "Mackenzie King and the Writing of Canada's Anti-labour Laws." *Canadian Dimension.* January: 42-48.

Russell, Diana. 1975. *The Politics of Rape: The Victim's Perspective.* New York: Stein and Day.

Rutman, Leonard. 1987. "J.J. Kelso and the Development of Child Welfare." In Moscovitch and Albert (eds.), *The Benevolent State.* Toronto: Garamond Press, pp. 77-95.

Saga, C.L. 1984. "Regulatory Offences, Infractions and Alternative Compliance Measures." *University of Toronto Faculty of Law Review.* 42(25).

Sample Survey and Data Bank Unit (University of Regina). 1984. *Breaking the Silence: Descriptive Report of a Follow-up Study of Abused Women Using a Shelter.* Ottawa: National Clearinghouse on Family Violence.

Sarat, Austin. 1985. "Legal Effectiveness and Social Studies of Law: On the unfortunate persistence of a legal tradition." *Legal Studies Forum.* 9(23).

Sargent, Neil. C. 1989. "Law, Ideology and Corporate Crime: A critique of instrumentalism." *Canadian Journal of Law and Society.* 4: 39-75.

Saywell, J. 1951. "Labour and Socialism in British Columbia: A survey of historical development before 1903." *B.C. Historical Quarterly.* 15: 129-50.

Schecter, S. 1977. "Capitalism, Class and Educational Reform in Canada." In Leo Panitch (ed.), *The Canadian State: Political Economy and Political Power.* University of Toronto Press.

Schrager, L. and J. Short Jr. 1980. "How Serious a Crime? Perceptions of Organizational and Common Crime." In G. Gels and E. Stotland (eds.), *White Collar Crime: Theory and Research*. Beverley Hills: Sage Publications.

Schrecker, Ted. 1989. "The Political Context and Content of Environmental Law." In T. Caputo *et al.* (eds.), *Law and Society. A Critical Perspective*. Toronto: Harcourt, Brace, Jovanovich.

Schwartz, R.D. and J.H. Skolnick. 1962. "Two Studies of Legal Stigma." *Social Problems*. 10: 133.

Scull, Andrew. 1977. *Decarceration*. New Jersey: Prentice-Hall.

Scull, Andrew. 1981. "Progressive Dreams, Progressive Nightmares: Social control in 20th century America." *Stanford Law Review*. 33: 301-16.

Scull, Andrew. 1984. *Decarceration: Community treatment and the deviant* Second edition. Toronto: Prentice-Hall.

Seccombe, W. 1986. "Marxism and Demography: Household forms and fertility regimes in the Western European transition." In J. Dickinson and Bob Russell (eds.), *Family, Economy and State*. Toronto: Garamond Press.

Segal, Lynne. 1987. *Is the Future Female? Troubled Thoughts on Contemporary Feminism*. London: Virago.

Sevenhuijsen, Selma. 1986. "Fatherhood and Political Theory of Rights: Theoretical perspectives of feminism." *International Journal of the Sociology of Law*. 14(3/4): 329-340.

Shaw, Susan. "Leisure in the Contemporary Family: The effect of female employment on the leisure of Canadian wives and husbands." *International Review of Modern Sociology* (forthcoming).

Shearing, C. 1981. "Subterranean Processes in the Maintenance of Power: An examination of the mechanisms coordinating police action." *Canadian Review of Sociology and Anthropology*. (August). 18(3): 283-98.

Sheehy, Elizabeth and Susan Boyd. 1989. *Canadian Feminist Perspectives on Law: An Annotated Bibliography of Interdisciplinary Writings*. A special publication of *Resources for Feminist Research*. Toronto: O.I.S.E.

Sherman, L.W. and R.A. Berk. 1989. "The Specific Deterrent Effects of Arrest for Domestic Assault." *American Sociological Review*. 49(2): 260-272.

Shkilnyk, A. 1985. *A Poison Stronger Than Love: The Destruction of an Ojibwa Community*. New Haven: Yale University Press.

Silberman, Charles E. 1980. *Criminal Violence, Criminal Justice*. New York: Vintage Books.

Silbey, S. 1985. "Ideal and Practice in the Study of Law." *Legal Studies Forum*. 9(7).

Silbey, Susan and A. Sarat. 1985. "Critical Traditions in Law and Society Research." *Law and Society Review*. 21(1): 16-75.

Silvera, M. 1983. *Silenced*. Toronto: Williams-Wallace.

Sinclair, Deborah. 1985. *Understanding Wife Assault: A Training Manual for Counsellors and Advocates*. Ontario Ministry of Community and Social Services — Family Violence Program, Toronto.

Skeoch, L.A. (ed.). 1966. *Restrictive Trade Practices in Canada: Selected Readings*. Toronto: McClelland and Stewart.

Small, Shirley J. 1978. "Canadian Narcotics Legislation, 1908-1923: A conflict model interpretation." In Wm. Greenaway and S. Brickey (eds.), *Law and Social Control in Canada*. Scarborough: Prentice-Hall, pp. 28-42.

Smandych, R. 1986. "Marxism and the Creation of Law: Re-Examining the Origins of Canadian Anti-Combines Legislation 1890-1910." In S. Brickey and E. Comack (eds.). *The Social Basis of Law* First Edition. Toronto: Garamond Press, pp. 53-65.

Smart, Carol and Selma Sevenhuijsen (eds.). 1989. *Child Custody and the Politics of Gender*. London: Routledge and Kegan Paul.

Snider, D. Laureen. 1978. "Corporate Crime in Canada." *Canadian Journal of Criminology*. 20(2): 142-168.

Snider, D. Laureen. 1979. "Revising the Combines Investigation Act: A study in corporate power." In P. Brantingham and J. Kress (eds.), *Structure, Law and Power: Essays in the Sociology of Law*. Beverly Hills: Sage Publications.

Snider, D. Laureen. 1982. "Traditional and Corporate Theft: A comparison of sanctions." In Wickman and Dailey (eds.), *White-Collar and Economic Crime*. Lexington: Lexington Books.

Snider, D. Laureen. 1985. "Legal Reform and Social Control: The dangers of abolishing rape." *International Journal of the Sociology of Law*. 13(4): 337-56.

Snider, D. Laureen. 1986. "Legal Aid Reform and the Welfare State." *Crime and Social Justice*. 24: 21-42.

Snider, D. Laureen. 1987. "Towards a Political Economy of Reform, Regulation and Corporate Crime." *Law and Policy*. 9(37).

Snider, D. Laureen. 1989. "Ideology and Relative Autonomy in Anglo-Canadian Criminology." *Journal of Human Justice*.. 1(1) (Fall): 27-42.

Snider, D. Laureen. 1990a. "Cooperative Models and Corporate Crime: Panacea or cop out?" *Crime and Delinquency* .

Snider, D. Laureen. 1990b. "The Potential of the Criminal Justice System to Promote Feminist Concerns." *Studies in Law, Politics and Society*. 10: 143-172.

Solomon and Madison. 1976-77. "The Evolution of Non-medical Opiate Use in

Canada, Part I, 1870-1929." *Drug Forum.* 5: 237-65.

Sparks, Richard F. 1980. "A Critique of Marxist Criminology." In N. Morris and M. Tonry (eds.), *Crime and Justice: An Annual Review of Research* (volume 2), Chicago: University of Chicago Press.

Spender, Dale. 1980. *Man Made Language.* London: Routledge and Kegan Paul.

Spender, Dale (ed.). 1981. *Men's Studies Modified: The Impact of Feminism on the Academic Disciplines.* Oxford: Paragon.

Splane, Richard. 1965. *Social Welfare in Ontario 1791-1893: A Study of Public Welfare Administration.* Toronto: University of Toronto Press.

Stanbury, W.T. 1986-87. "The New Competition Act and Competition Tribunal Act: Not with a bang, but a whimper." *Canadian Business Law Journal.* 12(2).

Statistics Canada. 1983. *Divorce: Law and Family in Canada.* Ottawa: Minister of Supply and Services Canada.

Statistics Canada. 1982. *Uniform Crime Reporting Statistics Of Sexual Offences in Canada and the Provinces: 1976-80.* Ottawa: Canadian Centre for Justice Statistics.

Statistics Canada. 1987. *Women in the Workplace.* Ottawa: Minister of Supply and Services Canada.

Statistics Canada. 1986. *Women's Work Interruptions.* Ottawa: Minister of Supply and Services Canada.

Stebbins, R. 1988. "Men, Husbands and Fathers: Beyond patriarchal relations." In Mandell and Duffy (eds.), *Reconstructing the Canadian Family: Feminist Perspectives.* Toronto: Butterworth, pp. 27-47.

Stephens, James F. 1883. *A History of Criminal Law of England* (volume II). London: Macmillan.

Stewart, Bryce M. 1926. *Canadian Labor Laws and the Treaty.* New York: Columbia University Press

Stone, Alan. 1971. "How Capitalism Rules." *Monthly Review.* 23: 31-36.

Stone, Christopher D. 1975. *Where the Law Ends: The Social Control of Corporate Behaviour.* New York: Harper and Row.

Stone, Christopher D. 1977. "Controlling Corporate Misconduct." *The Public Interest.* 48: 55-71.

Strong-Boag, Veronica. 1986. "Wages for Housework: Mothers' allowances and the beginnings of social security in Canada." In S. Brickey and E. Comack (eds.), *The Social Basis of Law* First Edition. Toronto: Garamond Press, pp. 91-106.

Sumner, Colin. 1979. *Reading Ideologies: An Investigation into the Marxist Theory of Ideology and Law.* London: Academic Press.